BRITAIN
OBSERVED

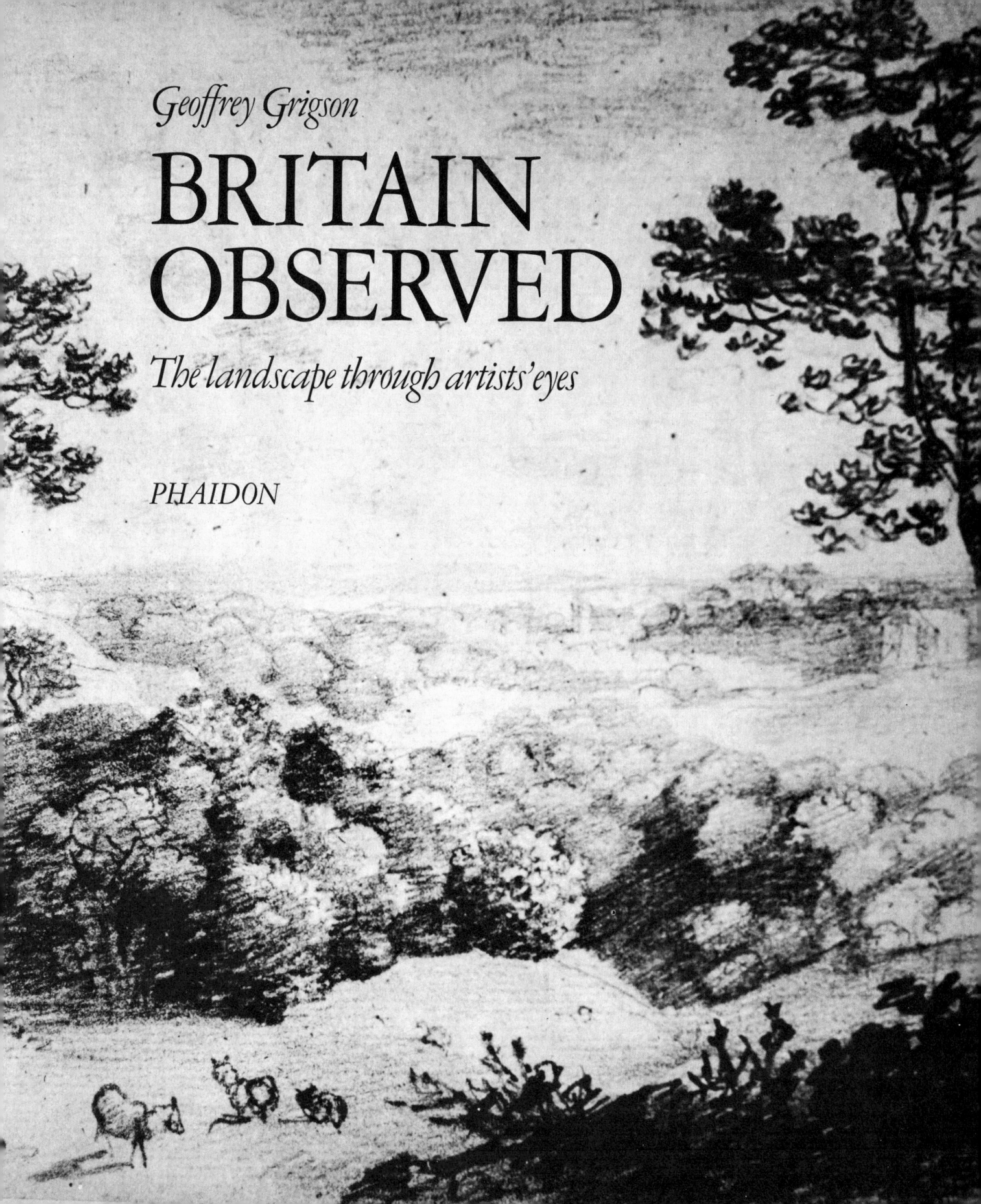

Geoffrey Grigson

BRITAIN
OBSERVED

The landscape through artists'eyes

PHAIDON

PHAIDON PRESS LIMITED, 5 Cromwell Place, London SW7 2JL
First Published 1975
Text © 1975 by Geoffrey Grigson. All rights reserved.

ISBN 0 7148 1597 7
Also published in a signed, limited edition of 300 copies,
ISBN 0 7148 1688 4

The lithographs on pages 180 and 203 are reproduced from W. Daniell's
Interesting Selections from Animated Nature, London 1809. On the
end-papers is an oil sketch by Constable, Cirrus Clouds (1822) in the
Victoria and Albert Museum, London.

Printed in Great Britain by Lund Humphries, Bradford

Contents

PREFACE

OUR FIELD OF VISION is more or less picture-shaped, a picture rectangle; which the painters naturally adopted. Painters analysed these rectangular views, at once personal and objective, with immeasurable results which spread far beyond the picture gallery. Bruegel, Rembrandt, Constable, Corot, Pissarro and Monet educated us to be more conscious of the world. They made the 'good view' a part of our lives (on the French Michelin maps a special sign indicates every exceptional *point de vue*); they established a modern value which now outlives the painting of landscape. Here, then, is a book of the more perfect vision of familiar places, or scenes, of lasting revelations of both place and person; a book which undertakes to show what some painters—not only from England, but a few from France, and from the Low Countries and elsewhere—have made of the scenery of Britain, since the painting of it began some four centuries ago. A book of art and a book of places.

Some artists—since they were talkative, and since art involves such depth of relationship between nature and men—also spoke their mind about landscape. So I have added at the end remarks made by some of the artists whose work I have reproduced, general remarks, with a sprinkling of comments about actual places which especially delighted them.

I must thank curators and dealers who have helped me with information and photographs for what, I am afraid, they will hardly think of as an 'art book', in particular Mr. Perriam of the Carlisle Art Gallery for showing me the work of William James Blacklock and giving me so much information about this neglected painter, Mr. John Green of the Laing Art Gallery, Newcastle, for telling me of Thomas Miles Richardson's oil painting of *The Tyne from Windmill Hills, Gateshead,* and Dr. Sigurd Willoch, Director of the Nasjonalgaleriet, Oslo, for information about the pictures of a minor favourite of mine, the Norwegian painter Thomas Fearnley. Keith Roberts of the Phaidon Press encouraged me to the making of a book I have had in mind for years. His colleague John Woodward, and how grateful I am for that, suggested that I should add the appendix from the artists' own writings. And I am grateful to old friends, Basil Taylor for one, whose work has helped me to a better appreciation of Constable and so of landscape, and who introduced me to William Daniell's solemn aquatint of the Thames, and Ben Nicholson for another, who won't approve of many of the inclusions, but whose letters and conversation (and landscapes) always have the ruthlessness of those standards which make for the best in art. Private owners have been kind; and Mr. Robert Bevan, too, who sent me remarks about landscape made by his father, R. A. Bevan; and Mrs. Kessler, who gave me information about Dufy in England.

FEBRUARY 1974   *Geoffrey Grigson*

7

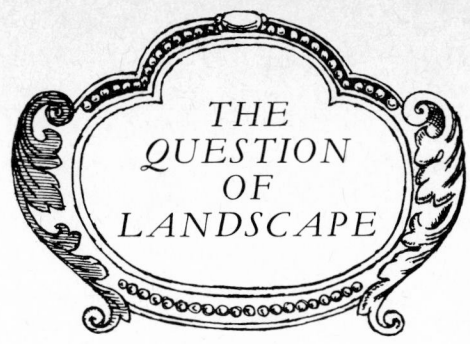

Landscape and places

CONSTABLE AND PISSARRO—once Constable had overcome the shock of sitting in the same room as a *French* artist—might complain that the picture is always its own subject, that painted landscape may be 'places', yet is not really 'about' places. They might urge that putting the two of them, with more than sixty other painters, together in a book because they all painted scenes or places in England, whether a Salisbury Cathedral or a Crystal Palace, is no decent gesture to the art they liberated and brought to maturity.

Perhaps they would be right—and perhaps they can be answered out of their own mouths and their own practice.

First, though, they might also insist—as they often did in their lifetime—that landscape is everywhere, never requiring either the cayenne pepper or the golden syrup of any kind of exaggeration. After he had been on a visit to Pissarro's eldest son Lucien, who had settled at Epping, one of the Pissarro children complained to his father that the country round Lucien's home was not very beautiful. Pissarro's response was that painters of landscape didn't require the Swiss Alps: they could do with little. Hadn't Corot made beautiful small paintings in Gisors with nothing to hand, or to eye, but 'a couple of willow-trees, a little stream and a bridge?'

'Happy are those who see beauty in modest spots where others see nothing. Everything is beautiful, the whole secret lies in knowing how to interpret.'

That was Pissarro, in 1893; and here before him, in 1832, is Constable (whom Pissarro admired so much, and who declared that he had never seen an ugly thing in his life):

'My limited and abstracted art is to be found under every hedge, and in every lane, and therefore nobody thinks it worth picking up.'

So much allowed, Pissarro wouldn't—and couldn't—deny that he put names to his canvases—*Pontoise, Rouen, Le Pont Neuf,* or *Penge* or *Lower Norwood* or *Kew Gardens*; Constable would not deny that places are nature, and that he preferred some places to others, not altogether for picture reasons.

Painters may find new places to fall in love with (Sisley's expression—see page 199), but usually they respond most of all to scenes in which their consciousness or their vision was formed. Pissarro was happier painting on the Seine or the Oise than on the Thames. Constable was happier painting the Dedham Vale than the Lakes ('I have heard him say that the solitude of mountains oppressed his spirits. His nature was peculiarly social and could not feel satisfied with scenery, however grand in itself, that did not abound in human associations'), though he took to Salisbury and Hampstead Heath. He never wanted—never needed—to go and look for scenes to paint in France or Italy. 'I should paint my own places best.' And he wrote that it was the banks of the Stour, where he grew up, which made him a painter—'I had often thought of pictures of them before I had ever touched a pencil'.

The fact is that we react in a mixed way to any picture, any work of art, even if it is deliberately reduced to the purest non-figurative construction of 'musical' arrangement of spaces, tones and colours (see Victor Pasmore on his transition from landscape

9

to musical, non-descriptive art, page 203); and about what may be called pure landscape art, or much of it, there is a kind and degree of welcome impurity, the artist making concessions to a very human taste he shares with those who enjoy his work. There are limits, but it seems to me right and respectable that we should, if we are English or Welsh or Scotch, welcome with an extra delight the Englishness, Welshness or Scotchness of the landscapes of our own country, the landscapes in either sense, in and out of the frame.

It is intriguing to see what has been made of the light, colour and forms of our own scenery in the vision of a Canaletto or a Pissarro or a Derain from abroad; it is intriguing always to see how the landscape painter individualizes his and our own preferred places. By ourselves, with no aid from the painters, we can recognize that Wharfedale or the Greta valley or the London Thames have characteristics which give us pleasure. In pictures the truth of these familiar characteristics is seen through the painter's truth and being. Cézanne's friend Emile Zola, attacking the *Salon,* famously wrote that 'A work of art is a corner of nature seen through a temperament' (1866). Samuel Palmer, aged 20, said in older language, 'Sometimes landscape is seen as a vision, and then seems as fine as art; but this is seldom, and bits of nature are generally much improved by being received into the soul' (1825). We may reasonably say that the landscape in the frame—and in the reproduction—is an extra revelation, an extra intensification, rather than an invention.

The Thames was there exquisite in half-lights and in

Constable: SALISBURY CATHEDRAL FROM THE SOUTH WEST. *Pencil,* $7\frac{5}{8} \times 8\frac{3}{4}$ *in. London, Victoria and Albert Museum.*

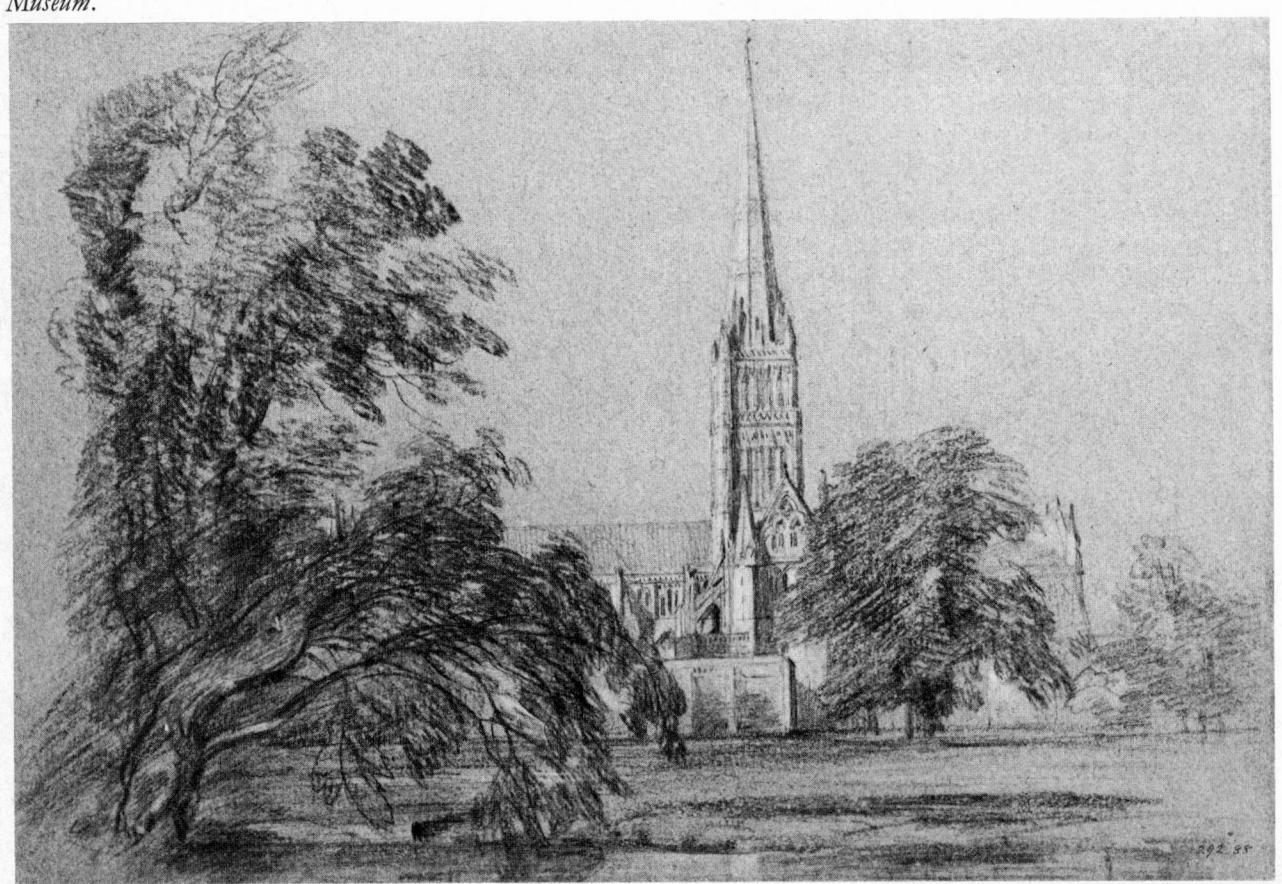

Victorian fog along the Chelsea and Battersea reaches. Our great-grandfathers were half aware of its beauty, though fog and damp get into the lungs; and then Whistler came. And Walter Greaves and his brother rowed this creature of the sapphire eye up and down the river at all hours, in all conditions of light and colour, and he made its peculiar Industrial Revolution beauties explicit in his Nocturnes and Symphonies. He made others see them and express them in other arts—Oscar Wilde in a poem he actually called *A Symphony in Yellow:*

> An omnibus across the bridge
> Crawls like a yellow butterfly,
> And here and there a passer-by
> Shows like a restless little midge.
>
> Big barges full of yellow hay,
> Are moored against the shadowy wharf
> And like a yellow silken scarf,
> The thick fog hangs above the quay.
>
> The yellow leaves begin to fade,
> And flutter from the Temple elms;
> And at my feet the pale green Thames*
> Lies like a rod of rippled jade.

As for the landscape in its two senses, if we are to enjoy the landscapes in paint, we can only begin, like the painter, with landscape in fact; to begin, that is, by enjoying our world, from which the landscapes in paint derive. The wrong starting point is the now rather too fashionable study of the history of art, which can so slyly insert itself, in a distorting, even a blinding way, between picture and spectator.

The history of a school, a style, a genre, has to take notice of what is simply connective. It cannot proceed serenely from best to best, oblivious of pictures which were simply vehicles of action or reaction, or which retain interest only as the exemplars of dead mannerism or a perverted vision. Approving or rejecting, it is only the spectator's eye which can operate without such constraints, in freedom.

This book is then a choice of pictures, in historical

sequence more or less, but by no means an historical survey of the rise and course of landscape painting in, and of, Great Britain. It begins with three Flemish painters, with Rubens, Van Dyck and Jan Siberechts, in the seventeenth century, it proceeds to the twentieth century, in which landscape painting after Derain, Ben Nicholson and Pasmore, has retreated again. It is really no more historical than that, such an arrangement ensuring that the landscape images, as they follow one another, do not jar in style.

If I say that landscape painting is now in abeyance (it is with the younger living artists of ability), I am not in the least suggesting that it will never return, in some way, or alleging that the best of such art since the seventeenth century is now a series of art gallery bygones which require to be explained by art historians. Landscape—the land—surrounds us, still. It is our milieu, we observe it, we respond to it, we are even becoming conscious again of environmental felicities—or the lack of them.

The accumulated vision of landscape art since Van Dyck took time off from painting lords and their ladies in Eltham Palace, amounts, then, to something we can largely estimate by our own everyday visual experience.

Modes change, but genuine images of the landscape kind are not alien to us like baroque mythologies or masterly barbarian carvings of the Urnes or Ringerike style. If I regard the first of the major pictures reproduced in this book, Ruben's allegory of *St. George and the Dragon,* I can legitimately derive more pleasure from its landscape of the Thames than from its foreground play-acting of Charles I as the saint and Henrietta Maria as the princess he has just delivered, complete with the bones and gobbets of earlier victims. Also it is legitimate to claim that Rubens lives more—or affects more of the living—in the unchanging content, or extent of his *Château de Steen* in the London National Gallery or of his *Rainbow Landscape* in the Wallace Collection, pictures which so moved Constable and Turner and James Ward and their contemporaries, than he does in his vastly vermicular mythologies and allegories or his vast jamborees of grand 'history' in the Louvre.

* For a green Thames, green or blue-green as can be, see Whistler's *Nocturne: Westminster Palace,* reproduced in Donald Holden's *Whistler Landscapes and Seascapes,* 1969.

The right quotation on the matter comes again from our greatest master of landscape, John Constable declaring—if with quite an excusable exaggeration—that 'There has never been an age, however rude or uncultivated, in which the love of landscape has not in some way been manifested.'

Constable asked 'And how could it be otherwise?'—since man 'is the sole intellectual inhabitant of our vast natural landscape,' and since man's nature 'is congenial with the elements of the planet itself, and he cannot but sympathize with its features, its various aspects, and its phenomena in all situations.'

Man's sympathy has not always proved as strong as Constable optimistically supposed it to be. But the principle holds.

The place and the ideal

The story of European landscape is part of the story of yesterday's extroversion of man's interest from himself-in-god to himself-in-nature, which has been followed by to-day's sequel of man for himself, as far as art goes, without god or nature. It is a northern genre. Italian painters of the Quattrocento set the incidents of the life of Christ and the Holy Family and the saints in their earthly scenic context, newly appreciated, which the painters rendered again and again with the most exquisitely timeless precision. The incidents dominate. But they lose their force, the figures diminish, the sinuosities of a river, the upwardness of a hill at the back of the sacred heads and haloes, the scrap of countryside in miniature framed by the sides of a window to the left or right of the Madonna and her Child, come forward and are enlarged. The accessory becomes the principal; and at last Dutch and Flemish northerners of the bourgeois culture of the seventeenth century can find their whole satisfaction in depicting an extent of sky coupled with an extent of land or water.

Inevitably this new landscape—also some of the new landscape-makers—crossed to a rich and awakening England. We began to use that Dutch word 'landscape'—*landschap*—as early as 1598, according to the *Oxford English Dictionary*. But what our seventeenth-century and eighteenth-century ancestors wanted at first was not images of the world by a Koninck or a Rembrandt, but a landscape-portraiture of power and glory.

Paint me the emblems of our blood and state—paint me Windsor Castle, or Whitehall Palace, or Richmond Palace along the royal Thames, or Nonsuch.

Paint me a likeness of the mansion I have just built complete with formal gardens I have just laid out on the bare terrain; and the picture will be the emblem of my own and my line's power and eminence.

In such a landscape portrait the clever and scrupulous artist could satisfy himself as well as his patron—for instance, Jan Siberechts, who was transplanted from Antwerp to England in 1672 by George Villiers, Duke of Buckingham. Here was an accomplished painter of landscape in its own right, who in England could live only as a portraitist of mansions. Working years later for the Willoughbys of Wollaton Hall, the coal kings of Nottingham, Siberechts painted what might be called two property-landscapes or status landscapes with Wollaton showing on the highest points.

One of these is the broad view of Nottingham and the Trent (Plate 5). The other is a landscape of Lenton Mill* (now swallowed by Nottingham): there is the mill house, horses draw a waggon and splash through the ford across the River Leen, a packman behind his pack animals rides across the middle distance—all this amounts to Siberechts' kind of landscape, independent of everything except itself. And then, as if it were a necessary afterthought, Siberechts remembers to top the hill above the Leen with that very grand mansion of the Willoughbys—turned into a very small ghostly shape skied on the horizon.

For Siberechts the *Lenton Mill* and the *Nottingham* were two landscapes; for his Willoughby patron we must suppose they were two 'Distant Views of my Wollaton Hall.'

When Tennyson a century and a half later wrote in 'The Lord of Burleigh' (1833–4)

> He is but a landscape painter
> And a village maiden she

* reproduced in T. H. Fokker's *Jan Siberechts*, 1931.

he was thinking of the kind of peripatetic artist, in the humbler wake of Jan Siberechts and many others, who still went around painting houses, by this time not palatial mansions, but the new country villa, the cottage ornée, the farmhouse, and—if he could manage likenesses—painting as well the owner and his wife and children. Constable was to act so for a time and on occasions. In 1816 he was commissioned to paint, not only General Rebow's Wivenhoe Park, outside Colchester (Plate 60), but the General and his wife and their daughter. There is a case, too, of such a wandering property and portrait painter designing a 'White Horse' for a Wiltshire farmer and being hanged as well for forging banknotes.

In the time of Siberechts and then through much, even most of the eighteenth century, the notion of landscape as a category with its own values, independent of associations with antiquity or the like, had still to root itself in English approval, or understanding.

No artist with a superlative skill in landscape, equal to Van Dyck's in portraiture (and with an international fame like Van Dyck's), had settled in England, or had been called for by the English situation; and painting in England was too young to allow a strong self-confidence in artists, as a rule, or in connoisseurs and customers who called the tune.

No confidence, no risks. Money is laid on certainties when a sense of inferiority has to be compensated for, art has to be high flying, and must follow the precedents. Pictures from Roman or Christian mythology were taken to evince imagination in its absolute, demanding of landscape no more than an appropriate setting.

Or not much more, until the surrounding world began to seem increasingly interesting and attractive. For such a new taste to be elevating, nature had to be more than its actuality, mud, cow-dung, discomfort and all. So painted landscape needed to conform to the philosophy of nature as an idea, an idea or ideal of perfection, a generalized perfected nature. Where was this nature to be found in existing art? Not in the new paintings from Holland which were too literal, but in the older pictures by Gaspard Poussin and Claude— landscape combined with myth and history. No paintings were more avidly collected, or more admired, than

those of Gaspard Poussin and Claude. They were nature improved, they were standards for home-made painting attempting to live up to the perfectness of the idea of nature. No English landscape could be English, it must wear the ready-mades of this Italianate ideal. If you were rich enough you could also reshape and plant the landscape around your Palladian mansion, 'improving' it in the same image of the Ideal.

England, Wales, even uncomfortable Scotland, were being explored for their scenery and their wonders, yet for decades it was scarcely thought—or respectably thought—that there was sense in what Constable was to call, in 1802, when he began to provide it, 'a natural painture'. Landscape *per se* struck the cultured English mind as vulgar and prosaic, an attitude still alive even as late as 1836, when in one of his Hampstead lectures Constable complained that landscape had 'hitherto escaped a distinction to which it is entitled.'

Real views from nature

In the eighteenth century and then at the very beginning of the nineteenth century there were two now celebrated expressions of this low esteem for anything which was not Ideal Landscape. One is the letter Gainsborough wrote politely and firmly, in the third person, to the Earl of Hardwicke (page 184), in the seventeen-seventies. Evidently the Earl, who had not long succeeded to his title, had asked Gainsborough for a picture which would also be a 'real view'— perhaps of Dover, where his family originated, or of his great family mansion of Wimpole Hall in Cambridgeshire or of the grounds of Wimpole (which Capability Brown began remodelling for him in 1767).

Gainsborough replied, as if the Earl should have known better, that 'with respect to *real Views* from Nature in this Country' he had never seen 'any Place that affords a Subject equal to the poorest imitations of Gaspar or Claude'; and that if his Lordship wished 'to have anything tolerable of the name of G', it must, figures and all, 'be of his own Brain.'

The other defence of ideal, or invented, landscape

was made by that mannered demonic artist of the passions and the *Sturm und Drang* of history painting, Henry Fuseli, lecturing to Royal Academy students, in 1801. Almost fifty years have gone by, and here is Fuseli attacking the 'real view' again, denouncing—there was more and more of it, time and sentiment having progressed—'the last branch of uninteresting subjects, that kind of landscape which is entirely occupied with the tame delineation of a given spot.'

He told the young artists, or art students, in front of him that the Dutch painters had bordered on 'negative landscape'; which was true. He told them that 'the landscape of Titian, of Mola, of Salvator, of the Poussins, Claude, Rubens, Elzheimer, Rembrandt, and Wilson, spurns all relation with this kind of map-work'.

'To them Nature disclosed her bosom'—Fuseli would have been quite ready to draw Nature in this work of disclosing her metaphorical breasts—'in the varied light of rising, meridian, setting suns; in twilight, night and dawn. Height, depth, solitude, strike, terrify, absorb, bewilder. In their scenery, we tread on classic or romantic ground, or wander through the characteristic groups of rich congenial objects.'

Fuseli saw what was coming; much, I suppose, as Tonks, head of the Slade School, saw what was coming when Cézanne, van Gogh, Gauguin, Seurat, Matisse, Derain, Picasso and Maurice Denis exhibited at the Grafton Galleries in 1910–11. Tonks, it was remembered by Paul Nash, called the Slade students together and put them on their honour not to go and see these new subversive pictures.

Landscapes which did not offer sufficiently classic or romantic ground for treading on, were topography. Topography—'mere topography'—became the name of contempt. The bogey raised in this way continued to flap round the painting-rooms and round the easels in the open air, inhibiting English landscape almost to its recent decline.

I do not myself believe that Richard Wilson, and then Gainsborough, were really quite so much against 'real landscape' as they pretended. Or at least I think it more likely that these two sensitive artists were half-consciously in two minds about it—about the need for

ever to invent and idealize. They were cultivated men, they deferred. They knew as much as anyone else about nature as an idea, and about approximations to the idea on canvas or in the landscape garden around the mansions of earl or banker. To argue differently would have been a kind of cultural and intellectual gaffe—if tempting. But then I think we can discern both the temptation and the tinge of guilt when Gainsborough, that most open of delightful men, remembers the strength of his early inclination to landscape, in his Suffolk childhood (page 185), or when he speaks of going off with his viol-da-gamba to sweet villages and painting landskips instead of portraits, or of his liking (page 184) for woods, rocks and waterfalls.

'I know not how it is,' says another portraitist, of Gainsborough's time, Joseph Wright of Derby, 'tho' I am engaged in portraits'—in the superior genre—'I find myself continually stealing off and getting to Landscapes' (page 185).

We take Gainsborough as more than a rococo painter of sheens of silk, more than a rococo contriver of landscapes for which he often built up models with pieces of coal and cork, and with moss and lichen and sand, and 'distant woods of broccoli'. But don't we feel—I think we do—that Gainsborough, and Wilson as well, would have been better landscape artists if they could have allowed the native, natural scene to impress itself on them more strongly, and more evidently?

Constable may have felt that too, much as he loved some of what we might call Gainsborough's semi-landscapes. They brought tears to his eyes. But his praise of Gainsborough touches on the defensive. He talks of the things he painted 'with exquisite refinement, yet not a refinement beyond nature'. He talks of a Gainsborough he saw at Petworth: 'No feeling of landscape ever equalled it'—and then: 'With particulars he had nothing to do, his object was to deliver a fine sentiment—& he has fully accomplished it. Mind—I use no comparison in my delight of thinking on this lovely canvas—nothing injures ones mind more than such modes of reasoning—no fine things will bear & want comparison with one another—every fine thing is unique.' It is as if Constable were saying, 'Well, there *should* have been a little more nature.'

Gainsborough seemed more 'natural', all the same, in Constable's time, and earlier, than he does to us. One eighteenth-century connoisseur, Horace Walpole, talked admiringly of the 'frankness of nature in Gainsborough's landscapes,' though we may find it overlaid, since we conceive of nature more literally and objectively.

It was Walpole—there should have been more such connoisseurs, as sensitive to the natural scene—who as early as 1762 (in his *Anecdotes of Painting in England*) had expressed surprise and regret that the English till then should have produced so few good painters of landscape 'in a country so profusely beautiful with the amenities of nature.'

Walpole had gone on 'As our poets warm their imaginations with sunny hills, or sigh after grottoes and cooling breezes, our painters draw rocks and precipices and castellated mountains because Virgil gasped for breath at Naples, and Salvator wandered amidst Alps and Apennines.' He wanted to know why, as no more than 'homely and familiar objects,' English painters had neglected 'our ever-verdant lawns, rich vales, fields of haycocks and hop-grounds.'

Those hop-grounds intrigued him: he found them pictorial, so I shall quote his whole hop-ground passage because I suspect it bears on the landscape to come of Samuel Palmer. The hop-grounds were paintable 'particularly in the season of gathering, when some tendrils are ambitiously climbing, and others dangling in natural festoons; while poles, despoiled of their garlands, are erected into easy pyramids that contrast with the taper and upright columns. In Kent such scenes are often backed by sandhills that enliven the green, and the gatherers dispersed among the narrow valleys enliven the picture, and give it various distances.'

Had Samuel Palmer just read that passage from Walpole, in Kent, in a new edition of the *Anecdotes*, when he remarked to himself in a notebook of 1826 that he would now go out 'to draw some hops that their fruitful sentiment may be infused into my figures'?

I believe he had. And wouldn't Horace Walpole have approved the tawny hop-ground that Palmer was painting before long at Underriver (Plate 83)?

Whether or no he had warmed to Horace Walpole or Kentish hop-grounds, Palmer had certainly warmed to Fuseli, one of his heroes, on the tame delineation of a given spot. In 1828 he is to be found declaring that though he is making studies from nature, he will never, God help him, become 'a naturalist,' which is to say a natural painter, 'by profession'.

Perhaps we could translate Palmer and Fuseli, and say that they are really asking for what we should call imagination in landscape. Zola told Cézanne that the good painter combined poet and workman. Fuseli and Palmer wished for more than the work, and Palmer's poetry was introducing what he felt to be the divine, filling out in that way his forms, and inventively—and very originally—increasing the splendours of his naturalism.

That was how Palmer, for one, waved away the inhibiting bogey-man of English landscape. But neither the young Palmer nor the old Fuseli he so much admired, could as yet conceive of imagination in landscape manifested only by pictorial means, only by the ordering of the tones, the colours, the masses, the light, the forms.

The freaks

The movement towards Impressionism, as the maturity of landscape, was inevitable. Yet in spite of every picture which was neither tame delineation nor one of 'the productions of men who have lost sight of nature, and strayed into the vacant fields of idealism' —that is Constable speaking once more—there was still to come, still to interfere, in English landscape, the most bizarre reaction—in the convictions and the painting of the Pre-Raphaelites and their fellow-travellers, from 1848 into the eighteen-sixties. Or instead of bizarre reaction—though bizarre is the right adjective—perhaps Pre-Raphaelitism should be assessed as decidedly the most bizarre extension and rejuvenation of old delusions, paradoxically transformed. Here was idealism continued—in the dress of realism.

It was not too good for landscape. When landscape

at once natural and imaginative—imaginative in natural terms—should have triumphed at last, here were young, gifted, ambitious artists, including Holman Hunt, Millais and then Arthur Hughes, pushing landscape back into the corners, and once more advancing and enlarging stories designed to edify. Constable might never have painted (he had been dead less than a dozen years when the Pre-Raphaelite Brotherhood was formed), Corot and the *peinture-verité* masters of the Barbizon school might never have been at work, a road might not have been leading clear to Pissarro, Monet, and Whistler.

Opposed and derided at first, these naturalistic or realistic moralizers and didacticians, and sentimentalists, were really in line with social tendencies in England, and soon enough found well-to-do patronage.

This long enduring force of idealism in Engish landscape had a curious result, that the succession of genuine landscape, uncontaminated by easy sentiment or exaggeration or anecdote, came from what I must call the freaks.

These are the artists, many of them not included, or else not much attended to, in the conventional accounts of English painting, who established their

Whistler: MILLBANK. *Etching, 4 × 5 in. London, British Museum.*

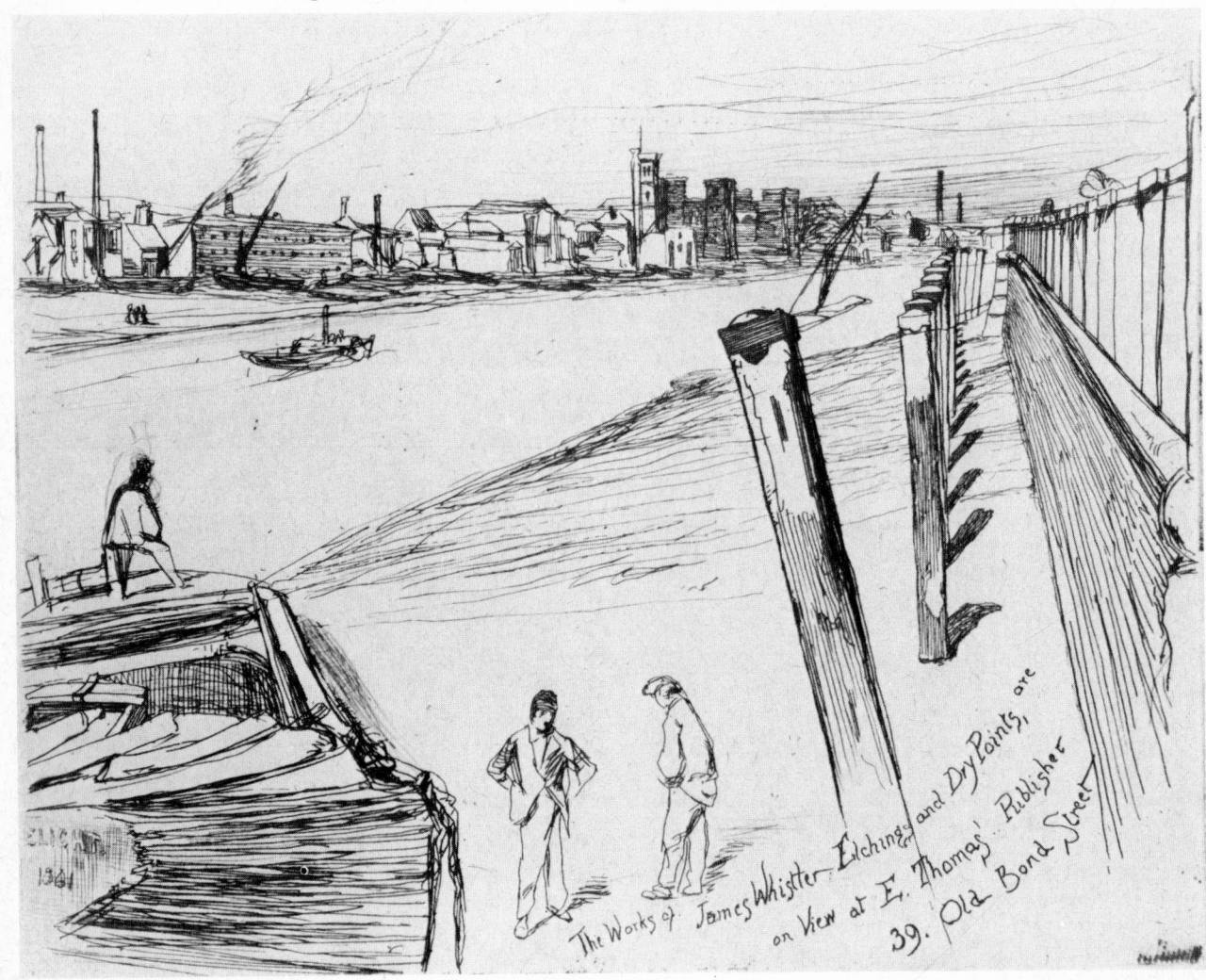

vision, and then found it did not pay, that it was against the market; and stuck to it never the less.

Smaller freaks, middling freaks, and large freaks and demi-freaks, we have them all. Constable (Plates 59–66) has been our largest and grandest freak: he had conviction, fortitude (and money), he did not allow himself to be bullied into compromise; and he has won, if posthumously—it is a pity that artists do not get their reward always in their lifetime—by the fresh strength of his landscapes, which are all the same 'taken from real places'.

Gigantic as a Picasso, we have in Turner (Plates 52–4; 56, 57) both freak and considerable compromiser. He compromised—smelling danger when he was accused, as a young man, of 'pushing his colours about', and of 'vicious practices', and of being 'a white painter'—until his position was impregnable; he became freak thereafter, in those catherine-wheels of light (which you will not find in this book, for

which I judge they are not—yes—topographic enough).

Whistler—there is the major freak (Plates 111–114) in whom imaginative sanity returned; a painter shamelessly rejected by many of his contemporaries (Burne-Jones crept to Ruskin's counsel in the libel action of *Whistler v. Ruskin* in 1878, to assure him that to British artists Whistler had been 'a matter of joke of long standing'). Few of his major landscapes were thought to deserve a place in our public collections, or have found a place in them since.

Middling and small freaks of landscape—among these are artists who hid from the unprofitable light of exhibitions, artists who were luckily for themselves independent, if not indifferent to their lack of success, artists who are known by a single landscape or two, artists who begin at last to emerge from a long obscurity or from a misleading characterization of their art. Among these I would number Charles Keene (Plates 87–9), who was far more, as his friend Edward

Whistler: VAUXHALL BRIDGE. *Etching*, $2\frac{5}{8} \times 4\frac{1}{2}$ *in. London, British Museum.*

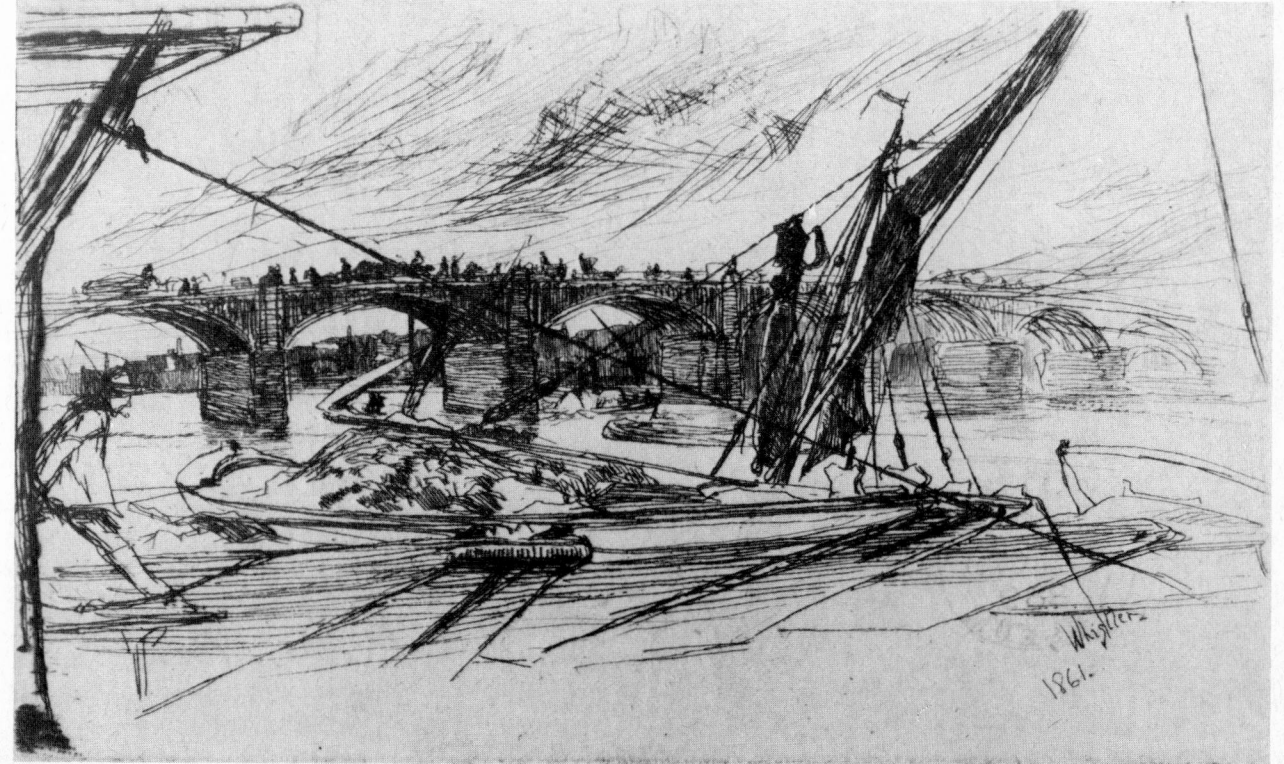

Fitzgerald indicated, than 'a droll in *Punch*', his over-publicized work for which gave him his bread and butter; Jacques-Laurent Agasse, from Geneva, a London artist 'of independent, unconciliating manners', who 'lived poor and died poor' (Plate 58); George Robert Lewis (Plates 76, 78), one of a celebrated family of artists, of German origin, who retreated from London to Hereford as a drawing-master; W. J. Blacklock (Plates 85, 86), who left London because of ill-health, and went blind and died, up north, before he could establish his name; and George Price Boyce (Plates 99–101), demi-Pre-Raphaelite, for a while, yet friend and admirer of Corot, whose means enabled him to paint privately, in his own original idiom, though he contributed to the exhibitions.

Thirty years ago, Samuel Palmer and Cornelius Varley would have been located in one or another of these groups of the obscure; or Wright of Derby, in as far as he was a painter of landscapes.

The artist's was, as it often remains, a difficult, insecure life. Again and again talented landscape painters gave way and adapted themselves to fashion, to the market. One of these was John Linnell, who abandoned a personal 'romantic objectivity' (Plates 71–3) for a soft pietism of landscape—Old Testament prophets or Christ in Surrey landscapes under clouds of cottonwool—which brought him wealth in the end. Another was Francis Danby (Plate 84) who looked round for a profitable manner, against his gift if need be. In 1858 Danby wrote despondently to his patron of 'the prevailing gaudiness of modern exhibitions'—'But now so general is the taste for bright and staring colours that he who does not go with it must appear an oddity. It is evident that then, in self-defence, in cases where I exhibit my pictures publicly I should submit to the general tone and flow with the current.'

These landscape painters were men whose necessary vitality or fertility sometimes issued in large families, as well as in canvas after canvas or panel after panel. Danby was among them, having one wife, and one mistress, and no less than ten children to support. Linnell was another patriarch who had to earn for sons and daughters.

The logic of their art as a self-sufficient category dependent upon nature pushed the painters of landscape one way, the inheritance of an academic concept of High Art went on pushing the other way.

'You say we paint too much from Nature; that is a great mistake,' Blake's friend and Danby's friend George Cumberland had written to his landscape-painting son in 1819. 'Even Linnell does not enough observe her, except in sketches from her. All abandon their early studies . . . almost all our artists. The moment you quit her you are lost in landscape painting'*—as Corot or Constable would have agreed.

The strain on the vision of many practitioners was evident, and for them the result was often a forced and weakened overproduction, in a sad and worried life (Cotman's life, for instance, or the life of Samuel Palmer).

Delacroix in his *Journal* speaks of the artist needing enough money to give him independence and 'freedom from those anxieties and those ignoble shifts to which one is put by money embarrassments'—that indispensable state 'which permits one to give oneself to high enterprises, and which prevents the soul and the mind from going downhill.'

Few English landscapists more than began in that happiness. And too many of them, without his stamina, his courage or his truth to himself, learnt, with Millet in France, that 'art isn't a picnic but a grinding mill.'

The Impressionists

It was twelve years after Francis Danby wrote the letter of disillusionment and surrender I have quoted, that the Franco-Prussian war brought Monet and Pissarro from Paris to London (and Daubigny, and the genre painter François Bonvin, who painted a Thames-side picture or two, at Gravesend). Pissarro recollected (page 197) that he and Monet (neither of them very young or immature artists at the time, Monet 30, himself 40) had the idea of submitting their landscape studies to the Royal Academy—'Naturally we were rejected.'

* This, and Danby's letter above, are quoted from *Francis Danby: Varieties of Poetic Landscape*, 1973, by Eric Adams.

What the Academicians rejected was landscape as absolute and as tender as Monet's *Thames and the Houses of Parliament*, now in the National Gallery in London (Plate 116) or Pissarro's *Crystal Palace* (Plate 115). These are landscapes which are pictorial, finally and simply; in which the Houses of Parliament or the Crystal Palace, in its Sydenham surroundings, are items of shape, placing and colour or tone, no more than that; so 'Naturally we were rejected'—and by a selection committee, in 1871, of academicians none of whom is remembered except, with mixed response, G. E. Street, the Pre-Raphaelite architect, and William Powell Frith, the painter of *Derby Day* (who was to give evidence against Whistler, in the *Whistler v. Ruskin* trial seven years later). If Watts R.A. had been one of the selectors, or Millais R.A., or Leighton R.A.—all three might have served—would the landscape studies by Pissarro and Monet have stood a better chance?

I doubt it; and in that year's academy Millais exhibited *Victory, O Lord*—'in the composition of this picture the artist seized the moment when Moses, Aaron and Hur are seen on top of the mountain, while Joshua fights with the Amalekites at the foot, as described in Exodus XVII, 10, 11, 12, 13.' *Victory, O Lord* was well received, history painting still victor, while Monet packed up his dove-tinted landscape of the river, and took it back with him, now the Prussians were gone, to a Paris nearly as indifferent as London of the R.A.s to unsensational purity of landscape.

All along the obstacle course to landscape, as an independent and at last predominant category, it had been effect which was asked for, and striven for, obvious associations (rather than those broad or deep associations with humanity desired by Constable) which had been corruptingly played upon to charm money out of the rich and conventional. Indeed it was this exaggeration which Eugène Delacroix pinpointed as the fault by which the stature of the great English painters had been reduced, including painters of landscape (though not Constable, whom he deeply respected) as well as portraitists. Looking back, he wrote in 1860 'Lawrence, Turner, Reynolds and in general all the great English artists have the defect of exaggeration, particularly as to the effect, which pre-

vents them from being classed among the great masters. Those exaggerated effects, those dark skies, those contrasts of shadow and of light—to which they have been led, however, by their own cloudy and variable sky, but which they have overdone to an unmeasured degree—make one hear the voice of the defects they borrow from fashion and prejudice in louder tones than the voice of their virtues. They have magnificent pictures, but the latter will never offer the spectacle of that eternal youth of the real masterpieces—exempt, all of them, I venture to say, from bombast and effort.'*

That is the acutest of judgements of English painting in its most fertile period; and, small and great, it can be held to cover nearly everyone—except the freaks.

'After the fire a still small voice' Constable quoted against the prodigious and the astounding. How many other painters of landscape were for ever trying to keep that purity and innocence of vision, for ever guarding themselves against bombast, effort, exaggeration, and all those defects which artists do so often borrow from fashion and prejudice?

Even Constable, towards the end of his life, felt he might have betrayed himself a little. He wasn't sure. He looked round at the woods and hills of Arundel in Sussex (page 189) and their beauty made him suspect that he might too much have 'preferred the picturesque to the beautifull—which I hope will account for the *broken ruggedness of my style*.'

Landscape journeys

Coming back in a minute to some of the foreign painters of English landscape, we may call on Turner, since his sketchbooks survive, to discover from him something of the landscape painter's exploratory life, in the great period of the sublime, the picturesque, and the beautiful. Summer, especially early summer, when the light was more vigorous and there was less chance of rain and cold, was the time for such professional expeditions, for finding and sketching views, for building up a stock of drawings of every chance thing,

* from Walter Pach's translation of the *Journal*, 1937.

every mass of trees or movement of water or deployment of clouds or waddling of ducks, which might come into the finished pieces to be worked up, through autumn and winter, for patrons, for the exhibitions, for the aquatint publishers.

The way to sales and livelihood was not to wander off and please yourself. The painter worked in neighbourhoods which attracted the well-to-do summer 'tourists' and their families, he sketched the ruined abbeys, the waterfalls, the harbour, the rocking stone they might like to remember and admire again in a drawing-room portfolio of watercolours.

So the picture neighbourhoods were soon mapped out and established—such as the Lakes, North Wales, the Cader Idris country (where the painter could be pious in his memory of Richard Wilson), the Yorkshire Dales, Wharfedale especially, the Peak District, the Northumbrian castle-coast from the Tyne to Holy Island, Durham Cathedral and the Wear, the coast around Hastings, the Isle of Wight, the coasts of South Devon and North Devon, the Bristol Gorge, Norwich's Mousehold Heath, in its old greater, wilder extent; add to which there was always the Thames from Windsor to Chelsea or London Bridge.

Even so the expedition had to be planned carefully and carried out economically. There were orders to be arranged ahead of travel, there were patrons to be visited en route for new orders or in search of payment for views already 'taken' and delivered.

Distances had to be worked out, time would be short, weather unpredictable (in one of Turner's sketchbooks it is fascinating to come across a Cader Idris watercolour spotted and splashed by rain).

Several of his early sketchbooks, in particular, show how Turner worked out his itineraries, listing his mileage, and placing beforehand the castles, the churches, the abbeys, the bridges and so on, which it might be worth sketching. He would discover what was what from books by the antiquaries and the literary 'tourists'.

From a sketchbook of 1794, Turner then nineteen years old:

> Derby; near which is Dale Abbey
>
> Nottingham, 3 Churches, St Mary, Gothic, a large Castle, romantic situated. In the Market Place, one end Justice, the other a Cross supported by 4 Doric Columns. A Bridge of 19 arches.
>
> Linton, a mile from N., a Abbey.
>
> At Southhill or Southwell is a Collegiate Church. There is remains a Battlement Tower of a Castle N.
>
> Newark, a Bridge, a Gothic Church and Castle.
>
> At Stamford, R. of a Castle.
>
> At Crowland a triangular Bridge, pure Gothic. Great part of the Abbey still remains—the Steeple, with the West isle, with carv'd Figure.
>
> Peterborough Cathedral.

Or Turner on the first page of a sketchbook of 1810–1816:

> Lulworth Cove water for 80 ton burthen.
>
> Portland 4 miles from Weymouth.
>
> Ferry at the end called Smallbrook the water call'd the Fleet 5 miles.
>
> Cheselbank extends from Port to Abbotbury 9 miles long. Cheswell.
>
> The pebbles get smaller as the receded from Portland.
>
> Light House at Portland built by Mr Johns of Wey 68 feet high conical geometrical . . .
>
> Torbay to be seen the distance 25 leagues near is Cave's hole perforated thro' from E. to West.
>
> The inhabitants of Portland the ancient Belares. The Reevepole the Saxon mode of keeping accounts of land.
>
> Some traces of a Roman encampment behind the Portland Arms.
>
> Abbotbury founded by Orcus Steward to the household of K. Canute, St Catherines Chapel sea marks.
>
> Swannery and Decoy.

—and so on, not omitting the natural cliff arch of Durdle Door and the fact that the Duke of Monmouth landed at Lyme Regis, and that there were good corbel stones elsewhere and a Cromlech that might be drawn —'the Coit 14 feet 3 supporters 7 high.'

Everything was worth looking at, in case it might

come in useful, the landscape painters of this time having picturesque, sublime, antiquarian, historical, pastoral and literary tastes to satisfy, rather than the taste we call aesthetic.

Sometimes impressions crowded in too quickly. There were occasions when Turner had to resort to a note in words instead of notes in line or colour. He is in Derbyshire, he draws bridges, and barges unloading and barges moored. Suddenly he writes down, in his peculiar capitalization, 'Children picking up Horse Dung, gathering Weeds, Driving Asses with coals. Milk carriers to Manchester. Yorkshires into Barrels. Pigs, Geese, Asses, Browsing upon Thistles. Asses going to Coal Pits.'

Or Turner will remember or come across some

quotation he likes. Down it goes—triads from the Welsh (he is in North Wales, making drawings of Caernarvon Castle), from Pennant, whose *Tour in Wales* he must have been reading:

Snowdon Mountain, ravenous snow

melted, windy often.

In distress best is a relation.

Or a couplet from Pope—an affecting one much in harmony with the gentler landscapes of the time—gets itself included among sketches of river scenery he has been making within sight of Windsor Castle:

A shepherd's Boy (he seeks no better Name)

Let forth his Flocks along the silver Thame.*

Or (this time he is on the way back from working in

* From Pope's *Pastorals: Summer.*

Turner: MARTELLO TOWERS NEAR BEXHILL. *Etching,* 7 × 4½ *in. Boston, Museum of Fine Arts.*

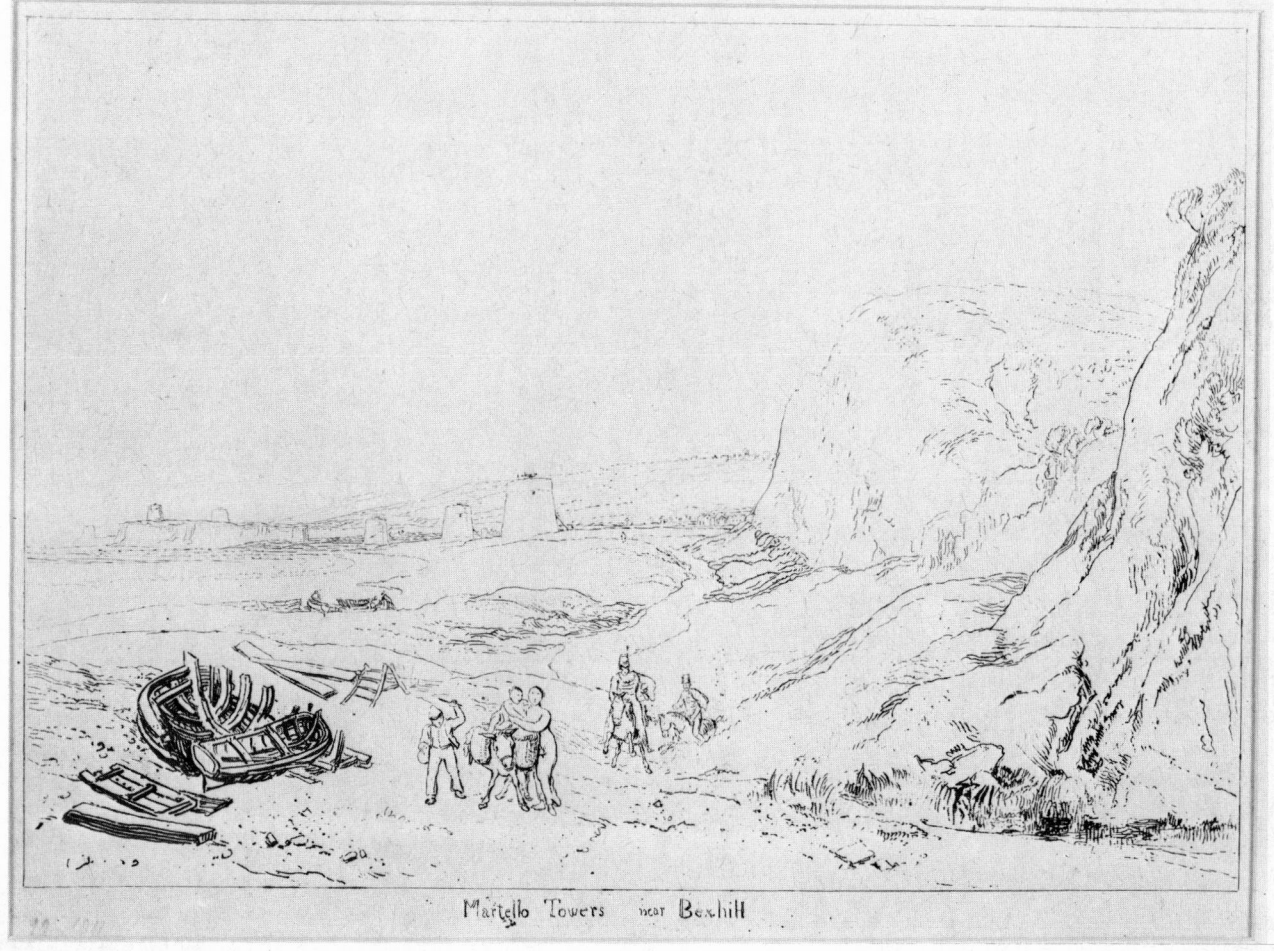

Martello Towers near Bexhill

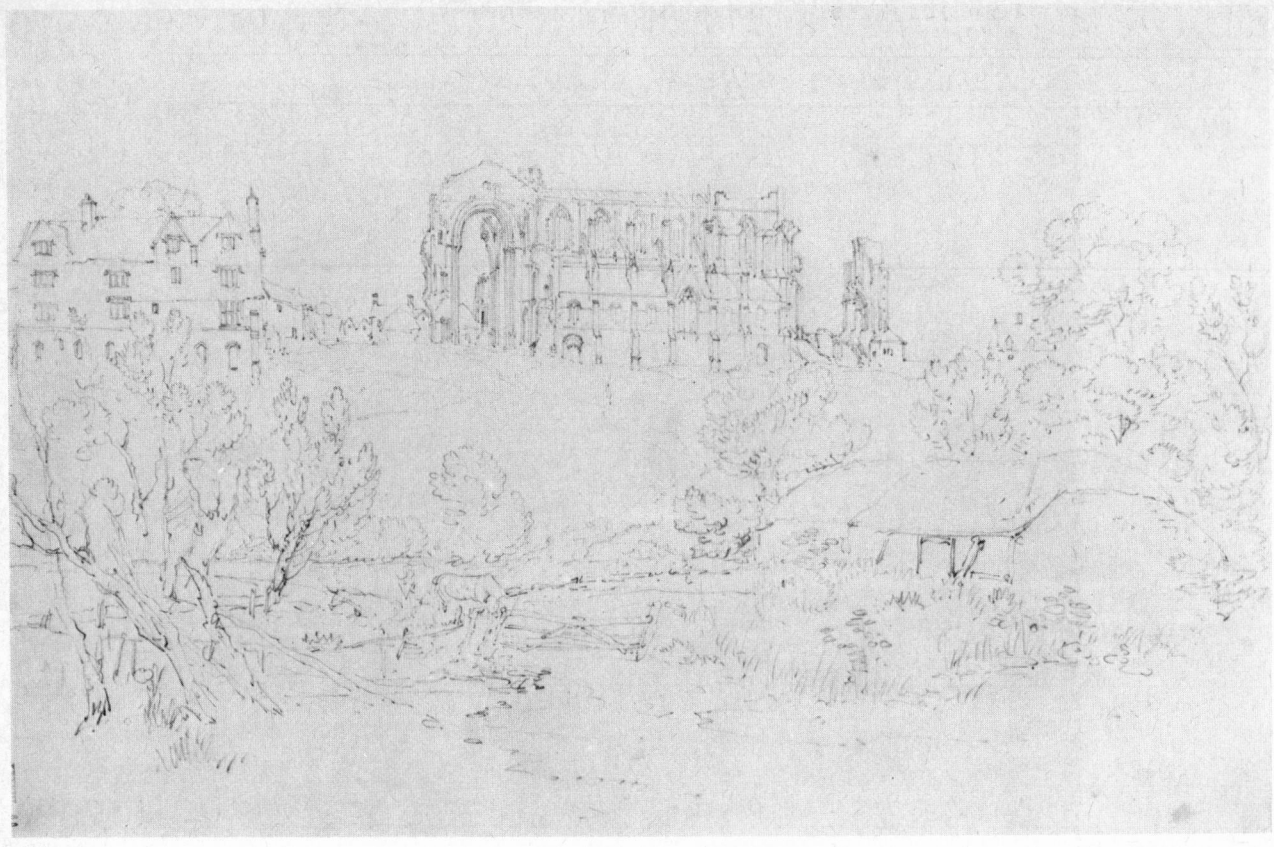

Turner: MALMESBURY ABBEY. *Pencil, 15 × 19 in. London, British Museum.*

Devon and Cornwall) Turner inserts an awkward scrap by himself, ungrammatical and illiterate, about the barrows around Stonehenge, of which there are four drawings in the sketchbook:

> But distant rising thro the darkning skies
> The blear expanse of Sarum's plain arise
> Where mouldering tumuli sepulchral steep
> Gives but a niggard shelter e'en to sheep.

Some day, like the sketches in stock, such a quotation may come in useful, attached to a finished drawing.

These sketching journeys meant long trips by coaster, often the quickest and least expensive way of travel for a London artist going north or even to Wales. (Coasting, so often preferable to rough and dangerous roads, may explain the 'long views' of such early draughtsmen as Hollar and his pupil and friend Francis Place). Horses were to be hired, but that cost money, and these summer artists trudged and trudged. One finds Turner, in preparation for work along the coast of South Wales, noting *Larn to Llanstephen, 5 miles along the shore,* and we can picture him making that short cut from Laugharne when the sea was far out across that huge width of sand.

. James Ward, another landscapist of enormous energy and endurance, walked 30 miles a day in 1811 on a sketching tour in the south of Scotland, his feet blistered and infected (to ease them he put tobacco leaves in each shoe), the rain driving down on him, nothing awaiting him in the evenings except filthy food, black cabbage soup out of a common bowl, bad eggs, salt fish, underbaked oatcakes, stinking ham, butter full of cow hairs, gravy compacted with coal dust; and then a bed which was dirty, damp, and running with bugs.

Samuel Palmer, who had trudged most of North Wales in his time, reached Clovelly in July 1849 so weak in the legs that he could hardly move: 'I crawl out with a boy to carry my things (being so weak) & crawl back again—*walking is out of the question.*'

One result of this working system, which lasted nearly a hundred years, is the existence not infrequently of many, many professional watercolours of the same celebrated place or curiosity.

One such curiosity is the Dropping Well at Knaresborough in Yorkshire, of which Francis Place made wash and pen drawings (Plate 9) as early as 1711. Another is Gordale Scar in the West Riding. Its shadowed cliffs of mountain limestone and its broken waterfall were professionally drawn by Smith of Derby in the mid-eighteenth century, by Edward Dayes, by Girtin in 1801, by James Ward about 1811 (Plate 47), and by Turner in 1816 (a drawing of Gordale was commissioned by his Wharfedale patron, Walter Fawkes of Farnley Hall); then by Inchbold (who was a Yorkshireman) in 1876; and in our own day, in 1939, in company with the present writer, by that explorer of the vision of his predecessors, John Piper.

What is touching is to think of the young landscape artists of the Romantic period, some of them deeply and eccentrically devout, and as filled as the poets of their time, and as the Barbizon painters were to be after them, with the new message and sense of nature, having ahead of them a life of endless hard labour and anxious calculation—to think, for instance, of the few who came together, in their twenties, in 1808, to found a winter drawing club they solemnly called 'The Society for the Study of Epic and Pastoral Design'.

Turner of Oxford (Plate 74), G. R. Lewis (Plates 76, 78), and Cornelius Varley (Plates 68, 69) were members, and as visitors to their meetings they invited Constable, and Havell (Plate 75).

Landscape ecstasies, landscape meditation—they were genuine enough, but they had to be transformed into saleable commodities of the publicly acceptable, if these young men were to live.

Along the Thames

A last, and special, word should go to the Thames, for it is the Thames—and properly—which has threaded our own landscape art and has linked through four centuries those artists from overseas who have drawn or painted in Great Britain. Along with the Seine, the Thames after all turns out to be the most painted river in Europe.

From abroad the Thames or the Thames valley artists begin with the smaller fry out of the Low Countries, with Anthonis van den Wyngaerde from

Schellinks: STONEHENGE AND SALISBURY PLAIN. $7\frac{5}{8} \times 28\frac{1}{2}$ *in. London, British Museum.*

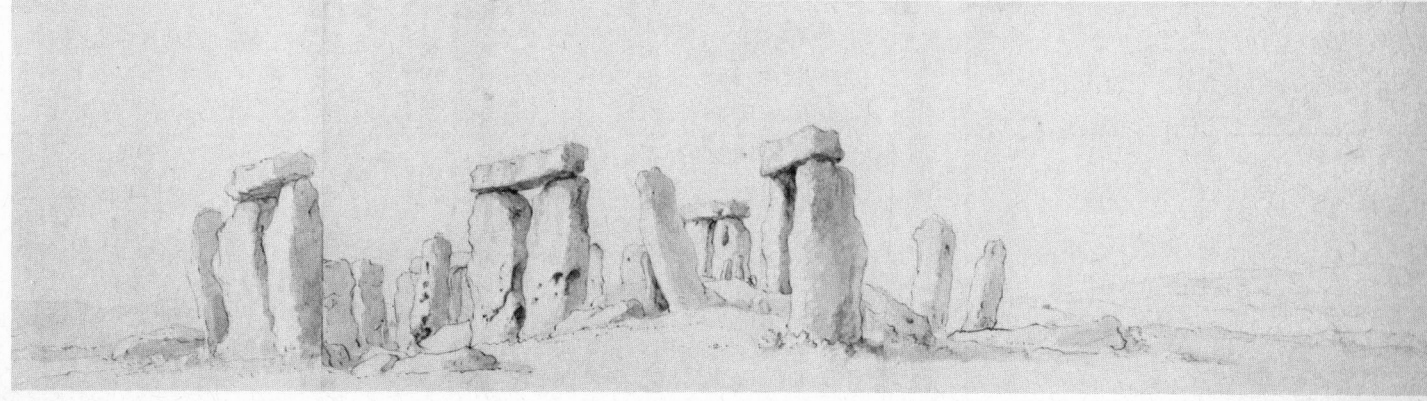

Antwerp or Brussels, flourishing in the 1550s, and Joris Hoefnagel (1541–1600), son of an Antwerp diamond merchant, who was in England in 1568 and 1569, Claude de Jongh from Utrecht, who died in 1663, the Amsterdam draughtsman Willem Schellinks (1627–1678), Abraham Hondius (Plate 10), Dutchman from Rotterdam, and a Londoner from 1665 to his death in the 1690s, not to mention Rubens for his incidental view of the Thames (Plate 1) and Siberechts (Plates 3–5). Wenceslaus Hollar, too, though Bohemian from Prague, came to England by way of Cologne, if not the Netherlands (Plates 6, 7).

So it goes on, our succession of Thames painters from across the Channel, Canaletto, Agasse, Corot, Daubigny, Pissarro, Sisley, Monet, the giant of them all in his unadulterated landscape, then Whistler, Derain, Dufy, and, as the result of another war, Oskar Kokoschka from Vienna, painter of a London, in his expressionist idiom, as panoramic as Canaletto's,

but not as exhilarating (painter, also, unexpectedly, of that English sentimentalist's haven, Polperro, in Cornwall).

Distinguished, too, are the English artists of the Thames—of whom a few are Wilson, Scott, Zoffany, Rowlandson, Girtin, Turner, Constable, Daniell, Linnell, Greaves, Boyce, Maitland, down to Victor Pasmore, who brings this *Britain Observed* to an end— Thames at the close as well as Thames at the beginning.

Constable's 'I should paint my own places best' must apply to visiting artists—how do you know what you love, or exactly how to love it, except by time and intimacy? But it does not apply to them all. Canaletto came to London in 1746. Wonderful he is, at first, in the famous paintings reproduced in this landscape survey, and in a few others, among them the grand panorama of London, *The Thames with Westminster Bridge in the Distance* (in the Narodni Galerie in Prague). In these it is as if the Thames had appeared to

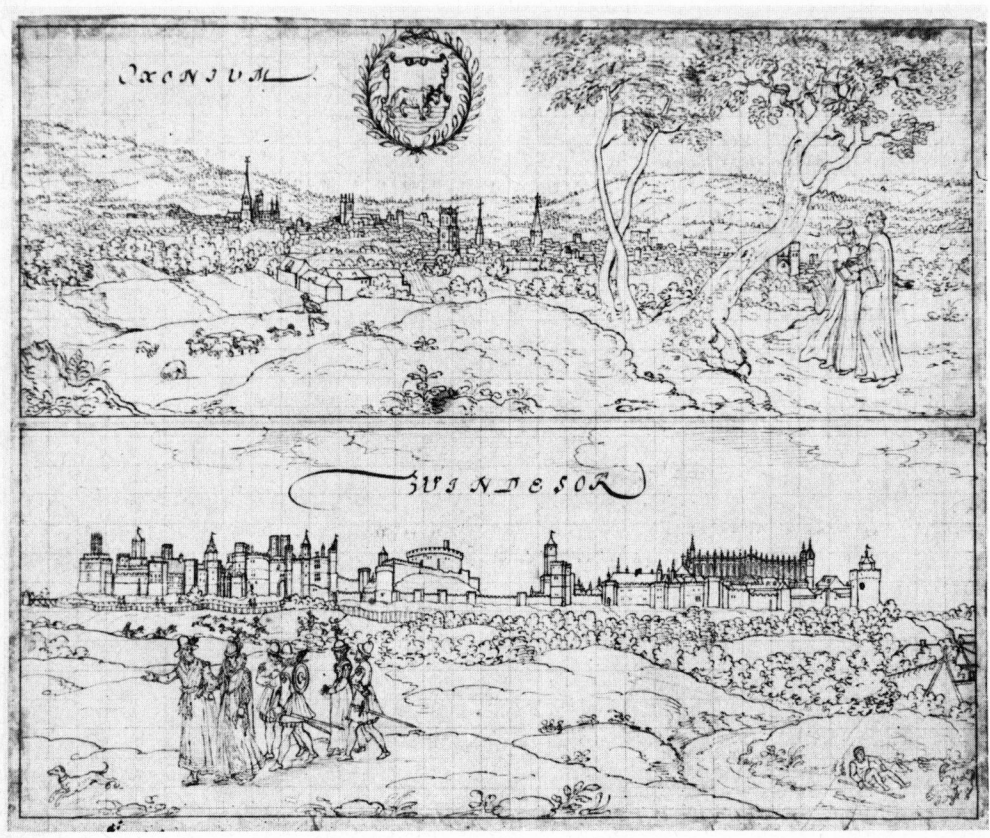

Hoefnagel:
VIEW OF OXFORD
AND WINDSOR.
$8\frac{3}{4} \times 10\frac{1}{2}$ *in.*
Royal Library.
Reproduced by
gracious permission
of Her Majesty
The Queen.

him a sparkling congenial enlargement of the Grand Canal. Almost comic he is, away from wide still water and city, in his painting of Alnwick Castle, in Northumberland.

Whistler—American or English? Or the artist with no country who naturalizes himself in Chelsea?—creates or sees a new Thames in the river which was waiting for him; a greater artist than we like to confess, even now. Pissarro, Monet—they project more than locality in a vision of light, which has nothing to do with aboriginal cradles, or frontiers, or local allegiances. Monet's London, his few early landscapes of 1870–71, of the parks and the river, then all his studies of Charing Cross Bridge, and Waterloo Bridge and the Houses of Parliament would fill rooms, if they could be assembled, of the National Gallery or the Tate or the Louvre, with no sense at all that he was painting sights alien to himself.

At first, contemplating English paintings by artists who were not English, I inclined to think of the painters as timid and incurious. All the rest of England was there for them, and Richmond or Kew was about as far as most of them ever went from Westminster Bridge. Yet why explore, painting being what it is, when the Thames was to hand? There were subjects enough, in that river, which we have since ruined, scenically, with such a hard and divisive embankment.

Painters from Flanders and Holland had come when the English required a new art in which they could be instructed, and when there was evident money to earn.

The English learnt, that first influx came to an end.

Thereafter it was a matter of curiosity about the metropolis on the Thames, or of learning about the new masters of portraiture or landscape, or of finding for a while a refuge, which might or might not be profitable. A painter or two looked in from the Scandinavian countries—Elias Martin (1739–1818) from Sweden, making wash drawings of St Paul's, and of the Thames foreshore (in the Nationalmuseum in Stockholm), and leaving behind him his strange wall landscapes in the saloon of Sunbury Court, in Middlesex; then Thomas Fearnley (1802–42) from Norway. That was more of an event, a painter, and a delightful one, of the Dresden School of Landscape, arriving in the 1830s, making friends with English artists, watching Turner putting last touches to his Academy pictures before the exhibition opened, admiring Constable, and painting in the Lakes in 1837 (Plate 70), and elsewhere. Perhaps his Yorkshire descent made him at home in the Lakes, though his most delicious paintings were Mediterranean.

One other Dresden painter visited London—and travelled outside London too, as Fearnley had done. This was Carl Gustav Carus (1789–1869), theoretician of landscape, the friend and the first biographer of Caspar David Friedrich.

Carus arrived in 1844. He travelled around England and Scotland with the King of Saxony, Frederick II, who was another landscape painter (and a botanist). At the Academy he was upset by Turner's exhibits (it

Schellinks: WINDSOR CASTLE. 13 × 45 *in. Amsterdam, Rijksmuseum.*

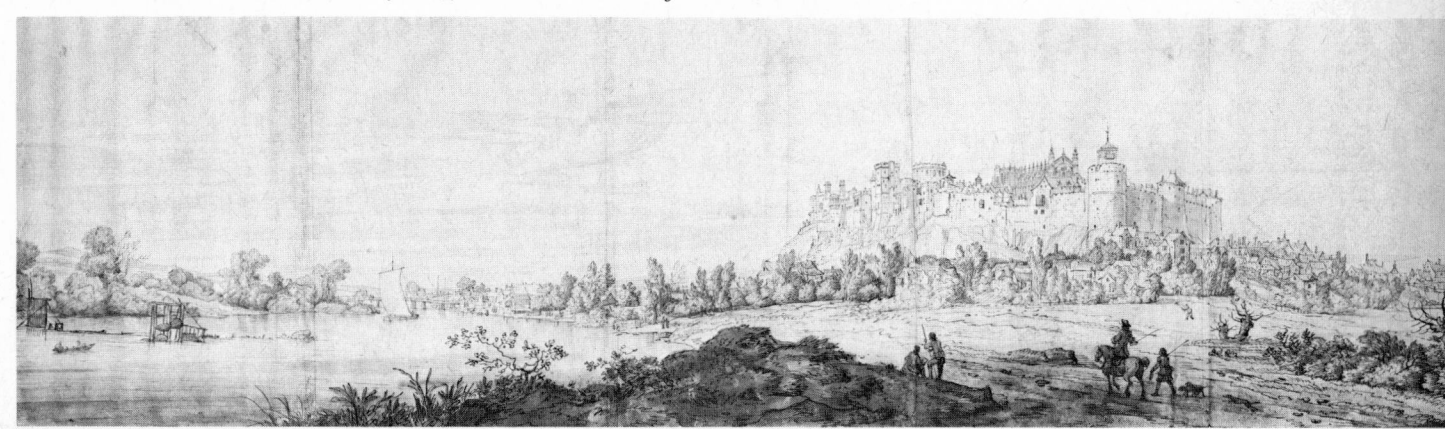

was the year of Turner's *Port Ruysdael, Van Tromp,* and *Ostend,* three Venetian oils, and also *Rain, Steam and Speed*) and found them absurd—'If a bright coloured sea piece were to be painted,' he wrote, 'on a wax tablet, then melted, and all the colours mixed up together, I fancy it would present much the appearance of this artist's paintings. I would give something to know *how* this painter sees nature and what there is in his eyes that causes him to see nature thus?'*

One thing Carus enjoyed was the richness of scenery in South Devon, which made him reflect that the landscape painter must receive the unconsciousness of nature into his consciousness. Carus believed that the landscape painter expressed a mood of his own inner life in what seemed a corresponding mood in the life of nature. But I have seen no English paintings by him (or by King Frederick).

England—English painting as well—meant a little more to the Barbizon painters. Corot was twice in England, in London, painting a few pictures on the second occasion when he was sixty-six (Plate 96). Jules Dupré (1811–99), one of the Barbizon reformers of

* C. G. Carus, *The King of Saxony's Journey through England and Wales in the Year 1844.* Translated by S. C. Davidson, 1846.

landscape and one of the good angels of the movement, had his English connections and was painting in England in 1834. He admired Constable. So did Charles-François Daubigny (1817–78), Corot's friend and Monet's friend, Barbizon pioneer whose landscapes of extent come near to Impressionism. He was in London in 1866 (and was to be there again, on his wartime visit, through the autumn and winter of 1870 and the spring of 1871) when he discovered the light and width of the estuary of the Thames, painting, for instance *The Thames at Erith* and making drawings of the winding, low embanked Kentish shore and the river barges.

So to the glory of the business, as far as concerns the *outre-mer* interpreters. If Daubigny's English paintings are weaker than the best of his French ones—'I should paint my own places best' applies to him all right—how glad we can be that Pissarro came, and came again and again; that Claude Monet painted so feverishly, solemnly and lyrically from his rooms at the Savoy and St Thomas's Hospital; that Vollard the dealer sent Derain across in 1906 to do the Thames over again *not* in Monet's way, but splendidly still, in that process which has at last taken painting altogether beyond landscape.

Hollar: WESTMINSTER AND THE THAMES, LOOKING NORTH FROM LAMBETH HOUSE, *c.* 1637–43. 6 × 15¾ *in. London, British Museum.*

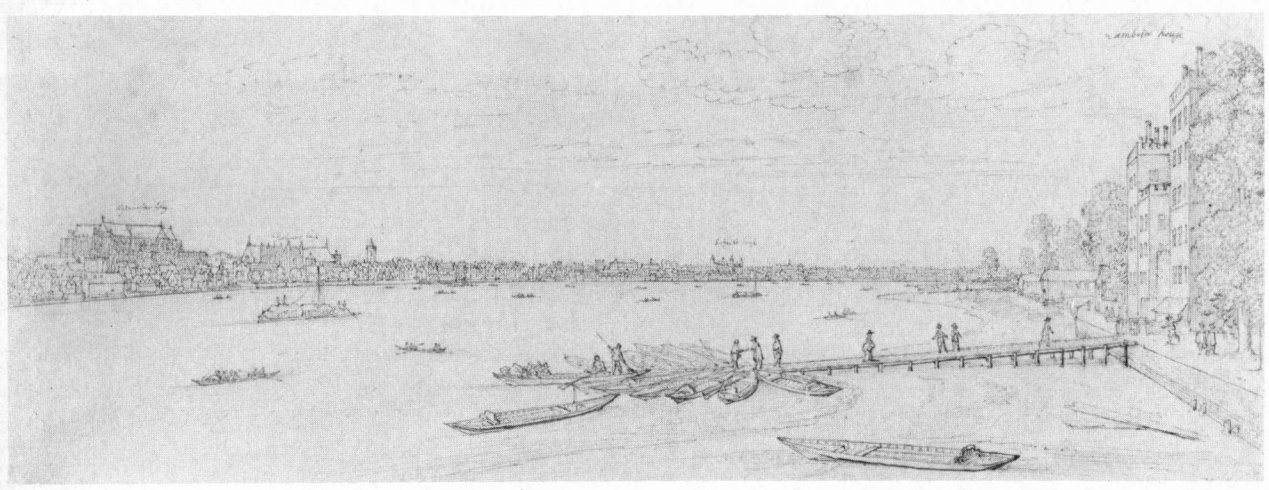

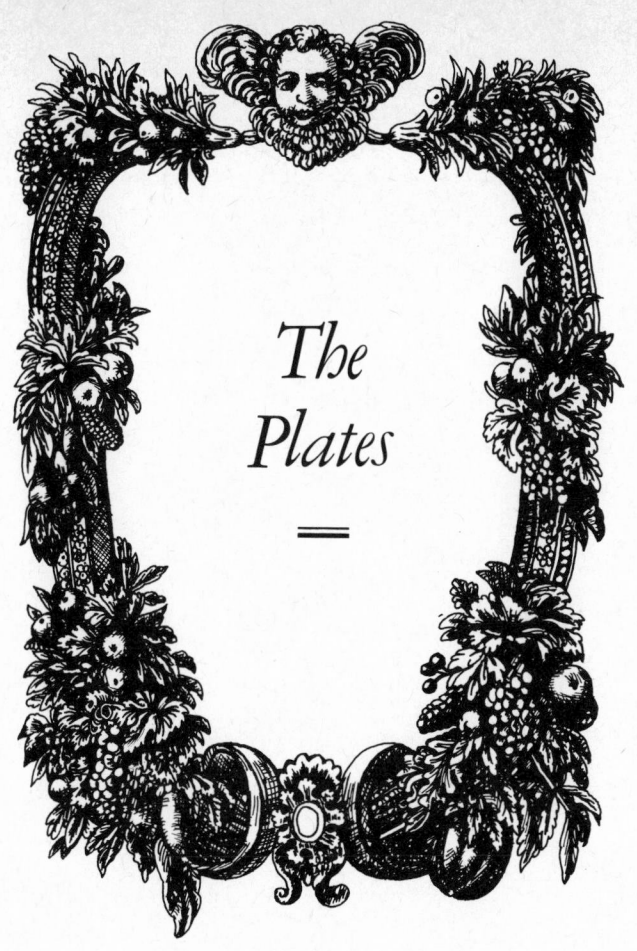

The
Plates

=

THE GREAT ANTWERP MASTER was in England from the beginning of June 1629 to the beginning of March 1630, and in the course of that year he painted the *Landscape with St. George and the Dragon,* showing Charles I as St. George and Henrietta Maria as the rescued Princess against a background of the Thames and a distant London arranged or re-arranged according to the artist's fancy. The major landscapes by which Constable and other English painters were to be so moved, arrived in London nearly two centuries later. These were the *Château de Steen* in the National Gallery and *The Rainbow Landscape* in the Wallace Collection. Constable spoke of *The Rainbow Landscape* as marking one of the 'four memorable points in the history of landscape'. In Rubens he found 'dewy light and freshness, the departing shower, with the exhilaration of the returning sun'—'In no other branch of the art is Rubens greater than in landscape; the freshness and dewy light, the joyous and animated character which he has imparted to it, impressing on the level monotonous scenery of Flanders all the richness which belongs to its noblest features. Rubens delighted in phenomena;—rainbows upon a stormy sky—bursts of sunshine—moonlight—meteors—and impetuous torrents mingling their sound with wind and waves.' It was Constable's friend Sir George Beaumont who gave the *Château de Steen* to the National Gallery.

I. ST. GEORGE AND THE DRAGON. *Oil,* $57\frac{1}{2} \times 78\frac{1}{2}$. *London, the Royal Collection. Reproduced by gracious permission of Her Majesty the Queen.*

Rubens has set his Charles I as St. George and Henrietta Maria as the Princess on the north bank of the Thames. In the distance, upstream, Lambeth Palace. Left, a rather arbitrary arrangement of St. Mary Overy church (Southwark Cathedral), the Banqueting Hall, and Westminster Abbey. See Edward Croft Murray, 'The Landscape Background in Rubens's St. George and the Dragon', *Burlington Magazine,* 1947.

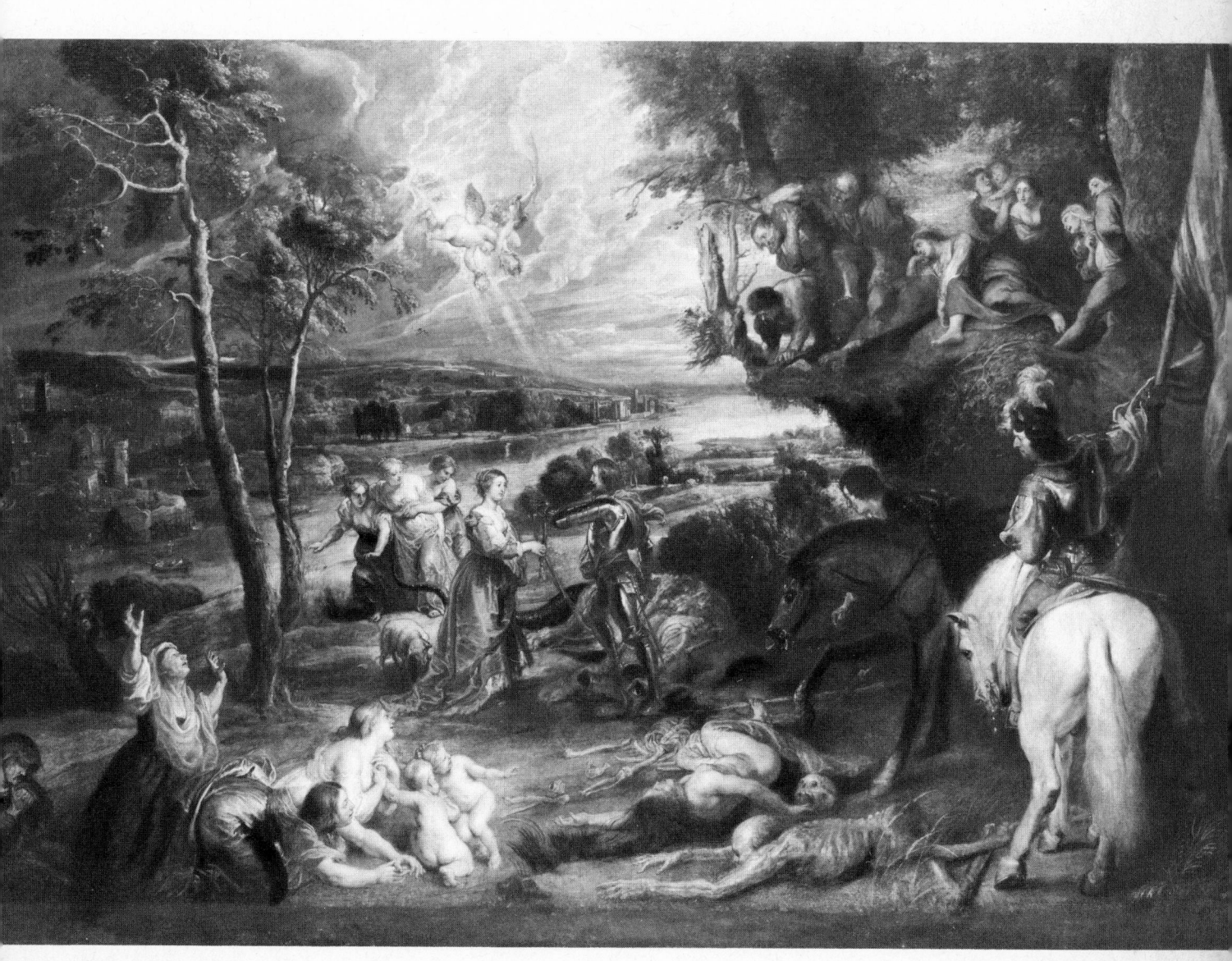

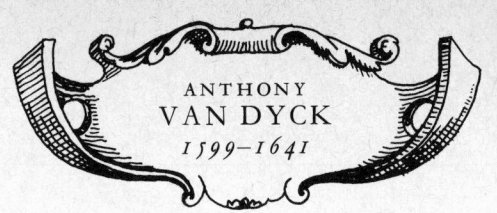

ENGLAND was Van Dyck's base, as court painter, from 1632 until his death, and it is possible that a number of undated, unlocalized landscape watercolours by him are of English scenes. One of sloping ground with trees overtopped by sails of boats on an estuary (in the Barber Institute, Birmingham) suggests the Kentish shore of the Thames, as it might have been within reach of Eltham Palace, near Blackheath. Van Dyck had his summer quarters in the palace and one can imagine even this suave master of exquisite manners and amiable disposition being a little tried at times by another noble lord and another noble lady, and taking refuge from his painting room and his assistants in a little Netherlandish landscaping along the uncourtly by-ways of Kent. These assured gentle landscapes, true to watercolour and independent of line, much excited connoisseurs of seventy years ago. They seemed to them to forerun the developed watercolour practice of the early nineteenth century.

2. UNFINISHED LANDSCAPE. *Watercolour, $8\frac{7}{8} \times 13\frac{3}{8}$ in. Chatsworth, Duke of Devonshire collection (Trustees of the Chatsworth Settlement).*

An unidentified scene, but more certainly English than the scenes of most of Van Dyck's other watercolours. The square tower appears to belong to a castle, not a church.

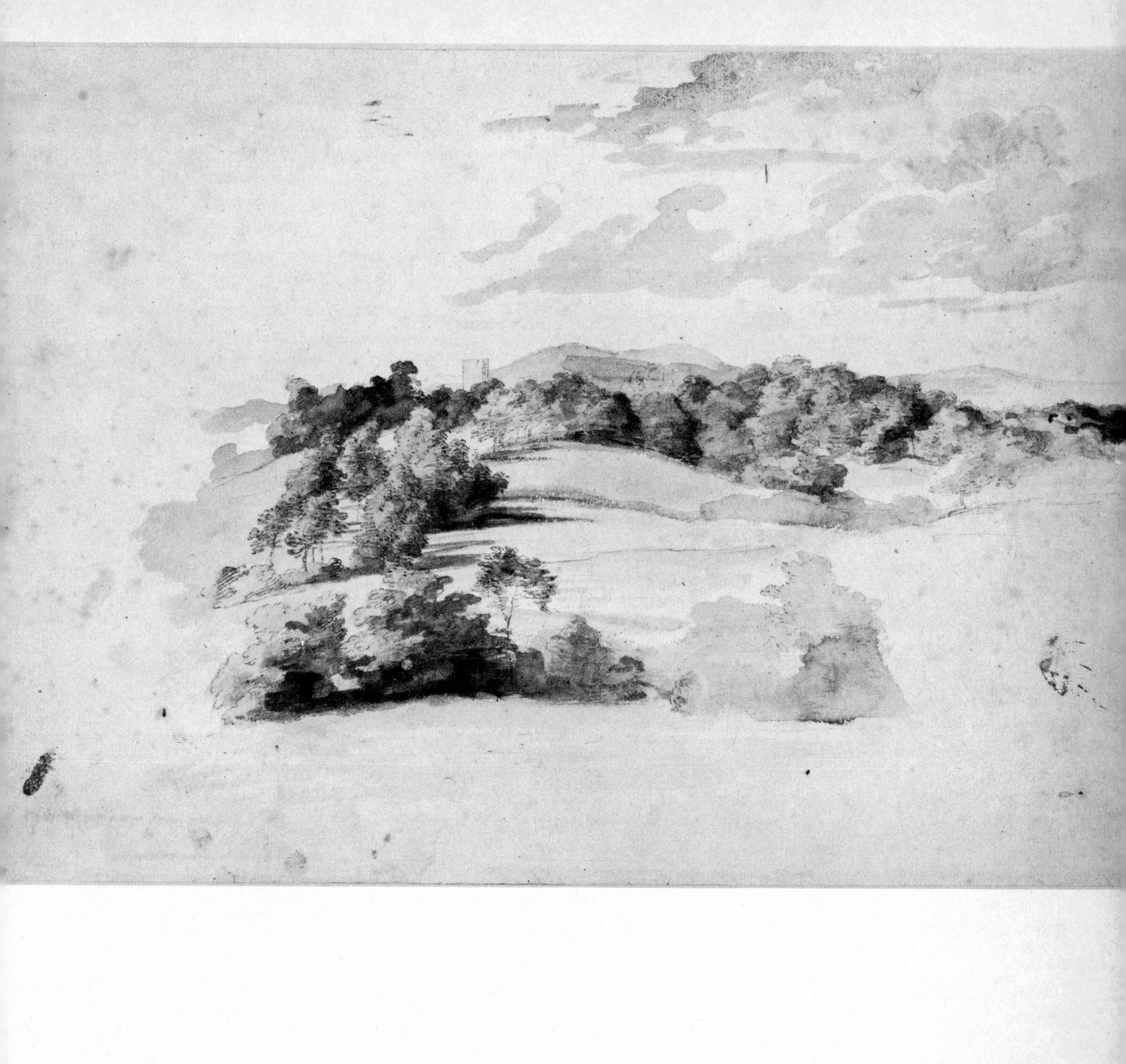

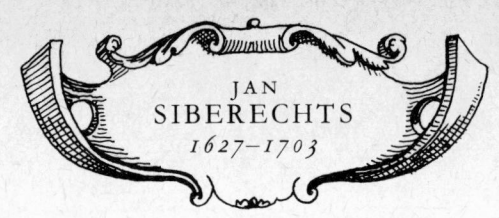

ONE OF THE ABLEST of the Flemish landscape artists to work in England, with advantage to the English landscapists who came after them in the eighteenth century. He had a passion for building up his pictures around and above a ford, the light of which would be broken by the passage of carts, or cattle, or peasants. It has been said that he lost something of his touch and silveriness in his English work, which all the same has more than a history book value. Coming to England from Antwerp in or about 1672, he lived by taking the landscape likeness of great houses up and down the country, including Cliveden, Longleat, Wollaton Hall, Chevely and Derbyshire's Chatsworth. But he also managed to paint more intimate landscape of the kind he liked. In his stay at Chatsworth the shapes and boldness of the Peak attracted him. Unmannered drawings by him catch the structure and sweep of hills. Siberechts settled in London, and was buried at St. James's, Piccadilly.

3. LANDSCAPE NEAR CHATSWORTH, DERBYSHIRE, 1694. *Watercolour,* $8\frac{1}{4} \times 14\frac{1}{4}$ *in. Amsterdam, Rijksmuseum.*

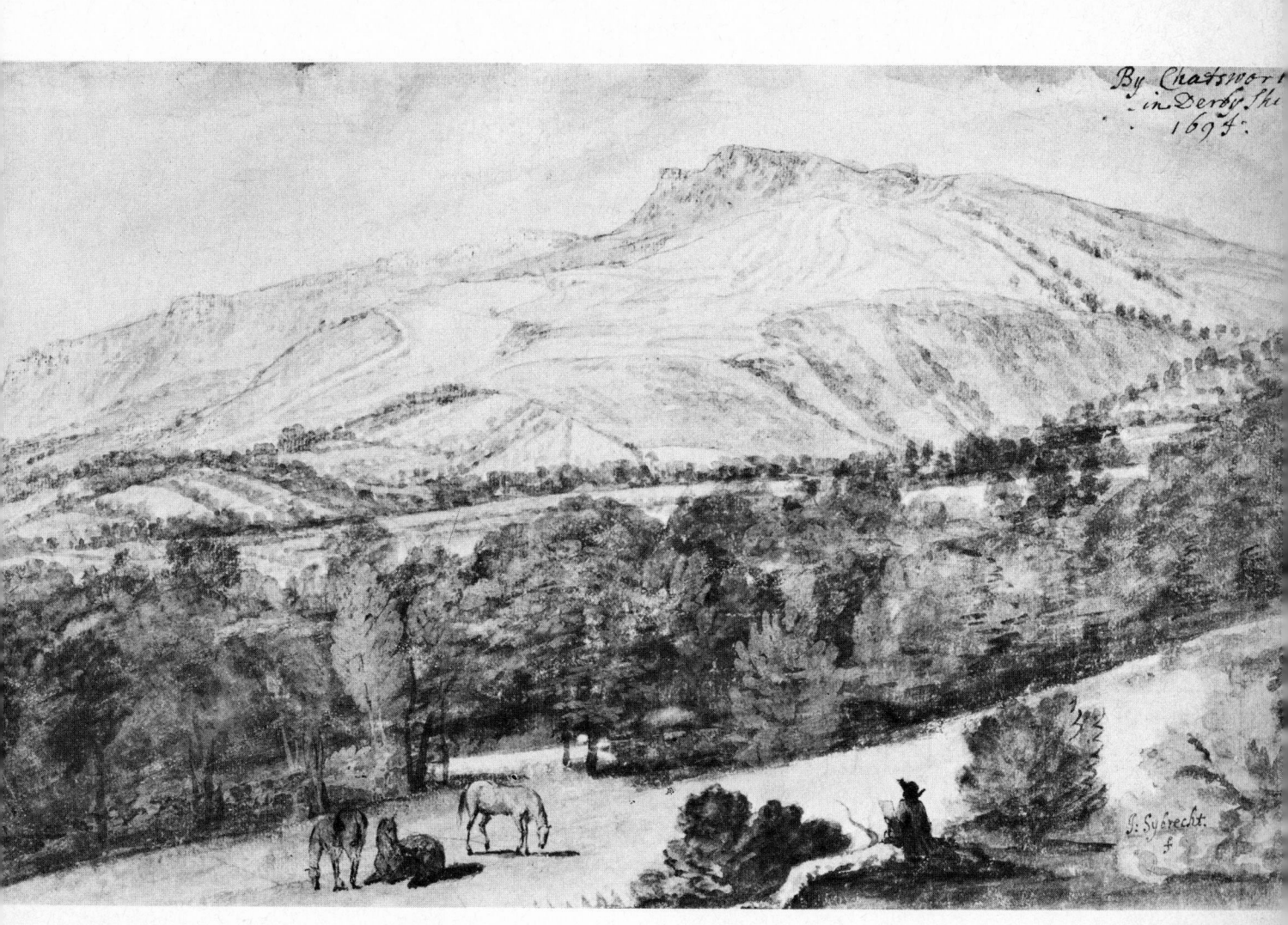

By Chatsworth
in Derbyshi
1694

J. Siberecht.
f

4. LANDSCAPE WITH RAINBOW, HENLEY-ON-THAMES. *c.* 1692. *Oil,* $32\frac{1}{4} \times 40\frac{1}{2}$ *in. London, Tate Gallery.*

Siberechts painted another view of Henley, reproduced in Leslie Parris, *Landscape in Britain*, Tate Gallery, 1973. It is dated 1692, and shows Henley at a distance beyond a more typical Siberechts foreground with cattle and peasants.

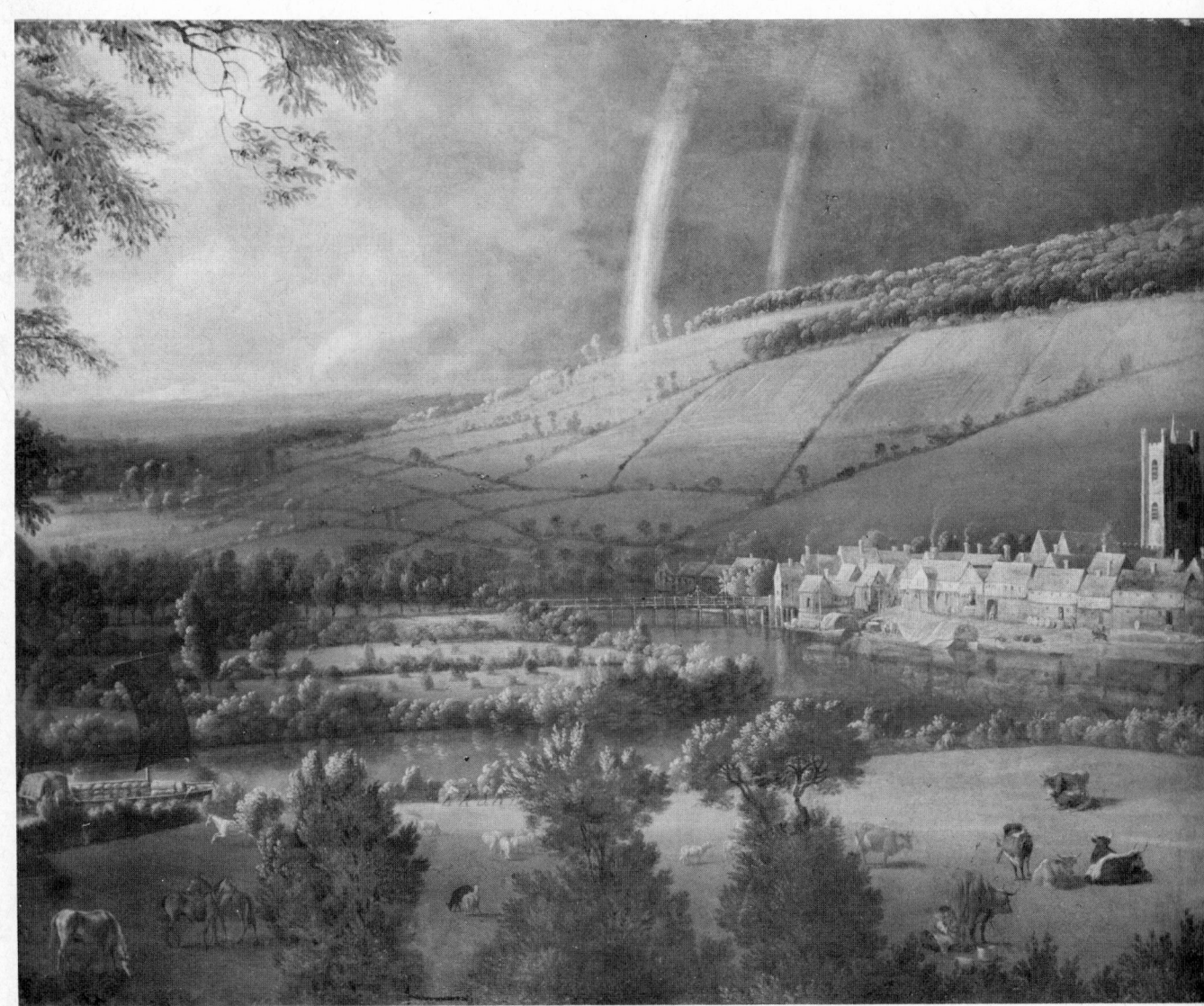

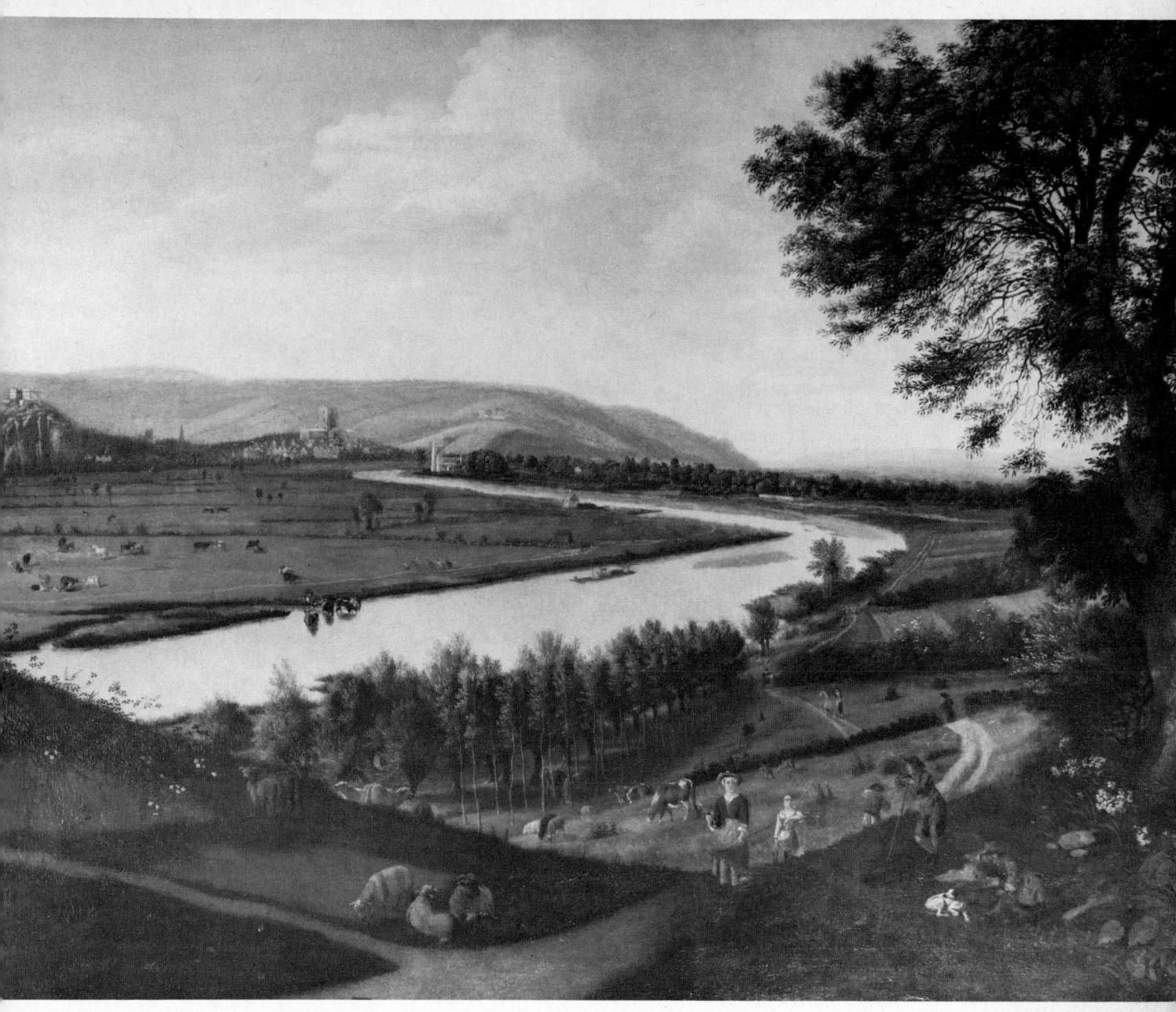

5. VIEW OF NOTTINGHAM AND THE TRENT. *Oil, 43 × 57½ in. Collection The Right Hon. The Lord Middleton.*

The pre-industrial Nottingham on the 'silver Trent' of such poets as Drayton, now the filthiest river in Great Britain. Painted for the Willoughbys, the coal magnates of Wollaton Hall, which shows on the hill top to the left. See page 12 for more about Siberechts and the Willoughbys.

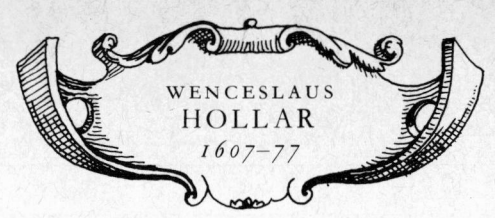

Words such as 'topography' and 'of historical interest' are rather too brusquely called up to greet the drawings and etchings of this energetic artist from Prague. He belongs to a century of awakened interest in travel and science; exactly the man for such a connoisseur as Thomas Howard, Earl of Arundel (celebrated for his Arundel Marbles), who met the young Hollar at Cologne, where he was then living, in 1636. He brought him back to London, and settled him in Arundel House on the Strand, overlooking the great waterway of the Thames. Hollar took to an English life. He went abroad to Antwerp in the Civil War period, came back in 1652, and stayed in England for the rest of his days, popularizing the idea of landscape by his wide views of coast and castle and palace. His panoramas are the illustrative or informative landscape art of a time when travel was less by road than by rivers, estuaries and coastal waters.

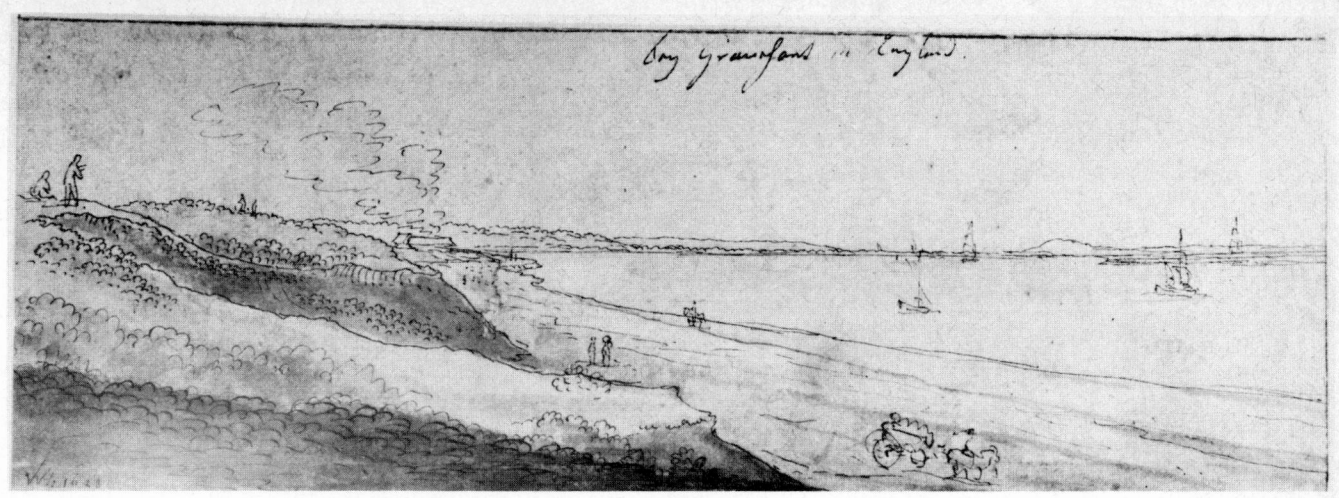

6. GRAVESEND. *Watercolour and pen, 25 × 7¹⁄₁₆ in. London, British Museum.*

7. THE EAST SIDE OF LONDON TOWARDS GREENWICH. *Pen, 5½ × 11¾ in. Collection of Mr and Mrs Paul Mellon.*

This was one of the studies Hollar drew for his *Long Bird's Eye View of London from Bankside*, etched in seven plates and published in 1647.

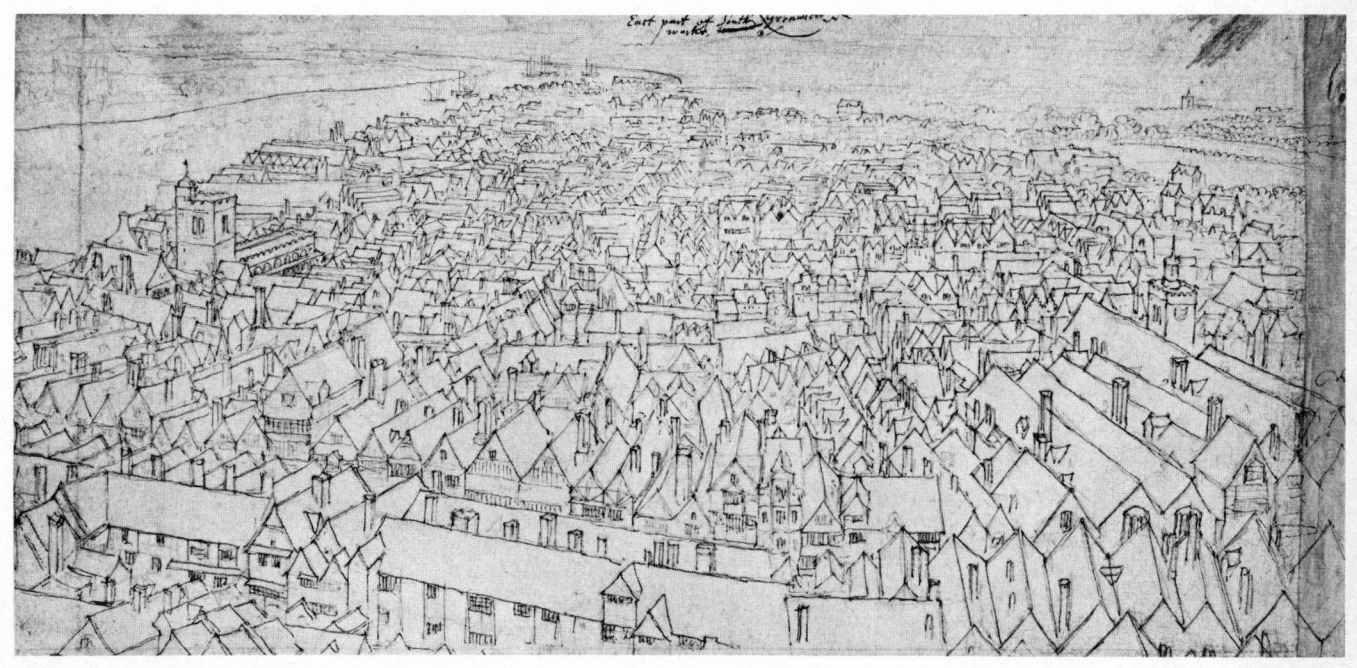

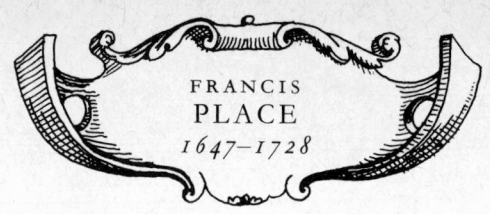

FRANCIS
PLACE
1647–1728

CONTACT IN LONDON with the Prague artist and etcher Wenceslaus Hollar helped to turn the young country gentleman Francis Place into 'the first English artist whose main preoccupation was landscape.' He grew up in Co. Durham, in the manor house at Dinsdale, near Darlington, in the fine country of the lower Tees. He learnt etching from Hollar, and displayed the semi-scientific curiosity proper to a virtuoso in the decades after the Restoration. He travelled and drew, and in time developed a broad and confident use of watercolour wash, making his records in Wales, along the Thames, in Yorkshire and in Northumberland and elsewhere, intrigued always by castles, ruins, hill-set towns, and coastal panoramas.

8. TENBY IN PEMBROKESHIRE, 1678. *Pen, wash and watercolour, $7\frac{1}{2} \times 21\frac{3}{4}$ in. Cardiff, National Museum of Wales.*

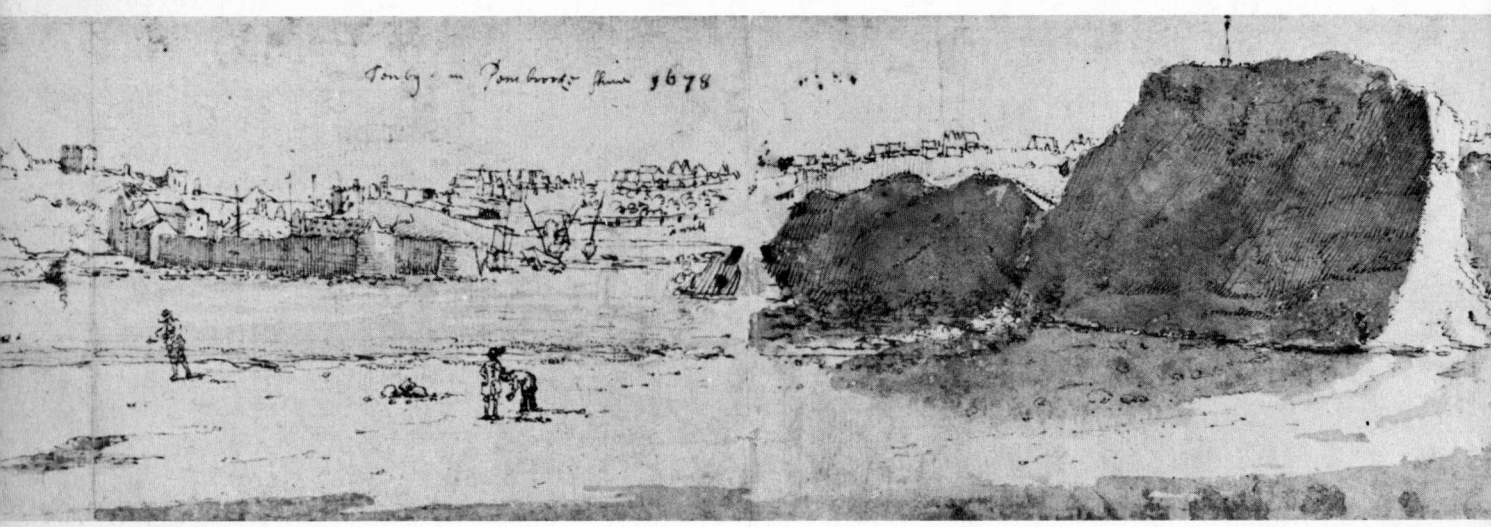

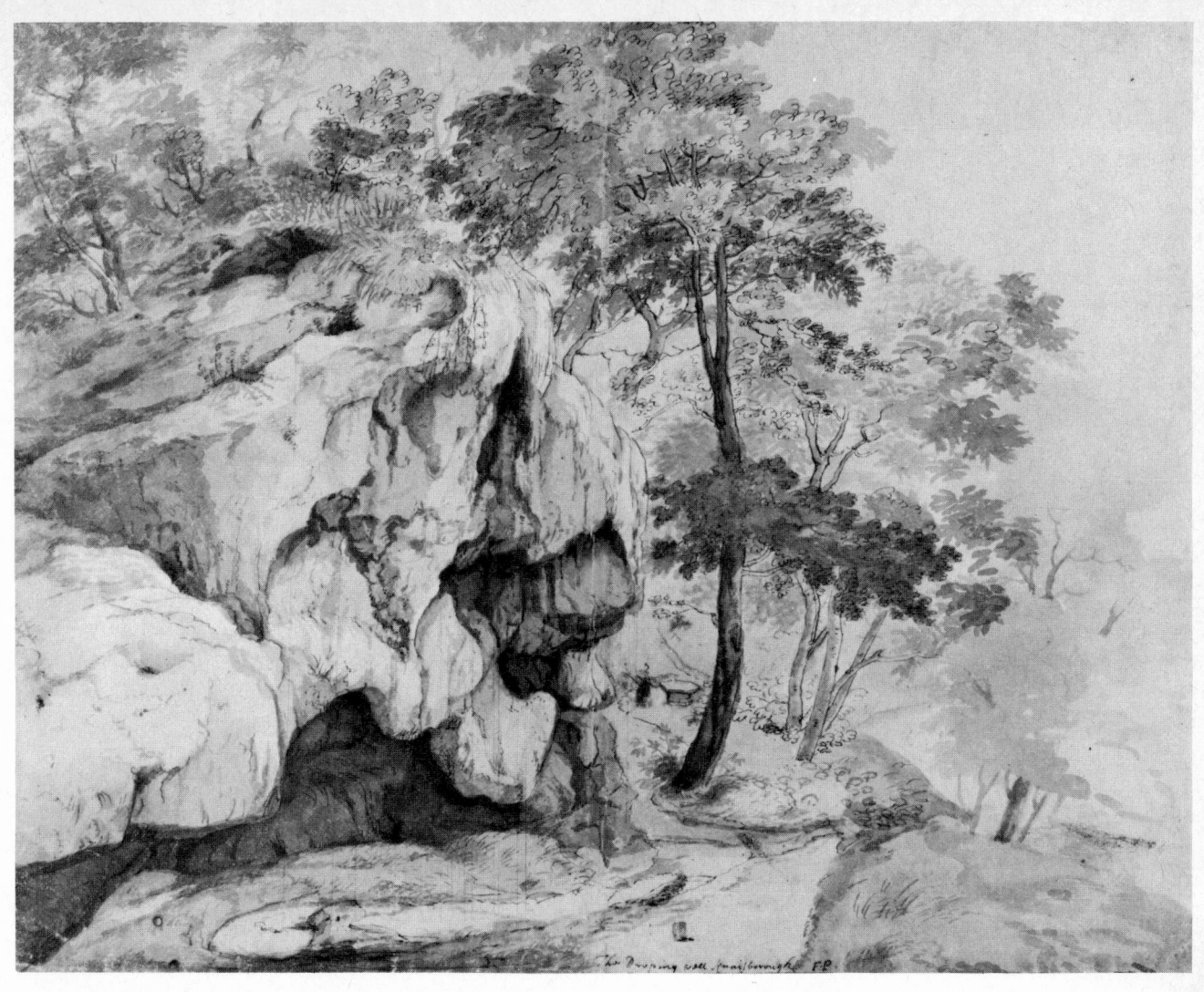

9. THE DROPPING WELL, KNARESBOROUGH, 1711. *Grey wash and pen,* $12\frac{3}{4} \times 16$ *in.*
London, British Museum.

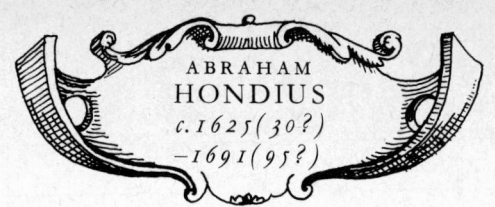

THIS DUTCH ARTIST from Rotterdam who set up in London about 1665 and lived there till his death, painted everything that would sell, dramas of wild animal life, dramatic landscapes as of cities on fire, and hunting pictures. 'He delighted in a fiery tint'. He is said to have been 'a man of humour and irregular life', 'exceedingly harassed and tormented with the gout', which killed him—in a public house off Fleet Street. His baroque feathery hunting pictures represented everywhere and nowhere. The English would have preferred his dog paintings. Vertue mentions an admired picture by him of more than thirty kinds of dog, each with its specific character and expression—a Landseer before its time?

10. THE FROZEN THAMES, 1677. *Oil, $43\frac{1}{8} \times 70\frac{1}{4}$ in. London, London Museum.*

Old London Bridge, and to the right Old St. Paul's, which had been destroyed in the Great Fire of 1666. Hondius painted this landscape no doubt as a memento of St. Paul's and of the great frost in the winter of 1665–6, which preceded the Fire. He seems to have used the same studies of the thawing of the ice on the Thames both in this picture and in his drama (Fitzwilliam Museum, Cambridge) of a ship icebound in the Arctic. The two pictures have much the same icy foreground, as well as a similar grouping of figures.

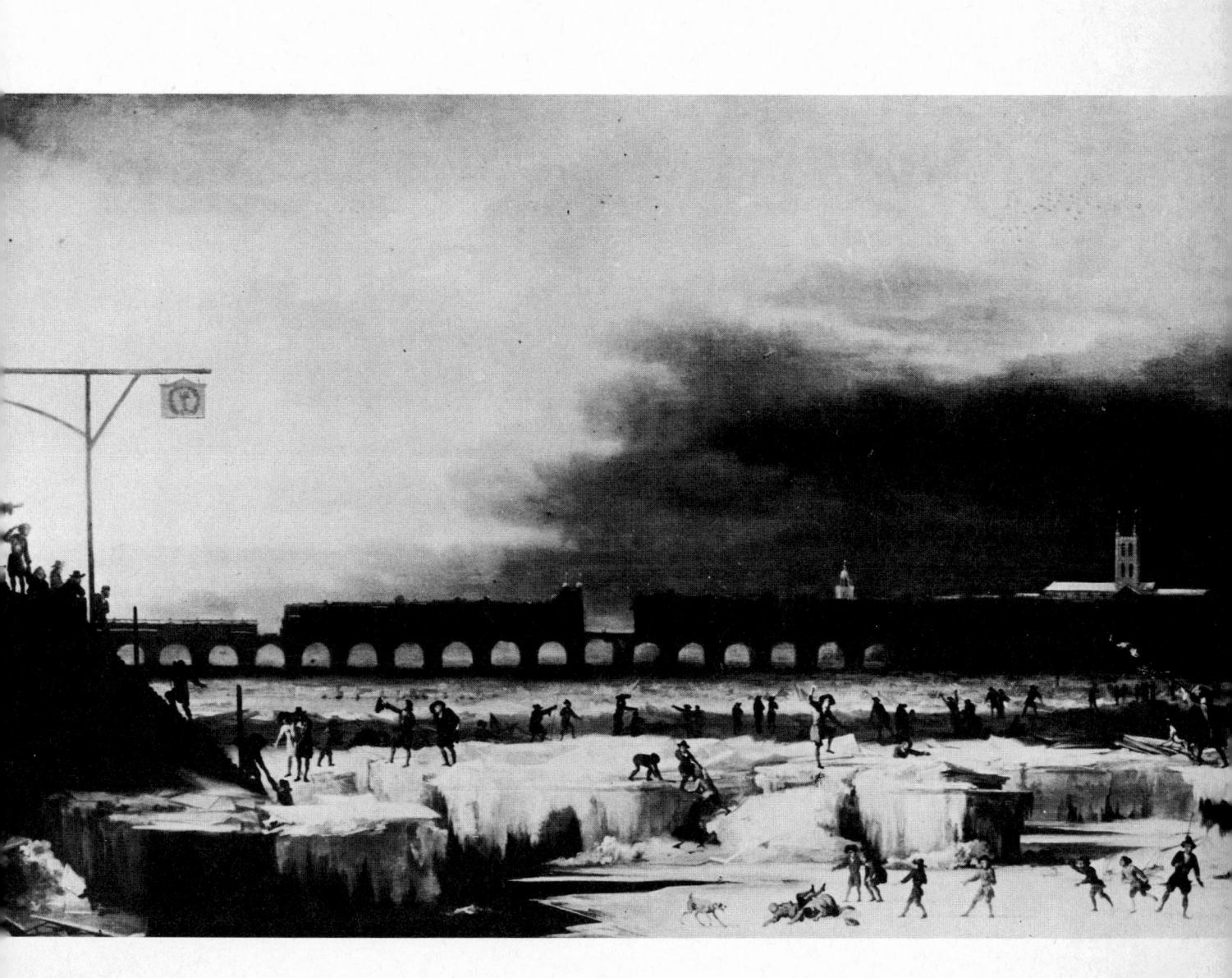

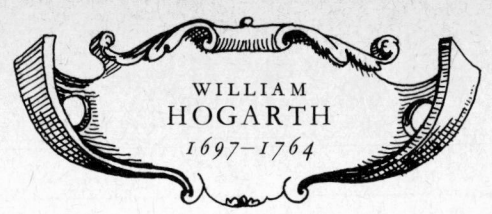

Morning, from the series he called 'The Four Times of Day', is a townscape exemplifying Hogarth's business with the human comedy. 'I wished to compose pictures on canvas', he wrote, 'similar to representations on the stage . . . scenes where the human species are actors.' The curtain goes up on the scene of 'Morning', not only displaying the virtuous stiff-backed pious lady on her way to church in Covent Garden and her encounter with the beggar woman, while the flower-girls and market porters play about with each other, but depicting as well the authentic London of Hogarth's visual experience. Special concepts or special sentiments of landscape do not interfere. Constable had to bring Hogarth into his landscape lectures, insisting that 'manner', which 'is more or less an imitation of what has been done already', was always plausible and always to be avoided, the safeguard being 'a close and continual observation of nature.' And he went on that landscape had been debased 'until Hogarth and Reynolds aroused the minds of our countrymen, and directed them to nature by their own splendid examples.' So he deserves his place in a book on landscape in England with this vision, whose effect the Londoner can still appreciate, of a squalid, chilly, snow-surfaced beginning to a West End day.

11. MORNING, *c.* 1736. *Oil, 29 × 24 in. Upton House, near Banbury, Bearstead Collection.*
    (National Trust).

The scene in Covent Garden is in front of St. Paul's Church.

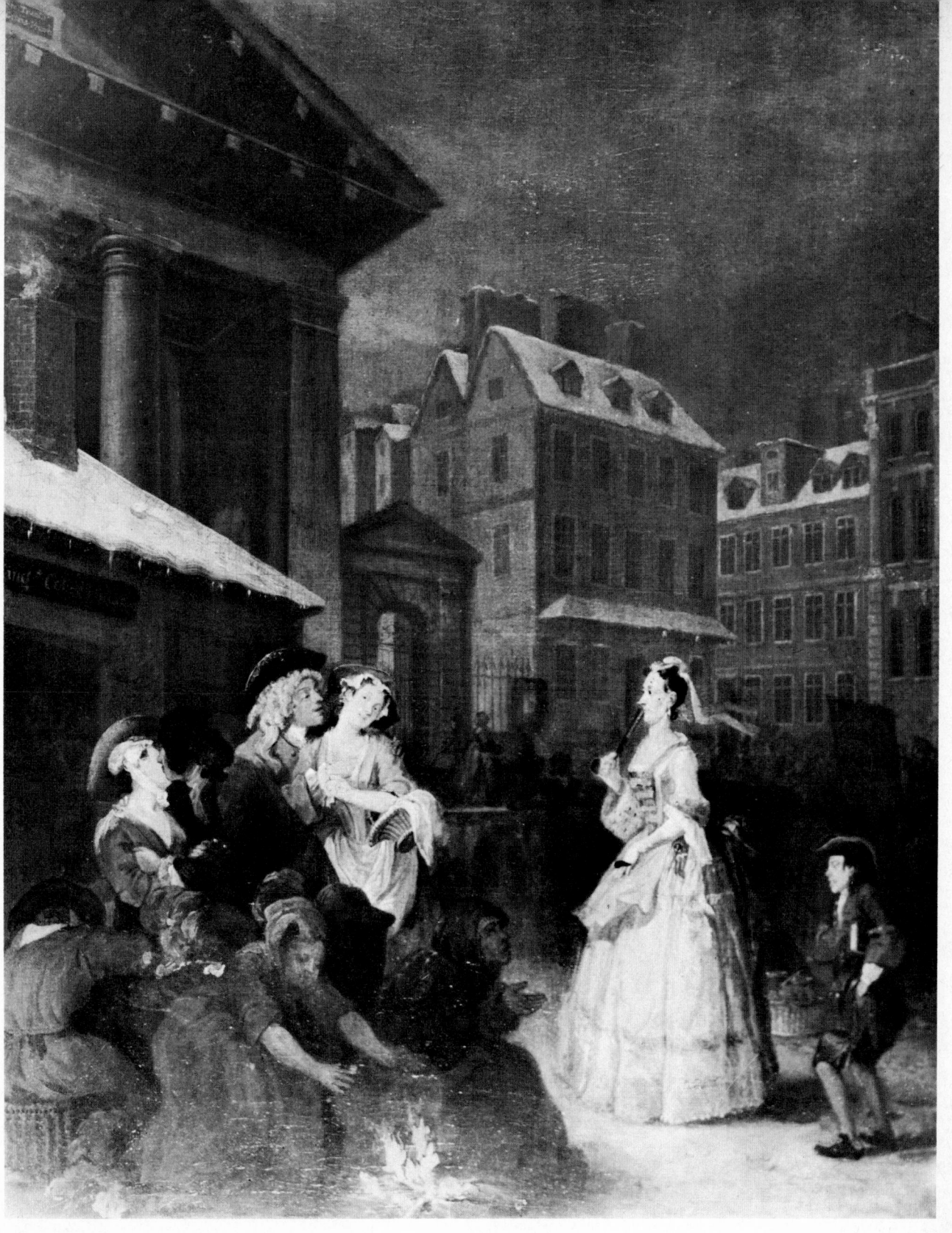

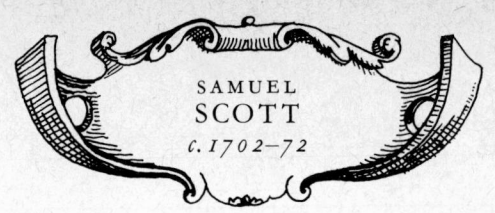

LONDON-BORN; at first, belatedly in the Dutch mode of the younger Willem van
der Velde (1633–1707), a painter of ships at sea, then a follower of Canaletto (who
worked in London from 1746 until about 1756), in pictures combining the still
waters of the Thames above London Bridge with the rising shores and the
architectural dignities of London (plus a ship or two). Employing a device used by
Canaletto and other Venetian view-painters, he dramatized some of these pictures
by employing the arches and piers of the new bridge at Westminster (opened in
1750) as a frame for distant and diminished buildings; but he lacked Canaletto's
power of creating a panorama of the Thames and the City and turning it into an
image of space, time, and mankind. Hogarth was one of Samuel Scott's friends.
He moved from London upstream to Twickenham; from Twickenham eventually
to Ludlow, and so on to Bath, where he died.

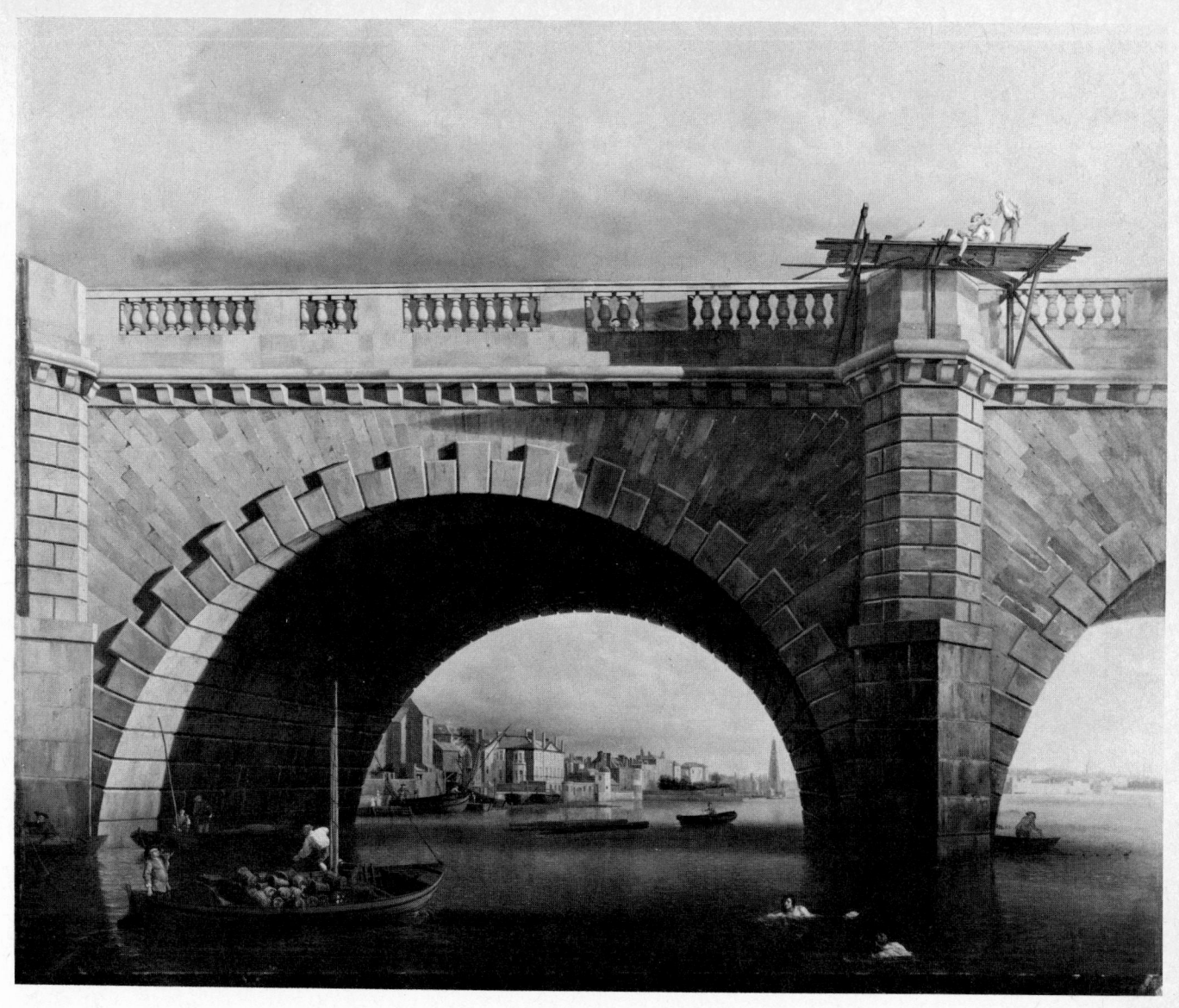

12. PART OF WESTMINSTER BRIDGE. *Oil, 53¼ × 64½ in. London, Tate Gallery.*

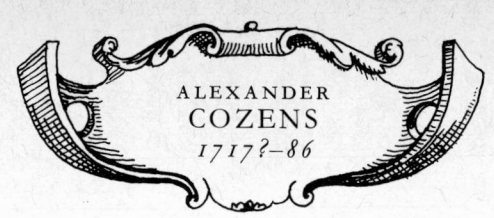

ALEXANDER
COZENS
1717?–86

His young millionaire patron William Beckford wrote of Alexander Cozens, then in his sixties, creeping about Fonthill 'like a domestic Animal'—'t'would be no bad scheme to cut a little cat's door for him in the great Portals of the Saloon.' This suggests his character, mild, uninterested in art politics or in anything, one may suppose, except drawing and painting and visions of perfect landscape, and systems of 'invention' which he explained in one little-noticed drawing-book after another. 'Cozens'—this is Beckford again—'is here very happy, very solitary and almost as full of Systems as the Universe.' He was born in Russia, where his father was a builder of ships, he worked in Rome as a young man, settled in London, and taught drawing at Christ's Hospital and Eton College. As an inventor of landscape and cloudscape Cozens was little concerned for locality, though he made a few landscapes, in watercolour as a rule, around London and as far afield as Dorset (near Weymouth), the Peak District, and North Wales. His son John Robert Cozens inherited and developed some of his characteristics. *Page* 183.

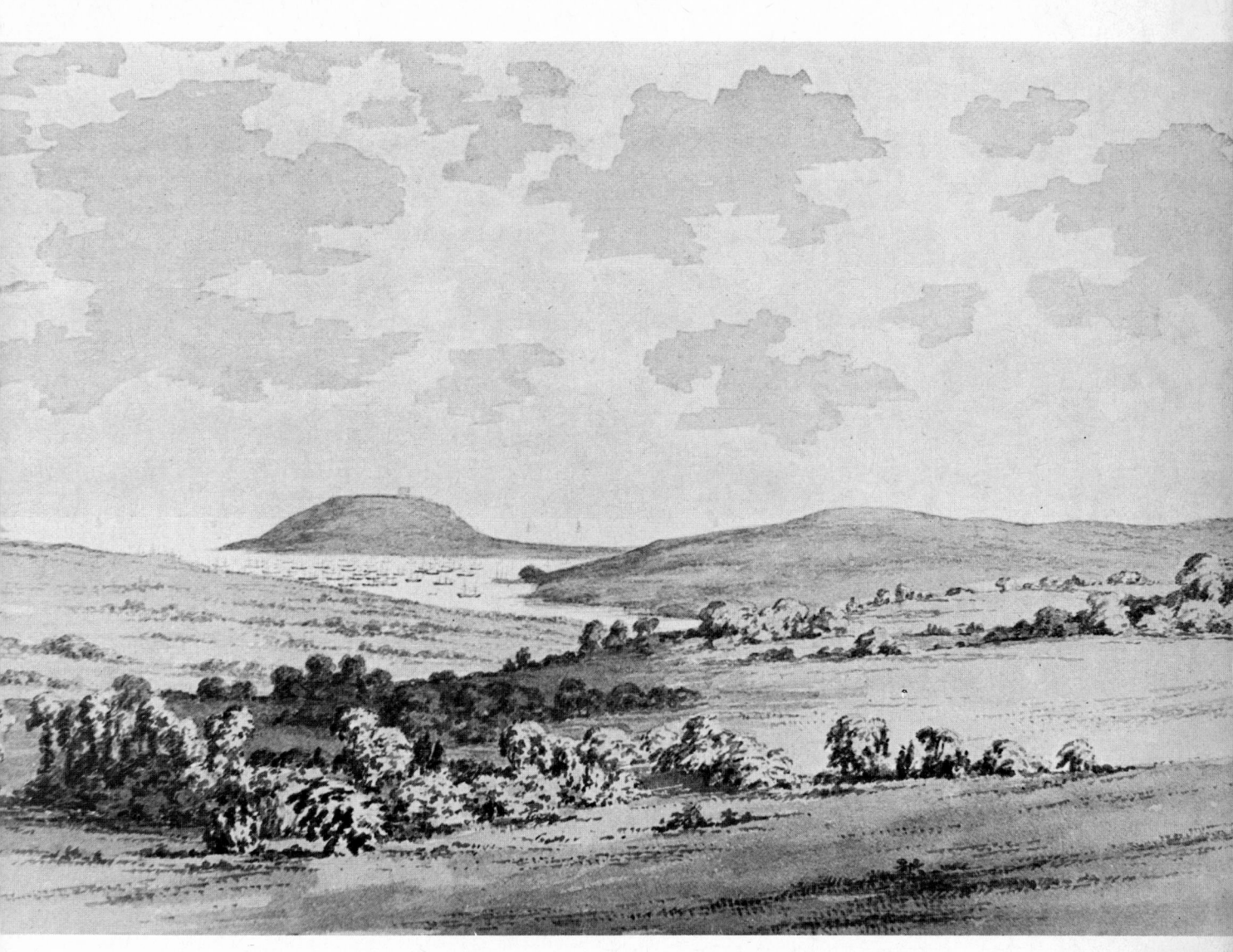

13. WEYMOUTH HARBOUR WITH PORTLAND IN THE DISTANCE. *Pen and water-colour, 8⅛ × 11 in. Manchester University, Whitworth Art Gallery.*

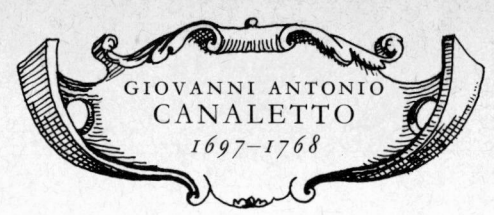

THE ENGLISH HOME from their travels had taken to Canaletto's imported views of the wonder city of Venice, and it was reasonable to suppose that they might take to Canaletto's views of London-on-Thames if he were to come over and supply them. He arrived at the end of May 1746, when one can hope that the weather showed London at its most sparkling and inspiriting; and he stayed, with an interval, until about 1756. Aristocratic patrons employed him to set their homes in view. His best pictures are the two great London views he painted for the Duke of Richmond and his long wide *View of Whitehall* (Duke of Buccleuch). He also painted up the Thames, as if along the Brenta, and went as far off as Northumberland to paint Alnwick Castle. His pictures away from London have been described as 'neat, rather old-maidish views'; and with reason. Canaletto was middle-aged when he came. London was a city, and could excite him, on its lake-like river. The rest of England wasn't London and wasn't Venice and could not stir this painter of light and air and water to a renewal of visual happiness and ecstasy. By contrast his *City of London from Richmond House* offers the excitement and calm of Wordsworth's sonnet written in the early morning on Westminster Bridge half a century later—

> silent, bare,
> Ships, towers, domes, theatres and temples lie
> Open unto the fields, and to the sky;
> All bright and glittering in the smokeless air
> —the river gliding 'at his own sweet will'.

14. WHITEHALL FROM MONTAGU HOUSE (*detail*). *Collection Duke of Buccleuch.*

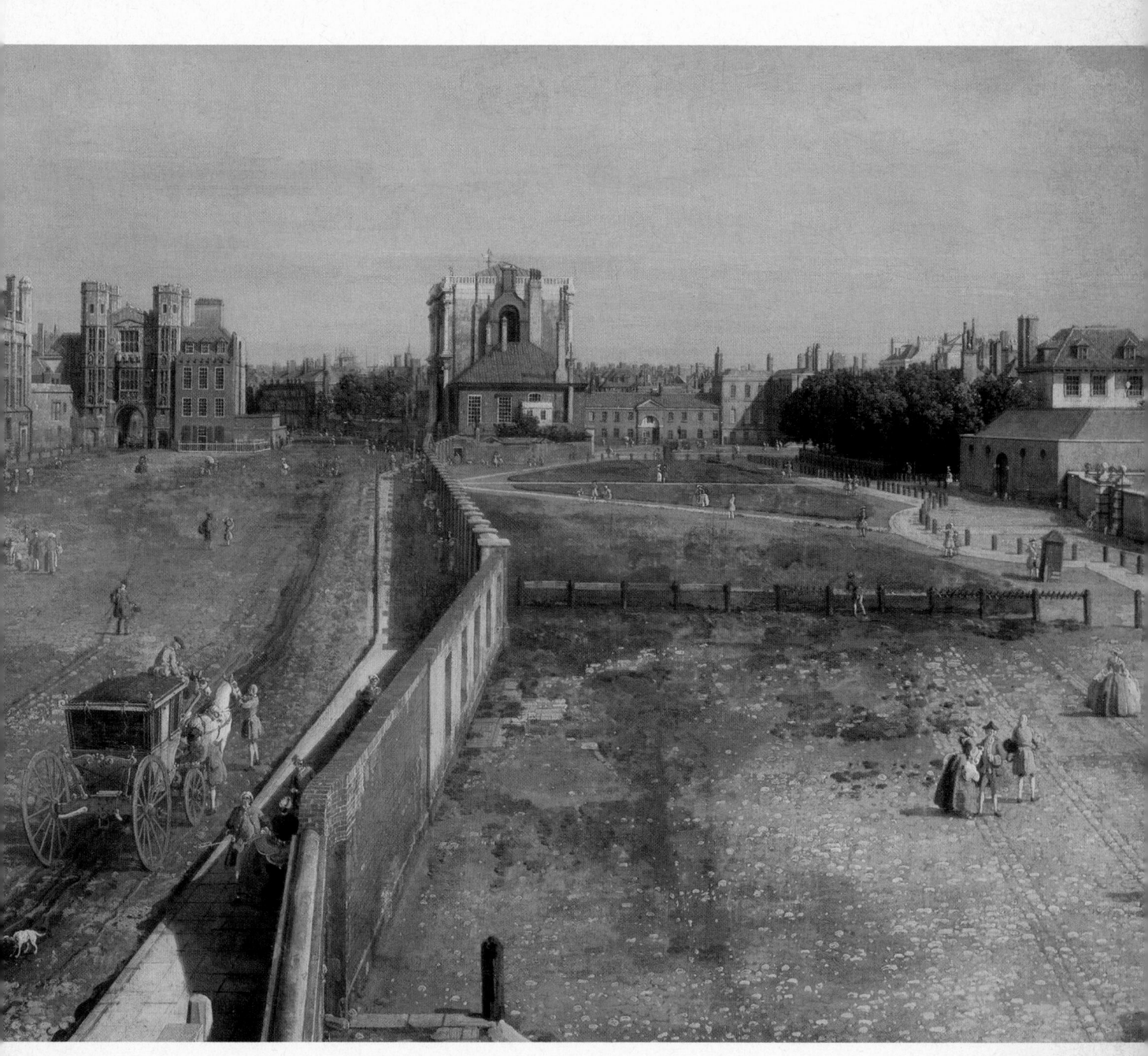

15. OLD WALTON BRIDGE, 1754. *Oil, 18¼ × 29½ in. London, Dulwich College Picture Gallery.*

The bridge was at Walton-on-Thames, Surrey, a short-lived wooden structure built in 1748 and replaced in 1750. It was something of a wonder in its day. The structural members were tangential to a circle—'It was claimed that any member could be removed without disturbing the timbers adjacent.' (N. Pevsner, *The Buildings of England, Surrey*).

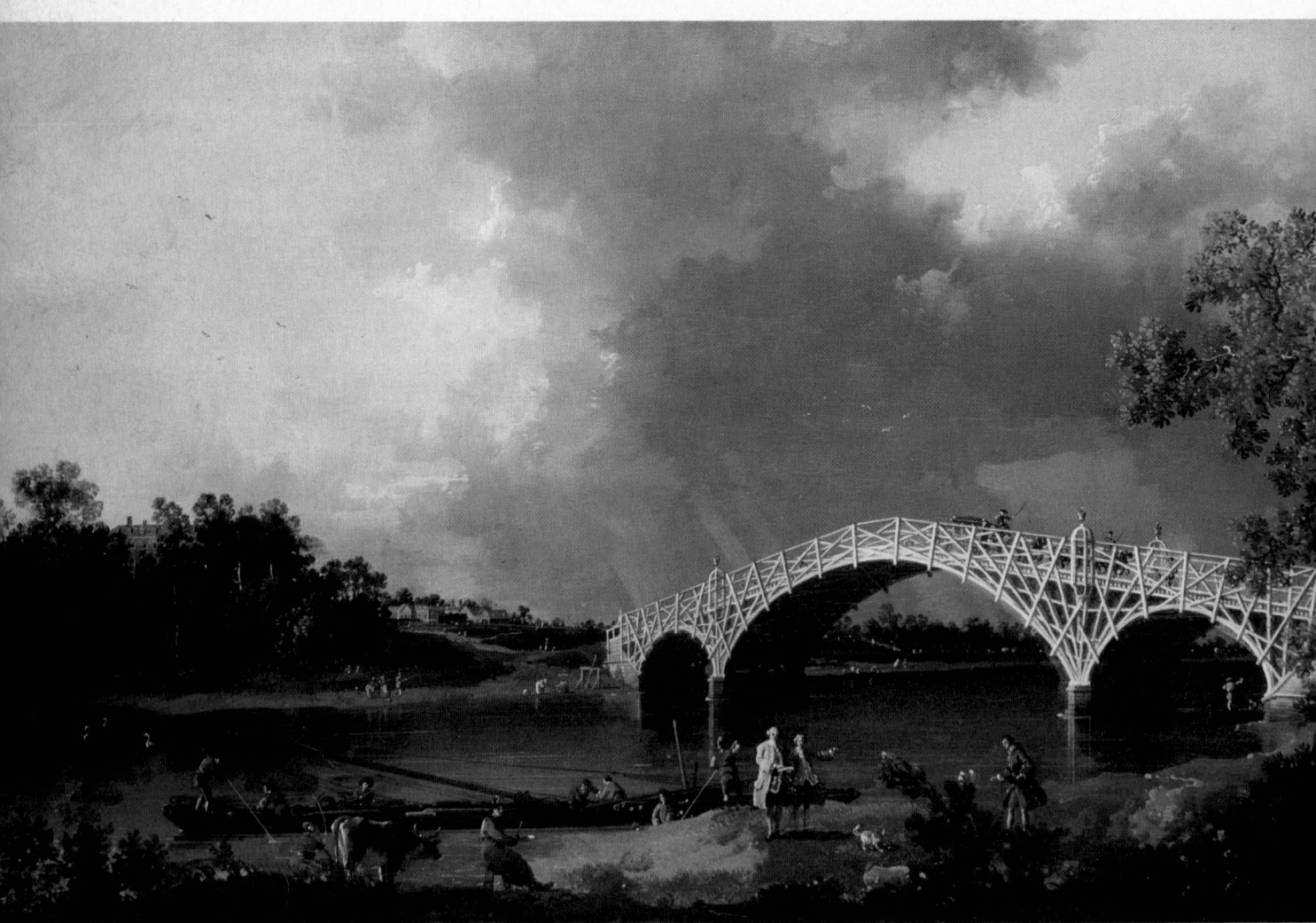

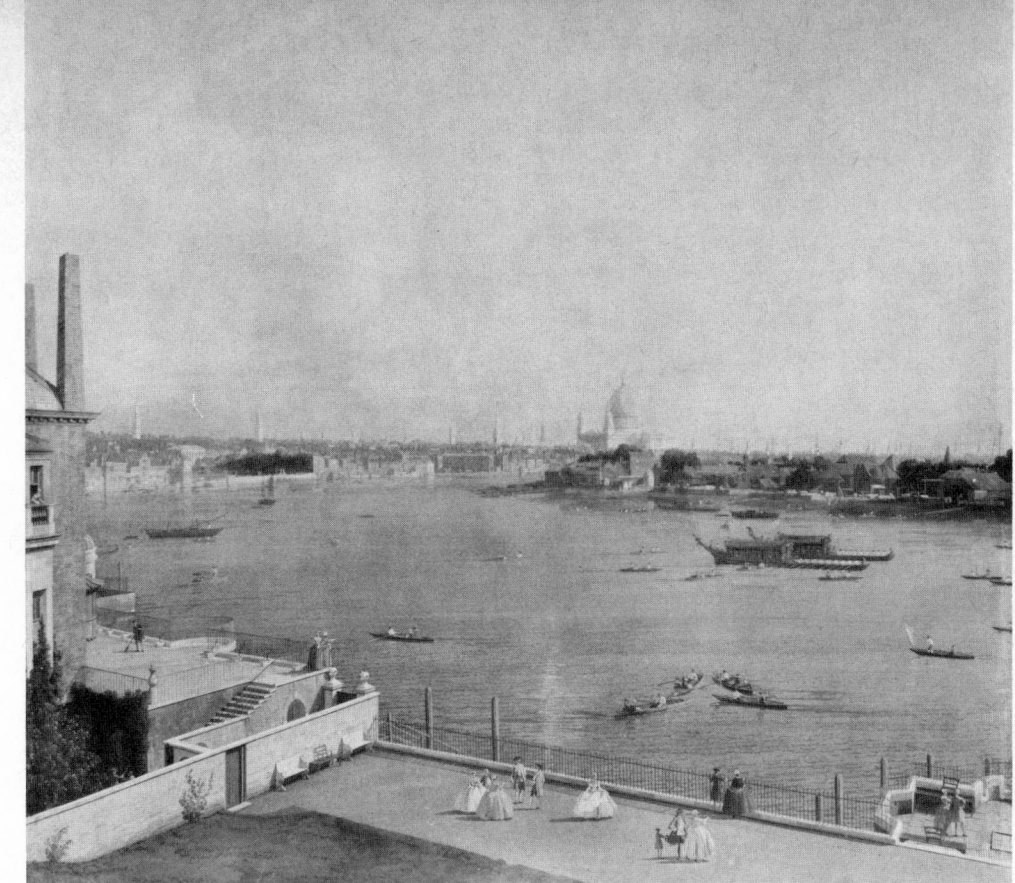

16. THE CITY OF
LONDON FROM
RICHMOND
HOUSE.
Oil, 43 × 47 in.
Goodwood House,
Duke of Richmond
and Gordon.

17. WHITEHALL FROM MONTAGU HOUSE. *Oil, 46½ × 93 in. Collection Duke of Buccleuch.*

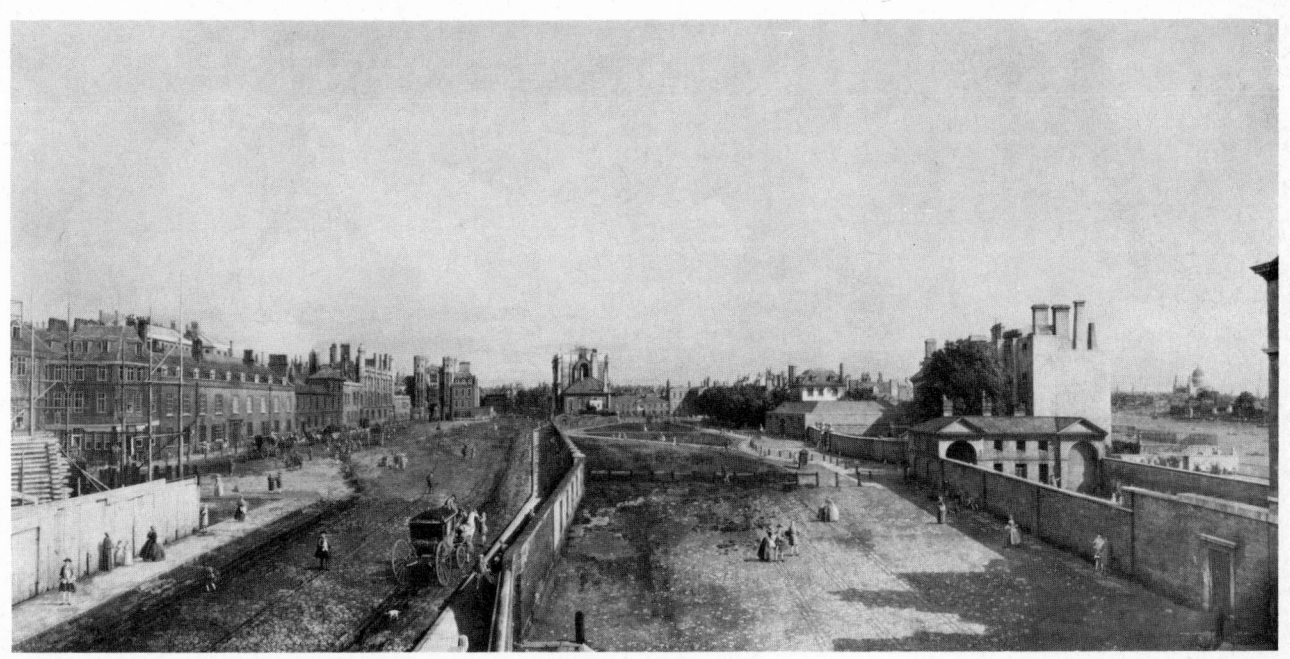

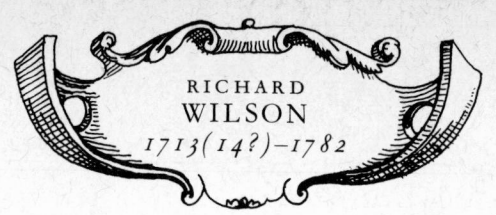
A PROBLEM about Wilson is to be sure of his own attitude to what might be called curly and more or less straight landscape. He poeticized his landscape, whether Italian, English or Welsh, yet it is hard not to prefer the pictures which more straightly correspond, if not to the given scene, then to the nature of scenery—pictures such as his *Northop, Flint*, his panoramic view of *Dover*, or his famous *Llyn-y-Cau, Cader Idris*. It isn't invention that one queries (as his old pupil Joseph Farington remarked 'Wilson when he painted views seldom adhered to the scene as it was') so much as the manner of the invention. Some of the anecdotes recorded of Wilson suggest a doubt in himself, consistently as he imposed sentiment on scene, so that it is all one whether the scene is abroad or at home or imaginary. Wilson's dilemma was perhaps that of the boy who grew up in the thrilling scenery of North and Mid Wales and the well educated man who read and recited Horace's poems, went to Italy 'sighing for classic ground' and came to know the accepted landscapists and exactly what the landscape sentiment of the age demanded. Wilson was born in Montgomeryshire at the rectory in Penegoes along the Vale of the Dyfi, Cader Idris in front, Plynlimmon at the back, and as a boy he also knew the scenery of the Vale of Clwyd and the Clwydian Hills, in Flintshire, with the distant mountains in view. It may be that the shimmering skies which he painted, and which are so lost in reproduction, developed from his childhood experiences of Welsh sunrises and great western sunsets down the Dyfi vale. As well as in Wales and around London and along the Thames, Wilson found his home views in Kent, Worcestershire, Bedfordshire, Hertfordshire, Devonshire, Berkshire, and Northants.
Page 1 8 3.

18. TREES AT HAMPSTEAD. *Black and white chalk on grey paper, $7\frac{5}{8} \times 10\frac{3}{8}$ in. London, Courtauld Institute.*

19. THE GREAT BRIDGE OVER THE TAAFE, 1775. *Line engraving, $13\frac{3}{4} \times 20$ in. London, British Museum.*
Engraved by the Frenchman, P. C. Canot, who settled in London in 1740, after a lost painting by Wilson. This is the famous single span over the Teifi at Pontypridd in Glamorganshire, built in 1755, after his first two attempts had collapsed, by a Welsh farmer's son William Edwards. Now half hidden by a more practical nineteenth-century bridge, it was considered as beautiful as the rainbow, and was often referred to as the Bridge of Beauty, and compared to the Rialto in Venice.

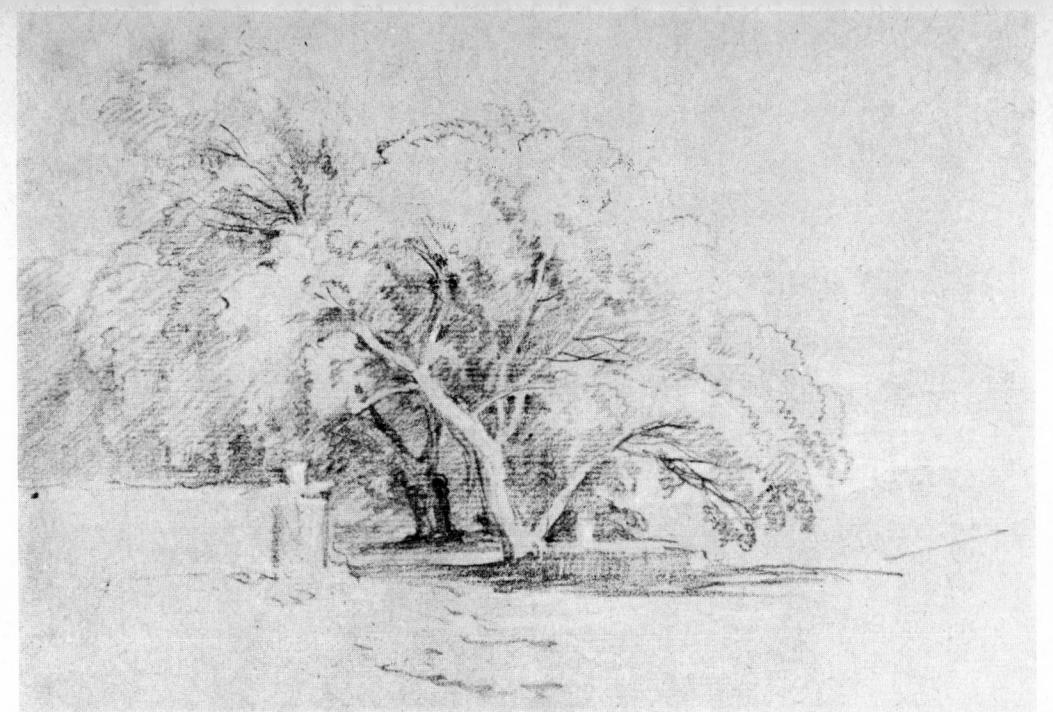

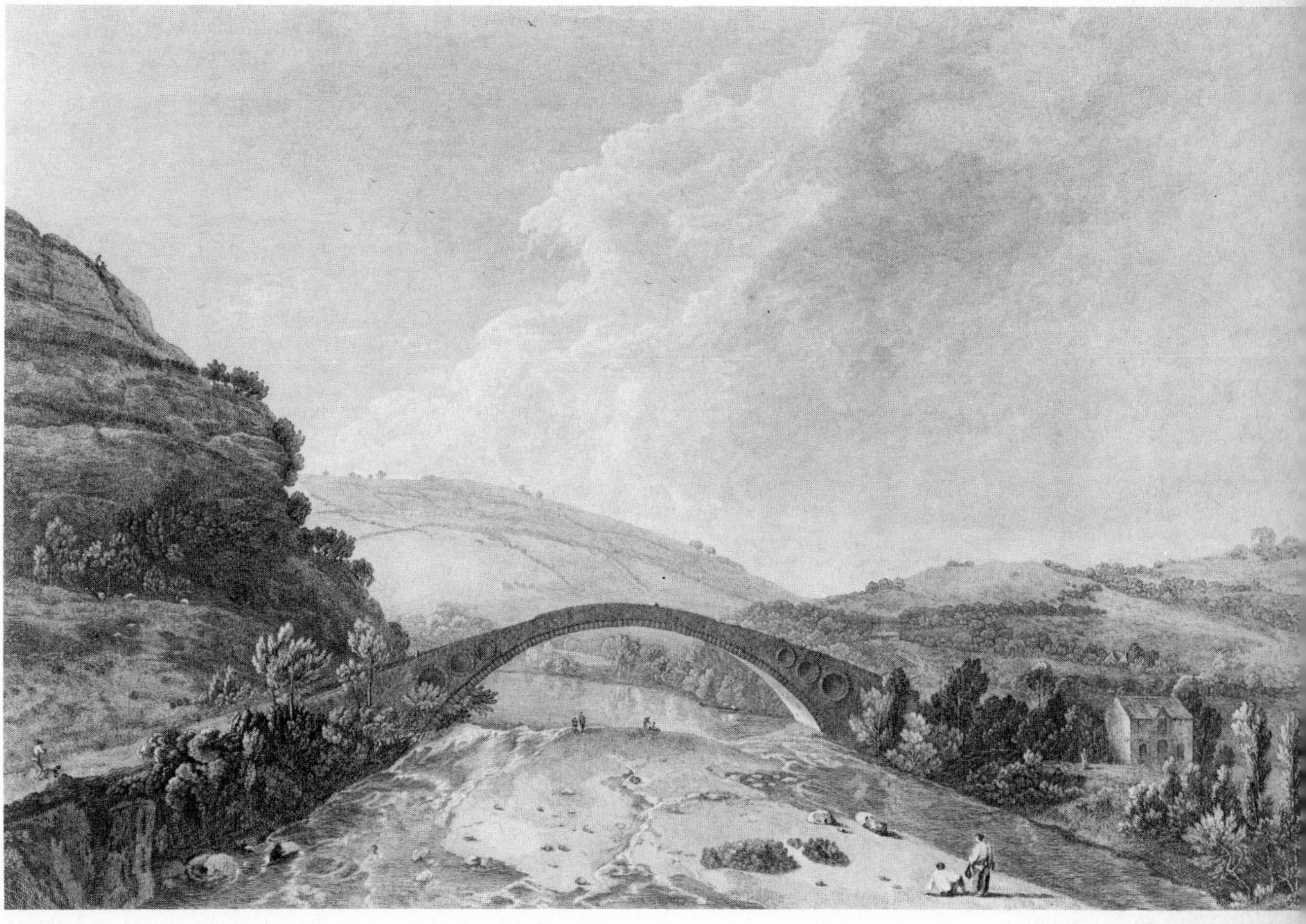

20. RIVER, ROAD AND VILLAGE, *c.* 1750–55. *Oil,* 35 × 47½ *in. Collection of the Earl of Wemyss.*
A view of the River Wye, perhaps above Hay-on-Wye.

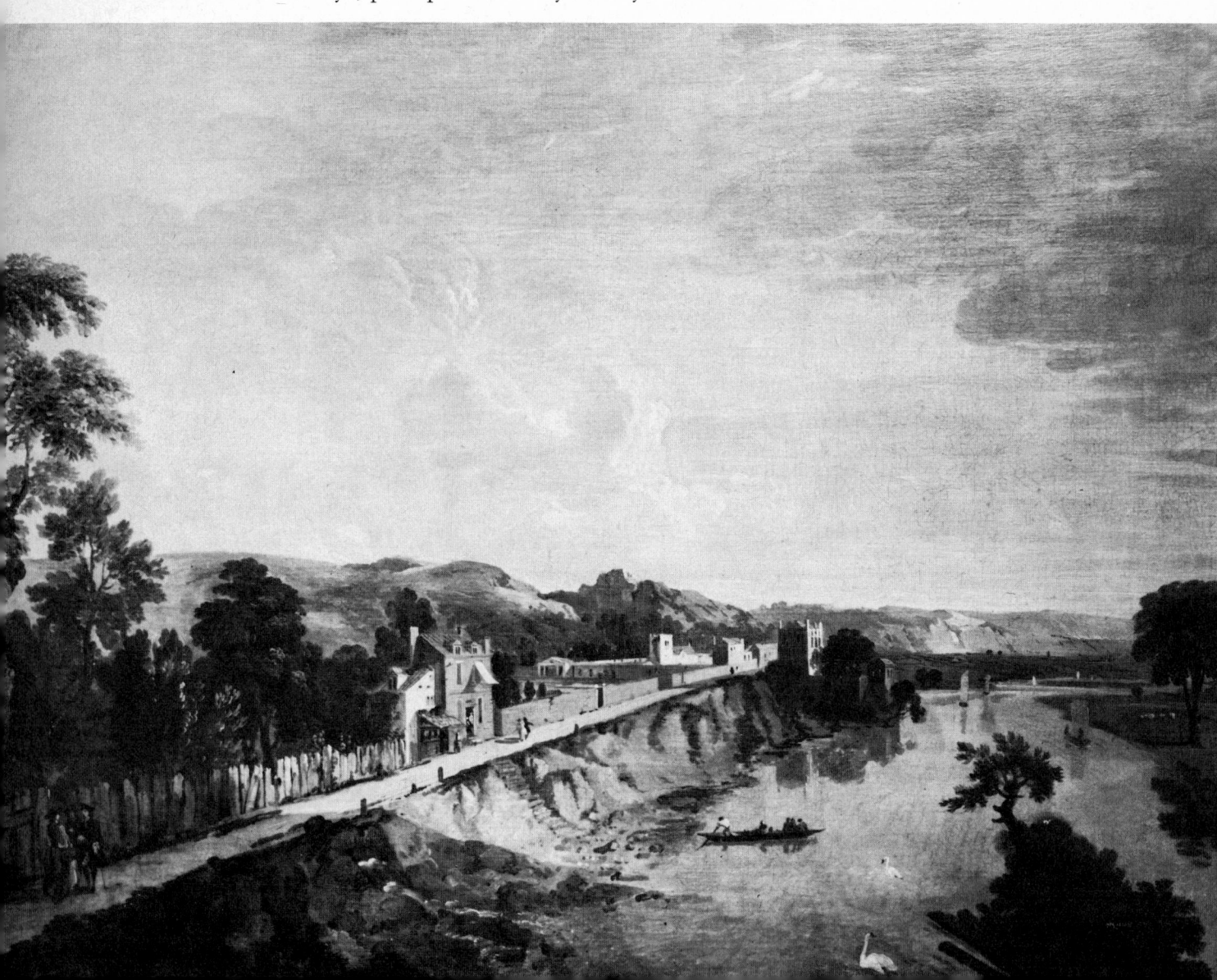

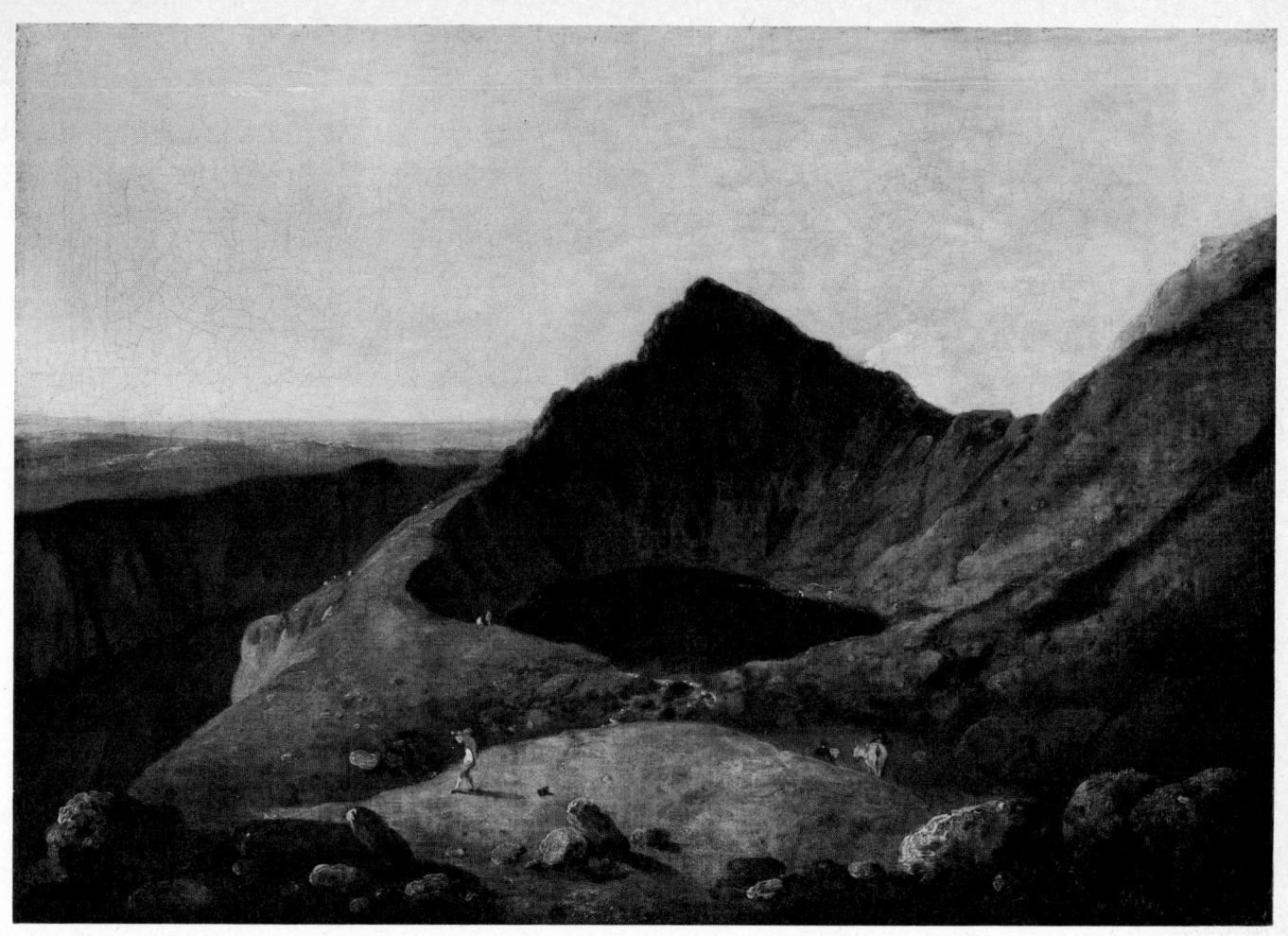

21. LLYN-Y-CAU, CADER IDRIS. *Oil, 20⅛ × 28¾ in. London, Tate Gallery.*

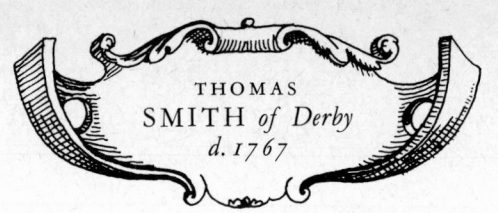

WHEN THOMAS GRAY the poet visited Gordale Scar in the West Riding in October 1769, on a 'gloomy uncomfortable day' which 'well suited the savage aspect of the place and made it still more formidable', he found that the landscape painters Vivares, Smith and Bellers had stayed in the ale-house at nearby Malham (where he dined) attracted by the same sight, of which they had published engravings. Smith, who was born and lived at Derby, was one of the pioneers of English landscape, travelling round after the grand and the exceptional, in the Peak, in the Lakes, in Yorkshire. In addition to engravings after his landscapes, there exist pictures by him of Kirkstall Abbey (Derby Museum and Art Gallery) and the Bristol Gorge (Manchester City Art Gallery).

22. HIGH FORCE, 1751. *Etching, 15 × 21½ in. Barnard Castle, Bowes Museum.*

The Tees which drums down at High Force, is here a moorland stream dividing Yorkshire from Co. Durham. After a few more miles it descends into the wooded delights of Rokeby, by which Cotman was to be so moved. This etching, from Smith's *Book of Landskips*, was engraved by James Mason who did much to spread a taste for landscape by engraving after Claude, Gaspard Poussin, Wilson, Scott, and others.

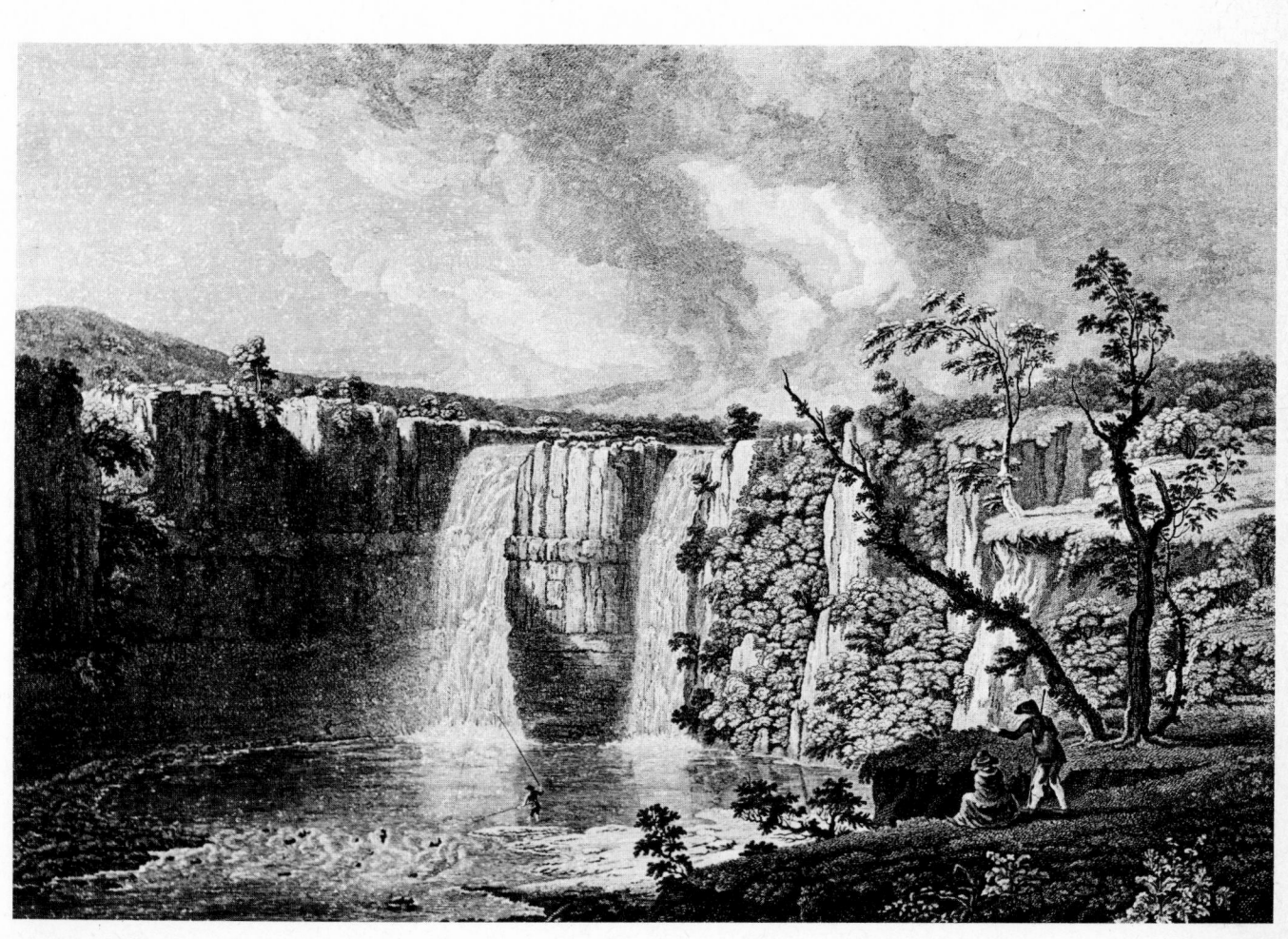

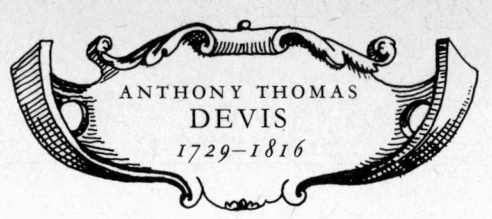

ANTHONY THOMAS
DEVIS
1729–1816

ONE OF A LANCASHIRE FAMILY of artists from Preston, where he was born. He came south, worked in London as a teacher of drawing, made landscape watercolours in many parts of England and Wales (Yorkshire, the Lakes, North and South Devon, the Vale of Neath, Bristol, Beachy Head, Suffolk, Surrey), and painted country houses in oil. He lived for many years until his death at Albury in Surrey, where his tomb can be seen in the graveyard of the old church, in Albury Park.

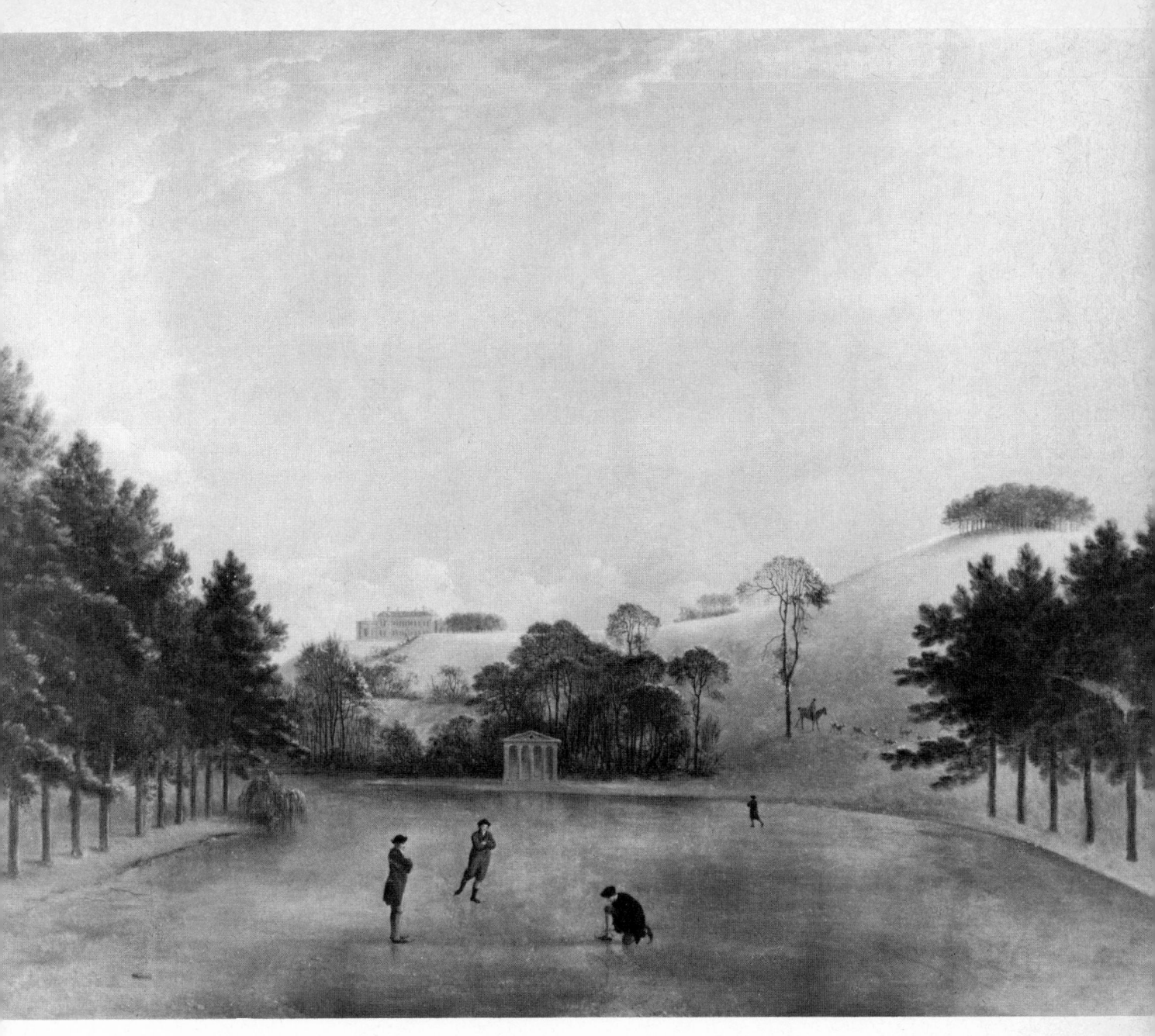

23. UPTON HOUSE FROM THE SOUTH. *Oil, $39\frac{3}{8} \times 49\frac{1}{4}$ in. Upton House, near Banbury, Bearstead Collection (National Trust).*

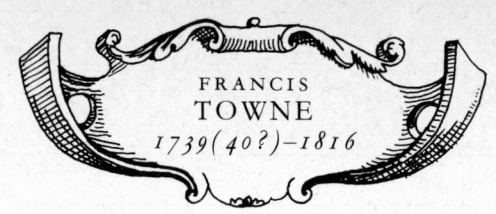

FRANCIS TOWNE'S WATERCOLOURS were discovered in 1920 at a time when English connoisseurs were at last becoming aware of Cézanne and Post-Impressionism. His cool mountain watercolours seemed to have a touch of what was then yesterday's modernism, and were at once overpraised, even to a pitch of comparing Towne with Cézanne. All the same, Towne's simplified representation of sheerness and rock and the sweep of great slopes is attractive. Within his clear line, it does present a drama without bombast or exaggeration. Shallowness and hardness supervene. Towne drew his best designs on a tour of North Wales in 1777, and in 1780 and 1781 when he looked with excitement at Italian and Alpine scenery. He made drawings in the Lake District in 1786. On the back of his views he is careful to write the name of the place and 'drawn on the spot by Francis Towne'. From the original he would make duplicates for this or that client in Devonshire and round Exeter, where for most of his life he was a successful and frugal drawing-master. Devonshire at that time had an active local culture, fostering many landscape painters and landscape amateurs.

24. THE SALMON LEAP, PONT ABERGLASLYN, 1777. *Pen and watercolour, 11 × 8½ in. Collection Miss Scott-Eliot.*

'Under whatever circumstances this pass is beheld, it will always strongly impress the tourist, whether it be in stormy weather, when the clouds are drifting rapidly over the summit of the cliffs, or whether it be in the full radiance of a summer-day, when each bit of rock has its own colour and beauty ... On the right rises a mountain precipice, probably over 800 ft. high, lowering over the road; its rugged surface is tinged with a russet hue, barely modified by a scanty tint of green from the partial vegetation growing upon it. At the foot the Glasllyn rolls its clear waters, which have a singular beryl-green colour. This scene forms the great charm to the neighbourhood of Beddgelert.' Murray's *North Wales*, 1868.

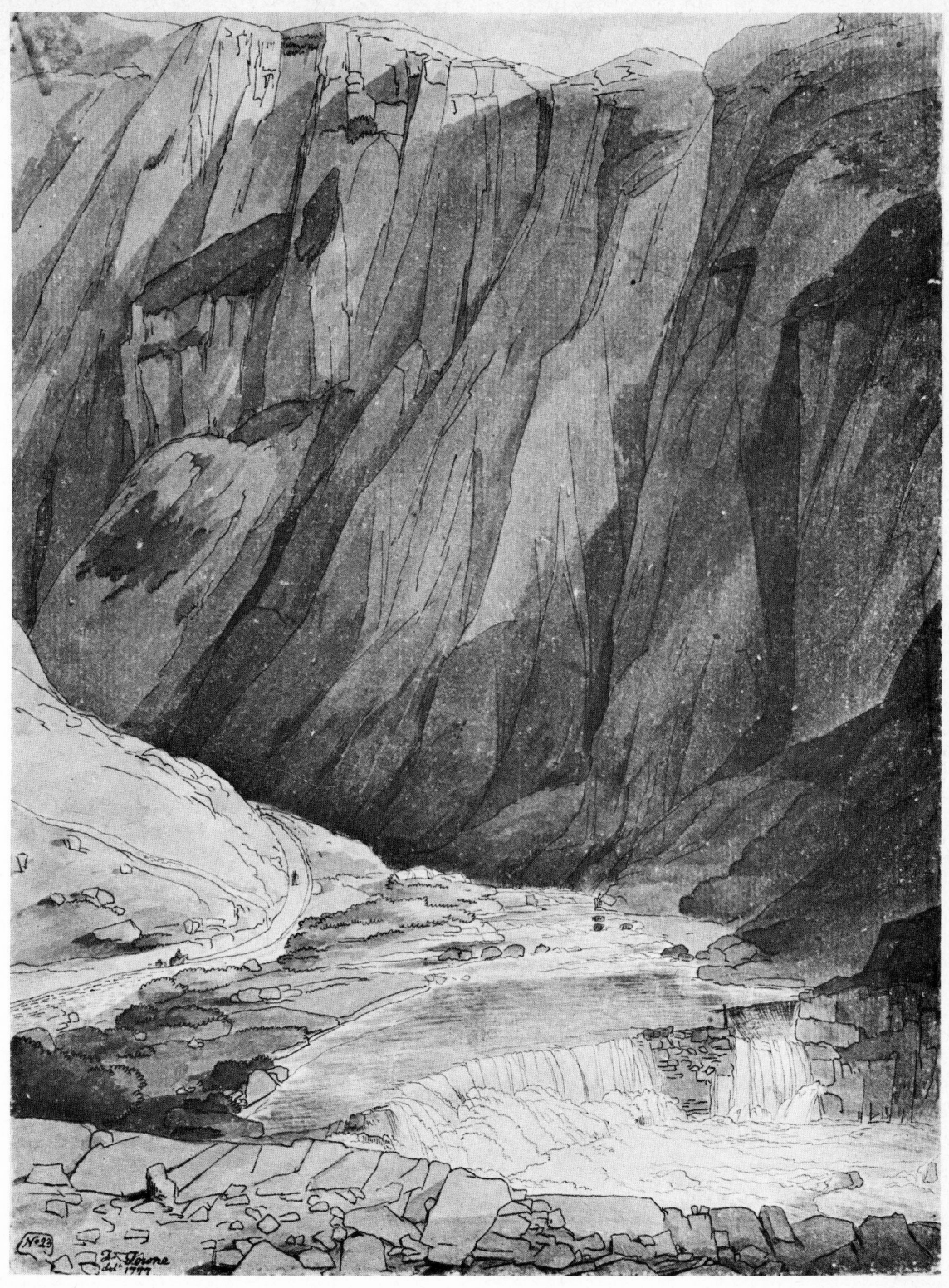

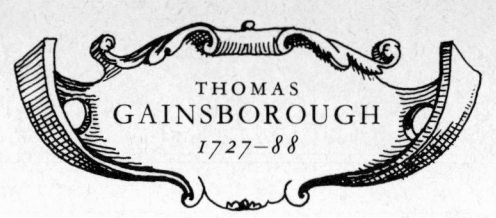

'HIS CONVERSATION was sprightly but licentious—his favourite subjects were music and painting.' Most of Gainsborough's landscape is a kind of music in its sequence and flow of shape and colour, tied to nowhere in particular. Constable could respond, but with a little reserve, to such rococo invention: 'The landscape of Gainsborough is soothing, tender, and affecting. The stillness of noon, the depths of twilight, and the dews and peals of the morning, are all to be found on the canvases of this most benevolent and kind-hearted man. On looking at them, we find tears in our eyes, and know not what brings them.' He responded to the tunes and exquisite manipulation of paint—'exquisite refinement, yet not a refinement beyond nature'—which we now accept more willingly and enthusiastically in the silks and the shimmer of Gainsborough's portraits than in his fancy landscapes. Having lived through the 'realities' of Constable, Corot, Sisley, Pissarro, etc., the Gainsborough landscape for us is of the kind Gainsborough was rather sorry to reject, the occasional early piece, either background or whole picture, in which Suffolk and Essex around Sudbury (where Gainsborough was born, one of the nine children of a clothier and crape-maker) look at us with a Dutch directness freshened and enlivened by Gainsborough's young receptivity. The Suffolk-Essex neighbourhood around Sudbury was the country he most felt. He told his first biographer that there was not 'a picturesque clump of trees, nor even a single tree of any beauty, no, nor hedgerow, stem or post' round Sudbury which he had not known and stored in his memory. He drew landscape around Ipswich, where he lived from 1748 to 1759; round Bath (1759–74); at Hampstead and Richmond, which he visited in the summer, in his London period (1774 until his death); at Foxley in Herefordshire, and in the Lakes in 1783.
Page 184.

25. SHIPPING ON A NORFOLK BROAD, *c*. 1756. *Oil,* 29 × 55½ *in. Private Collection.*

60

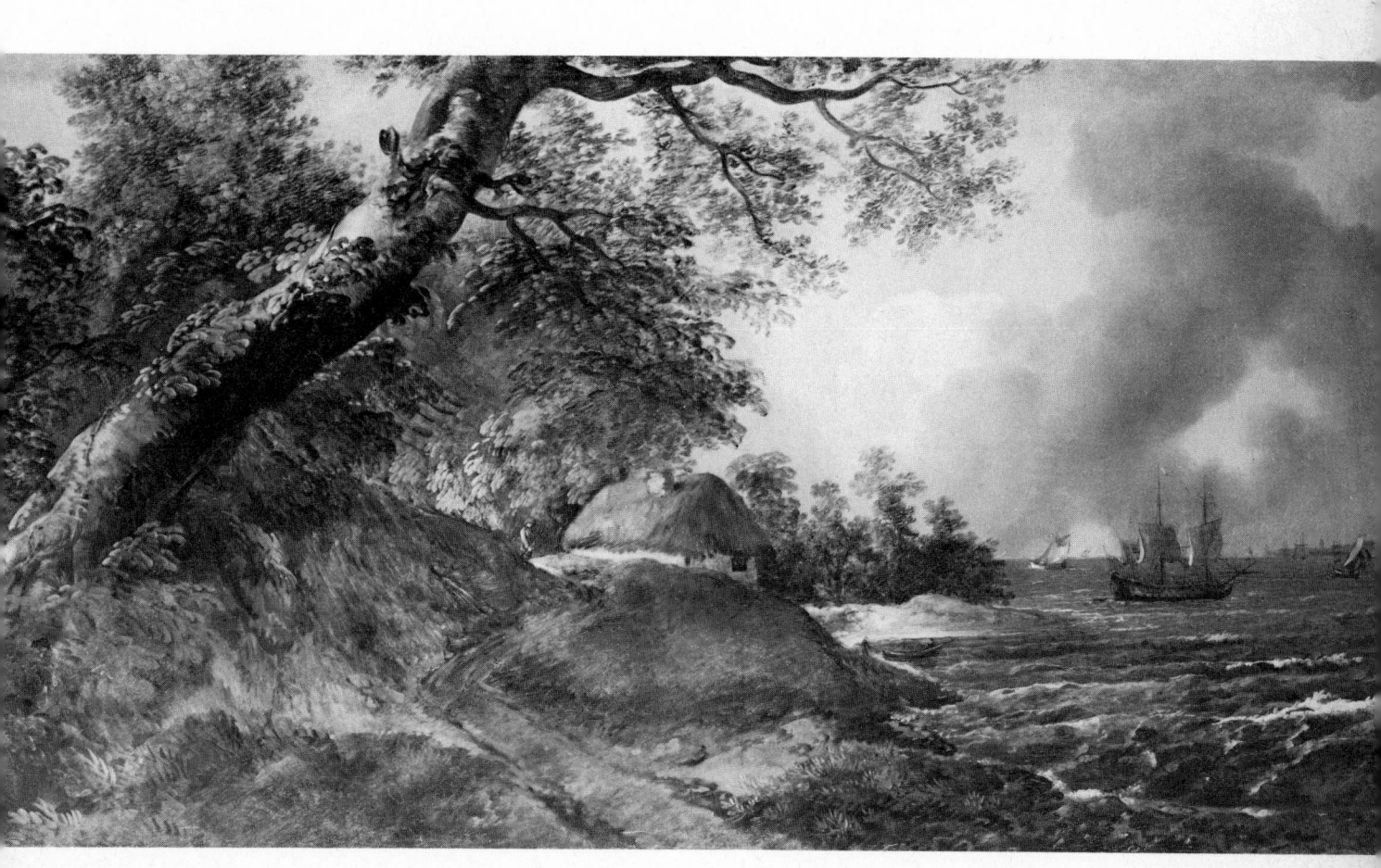

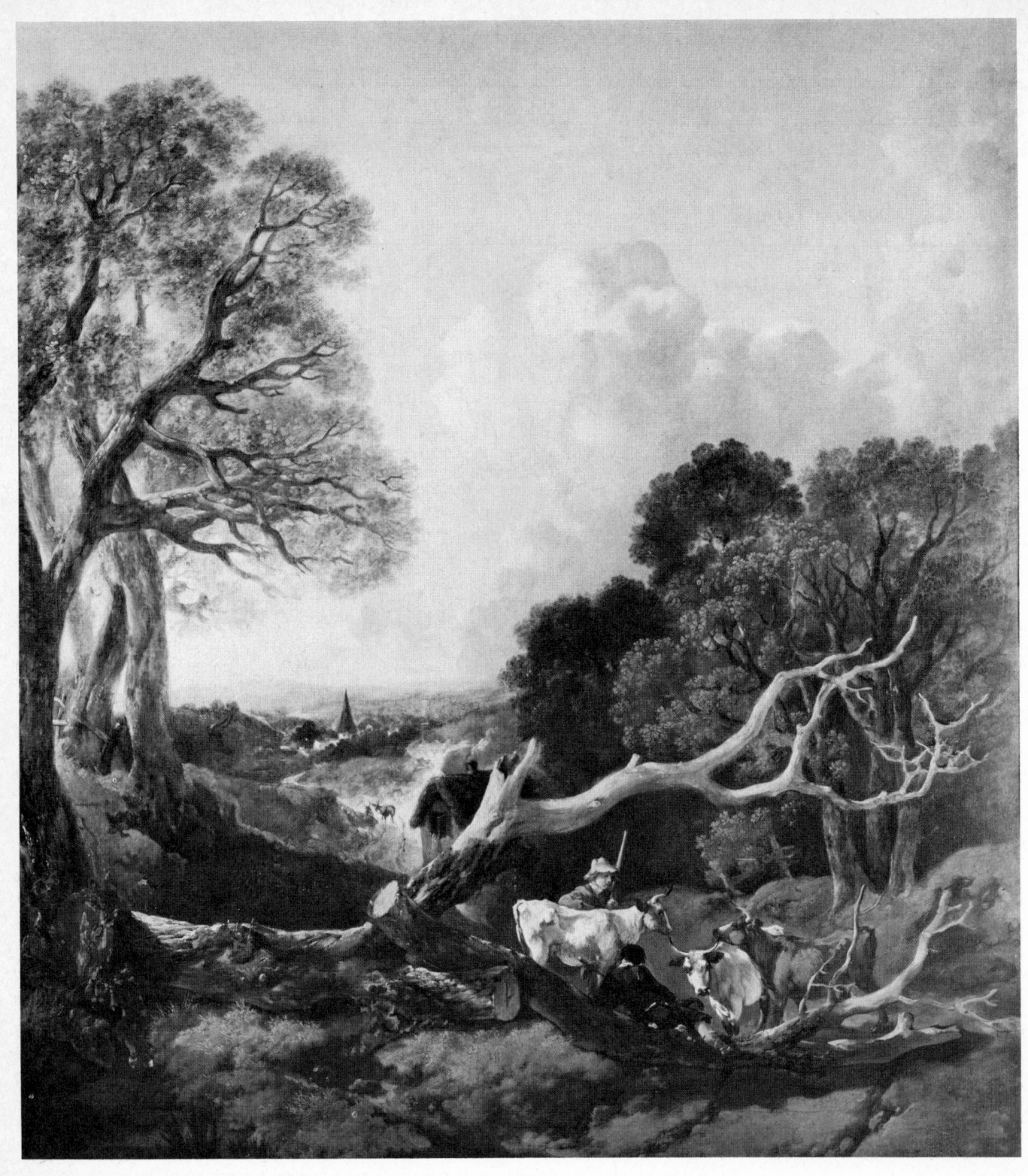

26. WOODY SLOPE WITH CATTLE AND FELLED TIMBER, *c.* 1750–53. *Oil,* 40 × 36⅛
in. Minneapolis Institute of Arts.

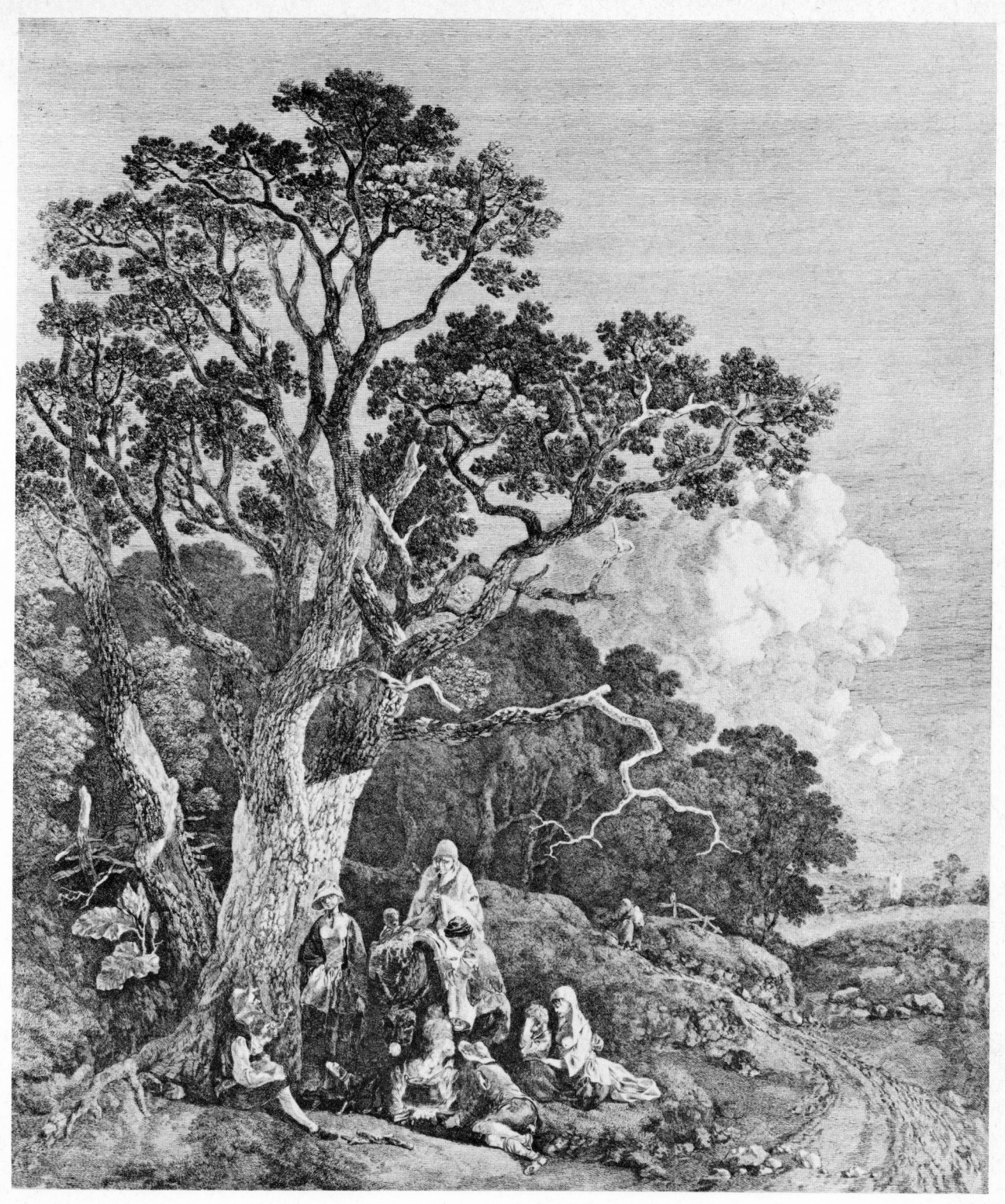

27. THE GYPSIES, *c.* 1753–4. *Etching,* 17 × 15 *in. London, British Museum.*

28, 29. GAINSBOROUGH'S FOREST ('CORNARD WOOD'), *c.* 1748. *London, National Gallery.*

Possibly, but not certainly, a view in the Suffolk parish of Great Cornard, on the edge of Sudbury. The title 'Cornard Wood' was given to the picture long after Gainsborough's death. For Gainsborough on this picture, see page 184.

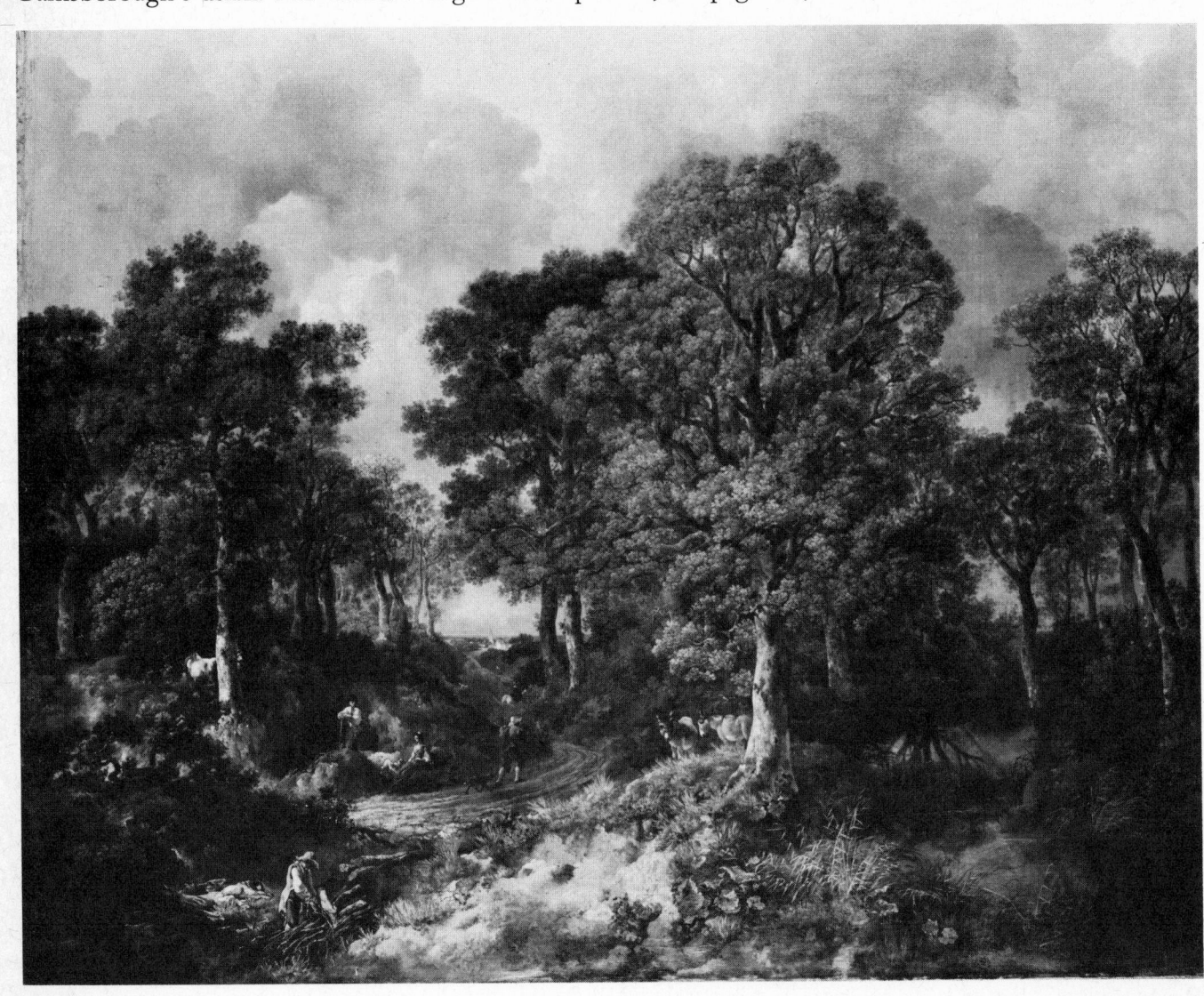

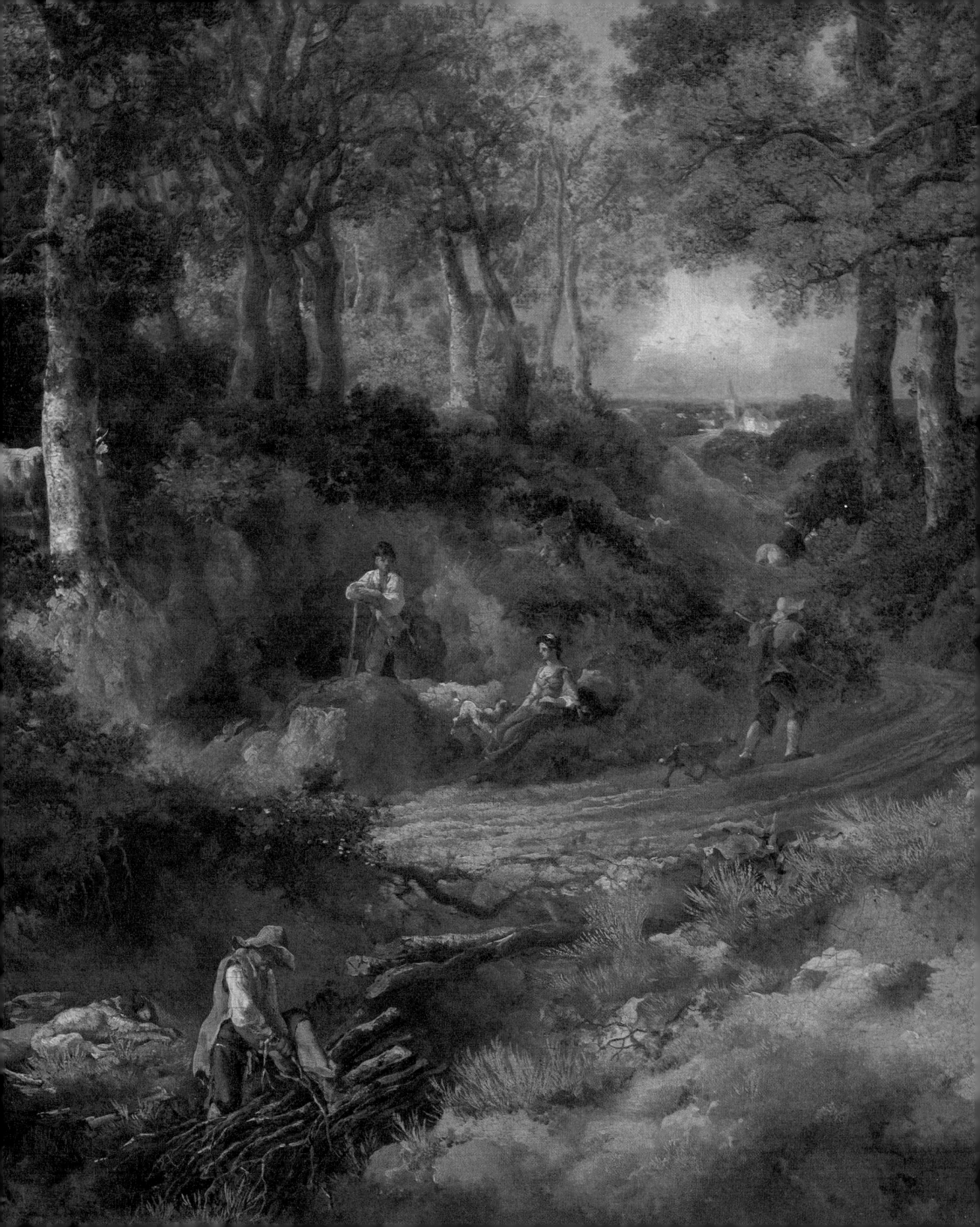

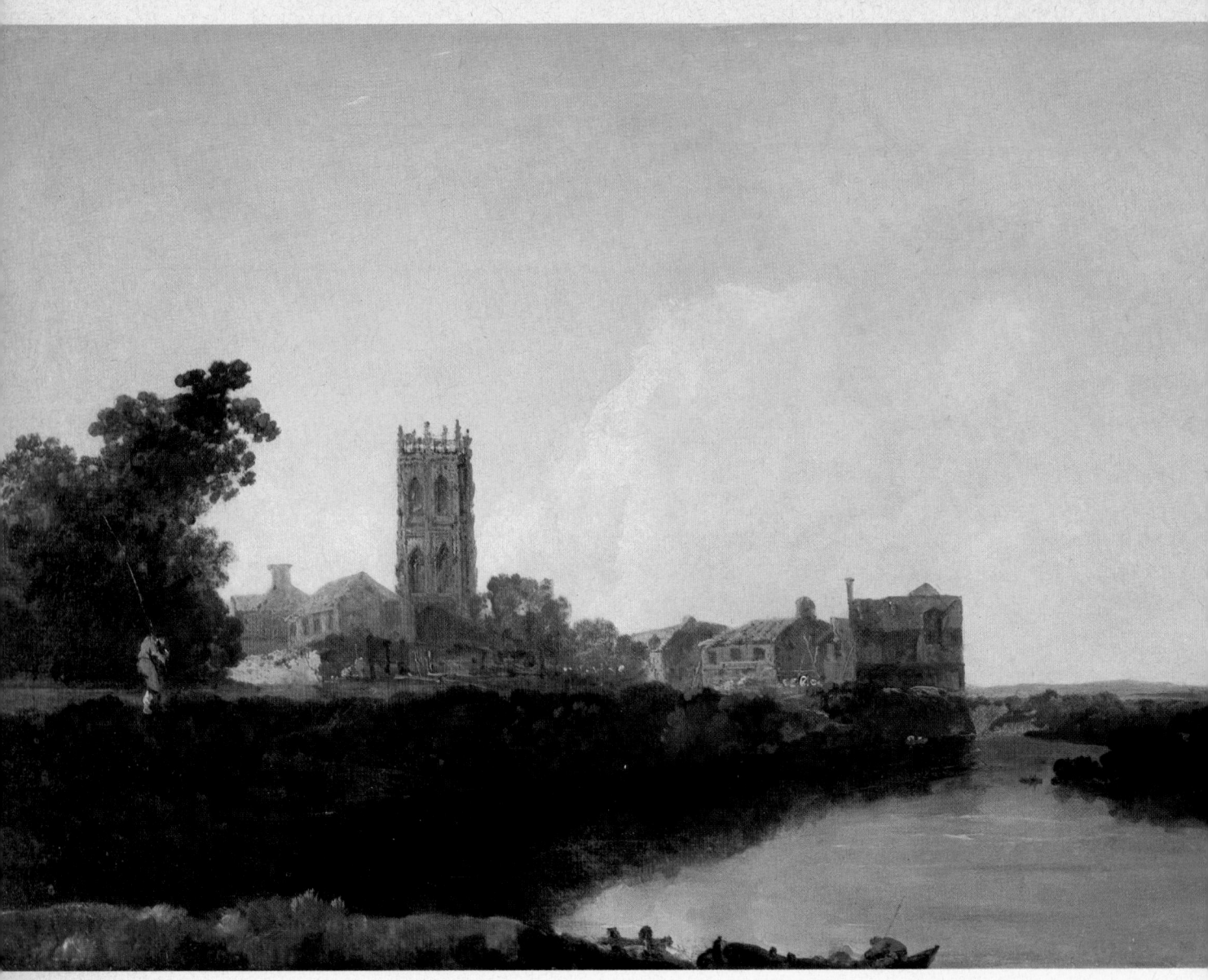

30. NORTHOP, FLINTSHIRE. *Oil, 15 × 21¾ in. Corsham Court, Methuen Collection.*
Church and village on the banks of the river Dee.

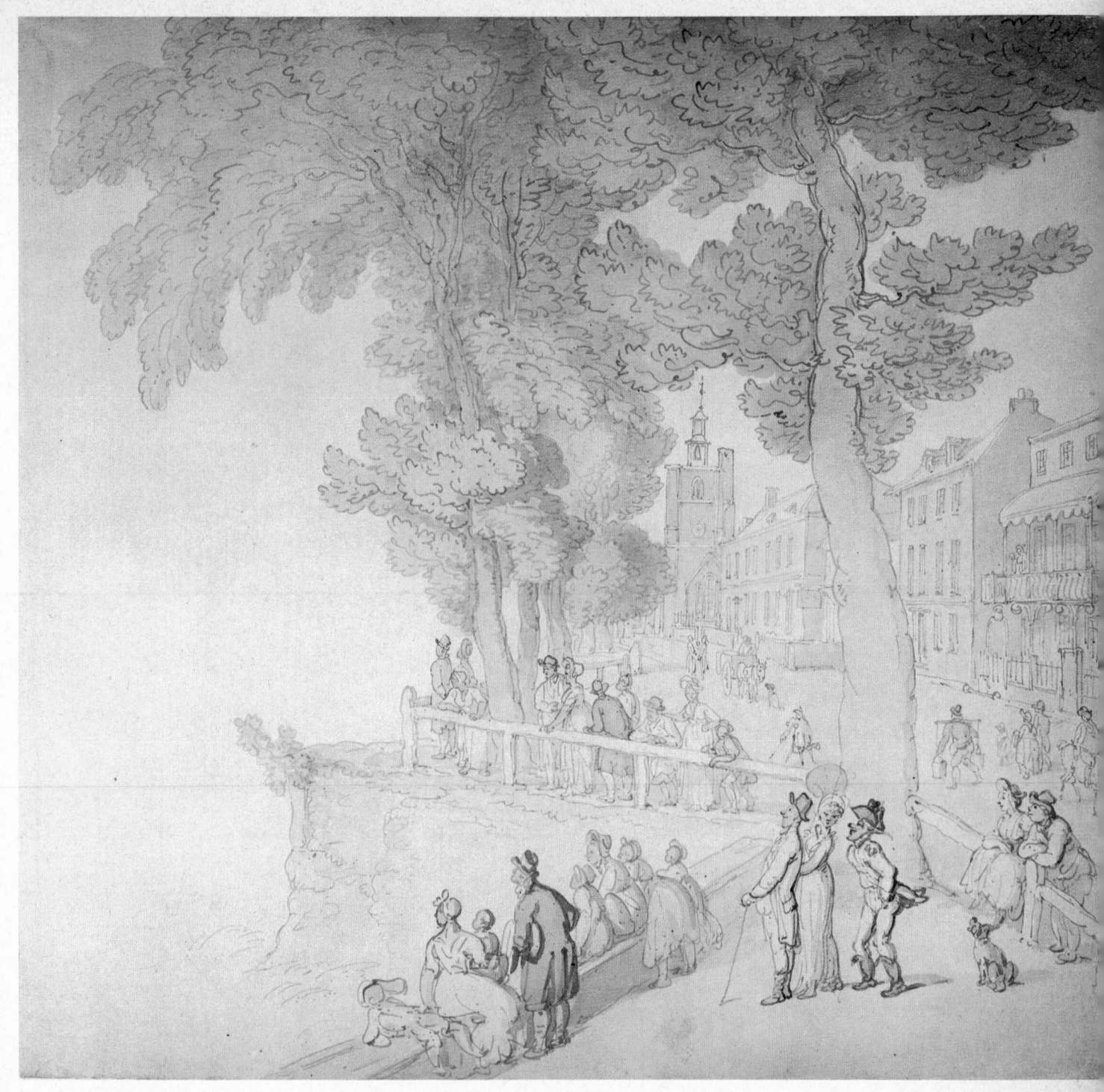

31. CHEYNE WALK, CHELSEA. *Watercolour,* 11 × 11$\frac{5}{8}$ *in. London, London Museum.*

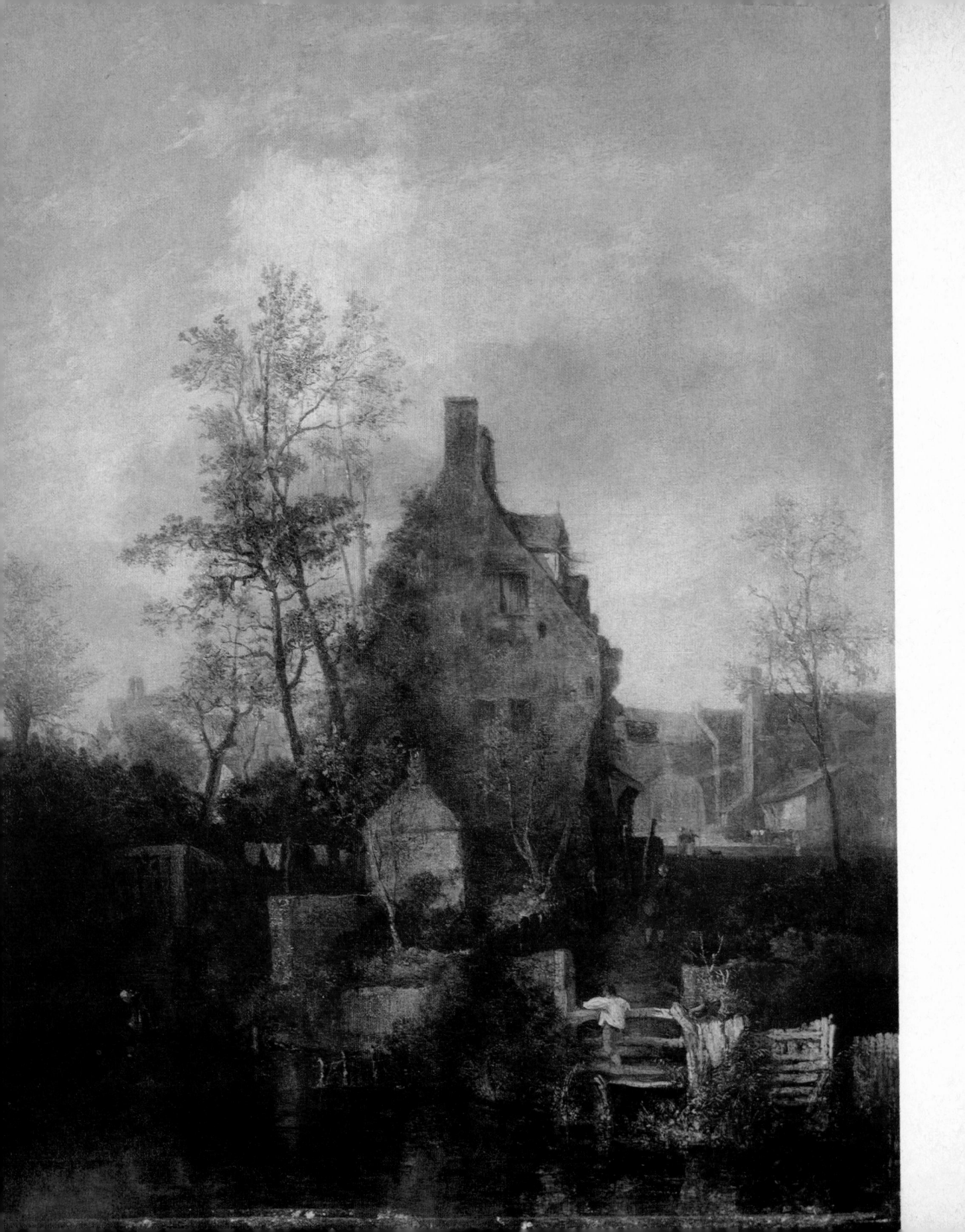

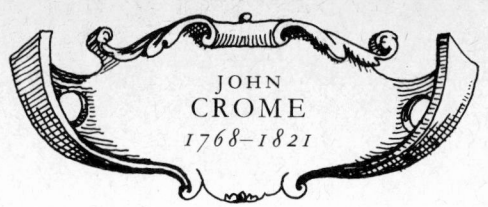

JOHN
CROME
1768–1821

CROME never established himself out of Norwich, where he was born and where he died, another of the Romantic landscape painters of humble family, his father a journeyman weaver and innkeeper. He came to painting by apprenticeship to a coach and sign painter in Norwich. As a teacher of drawing and sketching he soon had the chance of seeing Dutch landscapes in various family collections and of travelling with his pupils to picture country. He went to the Lakes in 1802 and 1806, and in between to South and North Wales and to Dorset. Thereafter he was seldom out of Norfolk, though in 1814 he travelled to Paris to see the Napoleonic hoard of pictures in the Louvre. Living less by his own work than by teaching and picture-restoring, Crome was not damaged by patronage and the Academy and a London existence. He was able to develop the solemnity of his landscape without interference, absorbing the light and breadth and long perspectives of the low East Anglian scenery in strongly composed pictures which take the eye from foreground to horizon via the lighted twist of roads or water. *Page* 186.

OUSEHOLD
EATH BY
ORWICH,
1813.
tching,
× 11⅛ *in.*
ivate
llection.

ORWICH:
EW OF ST.
ARTIN'S
ATE,
1808–13.
l, 20 × 15
Norwich,
stle
useum.

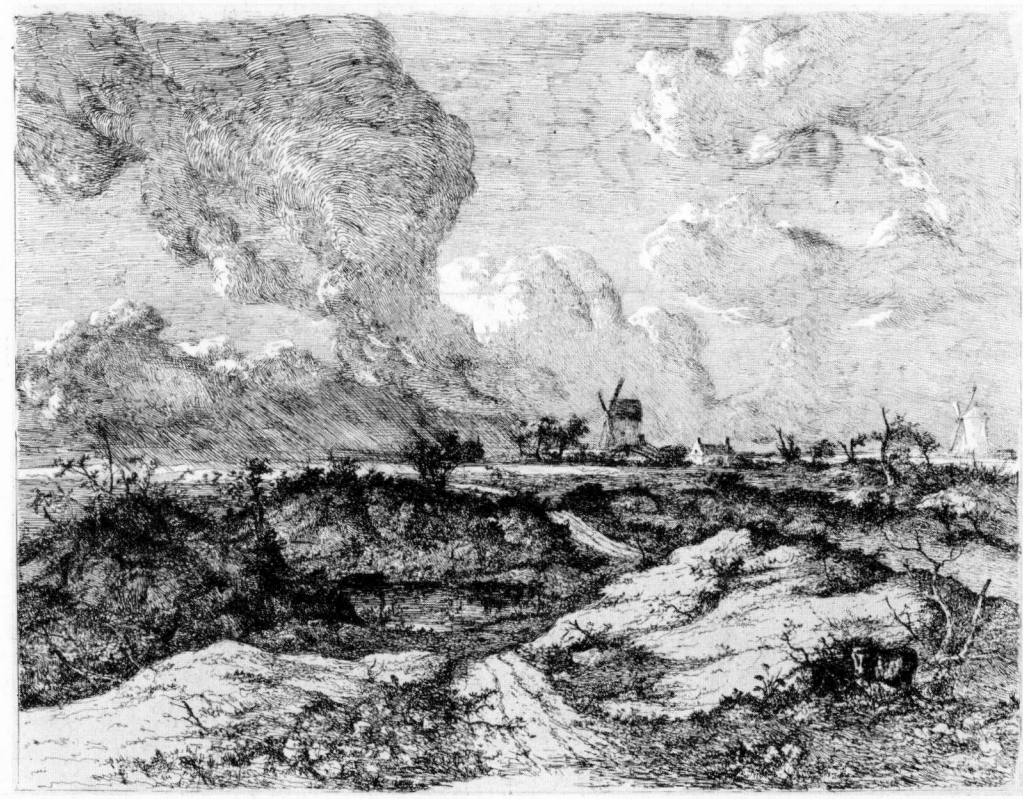

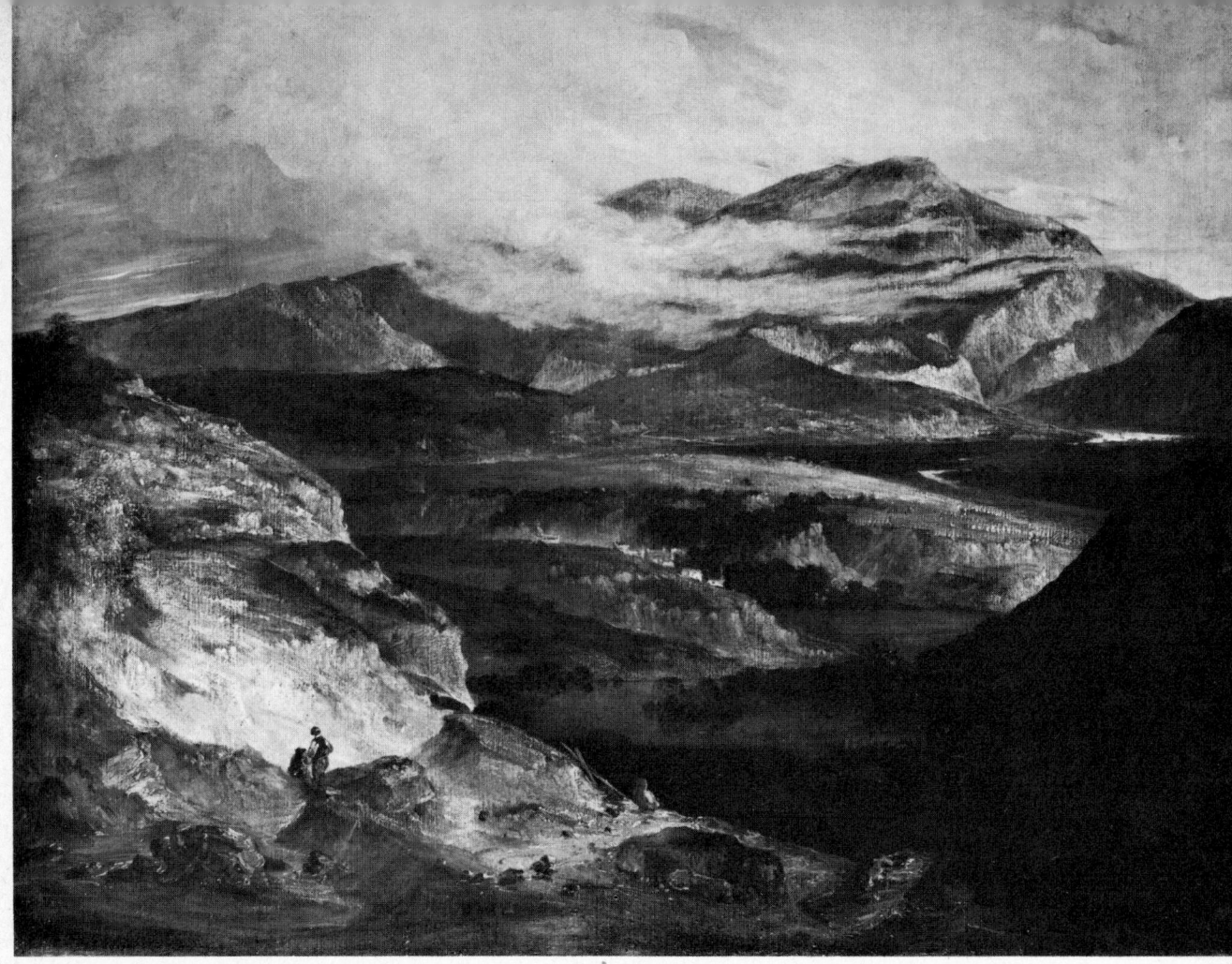

34. THE SLATE QUARRIES, *c.* 1804. *Oil,* 48¾ × 62½ *in. London, Tate Gallery.*

The Slate Quarries is a late and unlucky name to have given this picture, which in fact presents the view of Snowdon from Moel Hebog, across Nant Colwyn. Rising out of Crome's curve of cloud are the Llechog crest to the right and the summit of Snowdon to the left. The view was already a famous one when Crome visited Wales in 1804. His wreath of cloud covers the usual Beddgelert ascent of Snowdon from the farm of Ffridduchaf on the N.E. side of A487. Crome may have in mind Thomas Pennant's description of Snowdon in his *Tour in Wales:* 'A vast mist enveloped the whole circuit of the mountain. The prospect down was horrible. It gave the idea of a number of abysses, concealed by a thick smoke, furiously circulating around us. Very often a gust of wind formed an opening in the clouds, which gave a fine and distinct visto of lake and valley. Sometimes they opened only in one place; at others in many at once, exhibiting a most strange and perplexing sight of water, fields, rocks or chasms, in fifty different places. They then closed at once, and left us involved in darkness; in a small space they would separate again, and fly in wild eddies round the middle of the mountains, and expose, in parts, both tops and bases to our view.'

66

35. MOONRISE ON THE YARE, *c.* 1807–8. *Oil, 28 × 43¼ in. London, Tate Gallery.*

An East Anglian draining mill. Crome's patron Dawson Turner, the Yarmouth banker, antiquary and botanist, bought this famous moonlight from the artist. He wrote many years later that the picture shows the Yare near the point where it joins the Waveney, opposite Burgh Castle, the Roman Fort of the Saxon shore behind Yarmouth. This would make the winding river the Berney Arms Reach of the Yare. One of the bastions of Burgh Castle seems to be indicated to the right of the draining mill.

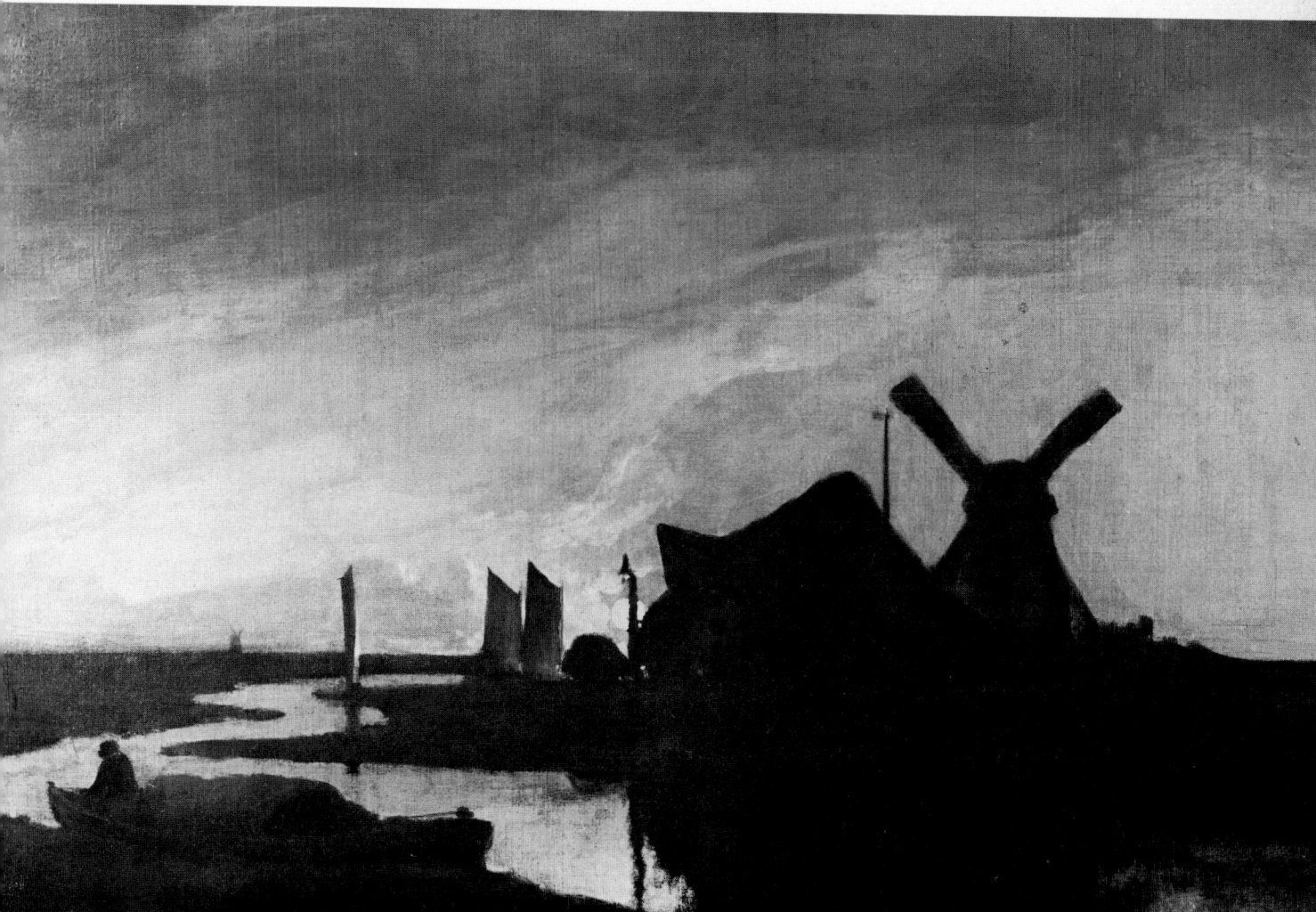

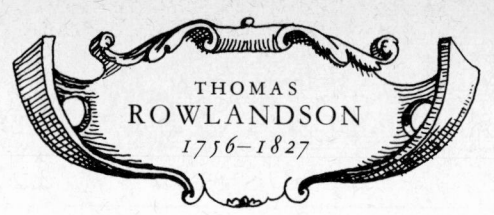

THOMAS
ROWLANDSON
1756–1827

THE VARIETY, the peculiarity and the everywhereness of life engaged Rowlandson; and its comedy. His landscape for the most part is where something happens
or is going on, and it may be graceful, happy, solemn, or grotesque. He could draw
anything, the most self-assured of all English artists, whose line, enclosing,
defining, intriguing, was active everywhere and anywhere. On the whole Rowlandson must be deduced from his work. Little is recorded about him, he was not given
to pronouncements, or to public postures about art. His Huguenot connection
took him to Paris in his student years and afterwards, and there is a French Rococo
influence in the quick fluidity of his line, though he was master of a persistent
style which was entirely his own. London was his theatre. He was London-born
and London-based, the son of a silk mercer. From his central theatre he made his
excursions, it might be to Yorkshire, to Wales, to Cornwall and Devon. He could
manage equally the enclosed and the open. In Cornwall, where he often stayed with
a banker friend and patron at Hengar House in St. Tudy, between Bodmin and
Camelford, he made some of his happiest and some of his most grotesque drawings,
extracting the essence of wild valleys below the moorland, in which streams
stumble along rocky beds, under canopies of oak. In Wales he would draw the
width and openness of a mountain pass going on and on and divided by the

36. UPPER VALE OF LLANGOLLEN. *Pen and wash and watercolour,* $5\frac{3}{4} \times 17$ *in.*
Aberystwyth, National Library of Wales.

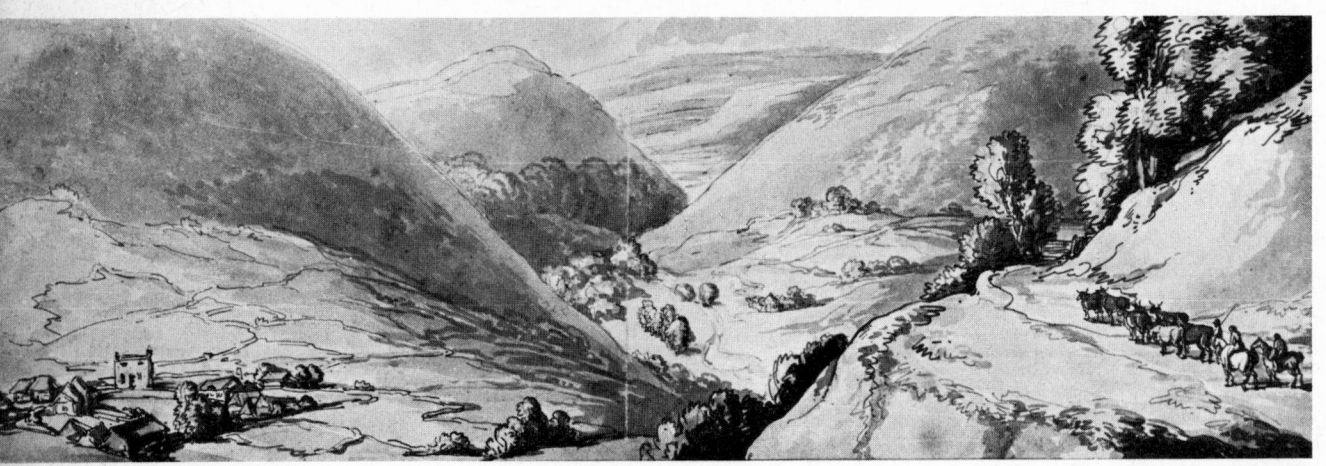

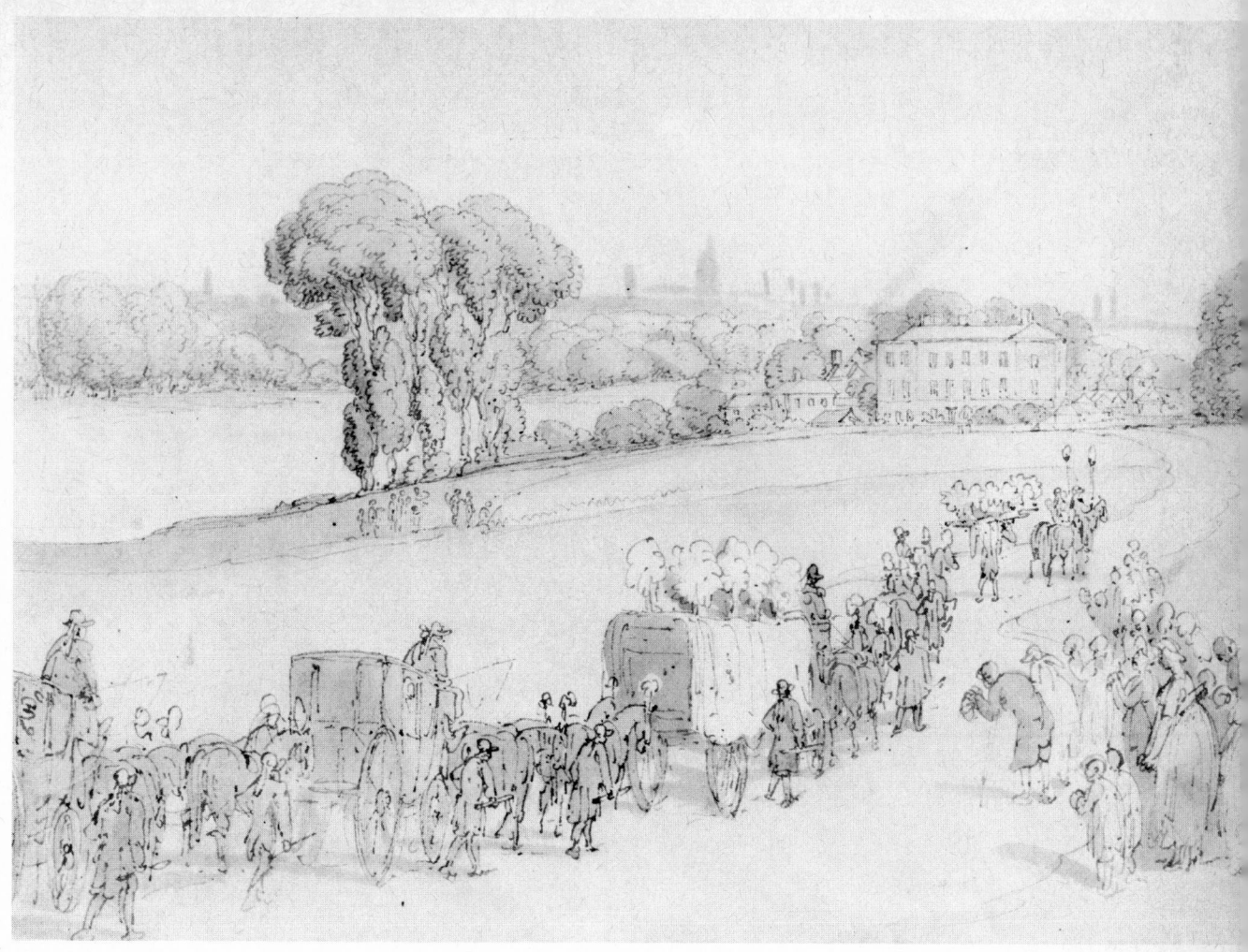

37. A FUNERAL PROCESSION APPROACHING A MANSION ON THE BANKS OF THE THAMES. *Watercolour*, 8 × 11 *in. Collection of Mr and Mrs Paul Mellon.*

wriggling of an uneven track, along which men and animals or waggons amble like beetles. Or from smooth grounds along the even flow of the Thames he would contrive images of country house felicity and calm.

Often Rowlandson creates a contrast between a level stillness and the activity of surrounding forms, whether of water or uneven rocks or decrepit buildings, just as his interiors often contrast the graceful and elegant line of youth with the wriggling picturesque outline of old age. Gnarled rocks, gnarled oaks, gnarled bawds and gnarled rakes have an identity in his tinted drawings, which he kept free of moral attitudinizing.

69

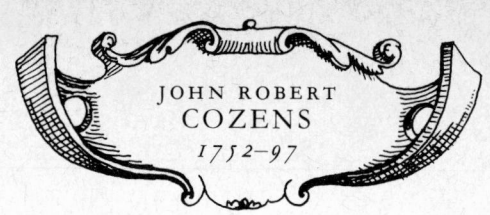

JOHN ROBERT
COZENS
1752–97

WHEN HE WASN'T IN SWITZERLAND, on the way south, or in Italy or in Sicily, one can imagine John Robert Cozens 'sighing for classic ground', like Richard Wilson. He lived too early to want to invent landscape out of English elements, or to be patronized for English subjects, and the few English watercolours by him which survive, are supposed to date from the last ten years or so of his life, after he came home from his second Italian journey, and before he went mad. He visited the Lakes, he made a few local compositions around London, not excited in them to his wide solemnities of atmosphere and distance, his grave musicality (one of the few facts known about him is that he played the violin and liked Handel's music). Like his father, the equally mysterious Alexander Cozens, he seems to have been a small man, retiring, and lost in himself and his landscape.

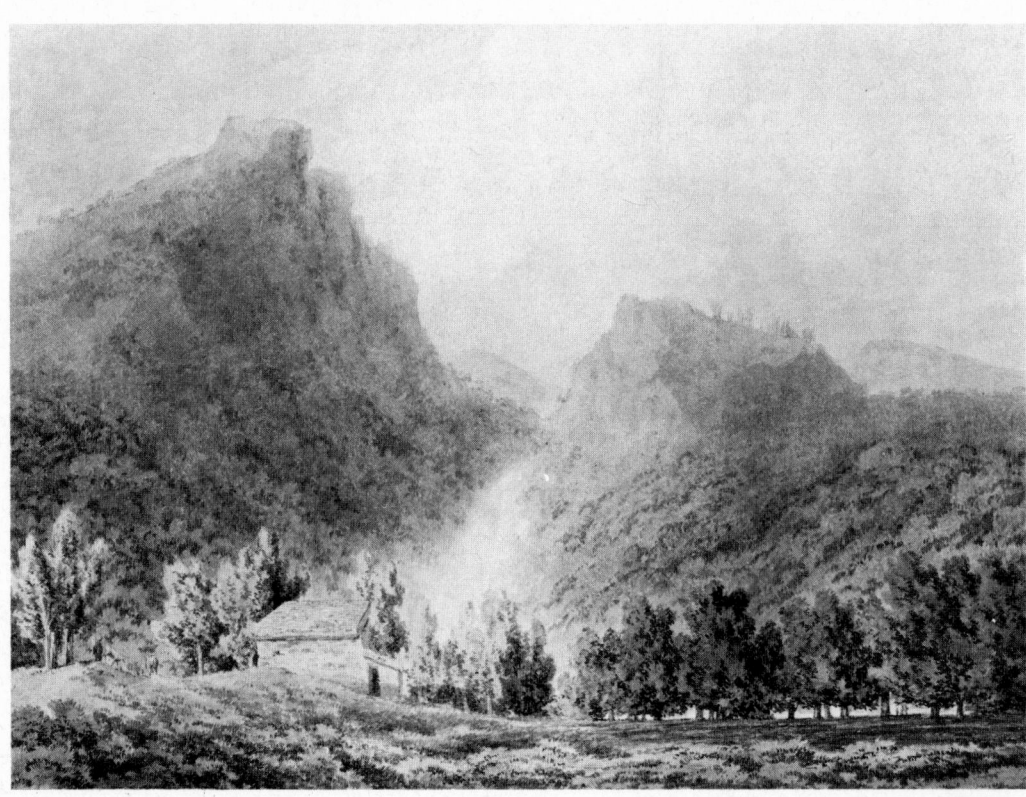

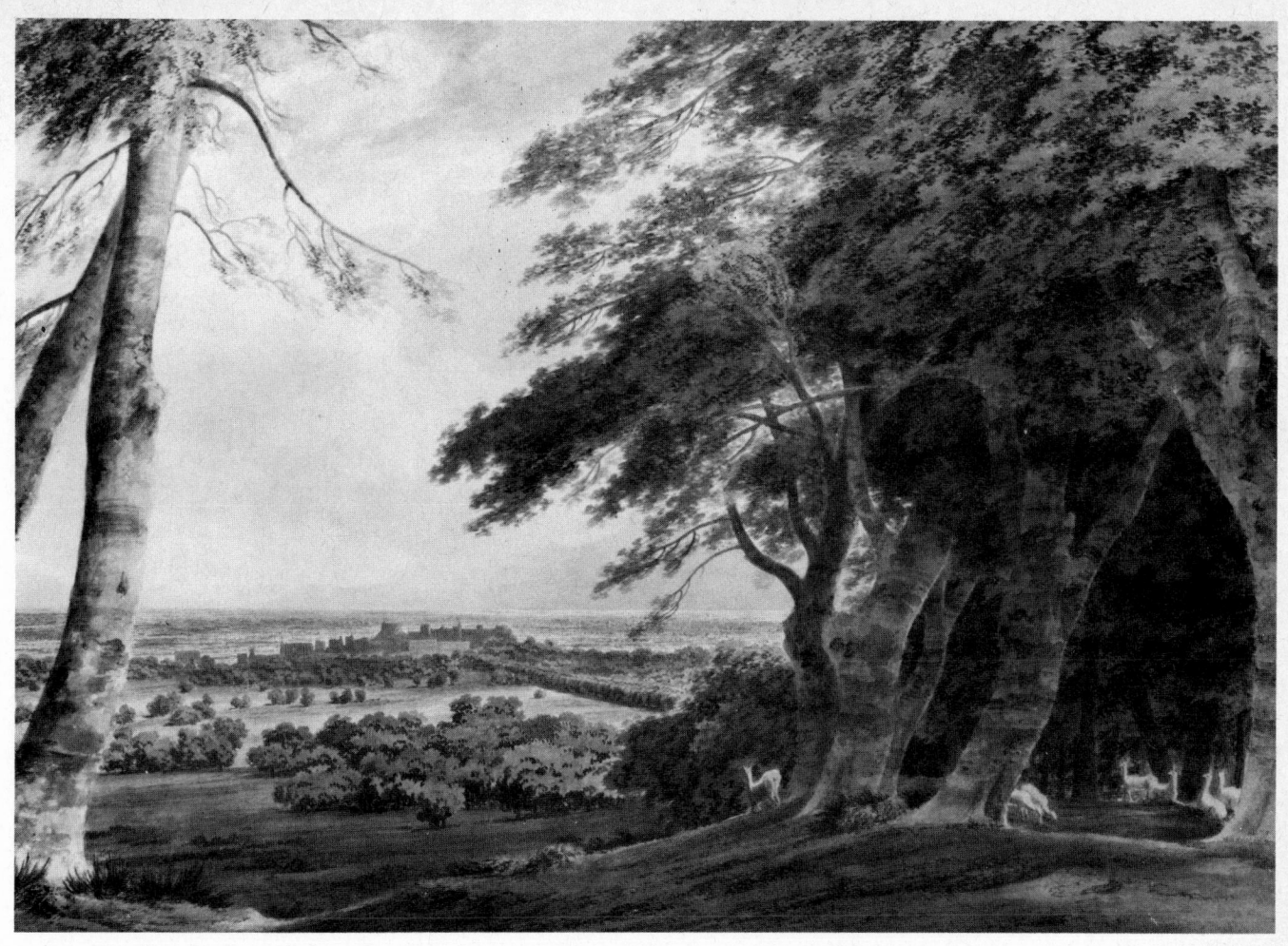

39. WINDSOR CASTLE FROM THE SOUTH-WEST. *Watercolour,* $19\frac{5}{8} \times 27\frac{5}{8}$ *in. Bedford, Cecil Higgins Art Gallery.*

38. THE WATERFALL OF LODORE. *Watercolour,* $14\frac{3}{8} \times 19\frac{3}{4}$ *in. London, Fine Art Society.*

Near Keswick, and long considered one of the sublimities of the Lake District, though visitors too often found a trickle instead of majesty, as artists and writers had led them to expect, Lodore requiring prolonged and heavy rain.

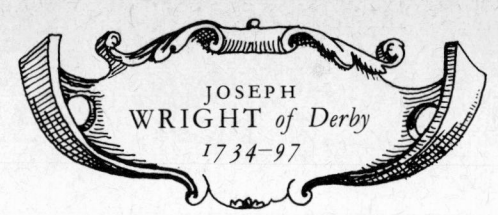

JOSEPH WRIGHT was born in Derby and lived there for most of his life, the son of an attorney and the brother of one of the principal doctors in the town. He came late to English landscape after making a name for his portraits, his 'philosophical' candlelights and his industrial scenes lit by the glow of iron. Derby and Derbyshire were then among the cradles of the industrial revolution and Joseph Wright's friends included such pioneers of science and industry as Arkwright the inventor of spinning machinery and the potter Josiah Wedgwood. He preserved an eye for things as they are, in contrast to his senior and friend Richard Wilson, who preserved an eye for things—other than shimmering atmosphere—as they are not. His vision was not blinded or prettified by a year in Italy (1774–5), which led him to paint grottoes, firework displays, and Vesuvius in eruption. From about 1780 he painted Derbyshire scenes of cliff and water composed less from the readymade tricks of the Ideal than from visual intimacy, local affection, and his scientific inclination. They are pure, calm landscape, by a painter concerned, not for popular attitudinizing, but for forms and surfaces and the play of light on limestone and water, and the light which these surfaces reflect. Like Courbet in the Jura, he is happiest in his native Derbyshire subjects, beside which his few Lakeland canvases are uncompelling.
Page 185.

40. LANDSCAPE WITH A RAINBOW—VIEW NEAR CHESTERFIELD IN DERBYSHIRE, *c.* 1795. *Oil,* 32 × 42 *in. Derby Museum and Art Gallery.*

The bridge presumably exists no longer, and the exact site of this landscape has not been identified.

41. LANDSCAPE WITH DALE ABBEY. *Oil,* 28½ × 39 *in. Sheffield, Graves Art Gallery.*

The ruins in the landscape are those of Dale Priory, a house of Augustinian Canons.

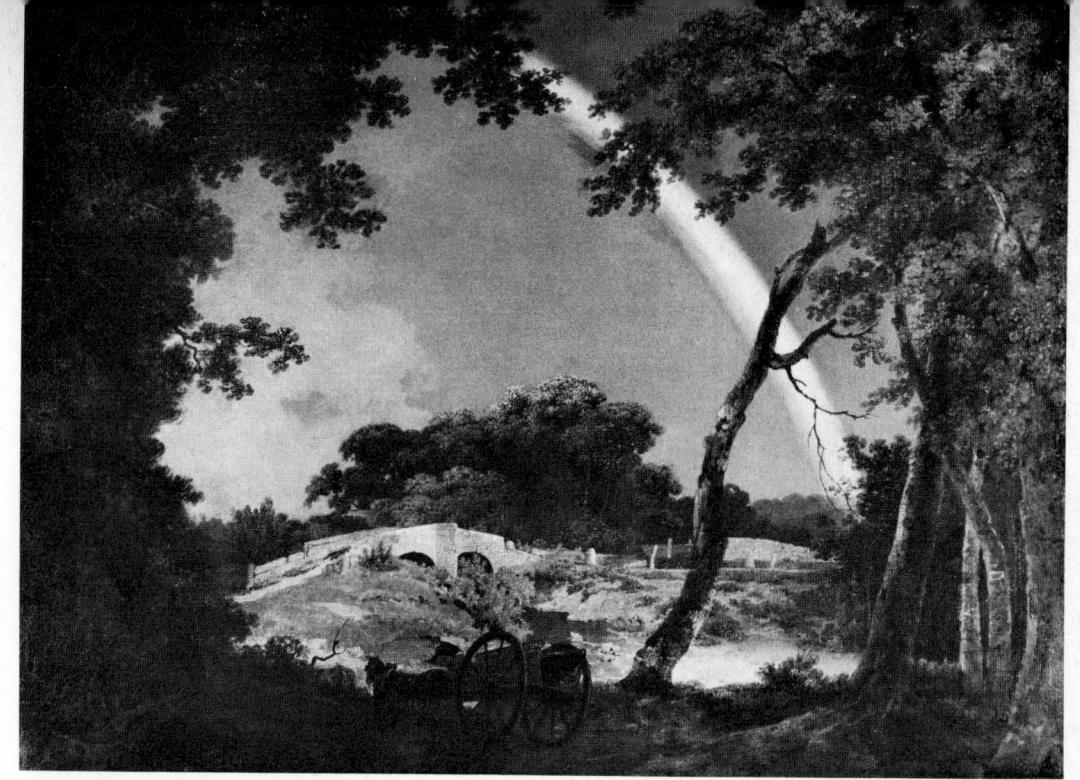

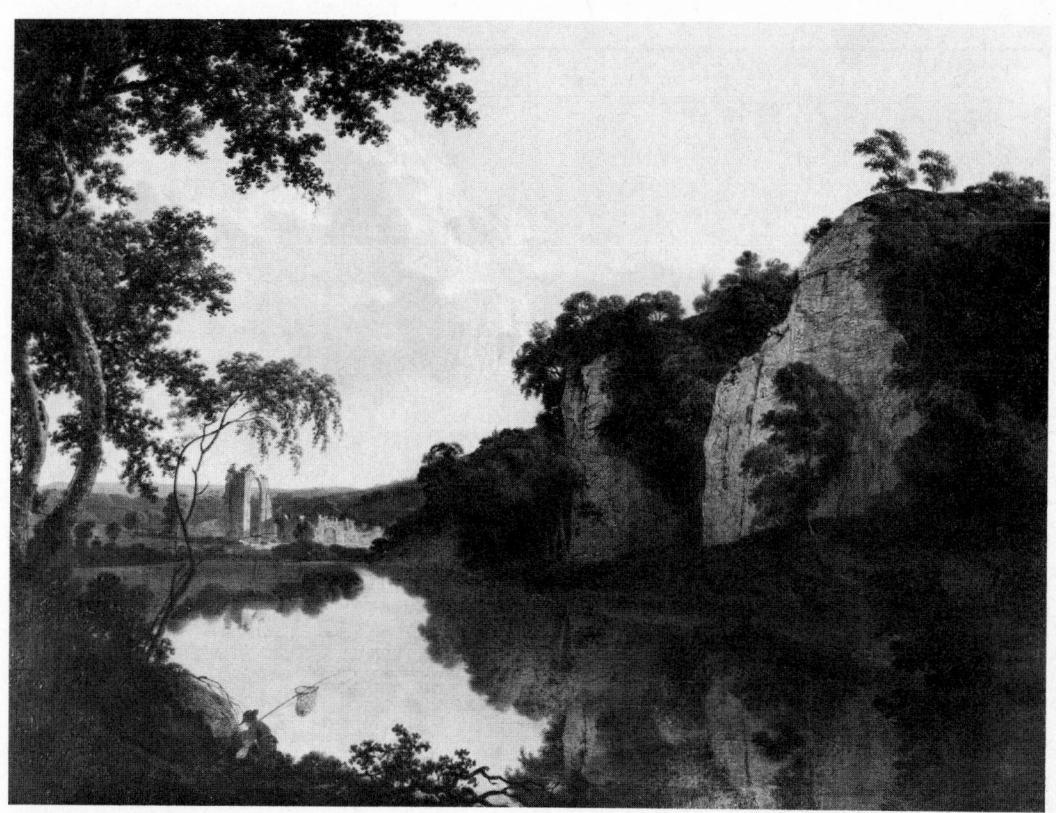

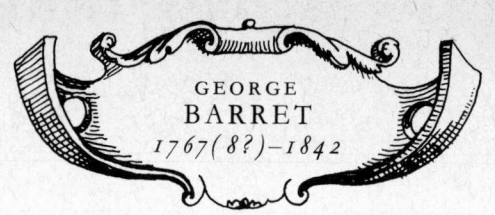

GEORGE
BARRET
1767(8?)–1842

GEORGE BARRET THE YOUNGER was one of the landscape painters forced by
patronage and prevailing tastes from an early naturalism, a romantic absorption in
nature and effects of light, into decidedly unreal poetic composition derived from
Claude. To begin with he was capable of such direct and attractive (but unsaleable?)
work as his *View on the Coast*. Poverty and a mild character appear to have been his
troubles. He began poor—when he was a boy he and his family were left destitute
by his father, the elder George Barret, who had been one of the first members of
the Royal Academy—and he died poor. With William Havell and Cornelius Varley
(Plates 68, 69, 75) he was one of the original sixteen members of the Old Water-
Colour Society founded in 1804.

42. VIEW ON THE COAST SEEN THROUGH A WINDOW, *c.* 1840. *Watercolour,*
$15\frac{3}{4} \times 10\frac{1}{4}$ *in. Windsor, The Royal Library, Reproduced by gracious permission of
Her Majesty the Queen.*

The view is along the southern coast of the Isle of Wight towards the lighthouse
below St. Catherine's Point, on the beach, which was built in 1840.

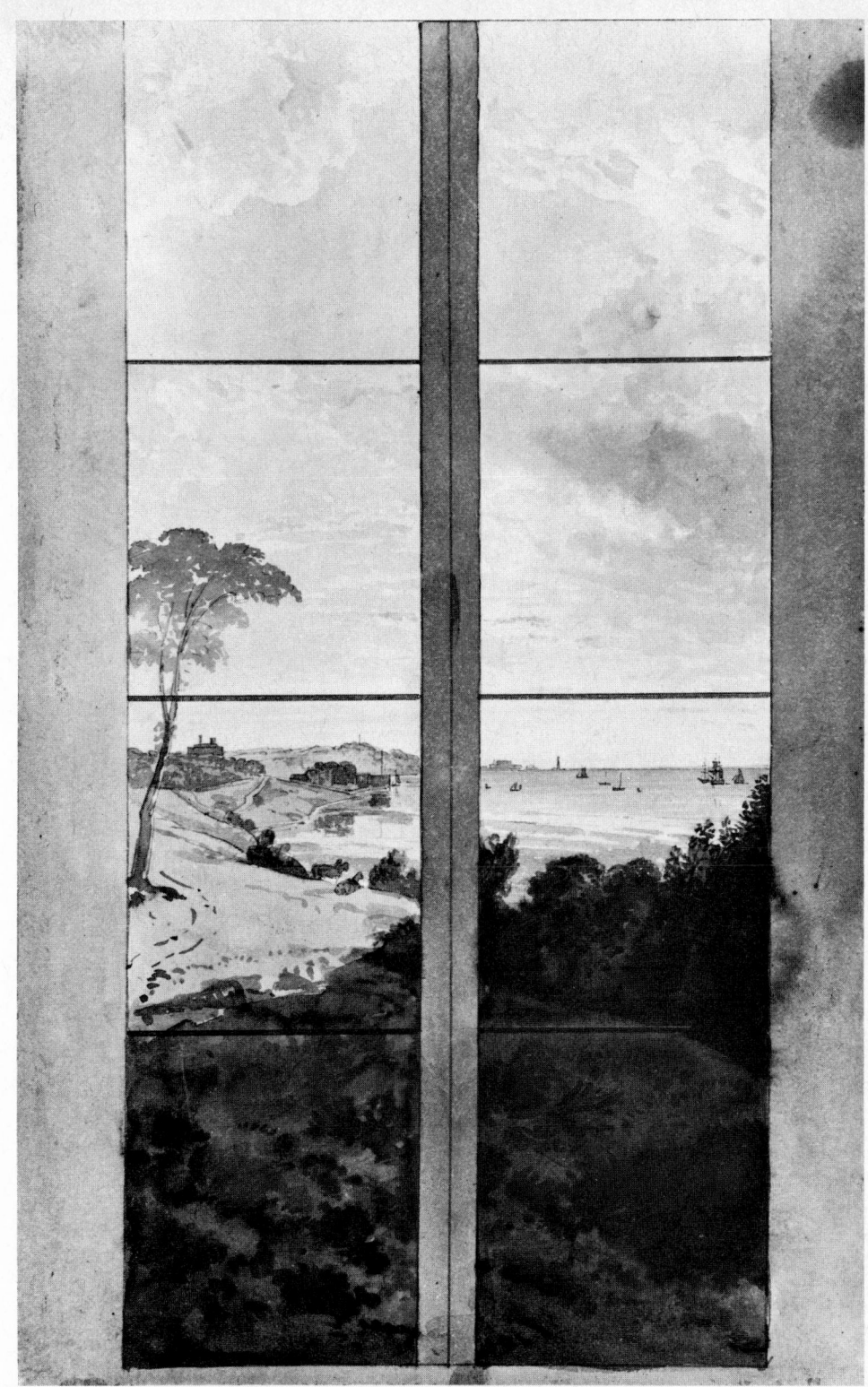

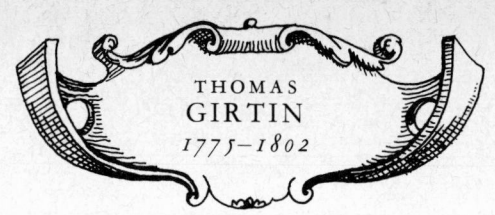

TURNER AND GIRTIN, son of a London brushmaker of Huguenot descent, were born in the same year and painted together when young. Then Girtin died when he was 27, after a short strenuous career and the rapid development of his subjective powers in watercolour. The unshaken praise for Girtin from his day until today has been automatic and hagiographic, as if based rather less on his work than on remarks by Turner and others, and on John Constable's estimate that he possessed 'genius of the very highest order.' He established an emotional imaginative rapport with the scene in landscapes which were neither adulterated nor dependent at the close of his life. Until then his design and his colours (like the beautiful sombre colours on a house-sparrow's back) combined with lumpiness of forms. The effect was stuffy. In his final watercolours a broad slow pace, a solemn rejection of the extras of romantic picture-making, and a winding of light into depth are among his great characteristics. He does not impose a catchy exaggeration on his selected aspects of the real or the sufficiently real. Clouds, for instance, pushed darkly over and down from dark heights stop short of the oppressive and become grave intimators of mortality; though one may prefer the silence of his very broad uncluttered landscapes or townscapes which exert at last a dying benediction. Overrated as he may be, it is hard to suppose that a more long lived Girtin would have sentimentalized his art or made it theatrical.

Girtin's encomiasts have always been upset by rather priggishly expressed accusations of 'vice', and passions overpowering the reason, and 'acts of excess', in which Girtin 'trifled away a vigorous constitution.' They were made after his death by his old teacher Edward Dayes. Priggish wording and counter-accusations against Dayes and horrified denials don't prove the accusations untrue or unlikely —or particularly damaging. The unsaintly John Wolcot, who had known Girtin, described him as 'generous and giddy', and Girtin's industry and imaginative power aren't contradicted if we suppose him to have been as fiery a particle as Keats, with habits as little like those of a curate.

43. OLD HOUSE BY A RIVER, *c.* 1796–7. *Watercolour over black lead,* $8\frac{1}{2} \times 13$ *in. Private collection.*

44. KIRKSTALL ON THE BANKS OF THE AIRE, 1802. *Watercolour,* $12\frac{1}{2} \times 19\frac{3}{8}$ *in. Collection of Mr and Mrs Paul Mellon.*

The completest ruins in England of a Cistercian abbey, in what was once the most delicious setting, until fouled by the industrialism of Leeds. Girtin's barge is prophetic.

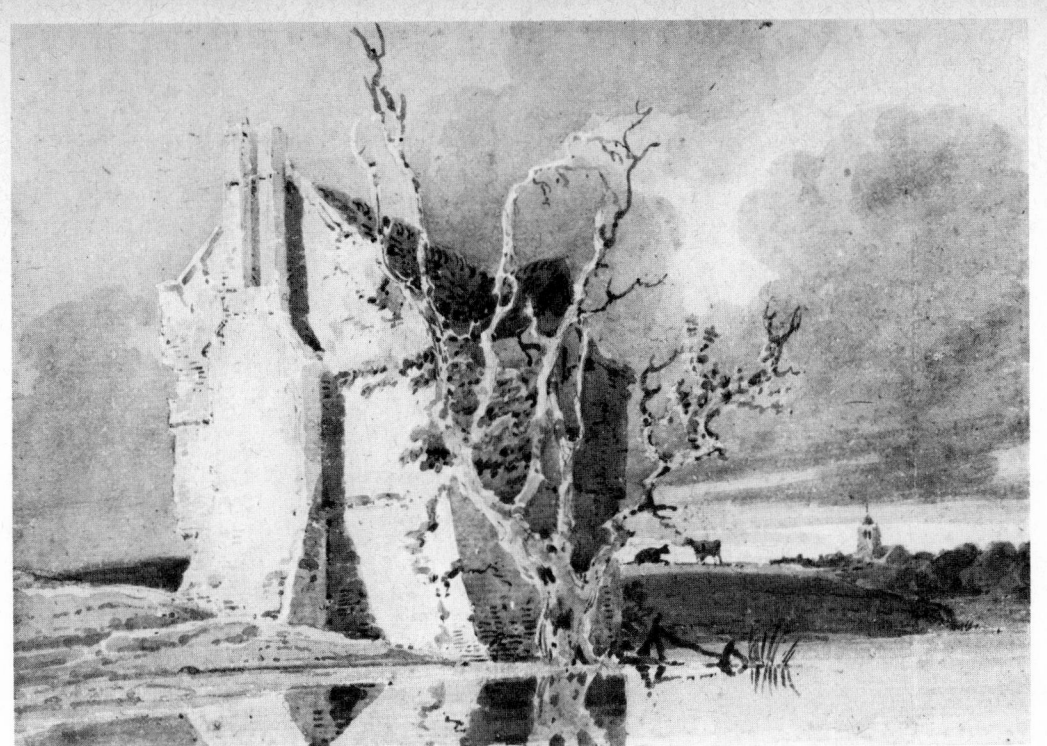

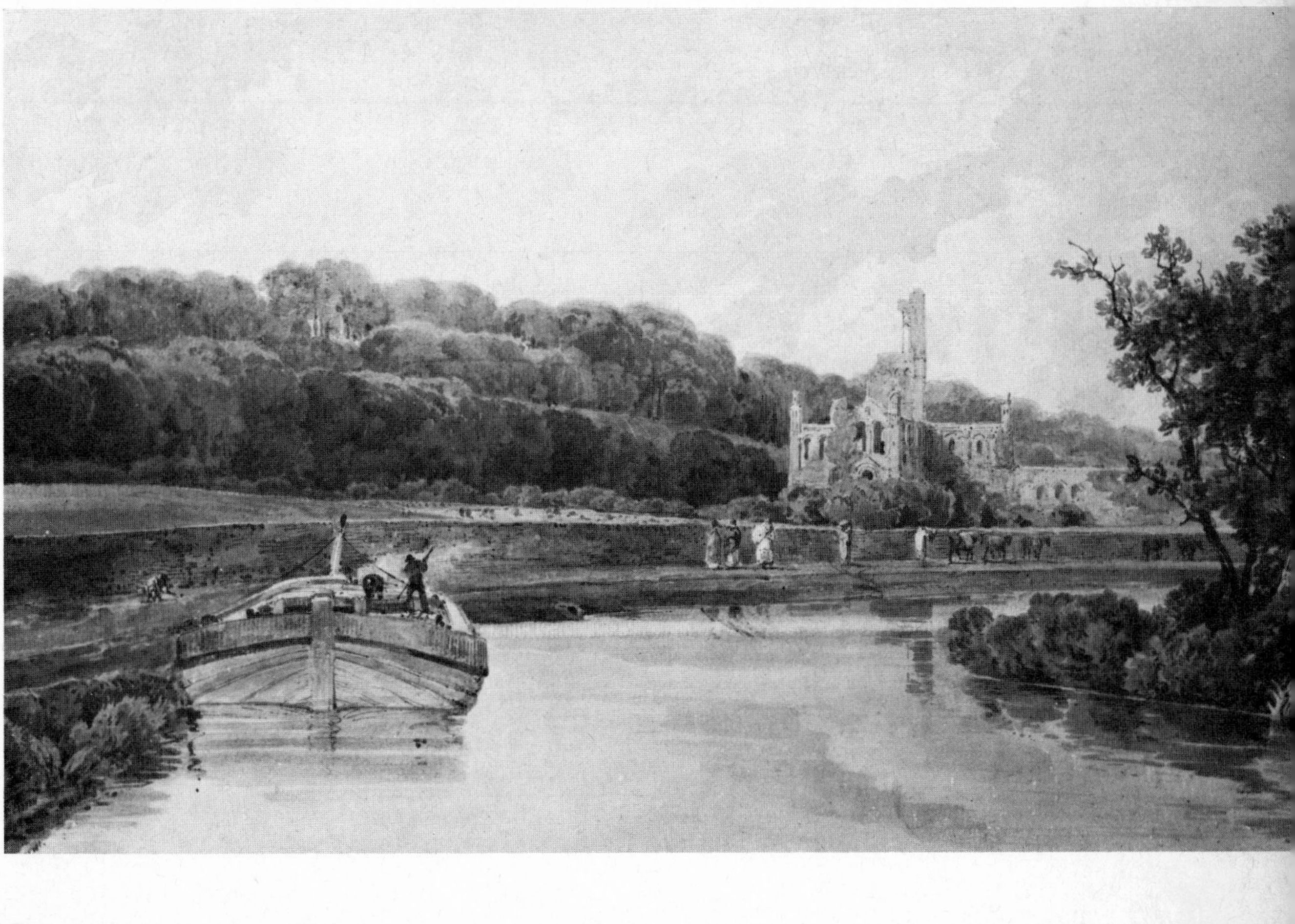

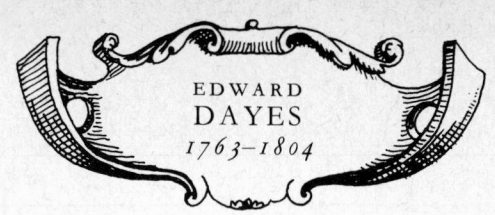

BECAUSE HE QUARRELLED with his pupil and apprentice Thomas Girtin, and left criticisms of Girtin, the London artist, Edward Dayes has always had a bad press. The facts are not really known, and are irrevelant. Certainly—but it is a free world —Dayes uttered disparaging opinions, always ready to talk (at any rate in his posthumous *Works*, 1805) of 'the callow capacity' of so powerful a string-puller in the arts as Joseph Farington, or to complain of 'the half-bred connoisseur' or of seeing 'the names of some of our prime nobility coupled with those of scoundrel-dealers, jobbers, and mongers of pictures, who play all manner of dirty tricks to deceive the public, and decry the present race of artists.' And he killed himself. Artists were not expected to behave in that way. But Dayes was an artist of various skills, engraver, miniaturist, composer of often dramatic—legitimately dramatic— watercolour landscapes. He was a man also of some learning in literature and antiquities as well as art. Dayes painted subjects on the Thames, in Derbyshire, Yorkshire, Wales, the Lakes, the North-East, etc.

Page 185.

45. THE PRIORY CHURCH, TYNEMOUTH. *Watercolour*, $19\frac{3}{4} \times 14\frac{5}{8}$ *in. Newcastle upon Tyne, Laing Art Gallery.*

The ruins (of 'the largest monastery in Britain to have been built within a castle') remain, near the now soiled edge of the North Sea. Dayes had a liking for the frame within the frame, the arch of a bridge or a ruin enclosing the further view (cf. Scott, Plate 12; and Agasse, Plate 58).

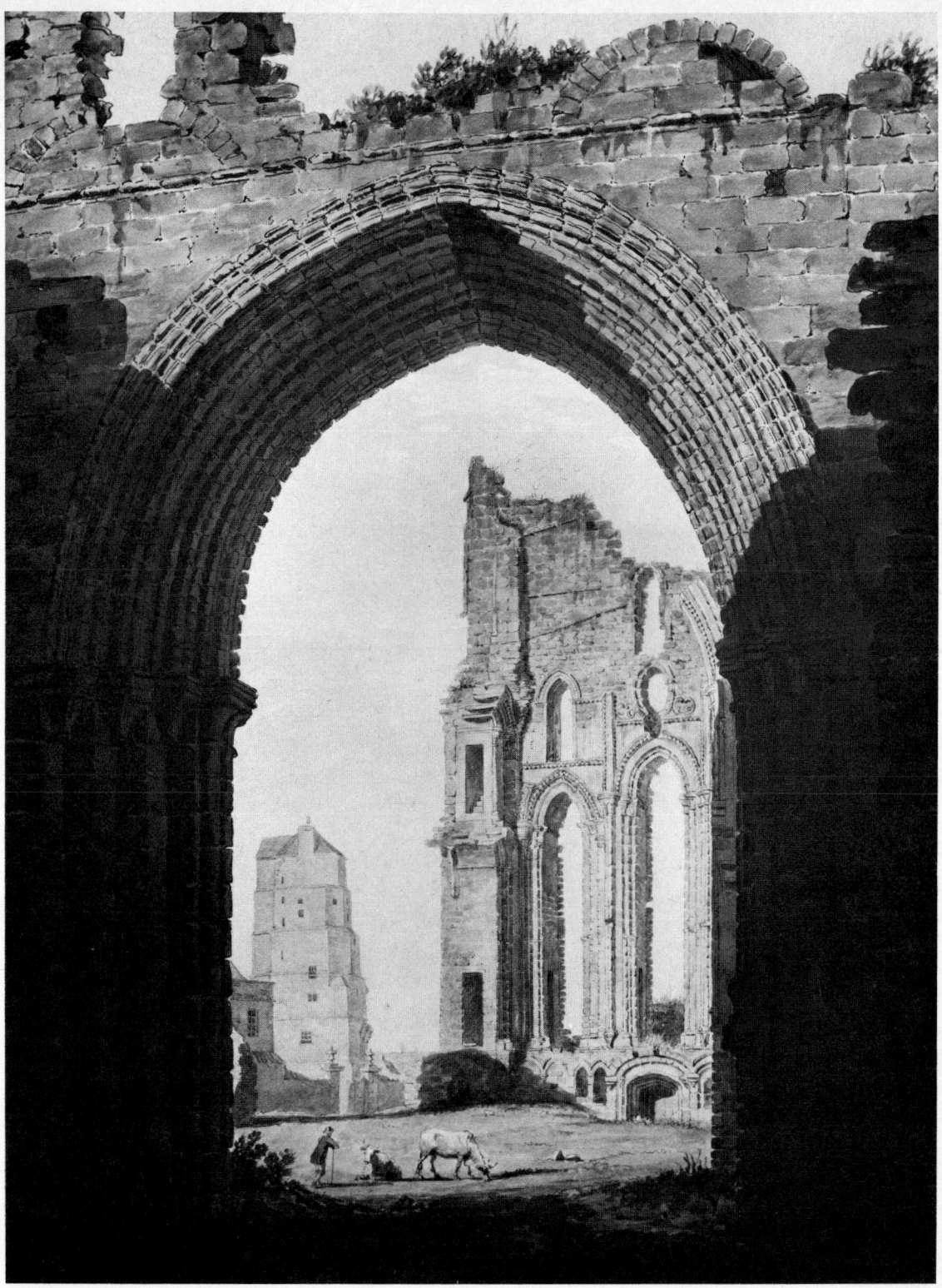

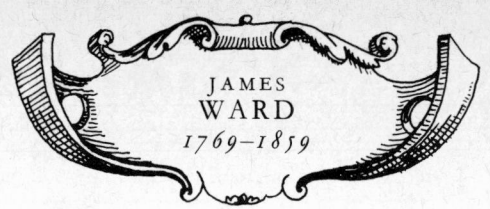

JAMES
WARD
1769–1859

His biographer (Reginald Grundy, *James Ward R.A.*, 1909) remarks that in his huge *Landscape with Cattle* in the Tate Gallery 'he records the marks on a butterfly's wing, and the minute forms of the weeds and grasses in the foreground, with the same close observation that he devoted to the rendering of the group of cattle.' He trusted to his skill 'to subordinate these details to the leading *motif* of his picture.' Ward often succeeded in this combination of breadth and detail, and his observed fact is one reason why pictures by him remain convincing. Between the sublime and the picturesque they frequently express his own peculiar, inquisitive, energetic being, instead of projecting only an extraneous fashionable sentiment. It is also recorded of him that when he toured Wales in 1802, for a series of engravings of prize animals, he came back to London with an extra 581 sketches from nature of 'every picturesque or uncommon object he encountered.' Humbly born (his father was employed by a fruit and cider merchant), with little education, he forced his way into painting out of the lowlier craft of engraving. He travelled, an insatiable draughtsman, through England, Scotland and Wales, and attempted everything, domestic sentimental genre, human as well as animal portraiture, sporting pieces, landscape, history, allegory, the sublime and the picturesque, and not infrequently the ridiculous, in a career which spanned English romanticism. Fuseli and De Loutherbourg were early influences, then Potter, and Rubens, by whose great *Château de Steen*, which he first saw in 1803, he was stimulated. His acquaintanceship included William Blake (Ward was religious and loved the apocalyptic), and his vigorous horse paintings and engravings had some effect on Géricault.

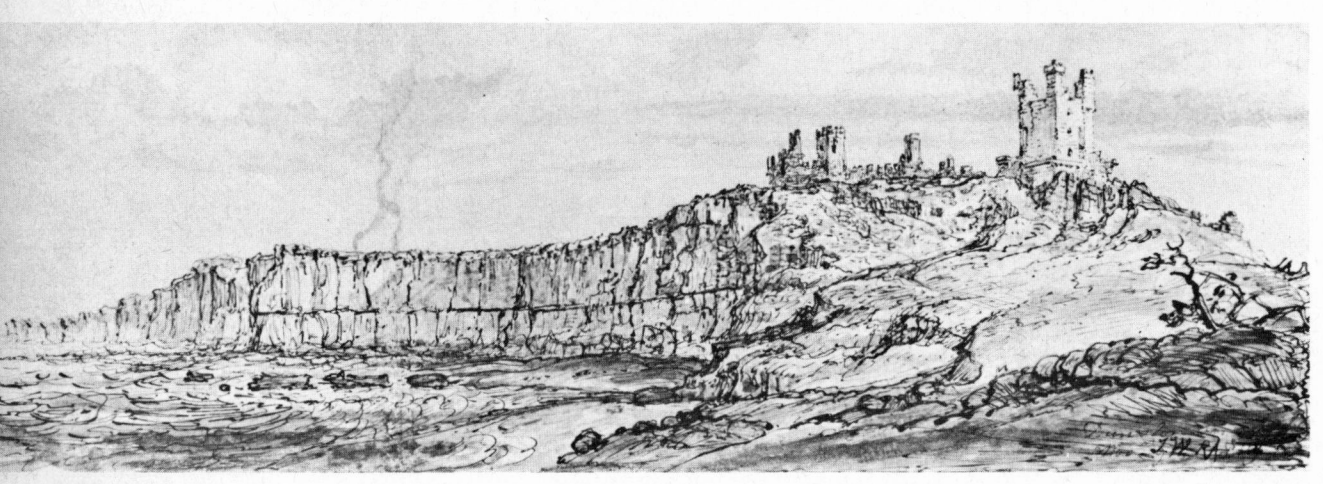

46.
DUNSTAN-
BURGH
CASTLE.
*Pen and
watercolour
5 × 14¾ in
London
Courtauld
Institute.*

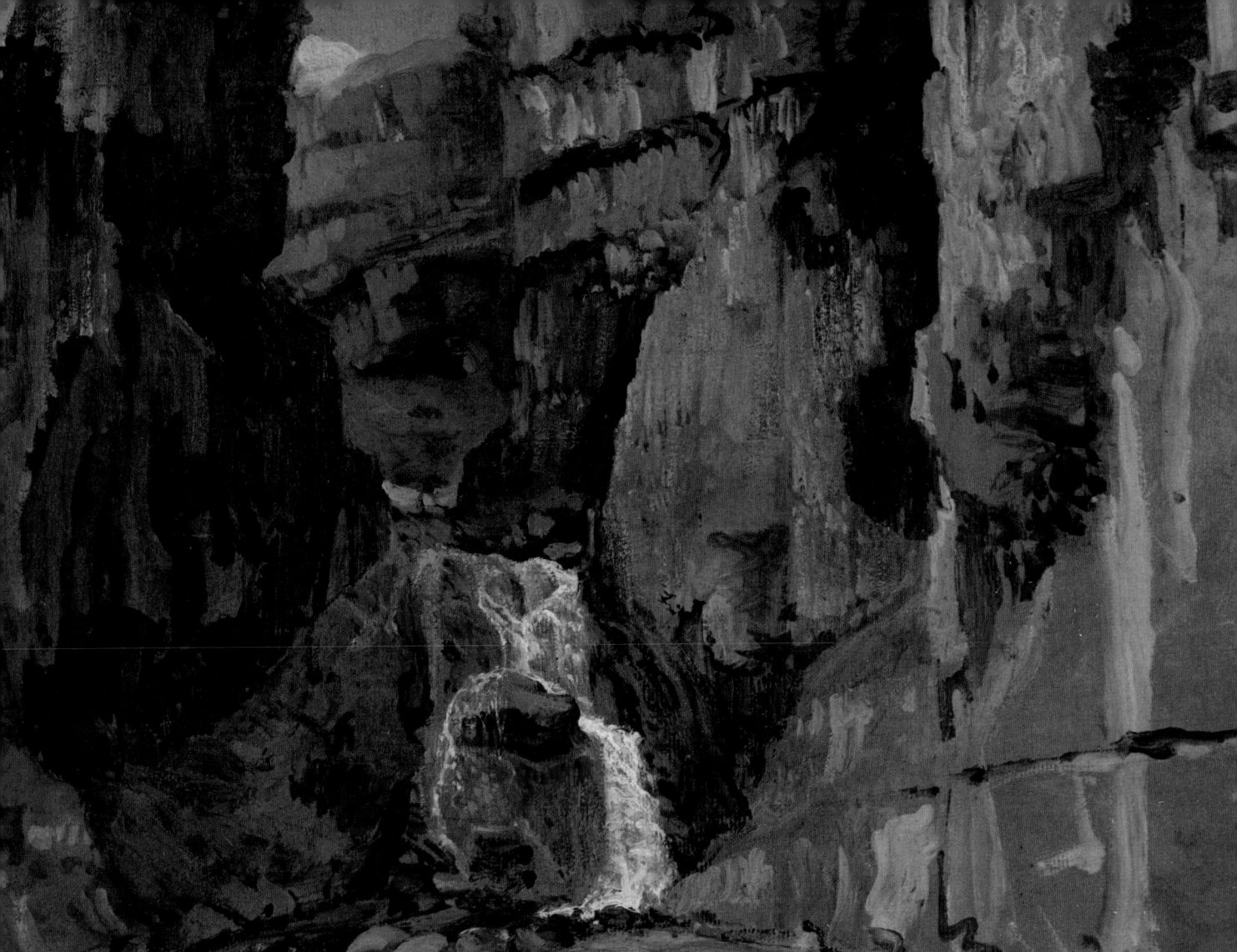

47. SKETCH FOR 'GORDALE SCAR' *c.* 1811. *Oil on paper* 12½×16⅞. *London Tate Gallery.*

One of several very accurate sketches which James Ward made for his immense picture *A Landscape, Gordale Scar, Yorkshire* (131 × 166 in.), which dominates its room in the Tate. The final picture greatly exaggerates the scale and grandeurs of this limestone gorge or series of fallen caverns, turning it into a highly effective image of the sublime. Ward had no doubt read the description of Gordale by the artist Edward Dayes (*Works*, 1805): 'The lover of drawing will be much delighted with this place: immensity and horror are its inseparable companions, uniting together to form subjects of the most awful cast. The very soul of Salvator Rosa would hover with delight over these regions of confusion.' He declared it better than any pass in North Wales, adding 'the right hand canopy, including the water-fall, presents a fine upright view, which shape is best calculated for the disposition of these rocks.'

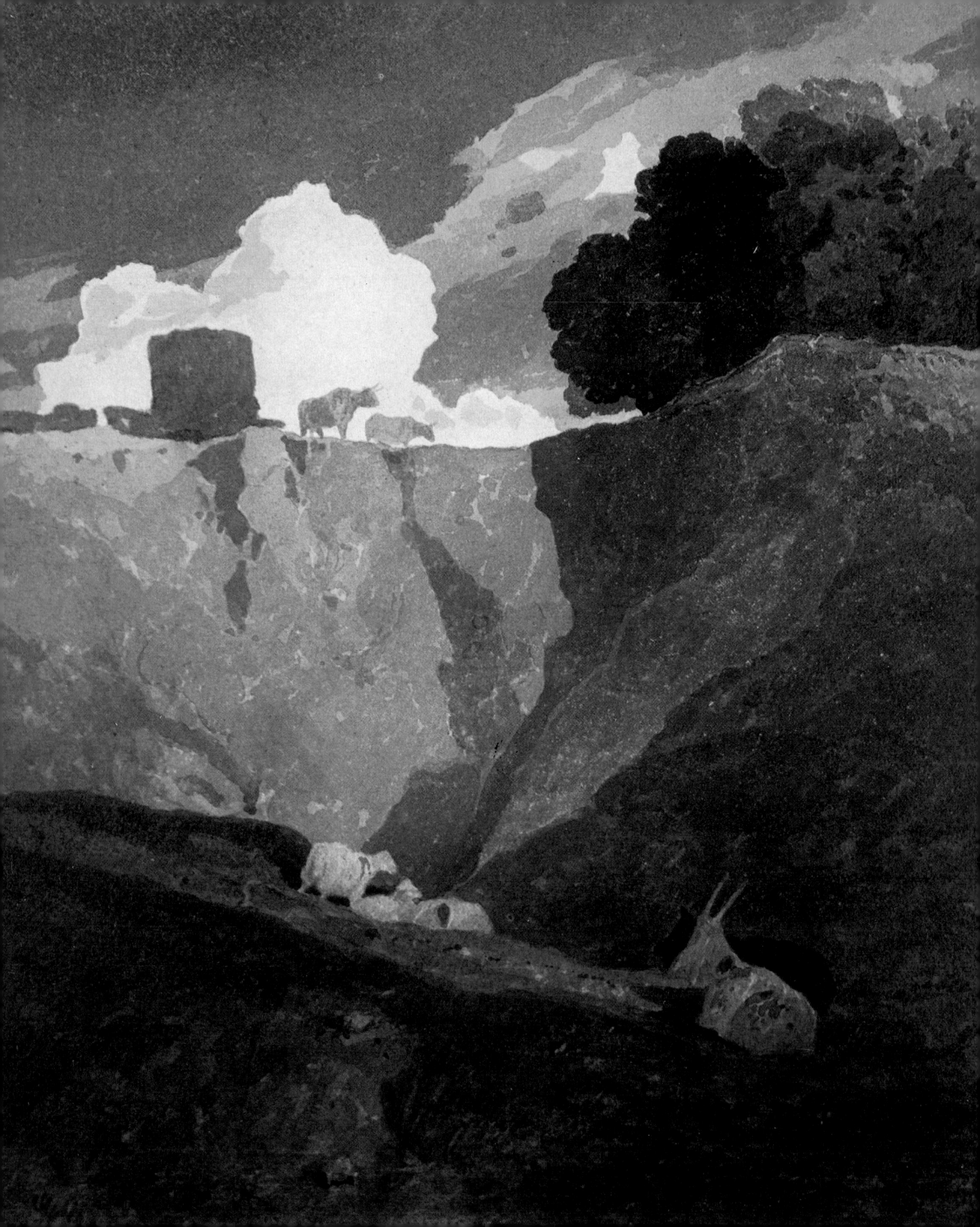

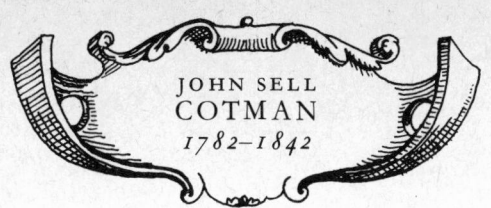

JOHN SELL
COTMAN
1782–1842

DRAUGHTSMAN, painter in watercolour and oil, and etcher, Cotman broke out of an unprivileged childhood in Norwich, where his father was first a hairdresser, then a draper in a small way. He drew almost from infancy, came to London when he was sixteen, working for a while in the most prominent of the fine art shops, before being employed in drawing and copying by the celebrated Dr. Monro, who had given work to Girtin and Turner. This introduced him to the then typical life of the young professional landscapists with no money behind them, who toured in the summer months for material which they worked up into exhibition pieces. They eked out sales by giving lessons in sketching to young ladies. Cotman's life, one of indecision and timidity except when face to face with his chosen landscape, was basically divided, in unsuccess, between London, Norwich and Yarmouth; with later tours in Normandy. He drew scenery in Wales, his own East Anglia, Yorkshire and elsewhere, quickly developing a style of objective naturalism in which a castle, a church, a ruin, a bridge, an aqueduct, or decrepit houses were depicted as unsentimentalized, untheatrical forms in a composition of cool shallow planes. It was Yorkshire scenery he felt most profoundly, near Rokeby where the Greta leaves the moors for great depths of woodland. From the Greta he made watercolours in which physically felt surfaces and planes are ordered into a near and distant vision of natural richness, landscape in no idiom but his own— an idiom which found few admirers.

The great year of his experience of the Greta was 1805, when he was 23. *Page* 190.

48. THE MARL PIT, *c.* 1808. *Watercolour,* $11\frac{5}{8} \times 10\frac{1}{8}$ *in. Norwich, Castle Museum.*

A marl pit on Mousehold Heath outside Norwich. Pits dug down to the chalk or chalky clay (the 'marl' used to fertilize sandy or sour land) marked the surface of many parts of England in this time of the watercolourists.

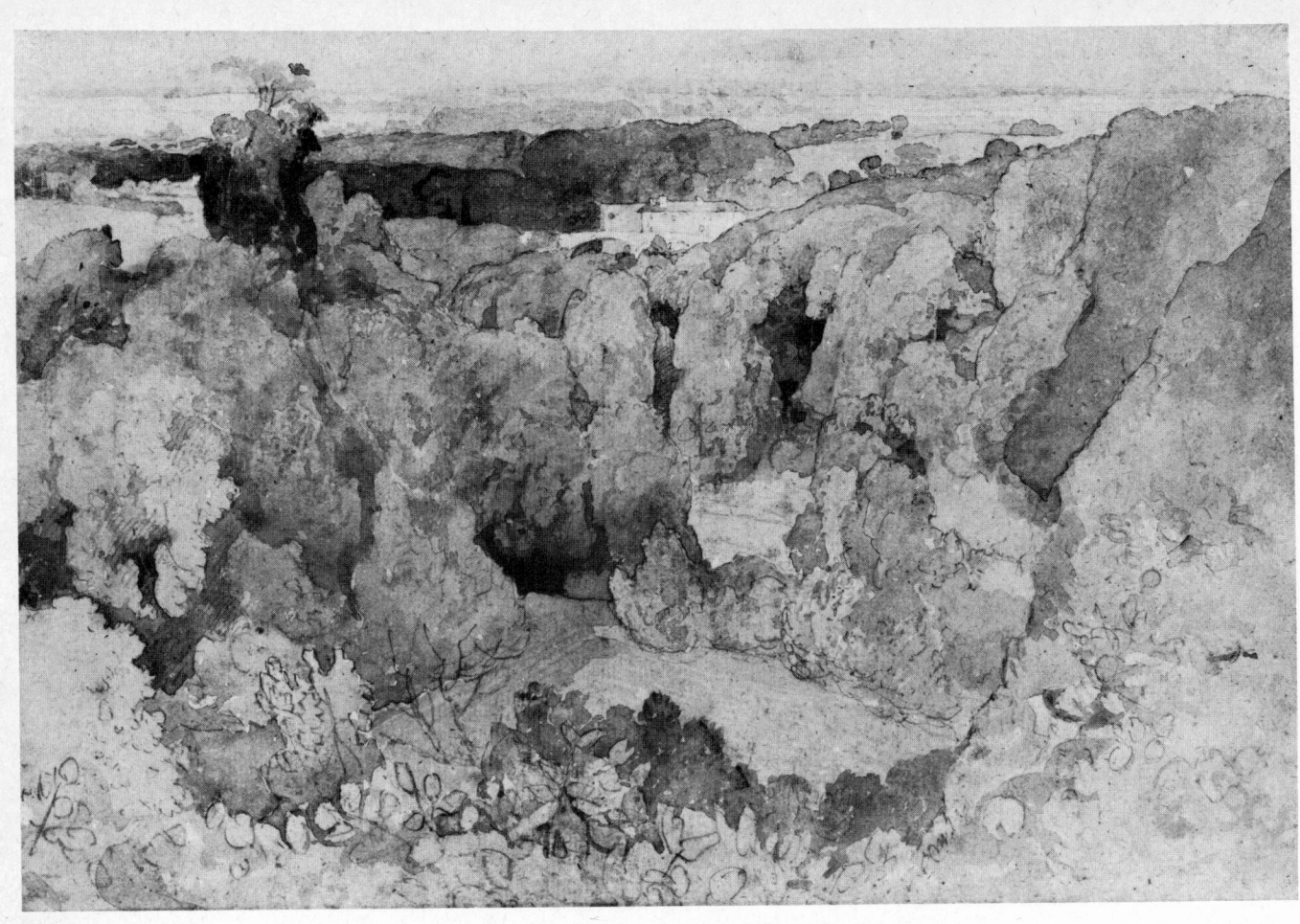

49. DISTANT VIEW OF GRETA BRIDGE, *c.* 1805. *Watercolour,* 10 × 15 *in. London, Tate Gallery.*

Yorkshire: Rokeby Hall and Greta Bridge seen from near Brignall, looking towards the famous Meeting of the Waters—the union of the Greta and the Tees, which have plunged from the moors into limestone depth and wealth of foliage. This is classic landscape, celebrated by Turner, Girtin, and Cotman in the best of his watercolours, by Coleridge (in his journals) and belatedly by Scott in his poem *Rokeby.* In one of his letters Scott declared that the Rokeby scene united 'the richness and luxuriance of English vegetation with the romantic variety of glen, torrent and copse which dignifies our northern scenery.'

50. THE SCOTCHMAN'S STONE ON THE GRETA, *c.* 1805. *Watercolour*, 10¼ × 15⅝ *in. London, British Museum.*

Cf. a note from Coleridge's journals for October 1799: 'River Greta near its fall into the Tees—Shootings of water, threads down the slope of the huge green stone —The white Eddy-rose that blossom'd up against the stream in the scollop, by fits & starts, obstinate in resurrection—It *is the life* that we live.

Black round spots from 5 to 18 in the decaying leaf of the Sycamore—'

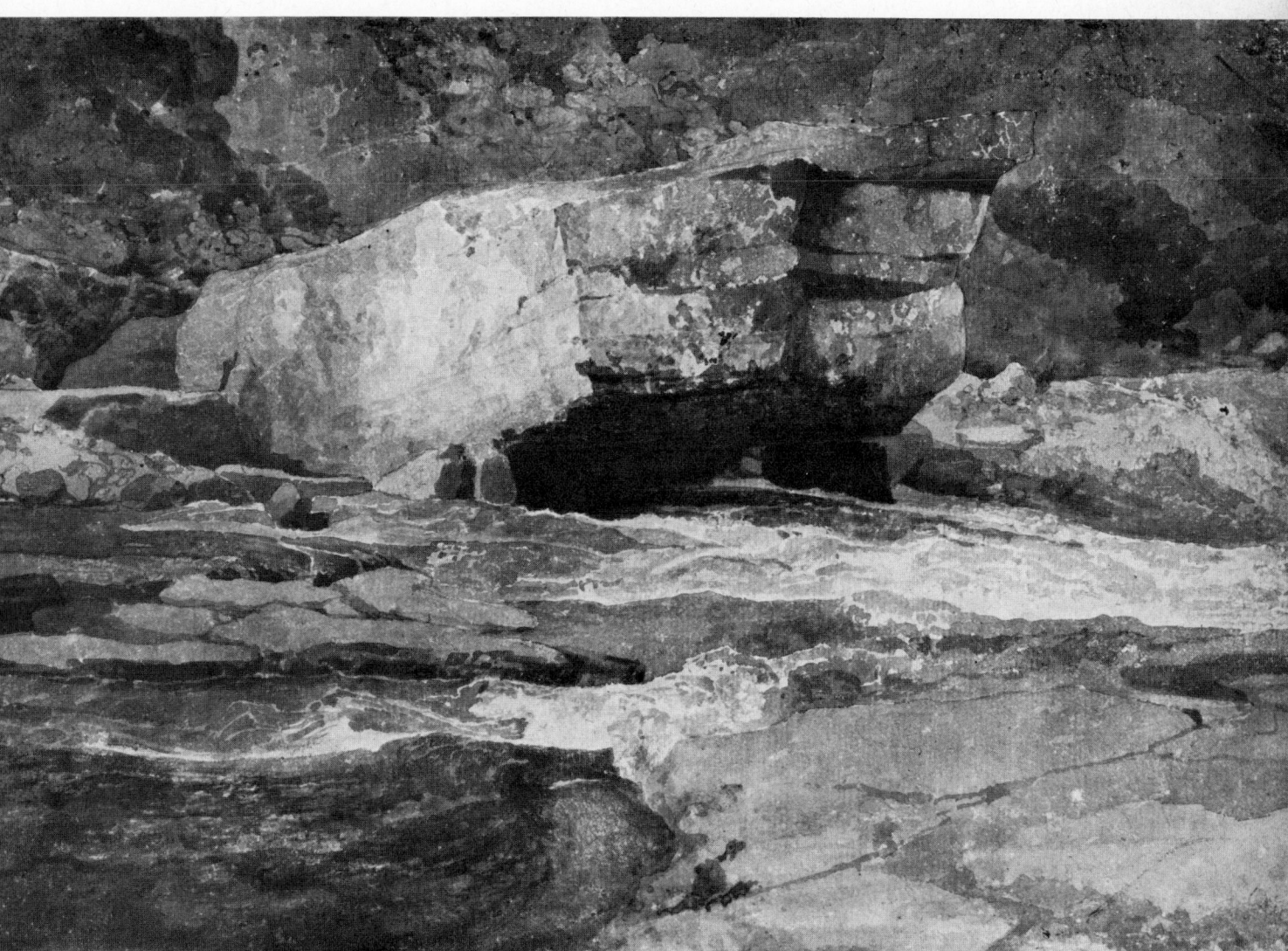

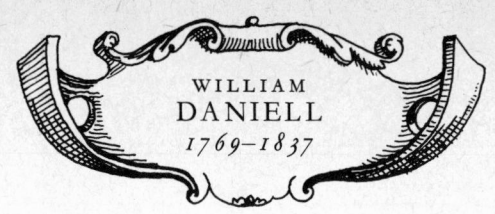

DANIELL has generally been written off as no more than a topographer of in-defatigable energy and application, though in fact he designed landscape of breadth and at times solemnity and dignity. His father, like his grandfather, seems to have been an innkeeper at Chertsey in the wide landscape of the Thames, where he grew up; his uncle was the artist and Royal Academician Thomas Daniell, to whom he owed his training in watercolour and in the new aquatint engraving which watercolour demanded. With his uncle he spent nearly seven years travel-ling through India, the outcome of which was their *Oriental Scenery* (1795–1808) in 144 coloured aquatints. In his thirties, between 1804 and 1805 Daniell produced his *Views of London,* six large coloured aquatints which include his solemn master-piece (1805) *Somerset House before the Embankment.*

Later he planned his great landscape series *A Voyage around Great Britain,* eight volumes folio (1814–25) of 308 coloured aquatints of scenery from Land's End to John o'Groats. He admired (and was admired by) Turner, but he did not give himself to picturesque exaggeration. The drama which he often establishes in his aquatint landscapes is legitimate, no more than strengthening the character and truth of each subject. Though Daniell never developed so strongly personal a naturalism, his affinities are more with Cotman, who was 13 years his junior; and he saw the merits of Crome. Daniell was disliked as a man (though he became an R.A.) and this perhaps began the underestimation of his work.

51. DOVER CASTLE, 1823. *Aquatint*, $6\frac{1}{2} \times 9\frac{1}{2}$ *in. London, Victoria and Albert Museum.*
From Volume VII of *A Voyage Round Great Britain*, 1814–24.

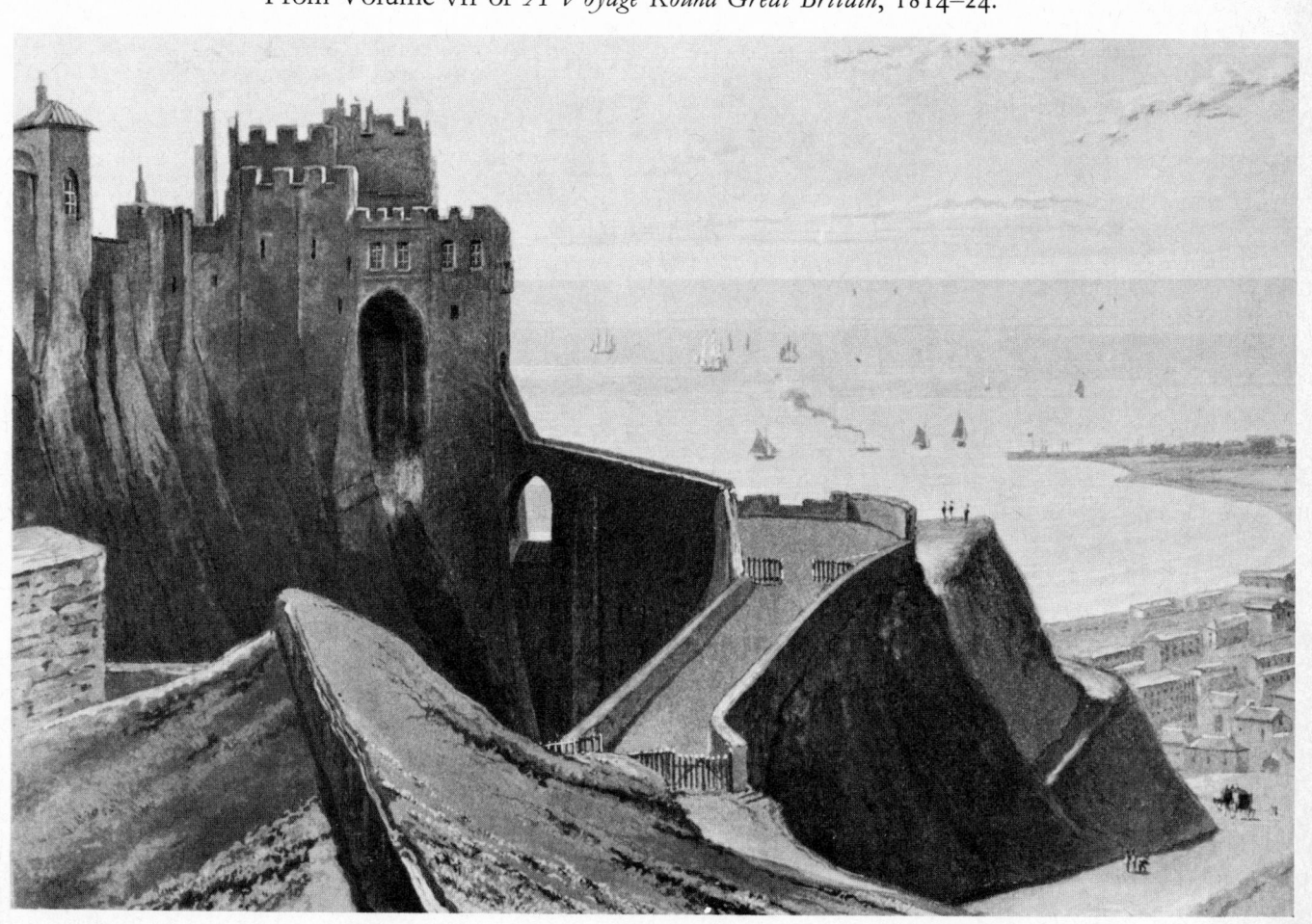

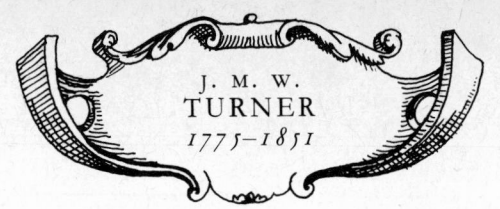

THE MOST ENIGMATIC of the major English landscape painters. Contrasting Turner's public and private art, his pictures for exhibition and his studies, Constable wrote on one occasion that 'some of Turner's best work is swept up off the carpet every morning by the maid and put onto the dust hole.' Even now the purest of Turner remains for the most part hidden in his many sketchbooks. In his grand exhibition pieces he adds a bravura of the dramatic, the picturesque, the ideal, the historical, according to expectation. Delacroix commented on this defect in his journal for 1860 (see p. 19). Turner's sketches, by contrast, are devoid of formula, the purest landscape, the purest vision or interaction of scenic suggestion and his own temper.

This son of a London hairdresser in Maiden Lane, 'a mere dim defile between houses clothed with the smoke of centuries', liked a natural world about as different as could be to the packed squalour of his childhood—the coloured space of skies, light, mountains, coasts, valleys and rivers, the theatre of the elements and the seasons in which the dramatic can become the quiet and serene. When he was a very young artist, friends he stayed with at Bristol called him 'The Prince of the Rocks', because he passed so much time on the limestone edges of the Bristol Gorge, above the woods and the tidal sinuosity of the Avon. He learnt light, shade, depth and form on sketching tours, which began, by the convention of the time, in South Wales (1792–3), and took him through all weathers, on foot, and on horseback, and by coasting vessels, around much of Great Britain. In search of wild and gentle scenery, castles, abbey ruins, cathedrals, harbours, he explored Derbyshire, the Midlands, East Anglia, the Isle of Wight, Yorkshire, Northumberland, Co. Durham, the Lakes, the Tweed, North Wales as well as South, the Highlands, the Fonthill Abbey district of Wiltshire—all by the time he was 26 and before he began the first of his continental tours in 1802. And that was only the foundation.

To Delacroix, when Turner called on him in Paris, he seemed like an English farmer, with 'a cold, hard face.' He liked his own company, he never married (though he was not averse to women), he was uncommunicative, and not given to writing comments on the scenery which pleased him, on his methods or on his aims. His letter below to Hawksworth Fawkes shows how little Turner had to say of the picture country familiar to him. The surviving drafts of the Academy lectures he gave, indicate a scarcely literate man struggling to compel words to explain thoughts and convictions which were by no means trivial. Turner's lifelong business, as he explained to Joseph Farington when he was still in his early twenties, was to drive the colours about—'Turner has no settled process but drives the colours about till he has expressed the idea in his mind.'

Ruskin, the great exaggerator of his mastery, considered that he loved most of all the Yorkshire Dales. Also he was particularly moved by the estuarine and steep woody and rocky scenery around Plymouth, and by the combination of land and sea at Mount Edgcumbe. *Page* 186.

52. EDINBURGH, FROM ST. MARGARET'S LOCH, WITH CALTON HILL ON THE RIGHT, 1801. *Watercolour*, $7\frac{3}{4} \times 5$ *in. London, British Museum.*

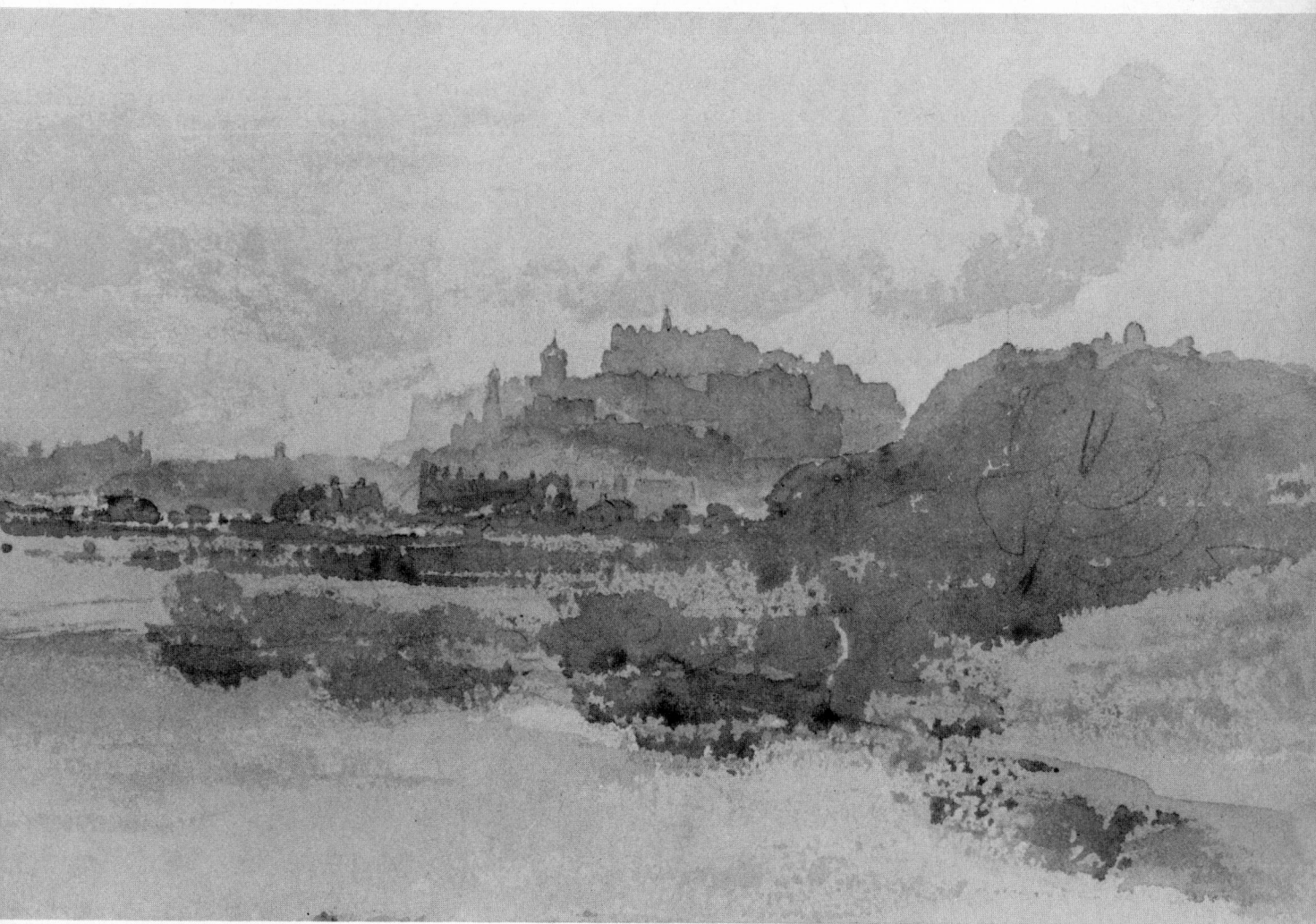

53. THE THAMES WITH RAINBOW AND BARGES, *c.* 1806. *Watercolour,* $6\frac{3}{4} \times 10\frac{3}{8}$ *in.* *London, British Museum.*

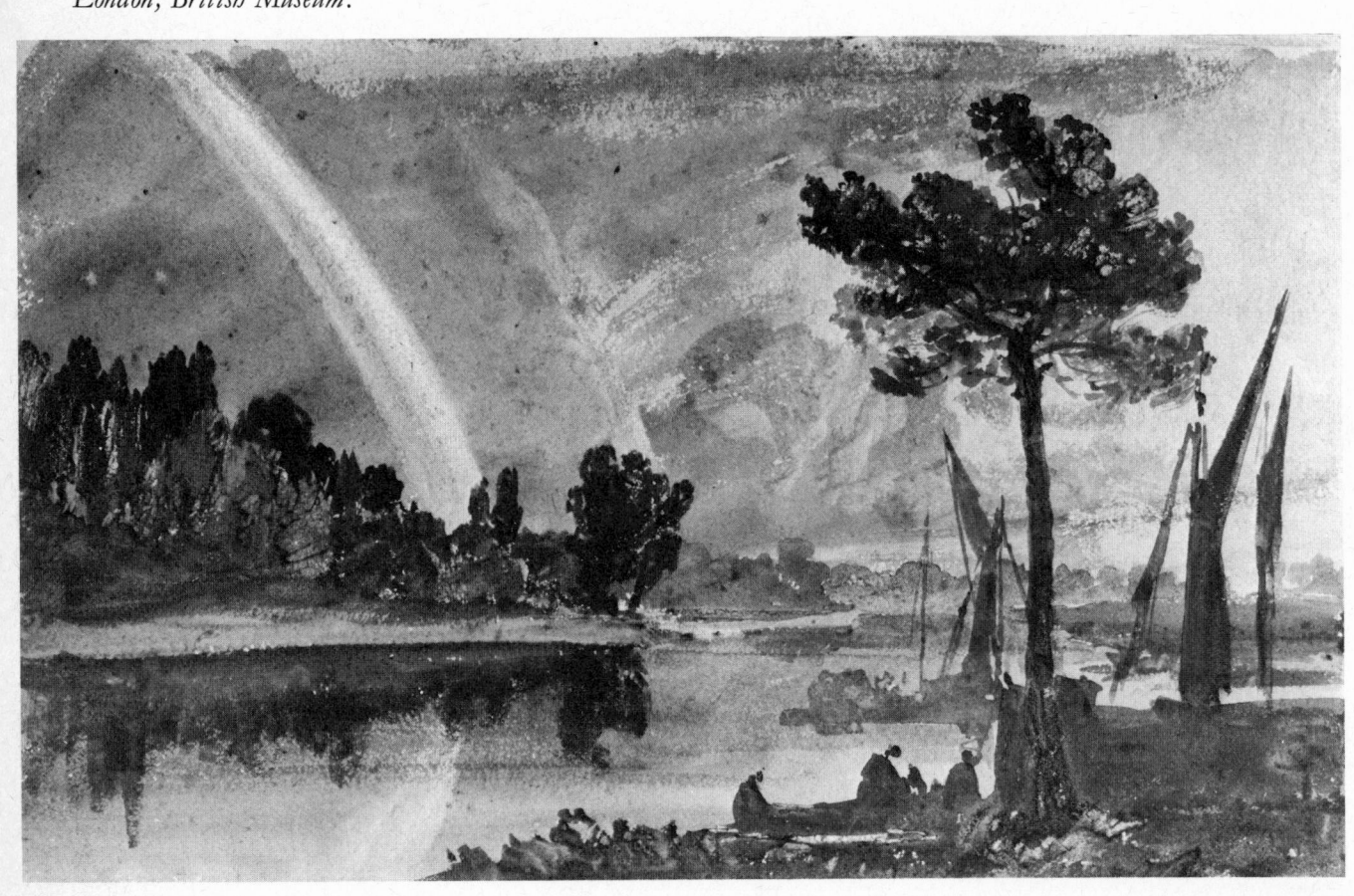

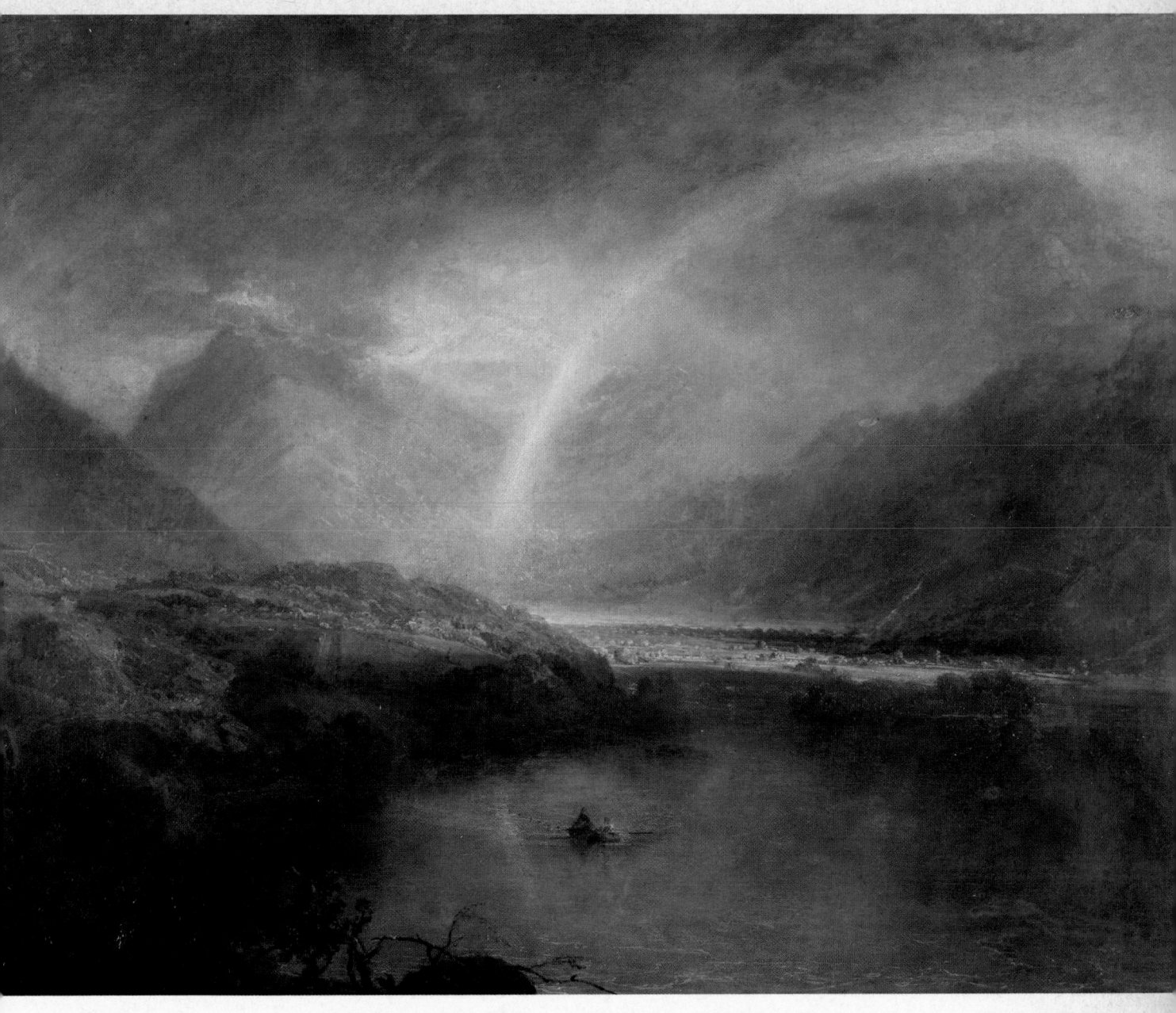

54. BUTTERMERE LAKE WITH PART OF CROMACKWATER, CUMBERLAND, A
SHOWER, 1797–8. *Oil, 35 × 47 in. London, Tate Gallery.*

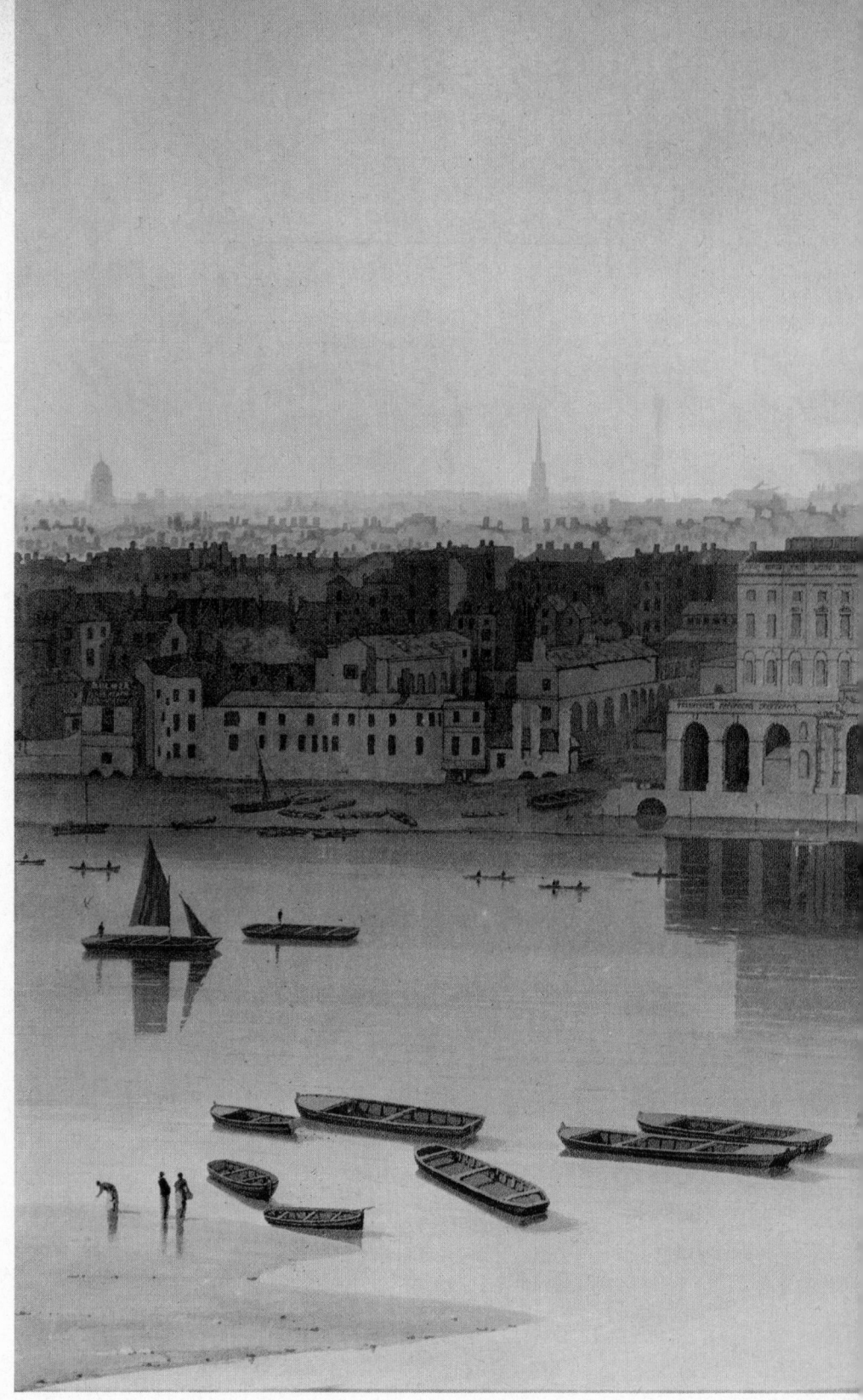

55. SOMERSET HOUSE
BEFORE THE
EMBANKMENT, 1805.
Aquatint, 16 × 26 *in.*
*London, British
Museum.*
This is No. 5 in
Daniell's *Views of
London*, 1804–5.

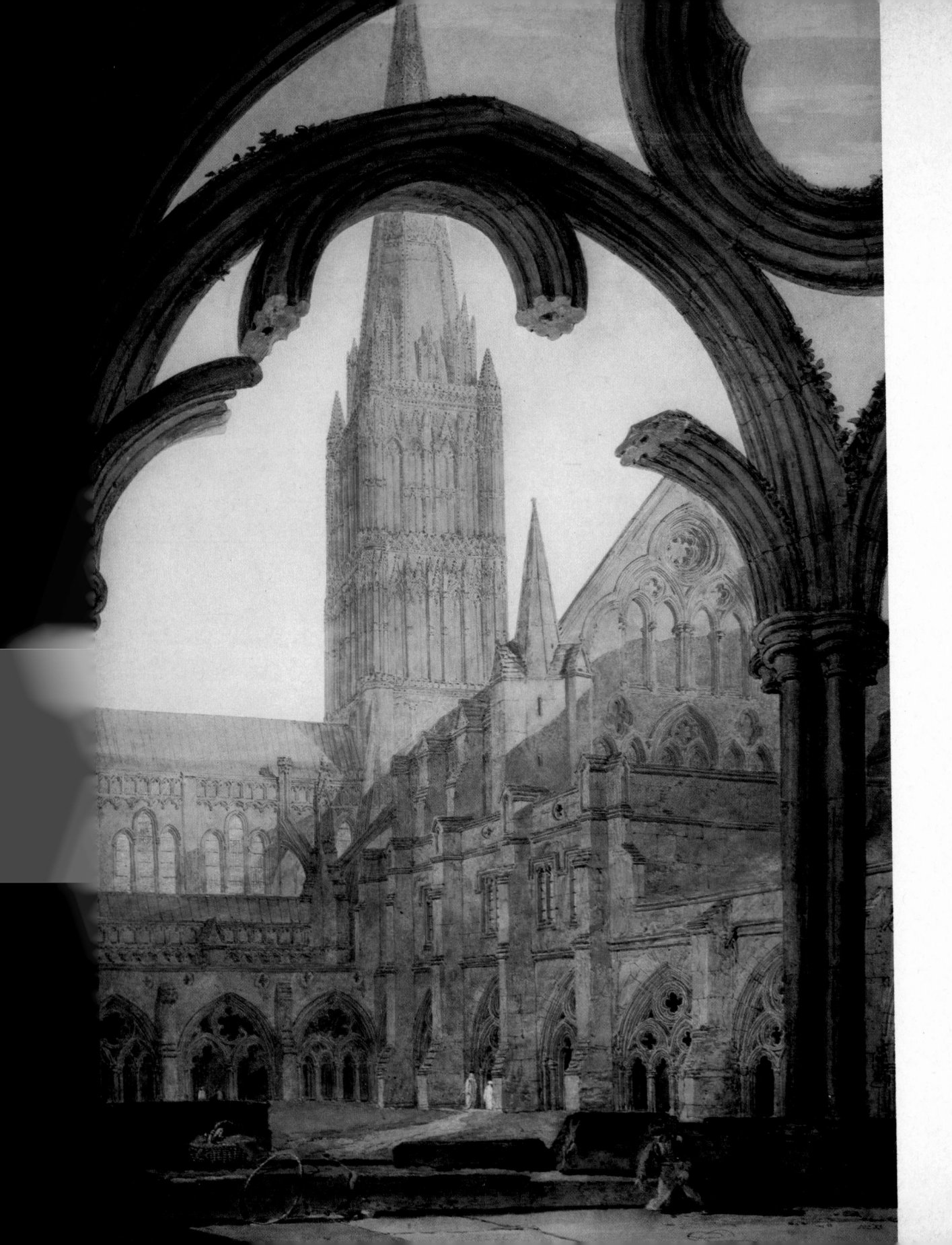

56. SOUTH VIEW OF SALISBURY CATHEDRAL FROM THE CLOISTERS, 1796–7. *Watercolour, 26¾ × 19½ in. London, Victoria and Albert Museum.*

57. TEIGNMOUTH HARBOUR, 1812. *Oil, 35¾ × 47½ in. Petworth House, National Trust.*

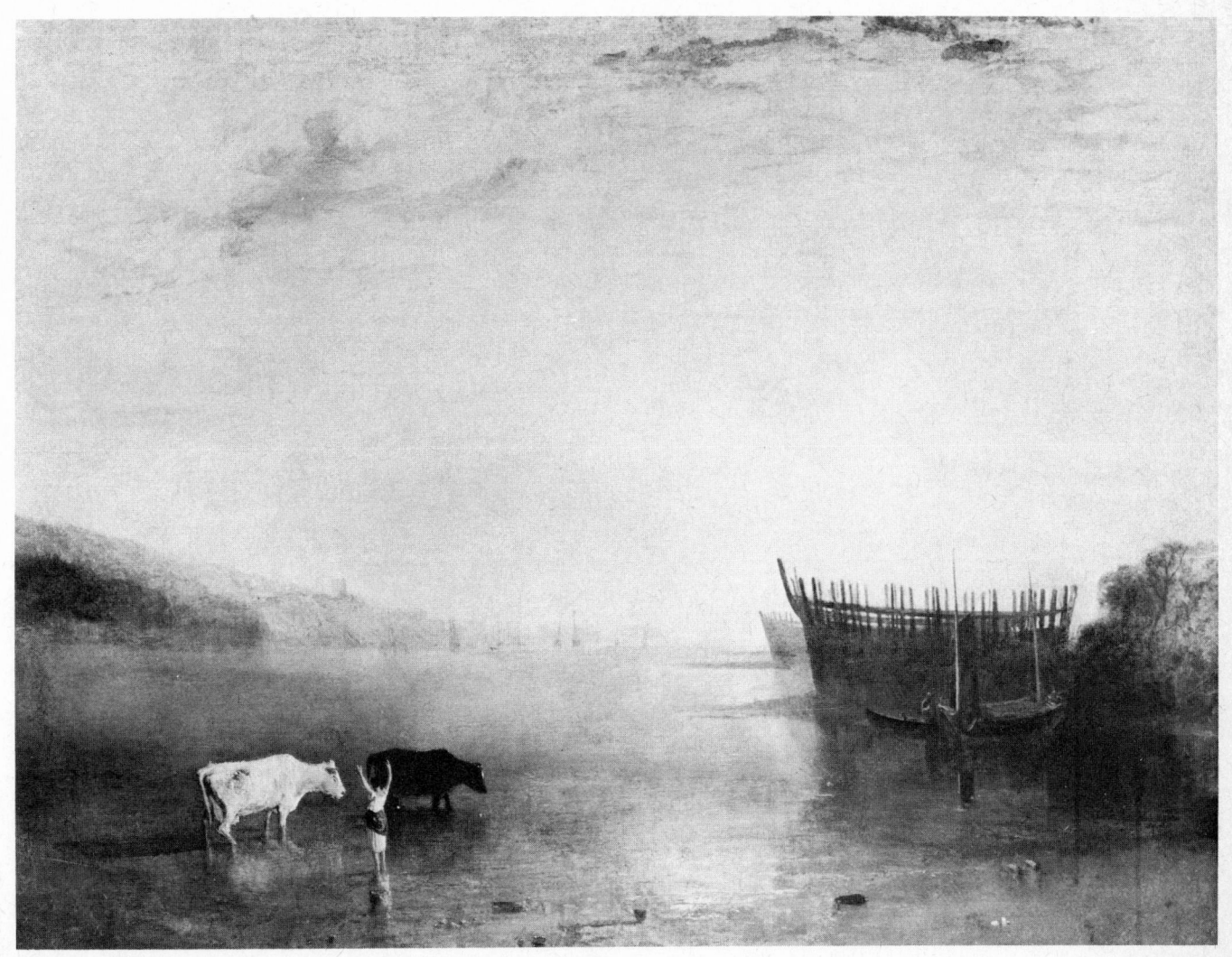

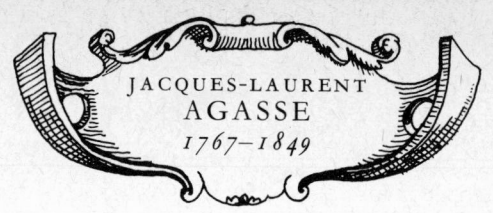

THIS GENEVESE ARTIST who came to England in 1800, two years after the French
had annexed Geneva, combined a training under David in Paris with an admiration
for the animal pictures of George Stubbs, who was old but still active when
Agasse settled in London. Stubbs, an eighteenth-century master, set his race-
horses and grooms in a more generalized 'common sense' landscape. From David
this later artist learnt to particularize. He distributed this particularity throughout
the forms of his work, whether the forms of landscape, dog, horse, or rider. He
had no interest at all in poetic or heroic falsities and was able to give his landscape
genre an objectivity and a cool charm of colour which purified it of sentimentality.
Pictures by him are no longer so common in England; they go back from the sale-
room to collections in Switzerland. In his long English career Agasse was content
with his few artistocratic patrons, who were more concerned with horseflesh than
high art. He kept much to himself.

58. LANDING AT WESTMINSTER BRIDGE, 1817–18. *Oil, 13¾ × 21 in. Winterthur,
Oskar Reinhart Foundation.*

Compare Samuel Scott's *Part of Westminster Bridge,* Plate 12, above. Through the
frame of the arch of Westminster Bridge Agasse shows the sunlit Waterloo
Bridge, designed by John Rennie, and then a new item in the Thames scenery. It
was opened in 1817 (and replaced in 1939).

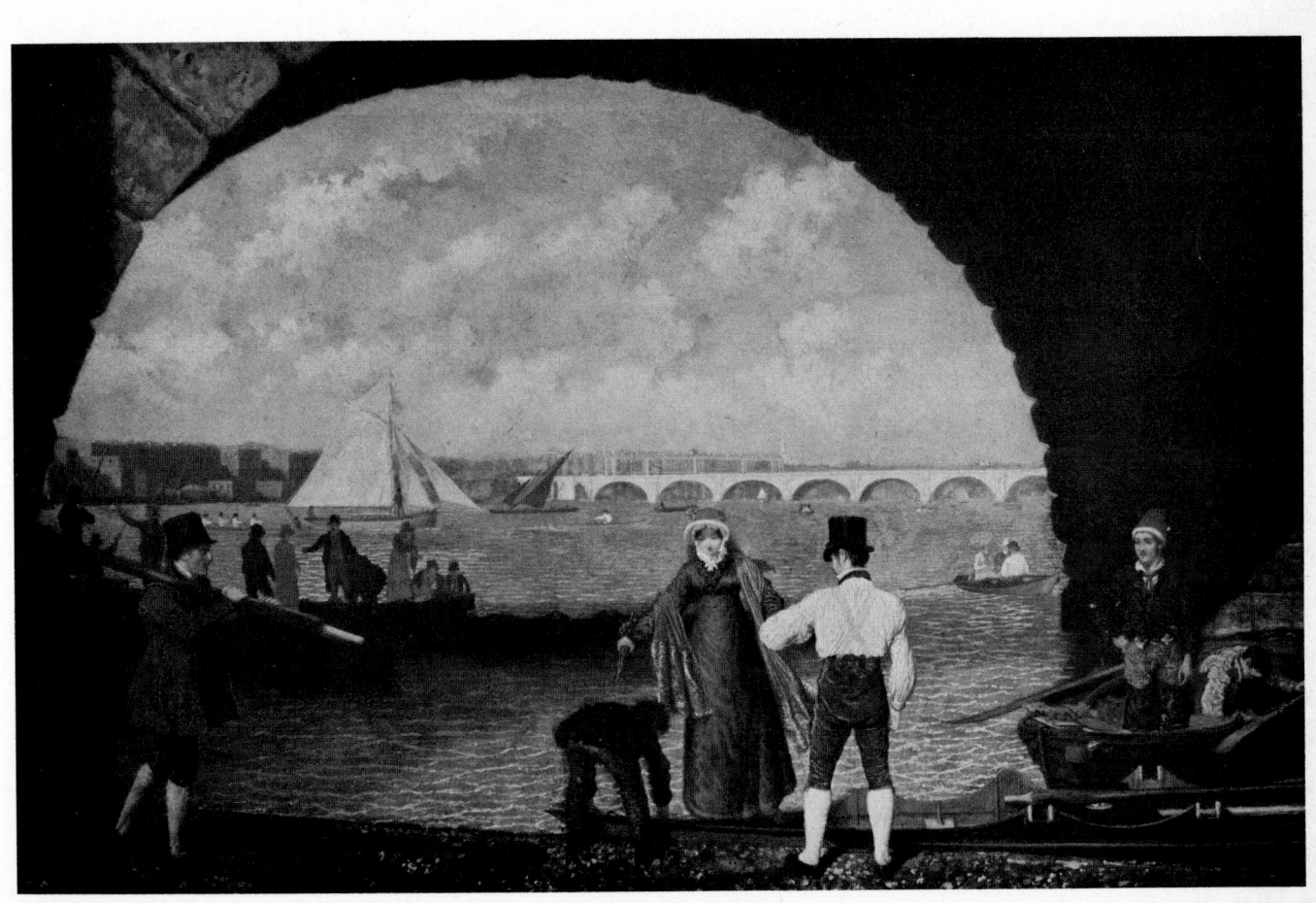

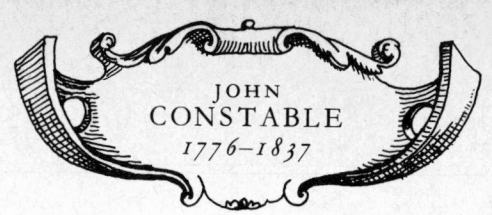
IN MANY WAYS Constable's life was one of anxiety for the free and full expression of his art. His father was a well-to-do miller and merchant, his upbringing in Suffolk, at East Bergholt, was comfortable, but he was one of several children in a family which eschewed fecklessness and valued being successful in a steady and sober way. A first anxiety—since his wish to become an artist was not opposed—was to prove himself in a profession full of hand-to-mouth failures. A second anxiety as he worked on and on in truth to his concept of a 'natural painture', was how not to antagonize that blind authority among leading artists and patrons which either blocked or permitted or even promoted success. His anxieties were never resolved, helped as he was by family love and security, by his wife's considerable inheritance and by his own interior firmness and strong individuality. Art affairs, life affairs, could worry him, clouds, light, sparkle, trees, painting, enthralled him once more and sustained him—although it was not until he was 53

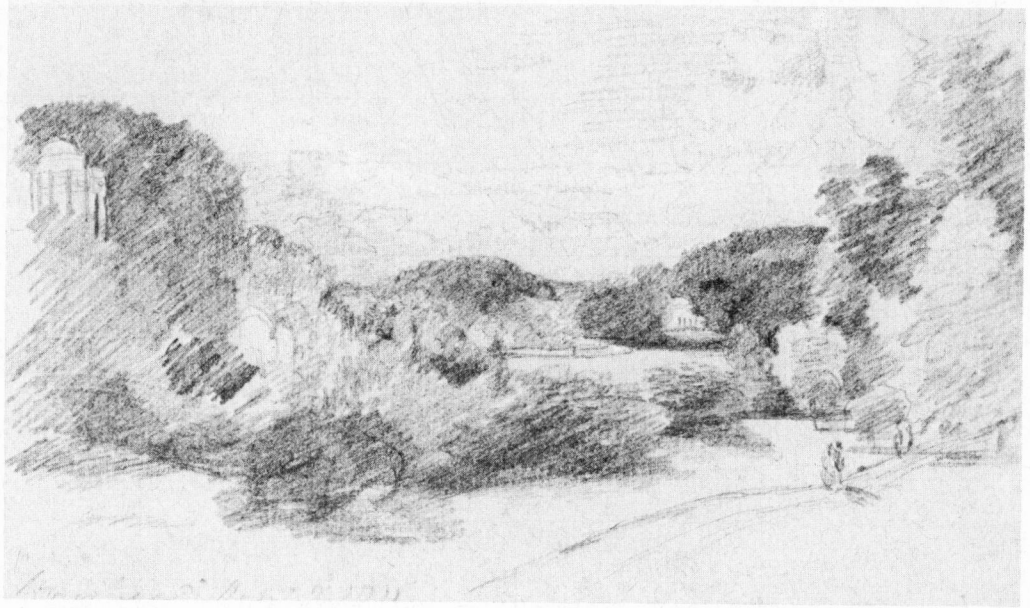

59. STOURHEAD, 1811. *Pencil,* $3\frac{3}{8} \times 5\frac{7}{8}$ *in. Cambridge, Mass., Fogg Art Museum, Harvard University.*

(A sketch of Henry Hoare's landscape garden at Stourhead in Wiltshire, now the property of the National Trust. On the left, the Temple of Apollo, and across the lake the domed Pantheon designed for Hoare by the architect Henry Flitcroft.)

that this grand conservative revolutionary was at last elected a Royal Academician
—to be able 'to write oneself Esquire', as an R.A., being then the mark of success
and position. From most English landscape painters Constable differed in refusing
to theatricalize his pictures in deference to theory or the market. So he limited
himself to the fundamentals of vision—to his subjective view of the objective—
without trailing around England, Wales and Scotland for subjects which were
accented by associations or the sublime or the intricately picturesque or the
sentimental. In 1806 his wealthy uncle paid for him to go on a painter's conventional expedition to the Lakes. He went, but he was not for mountains. He
preferred slow streams to fierce waterfalls; and he found his pictures as a rule in
the places or kinds of place familiar to him or in accord with himself—the Suffolk
and Essex meadowland of the Stour, the skies, slopes and trees of the Hampstead
ridge, a quick walk away from his home, Sussex beaches and Sussex downland, or
the river flats around Salisbury Cathedral. He was for ever afraid of falling into
manner or exaggeration. He remains the artist the English have most reason to be
proud of and thankful for, without reservation. *Page* 187.

60. WIVENHOE PARK, ESSEX, 1816–17. *Oil,* 22$\frac{1}{8}$ × 39$\frac{7}{8}$ *in. Washington, National
Gallery of Art.*

Painted by Constable for the owner of Wivenhoe Hall (which is just outside
Colchester), this portrays the quintessential 'landscaped' England of Georgian
times, a park of carefully grouped trees related to a winding lake made by damming
a small stream. Unlike Wordsworth, Constable preferred the landscape of man to
the landscape of the wild and the solitudinous.

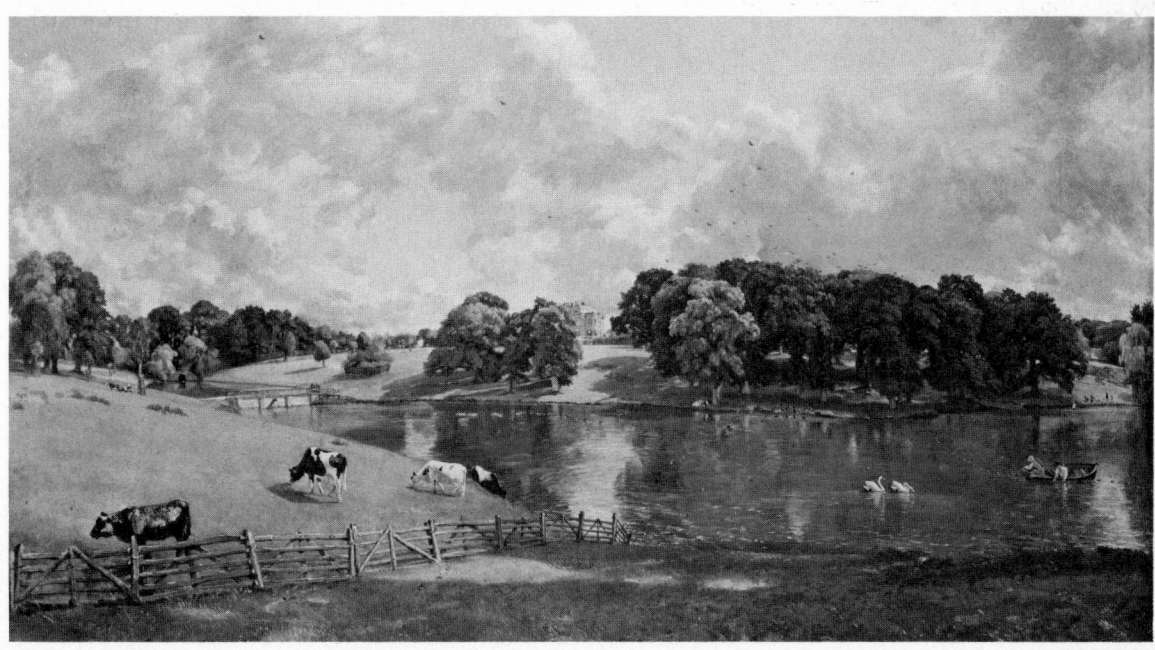

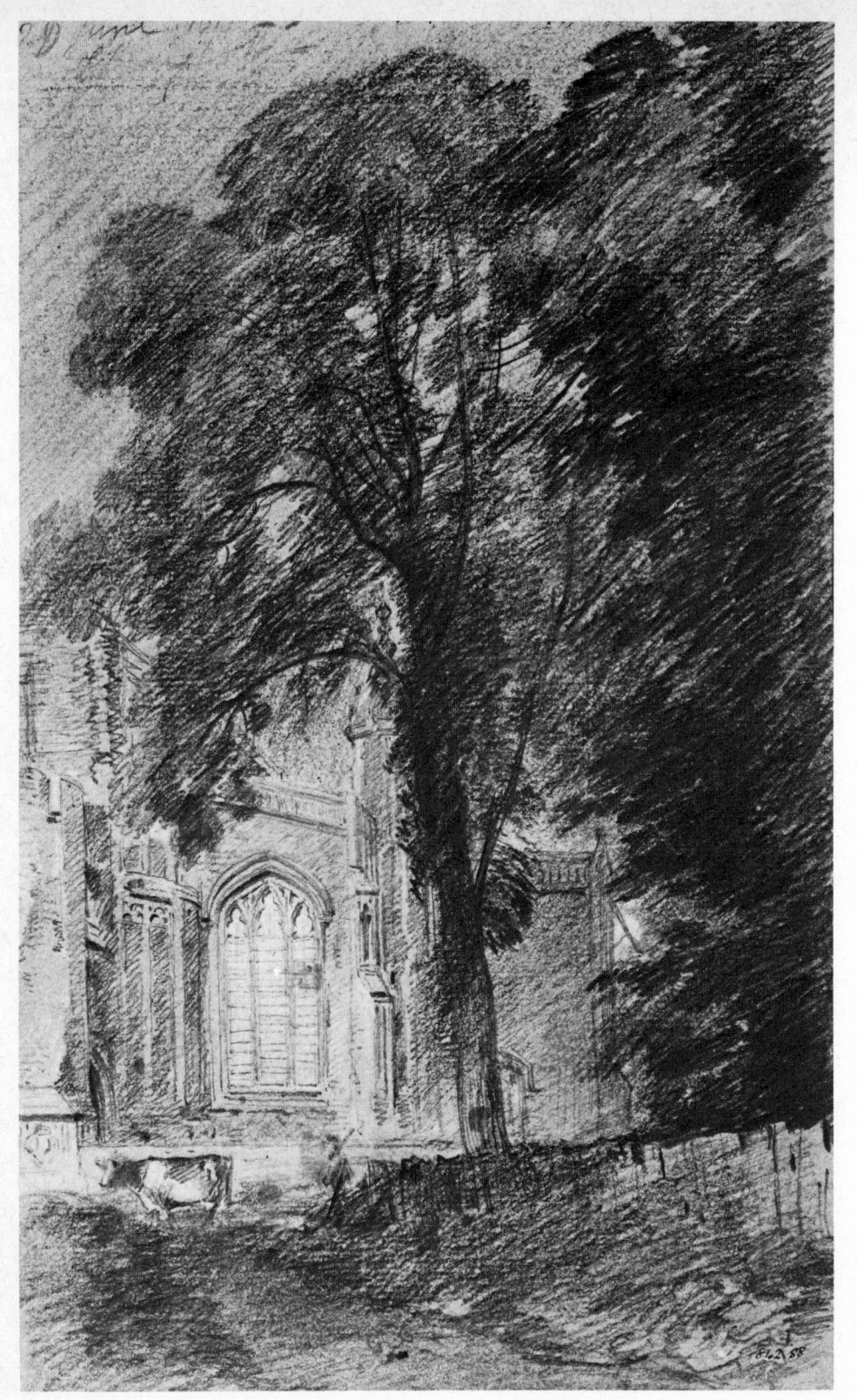

61. EAST BERGHOLT
CHURCH: PART OF
THE WEST END SEEN
BEYOND A GROUP
OF ELMS, 1812.
Black and white chalk,
$12\frac{1}{4} \times 7\frac{3}{4}$ *in. London,
Victoria and Albert
Museum.*
The church in which
Constable was
christened and in
which he and his wife
are commemorated.

62. WEYMOUTH BAY, *c.* 1816–17. *Oil,* $20\frac{3}{4}$ × 30 *in. Boston, Museum of Fine Arts.*

See note below on the two pictures of the Osmington shore (Nos. 63, 64). This is another of the Dorset pictures from Constable's honeymoon in the autumn of 1816. The view is from the Osmington cliff tops near Redcliff Point over Weymouth Bay to a barely visible Weymouth and to the Isle of Portland.

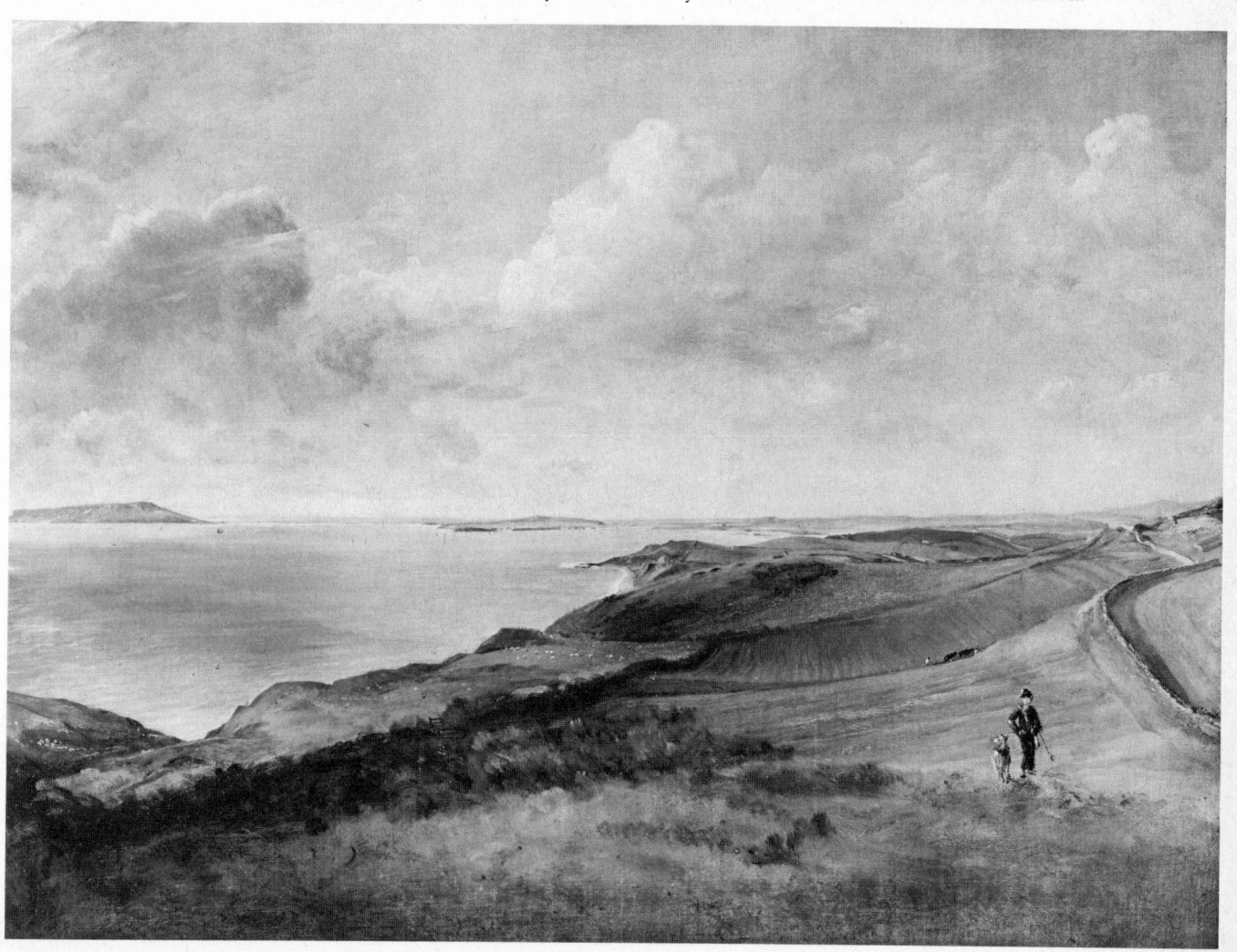

63. OSMINGTON SHORE, NEAR WEYMOUTH, *c.* 1816–17. *Oil,* 34⅝ × 40⅝ *in. Paris, Musée du Louvre.*

These two pictures of the Dorset coast and cloudscape derive from Constable's autumn honeymoon in 1816 at Osmington Vicarage, the home of his great friend John Fisher. Osmington village is tucked into a hollow, rising ground separating it from the cliffs and the sea, and the scene of the two pictures, so different in mood, at Bowleaze Cove, to which there is a path from the village. In a letter written to John Fisher five years later Constable recalls his experiences at Bowleaze Cove, quoting or misquoting from memory what was evidently a favourite passage from Byron's *Childe Harold*:

'How much I should like now to be at Osmington—but work I must & will—but the very thought of a walk upon

"—The lonely shoar
"—Where none intrudes
"By the deep sea—
"and music in its roar."

If I recollect the ashes have very beautiful mosses and the stems particularly rich in Osmington.'

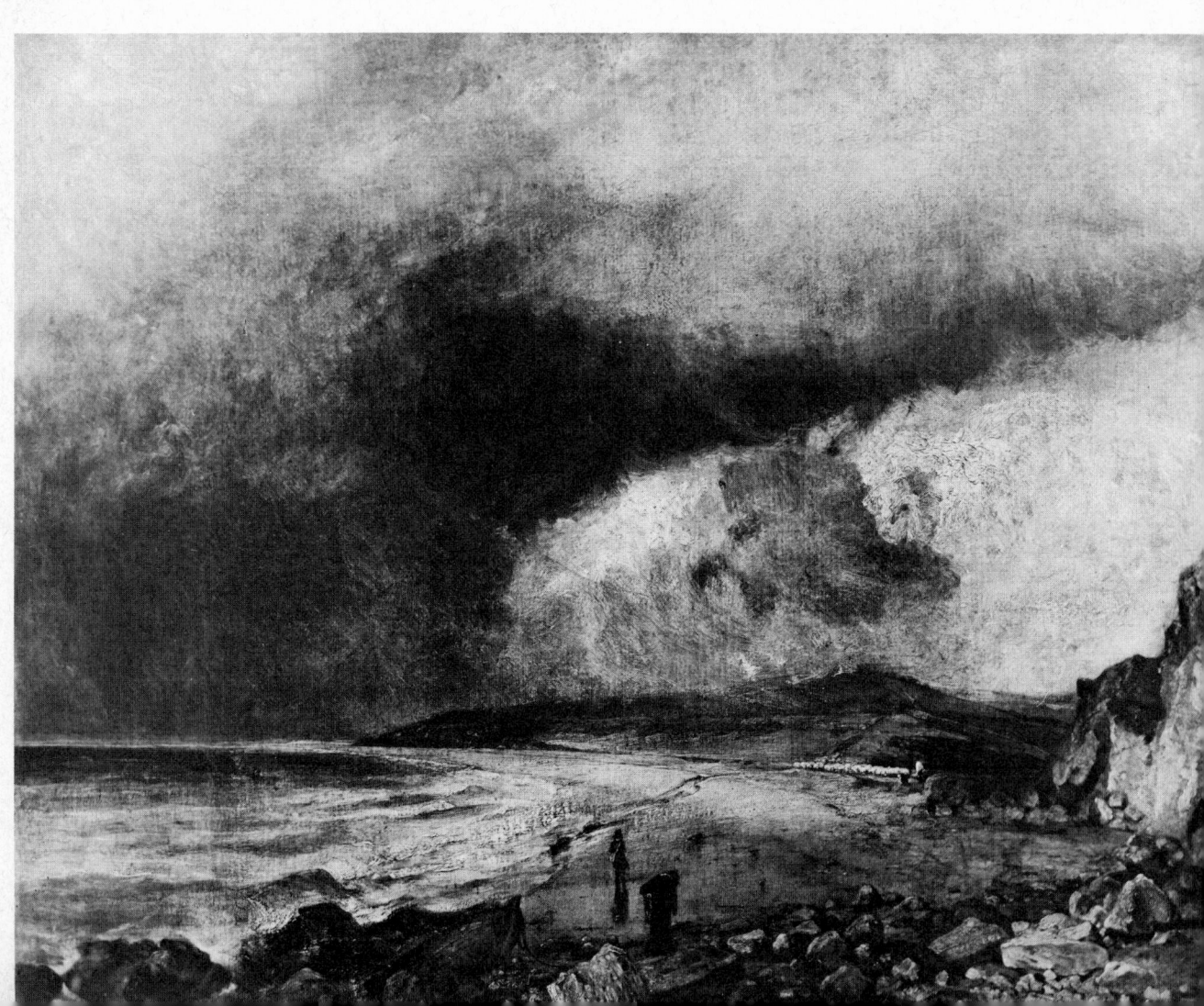

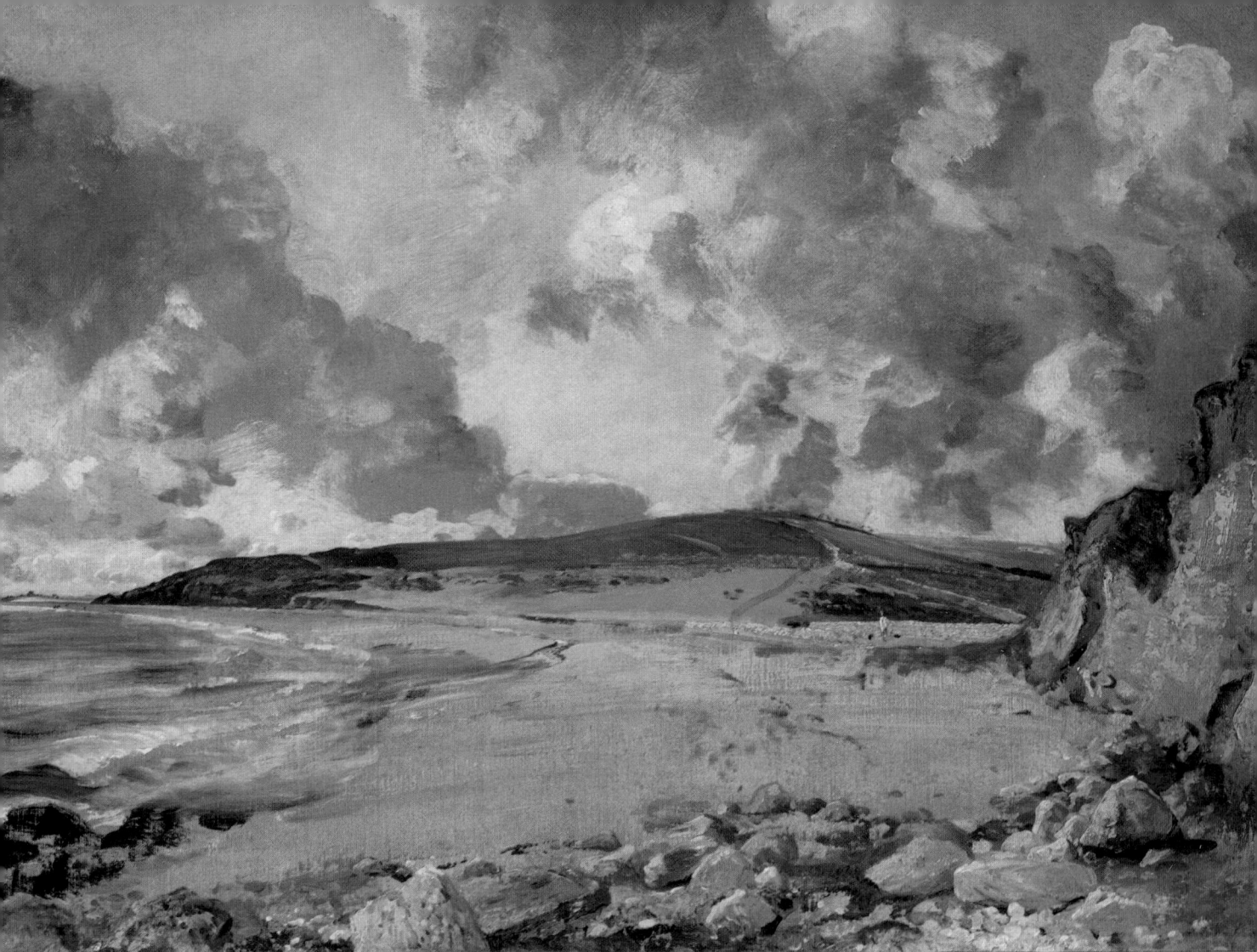

64. WEYMOUTH BAY, *c.* 1816–17. *Oil, 21 × 29½ in. London, National Gallery.*

The whole passage from Byron indicates Constable's feeling for landscape midway between the wild and the entirely humanized—and his love of man:

> There is a pleasure in the pathless woods,
> There is a rapture on the lonely shore,
> There is society, where none intrudes,
> By the deep sea, and music in its roar;
> I love not man the less, but Nature more,
> From these our interviews, in which I steal
> From all I may be, or have been before,
> To mingle with the Universe, and feel
> What I can ne'er express, yet cannot all conceal.

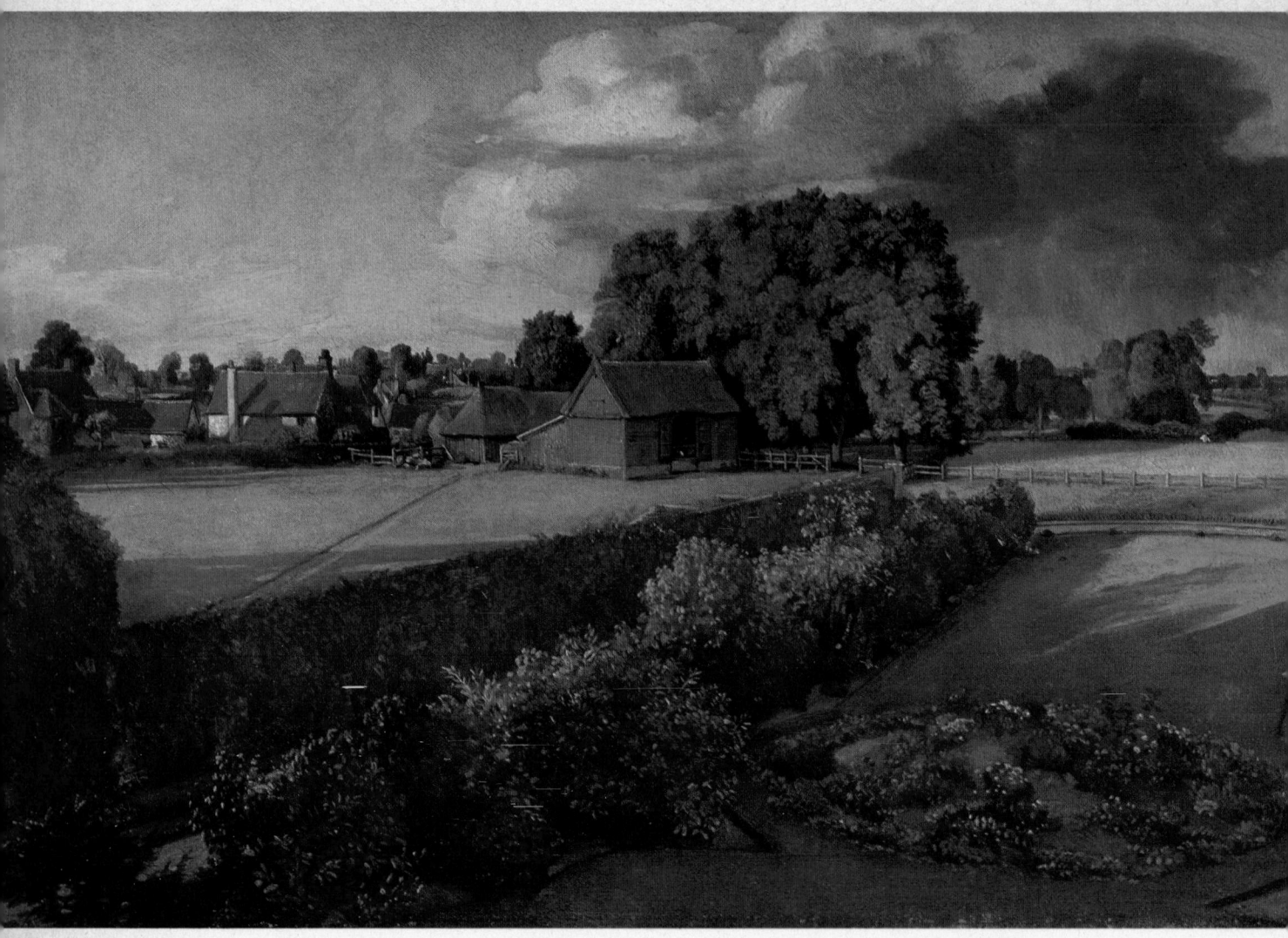

65. GOLDING CONSTABLE'S FLOWER GARDEN, *c.* 1812–16. *Oil, 13 × 20 in. Ipswich, Christchurch Mansion.*

A Suffolk landscape of Constable's own village, East Bergholt. No view could have been more familiar to him—from a window in the Georgian house in which Constable was born and reared with his brothers and sisters. The house had been built by his father Golding Constable.

66. DEDHAM VALE, *c.* 1810. *Oil,* $9\frac{3}{4} \times 12$ *in. London, Tate Gallery.*

Constable's native village East Bergholt is on the Suffolk side of the Stour, Dedham village on the Essex side. Constable's viewpoint is from high ground on the Suffolk side in Higham parish or Stratford St. Mary parish. See page 187 for Constable on the scenery of the Stour and East Bergholt.

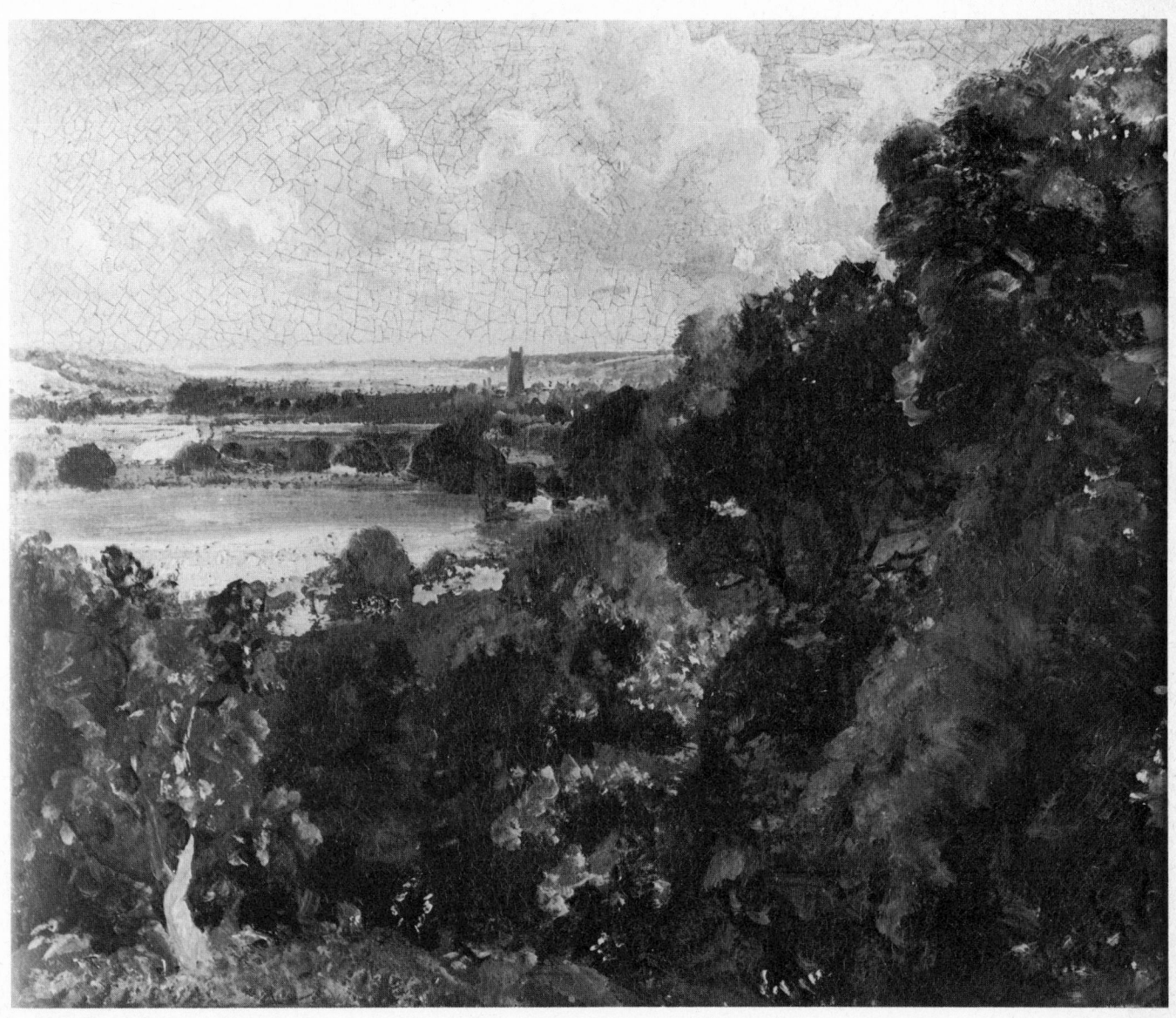

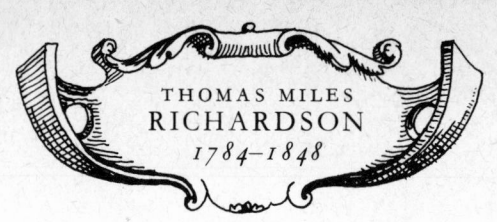

THOMAS MILES
RICHARDSON
1784–1848

RICHARDSON belonged to Newcastle upon Tyne. There he grew up, worked and died, one of the view-painters of the early 19th century who never established themselves in London. He admired David Cox, and the sight in Ackermann's window in the Strand of a drawing of Conway Castle by Cox had been decisive in a career which began with engraving, cabinet-making and schoolmastering. In landscape Richardson was moved by distance, twilight and a sense of the past. He engraved drawings to illustrate works by his brother, the Newcastle antiquary and bookseller Moses Richardson. Among his mostly northern watercolours there are views of Dunstanburgh, Alnwick Castle, Holy Island, Sweetheart Abbey, and Newcastle, and river-views, especially of the Tyne. He suffered like David Cox and others from the transition to an Early Victorian sentimentality, becoming repetitive and fluent and losing the firm poetry of his early work.

67. THE TYNE FROM WINDMILL HILLS, GATESHEAD, *c.* 1825. *Oil, 29½ × 48½ in. Newcastle upon Tyne, Laing Art Gallery.*

From a once famous view-point, outside the grimmest and least human of the towns of Co. Durham. 'To the west of the town are the Windmill Hills, on which are nine mills for grinding corn, and whence is obtained a fine view of Newcastle and Gateshead, and of the beautiful vale of the Tyne to the west of the bridge.' (Samuel Lewis, *Topographical Dictionary of England,* 1842.) Nearly half a century later George Price Boyce came to Windmill Hills, turned his back on the fouled view of the river and painted the hills themselves (Plate 100). Part of them is now kept as a municipal park.

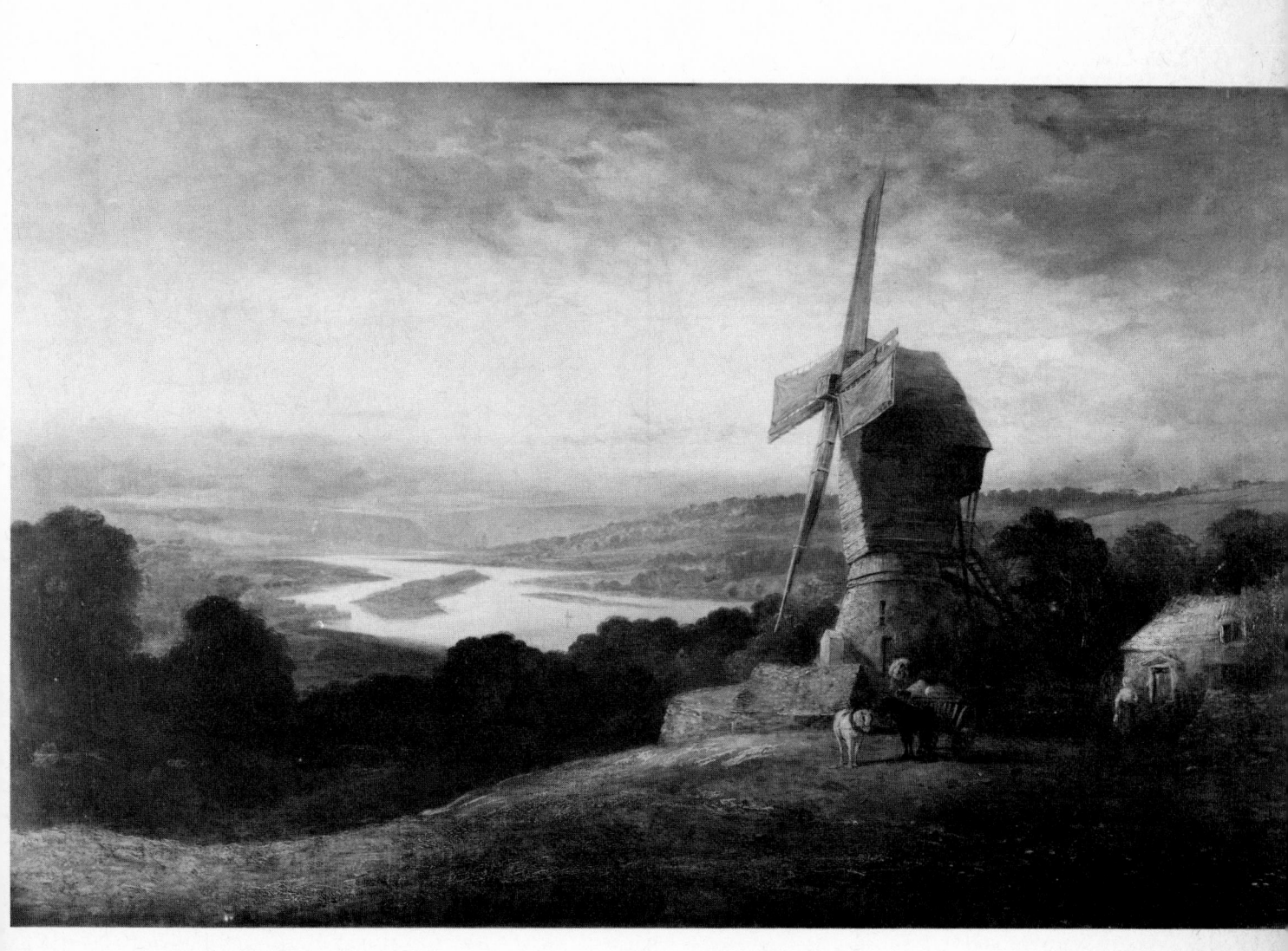

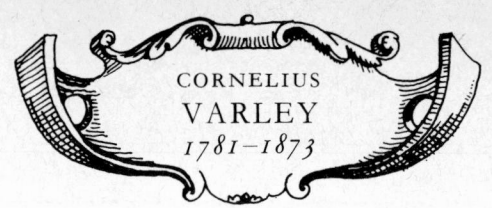

BORN IN HACKNEY, one of a family of artists of whom the best known was the drawing master and friend of Blake, John Varley, his elder brother. His favourite country was North Wales, which he visited several times in his twenties, certainly in 1802, 1803 and again in 1805. He had scientific curiosity, along with other landscape painters of his time, liking to analyse the phenomena of light and shadow and the formation of clouds. When young he painted broad watercolours of Welsh valley and mountain and sky, concerned with appearance and free from slavery to theories of the Ideal or the picturesque or to public demands for sentimentality in landscape. No doubt lack of appreciation of true landscape explains why Cornelius Varley more and more abandoned painting for optical and electrical investigation and microscopy. Artists of his generation, in the wake of Turner and Constable, include William Havell, David Cox, Peter de Wint and Turner of Oxford. *Page* 189.

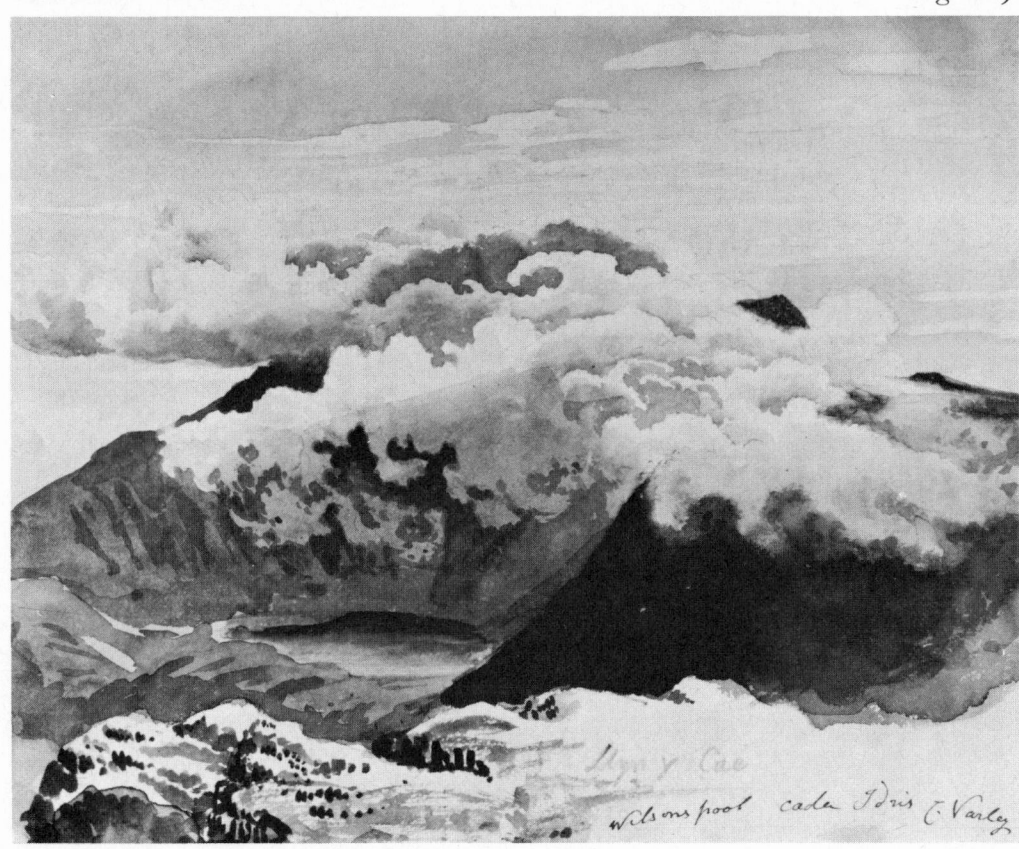

68. WILSON'S POOL, CADER IDRIS, 1803. *Watercolour, $7\frac{1}{10} \times 13\frac{1}{5}$ in. Private collection.*

Cader Idris and 'Wilson's Pool', Llyn-y-Cau: the mountain from the south side. Cf. Richard Wilson's famous picture (Plate 21), which was well known in Varley's day through engraving. For the circumstances in which these watercolours were made, see Varley's account on pages 189–90.

69. CADER IDRIS FROM LLANELLTYD, 1803. *Pencil and wash, $9\frac{3}{4} \times 16\frac{1}{2}$ in. London, Courtauld Institute, Witt Collection.*

Cader Idris from the north. In the foreground is Llanelltyd Church and the bridge over the river Mawddach. On the left, Cymmer Abbey. Cader Idris rises, top left, to Mynydd Moel.

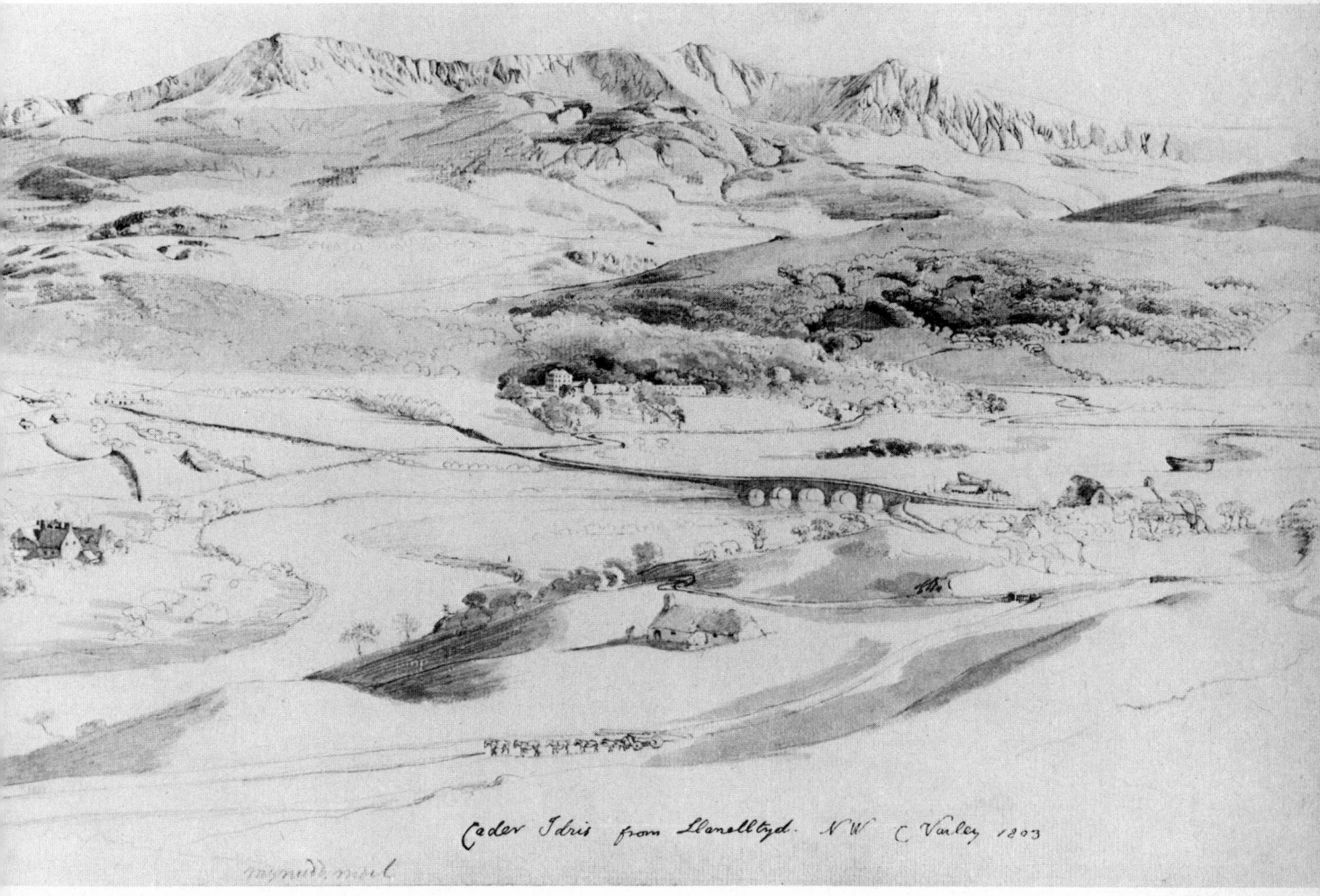

Cader Idris from Llanelltyd. N W C Varley 1803

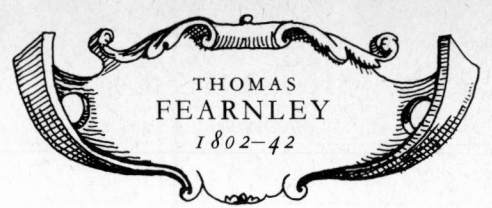

ONE OF THE PAINTERS of that romantic objectivism or wonder of landscape fact, which arose in Europe at the beginning of the nineteenth century only to be swamped by the academic high tide of idealism and sentimentalism. English by descent from a Yorkshire family, Fearnley was born at Frederikshald in Norway, on the east side of Oslo Fjord. He left Norway and worked for a time among the Dresden painters (Friedrich, Carus, Dahl, etc.), in contact with the idea of landscape as *Erdlebensbild*, images of the living earth. Dahl, the 'Norwegian Constable', gave him lessons in Dresden. From 1832 to 1835 he painted delightful landscapes in the south of Italy. After a first visit to England in 1835, he came back for a stay of two and a half years, painting and exhibiting in London, an admirer of Constable and Turner, and one of the few artists who have been on fruitful terms with the scenery of the Lake District. He died in Munich.

70. PATTERDALE, 1837. *Oil, $14\frac{3}{4} \times 16$ in. Oslo, Nasjonalgalleriet.*

The old St. Patrick's Chapel, an Elizabethan building replaced in Victorian times, at the southern end of Ullswater, in the Lake District. The yews remain.

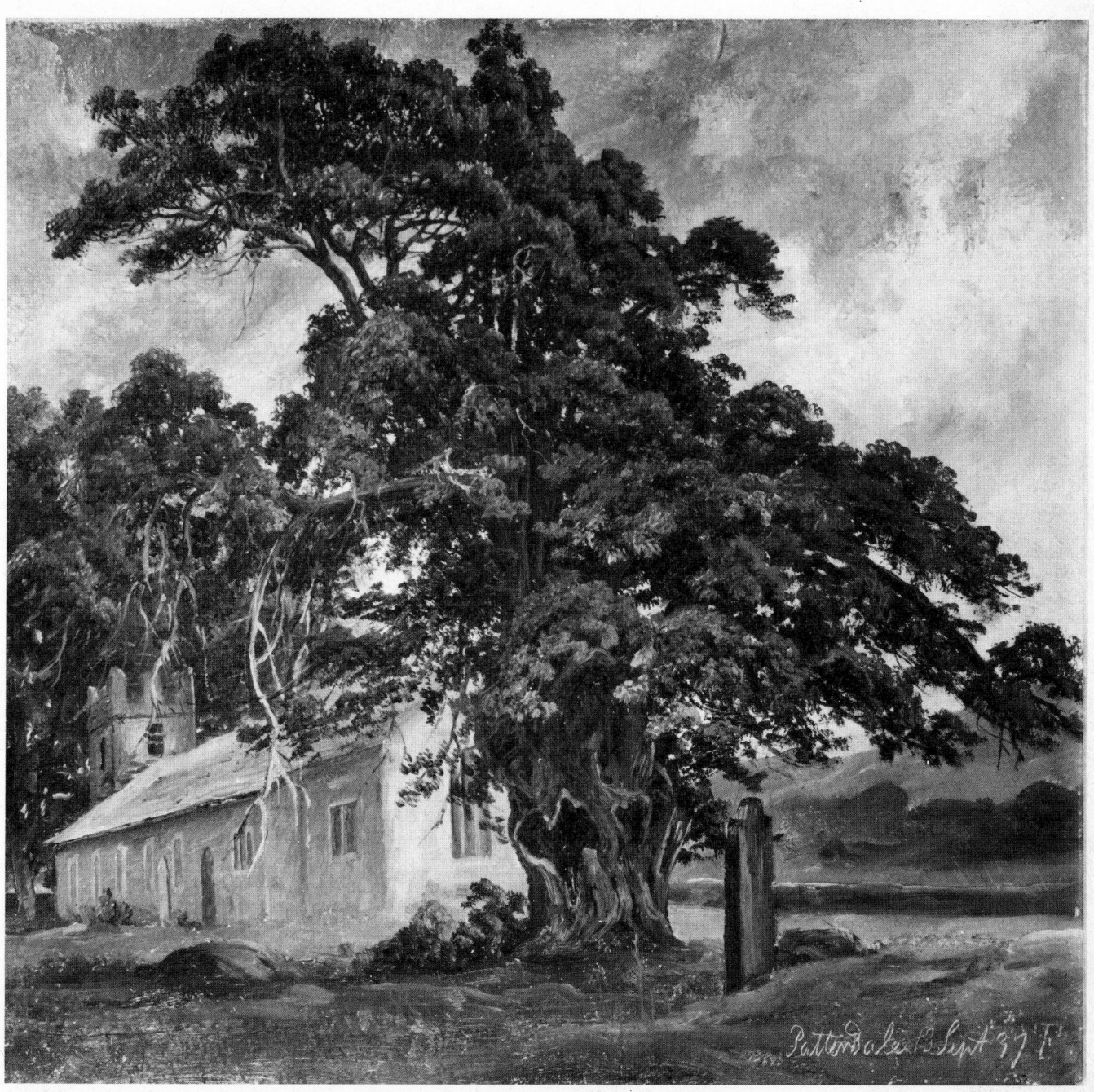

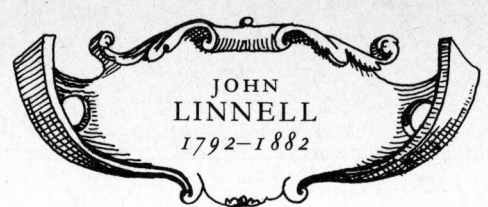

JOHN
LINNELL
1792–1882

LINNELL'S EARLY LANDSCAPES and portraits have an imaginative naturalism;
which he could not retain and at the same time earn enough to support a large
Victorian family. Since their temperaments were so different, it must have been
his religion (he became a Baptist, then joined the Plymouth Brethren) which made
him the admirer and helper of William Blake, in Blake's old age. The small
landscapes he painted before the 1830s, often on panel, (round Hampstead,
Southampton, Hastings, Reading, in North Wales, Buckinghamshire, the Isle of
Wight, the Peak District, etc.) display an unmannered freshness; and he was able
to direct the eye of the young Samuel Palmer (whose father-in-law he became) on
to the structure and forms of his Shoreham scenery, strengthening Palmer's
nature mysticism. Besides Palmer, other early friends and associates of Linnell's
who are represented in this book, included Cornelius Varley, Havell, George
Robert Lewis, and John Constable (who came to detest him). Linnell's fanaticism
increased, his landscape loosened to a muffled formula which he used pietistically
or in sentimental pastoralism. This was specially true of his landscapes of the
Surrey hills, painted around Redhill, where he settled in 1851. Such late work was
highly popular and made him wealthy.

71. THE
RIVER
KENNET,
NEAR
NEWBURY,
1815. *Oil,*
$17\frac{3}{4} \times 25\frac{5}{8}$ *in.*
Cambridge,
Fitzwilliam
Museum.

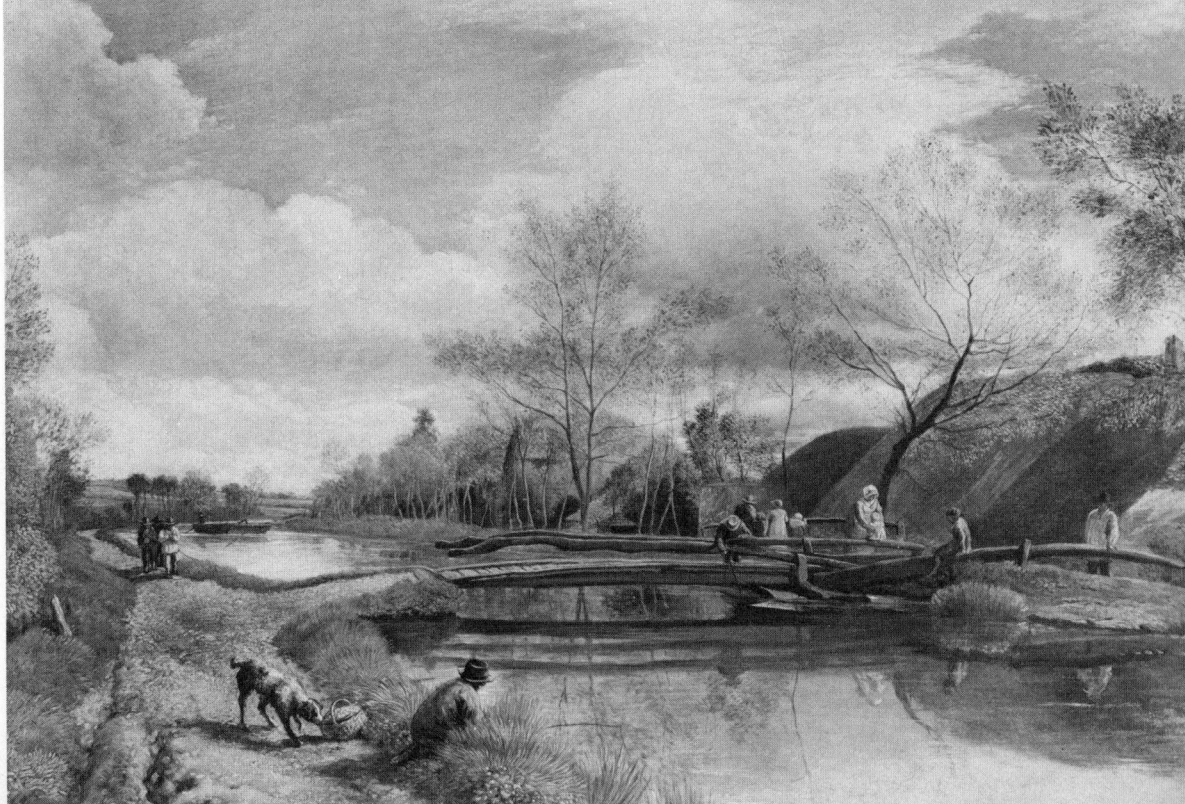

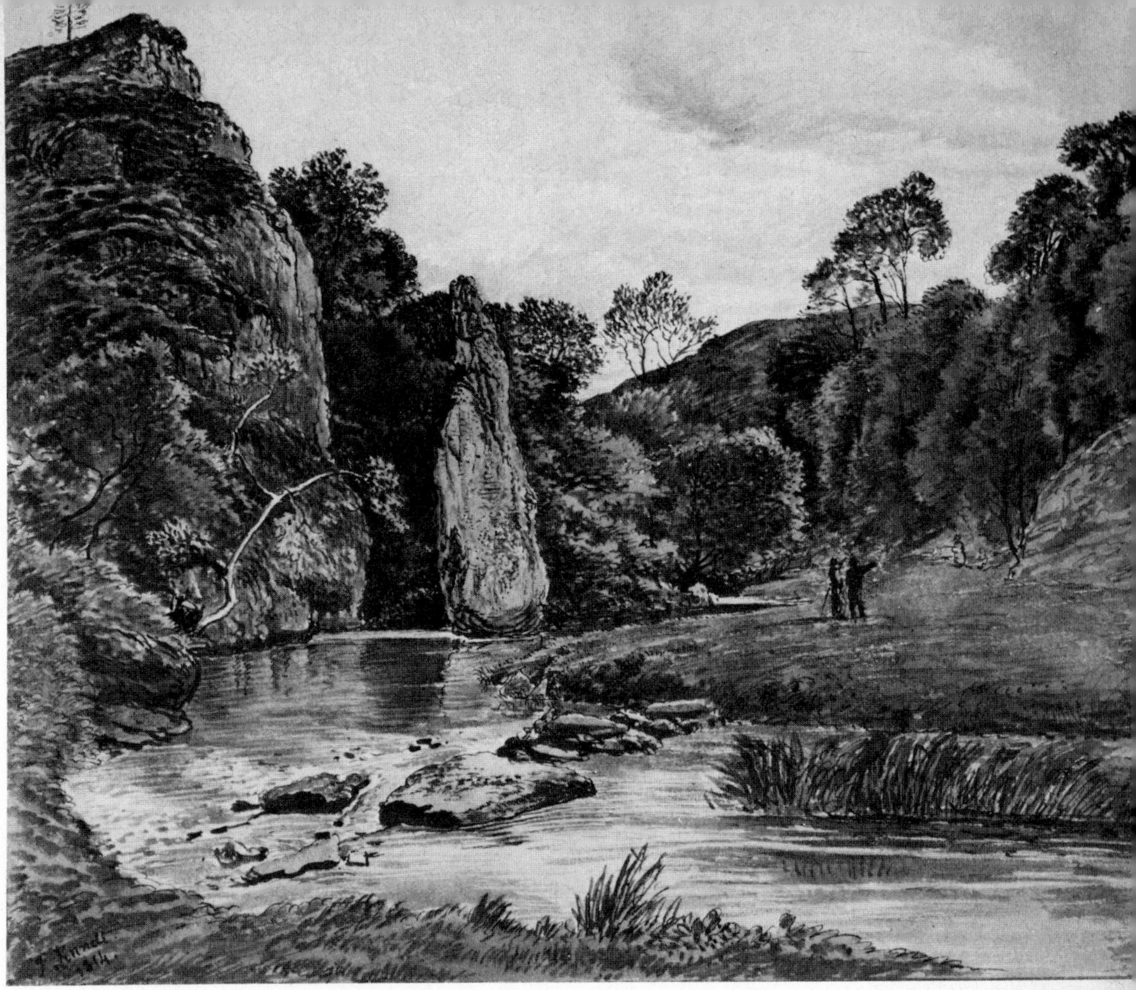

72. PIKE POOL,
BERESFORD DALE,
1814. *Pen and
watercolour over black
lead. Cambridge,
Fitzwilliam Museum.*
Linnell was in
Derbyshire in 1814
making drawings for a
new edition of *The
Compleat Angler*
published in the
following year. This
drawing was the basis
for one of the
engraved illustrations.

73. TWICKENHAM, 1806. *Oil*, $6\frac{1}{2} \times 10\frac{1}{16}$ *in. London, Tate Gallery.*

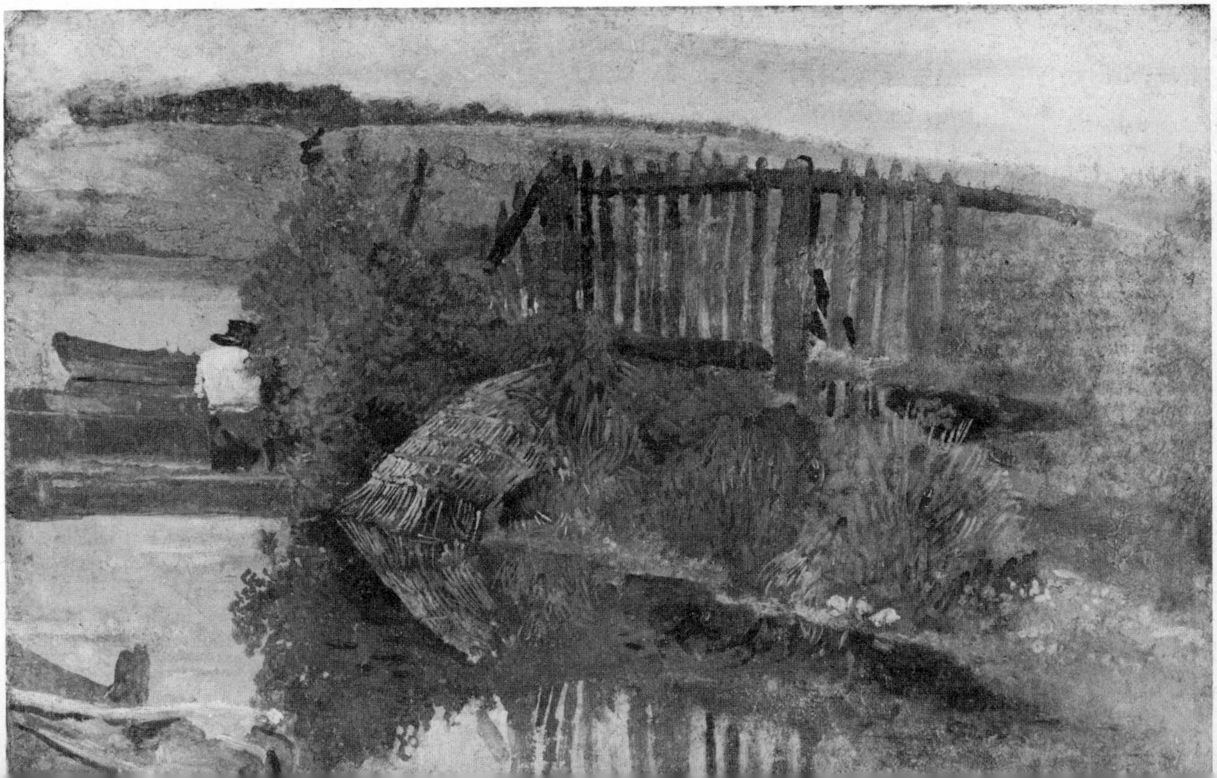

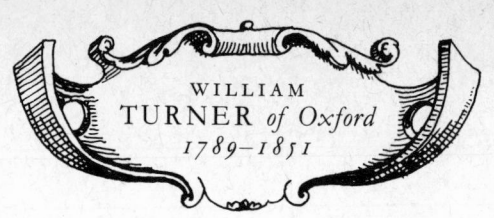

IT SEEMS POSSIBLE that William Turner of Oxford is undervalued among the English landscape painters. For eighty years (beginning with Roget's *History of the Old Water-Colour Society*) his watercolours have been mildly and dismissively praised, one authority after another, down to Martin Hardy in his *Water-Colour Painting in Britain*, parroting Roget's remarks. Turner was born in Oxfordshire, at Black Bourton, in the low country of the Thames, near the Kelmscot of William Morris. He was a self-effacing, retreating man. From early success in London he returned to Oxfordshire, and set up as a drawing master in Oxford. He lived in the county until his death, only leaving it in search of the kind of gentle, pastoral scenery he most liked (Sussex, the Malverns, Salisbury Plain, Devonshire, Wales, Northumberland, the Lakes, etc.). In 1808, with Cornelius Varley (Plates 68, 69), he had been among the original members of the Society for the Study of Epic and Pastoral Design; of which another member was George Robert Lewis (Plate 76), who lived in similar seclusion in Hereford. One of the old Turner's pupils remembered that behind his house in Oxford, in John Street, 'he had a small garden in which he grew plants suitable for introduction in the foregrounds of his pictures.' Turner can be dull, and he repeats himself; but not a few of his pastorals are solemn and moving, without sentimentality or meretriciousness of effect. His standard reputation seems to reflect that Victorian idea of art which rejected honest gravity of poetic vision for every variety of false sentiment, finding little room for Corot and none at all for the Impressionists.

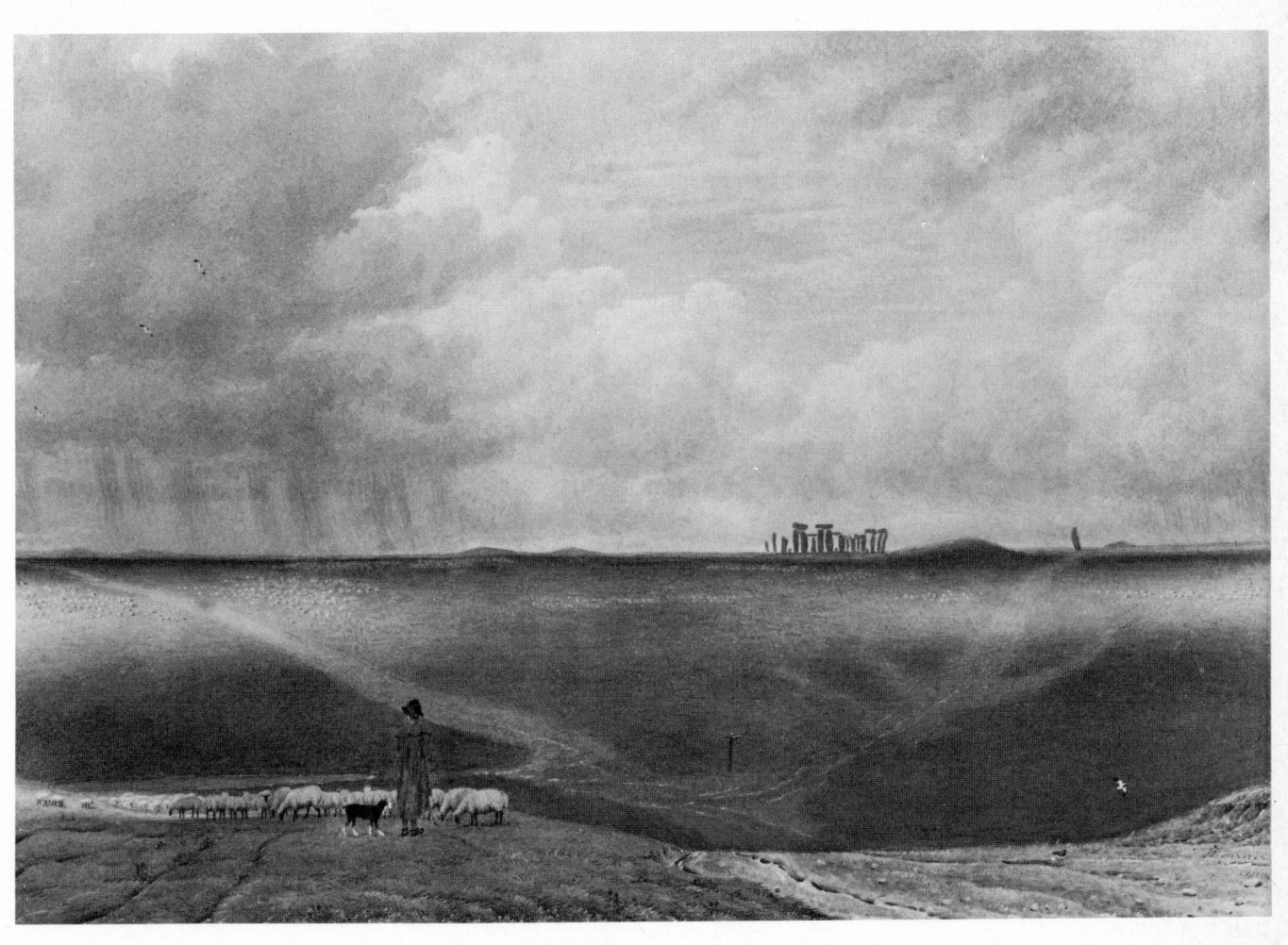

74. STONEHENGE. *Watercolour, 9⅞ × 16 in. Oxford, Ashmolean Museum.*

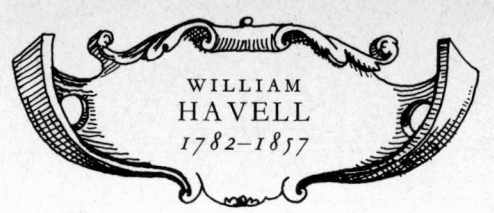

WILLIAM
HAVELL
1782–1857

A LANDSCAPE PAINTER, of Cotman's generation, and seven years younger than Turner whom he passionately admired for his command of sunlight. He grew up to know the Thames at Reading, where his father was a drawing master. He drew in Wales with his friend Cornelius Varley (page 189); and in 1807 he went to the Lakes, living some two years at Ambleside, where he made studies in oil and watercolour of light, water and mountain. A picture 'in which he has painted sunshine so near to truth that it absolutely makes the eyes ache to look at it' was rejected by the Academy in 1815. Cotman greatly admired this picture and made a note of its revolutionary brightness, which Havell thought a step beyond Turner: 'Most splendidly coloured: Trees very green: rich: orange green: tones vigorous'. Years afterwards he based one of his own watercolours on it. Havell made landscapes of the Thames and of coastal scenery at Hastings. He went East in 1816, visiting China, India and Burma. He also painted in Italy.

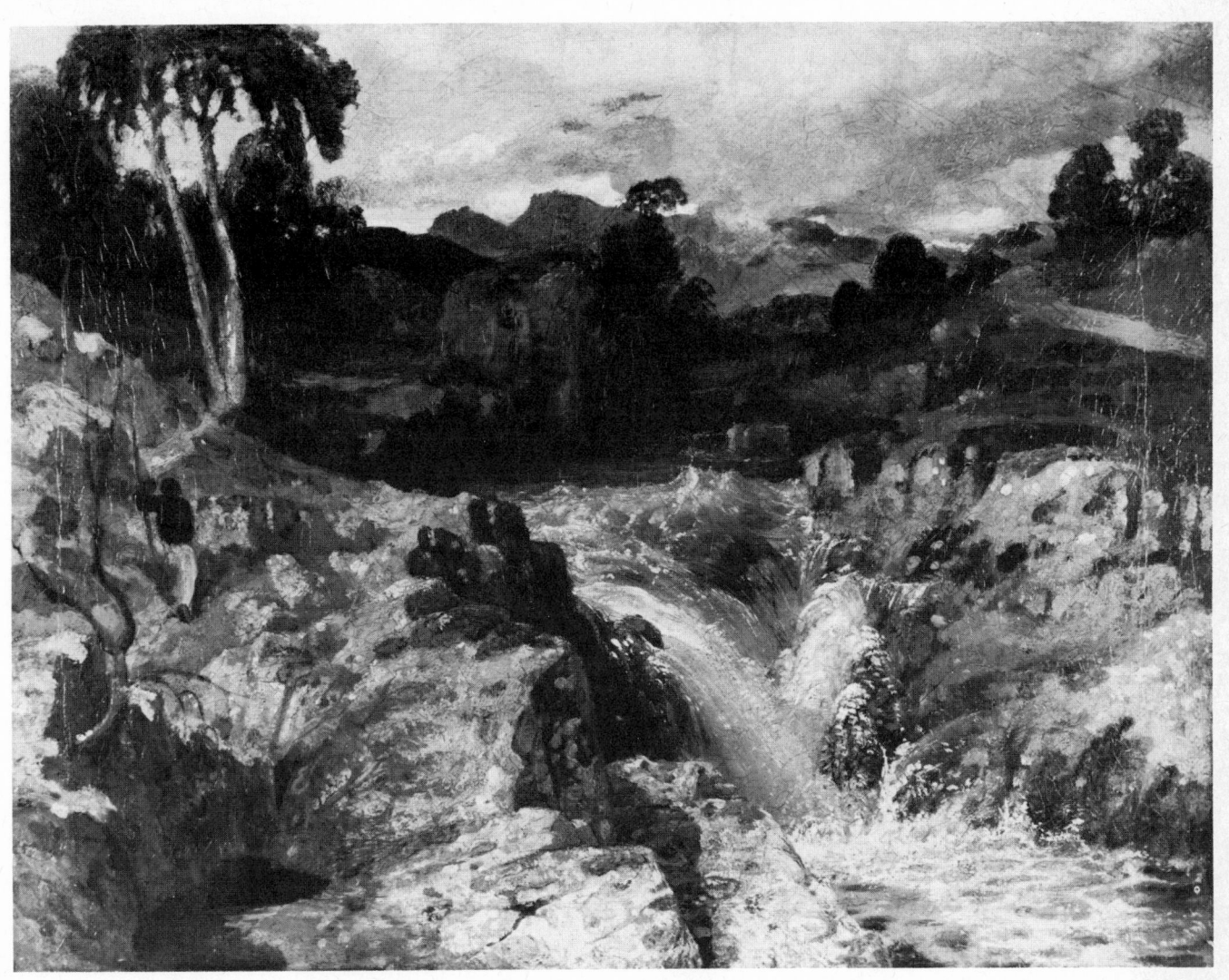

75. SKELWORTH FORCE, WESTMORLAND, LANGDALE PIKES IN THE DISTANCE, 1807–9. *Oil*, $24\frac{1}{4} \times 26\frac{1}{2}$ *in. Miss Joyce Havell.*

There is an extraordinary difference between such Lakeland oil studies by Havell, fresh and direct and full of sparkle, and the watercolours of the same time which he worked up for exhibition—and a living.

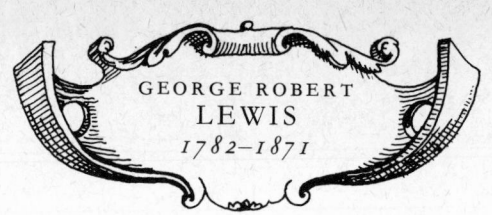

THOUGH HE PAINTED PORTRAITS and subject pictures as well as landscape and lived a very long life, works by G. R. Lewis are unaccountably rare; to judge from his much loved Herefordshire harvest picture, reproduced here (Plates 76, 78), they should be worth finding. His father was a German refugee from Hanover, who changed his name from Ludwig to Lewis, his brother was the landscape painter and engraver F. C. Lewis, whom Constable disliked as a camp-follower of art, and his nephew, best known of the family, was John Frederick Lewis who painted Near Eastern subjects with a detailed precision. Lewis belonged to the so called Chalon Sketching Society—'The Society for the Study of Epic and Pastoral Design', founded in 1808, of which two of the original members were Cornelius Varley and William Turner of Oxford. His friends included Joshua Cristall and John Linnell. George Lewis travelled and drew in France, lived for some time in Hereford, painting Herefordshire and border country landscapes. He was known for his tree drawings, and was also one of the first to publicize the Romanesque carvings of Kilpeck church, which he illustrated (though not very well) in a portfolio he published in 1842. He was born in London, and died in Hampstead.

76. VIEW IN HEREFORDSHIRE: HARVEST, 1816. *Oil,* $16\frac{3}{8} \times 23\frac{1}{2}$ *in. London, Tate Gallery.*

Lewis's view is from Haywood Lodge, 3 miles south-west of Hereford, to Dinedor Camp and (right) the high ridge of Marcle Hill.

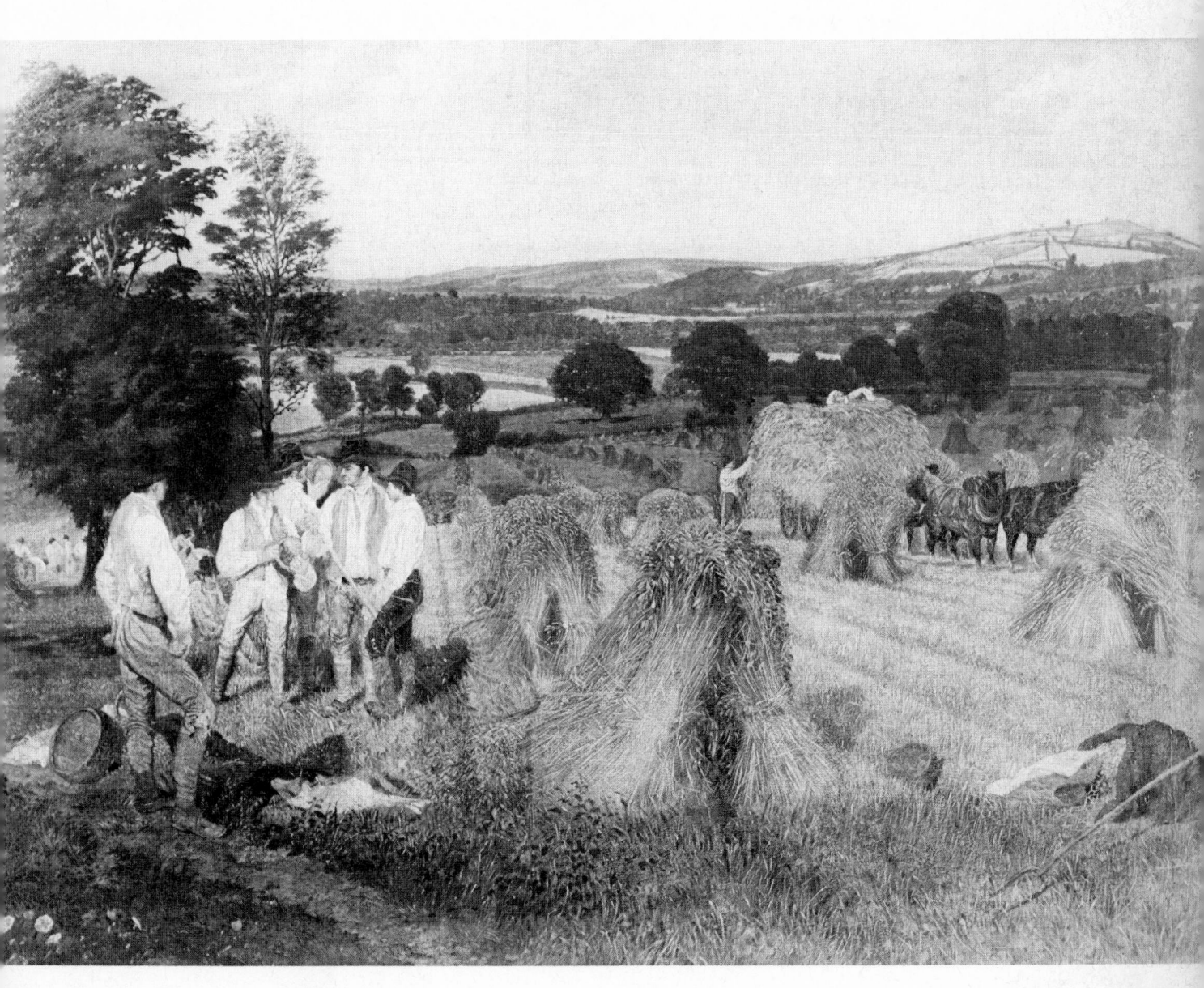

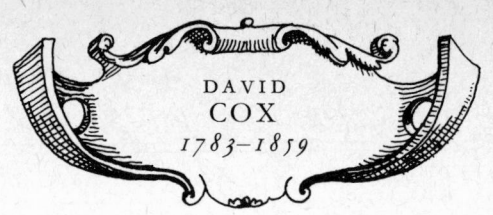

DAVID
COX
1783–1859

GEORGE MOORE once wrote of an artist whose eyes were strangely his own 'in a time of slushy David Coxes'. The adjective seems too often right. If there is an unexpected freedom about David Cox's watercolour landscapes, the colours and the forms slush this way and that, the total image has the effect of being thin and weightless as if an underlying reality had never been comprehended. His firmest work came early, surprising us with a realization that Cox was in fact of the generation of Cotman, and was younger than Turner and Constable by less than ten years. His career had a common pattern—growing up poor and humble (Cox's father was a whitesmith and blacksmith at Deritend, outside Birmingham), coming to art by a lowlier if related profession (he painted theatre scenery), travelling up and down the country for his landscape subjects, accommodating his style to the market, and labouring endlessly as a drawing master. His sketching took him to Wales (which he loved), the Lakes, Yorkshire, North Devon, Derbyshire, castles, abbeys, ferries; and his titles, 'Asking the Way', 'The Missing Lamb', etc., are indicative of too weak a desire to please. He worked in London and Hereford, and in 1841 retired to Harborne, on the edge of Birmingham.
Page 190.

77. ALL SAINTS' CHURCH, HASTINGS, 1812. *Oil, 5¾ × 8¾ in. Birmingham, City Art Gallery.*

Cox was thirty years old at the time of the publication (1813) of the first number of his *Treatise on Landscape Painting and Effect in Water Colours,* where this painting is reproduced in aquatint. The best of the aquatints in the *Treatise* and small oils of the same period have a gravity and intensity he lost altogether in his endless run of Victorian potboilers. This accords, conventionally expressed as they may be, with the *General Observations on Landscape Painting* which introduce the *Treatise.*

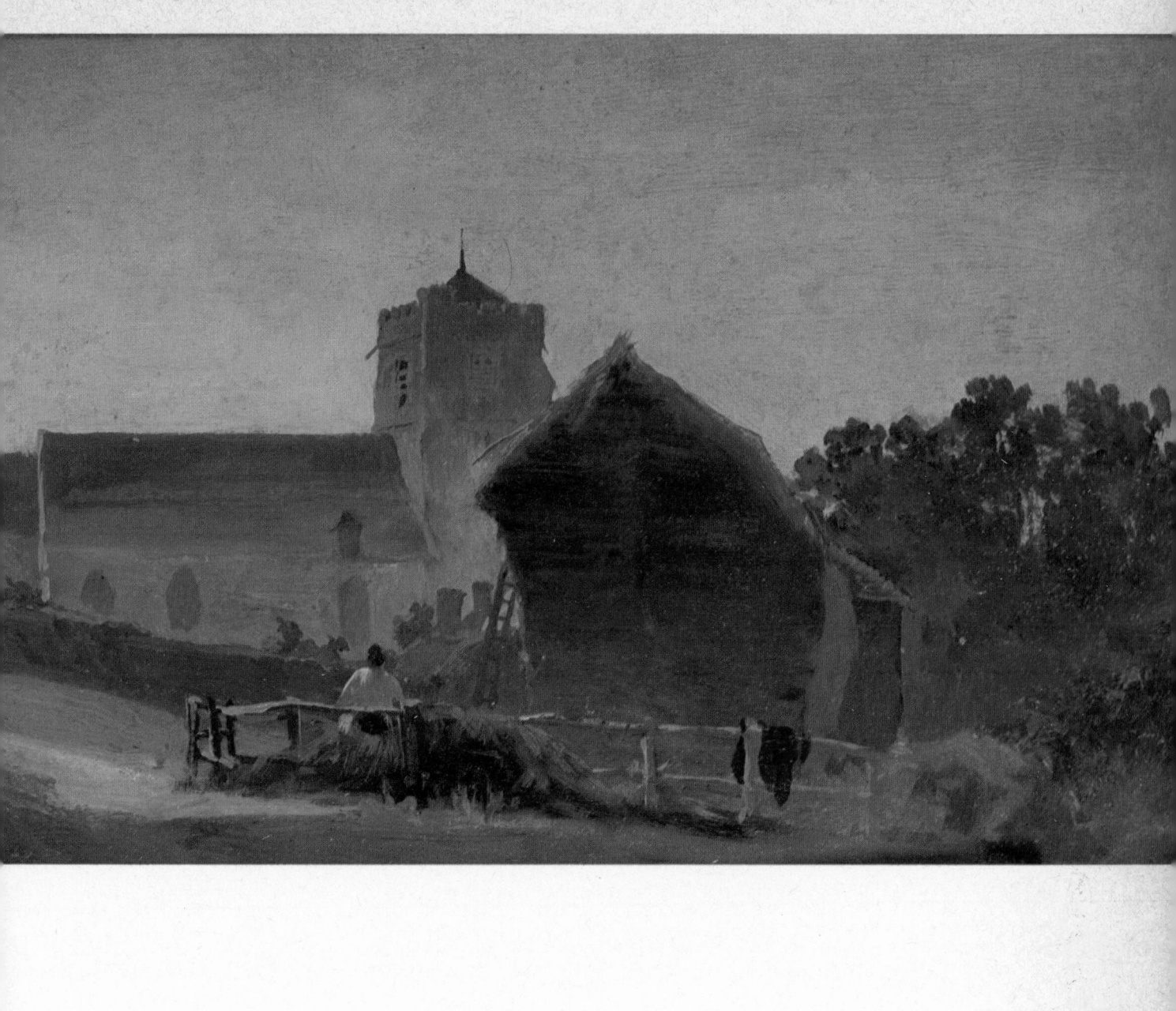

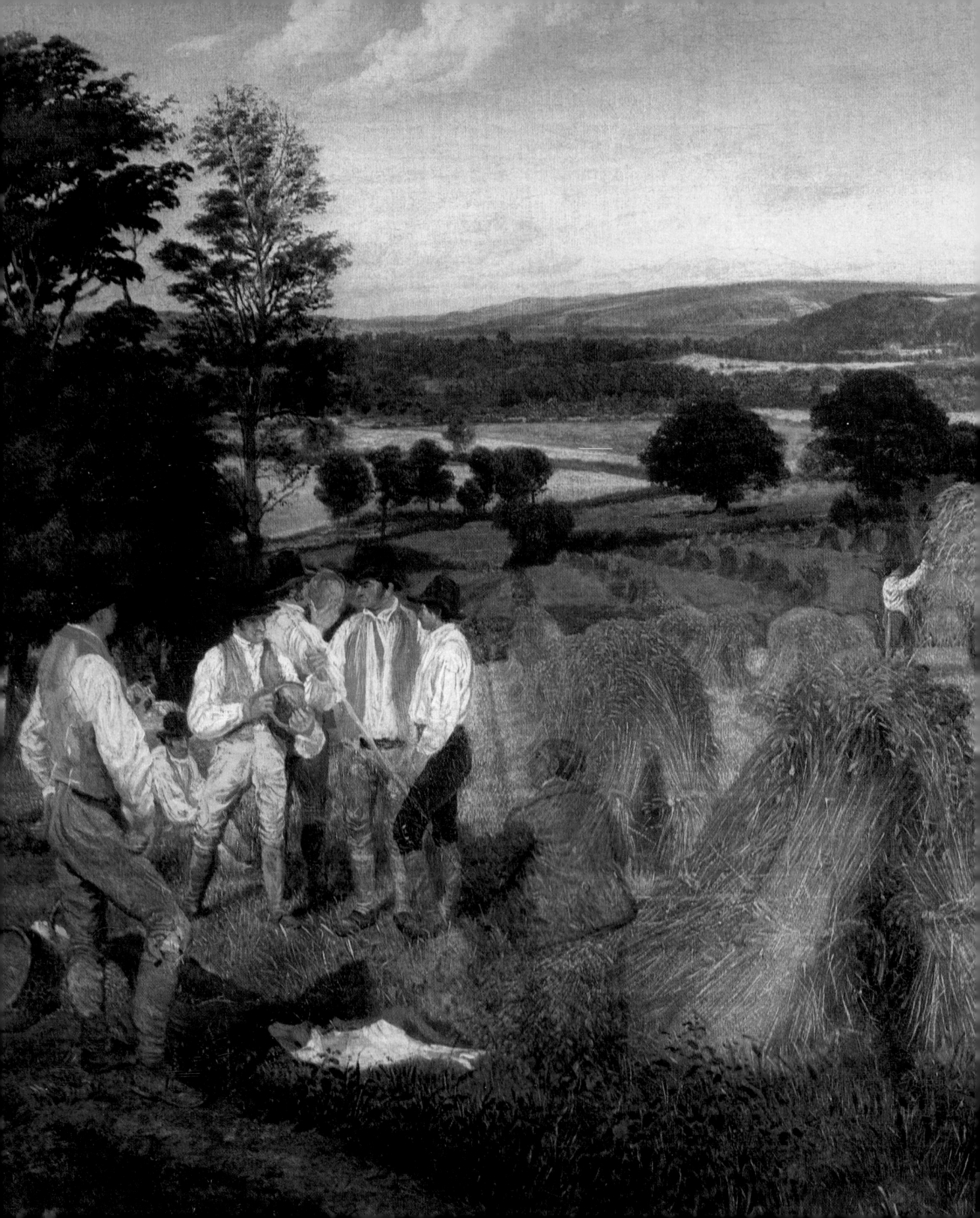

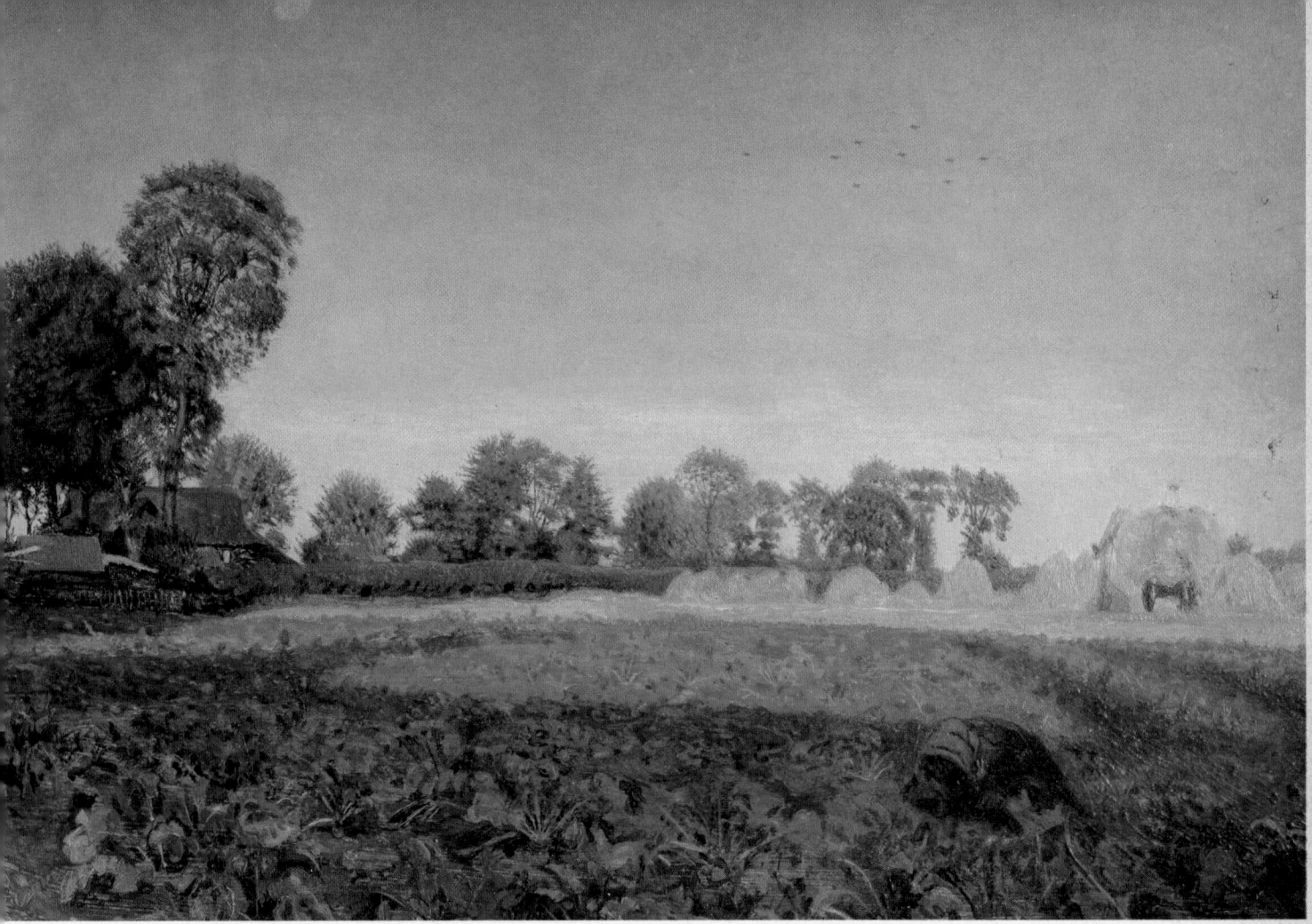

79. CARRYING CORN, 1854. *Oil, 7½ × 10½ in. London, Tate Gallery.*

Brown found his subject of turnips and carrying the corn at Hendon, in Middlesex, in farming country now built over and densely populated. For his work day by day on the picture, see pages 195–6.

78. VIEW IN HEREFORDSHIRE: HARVEST, 1816 *(detail). London, Tate Gallery.*

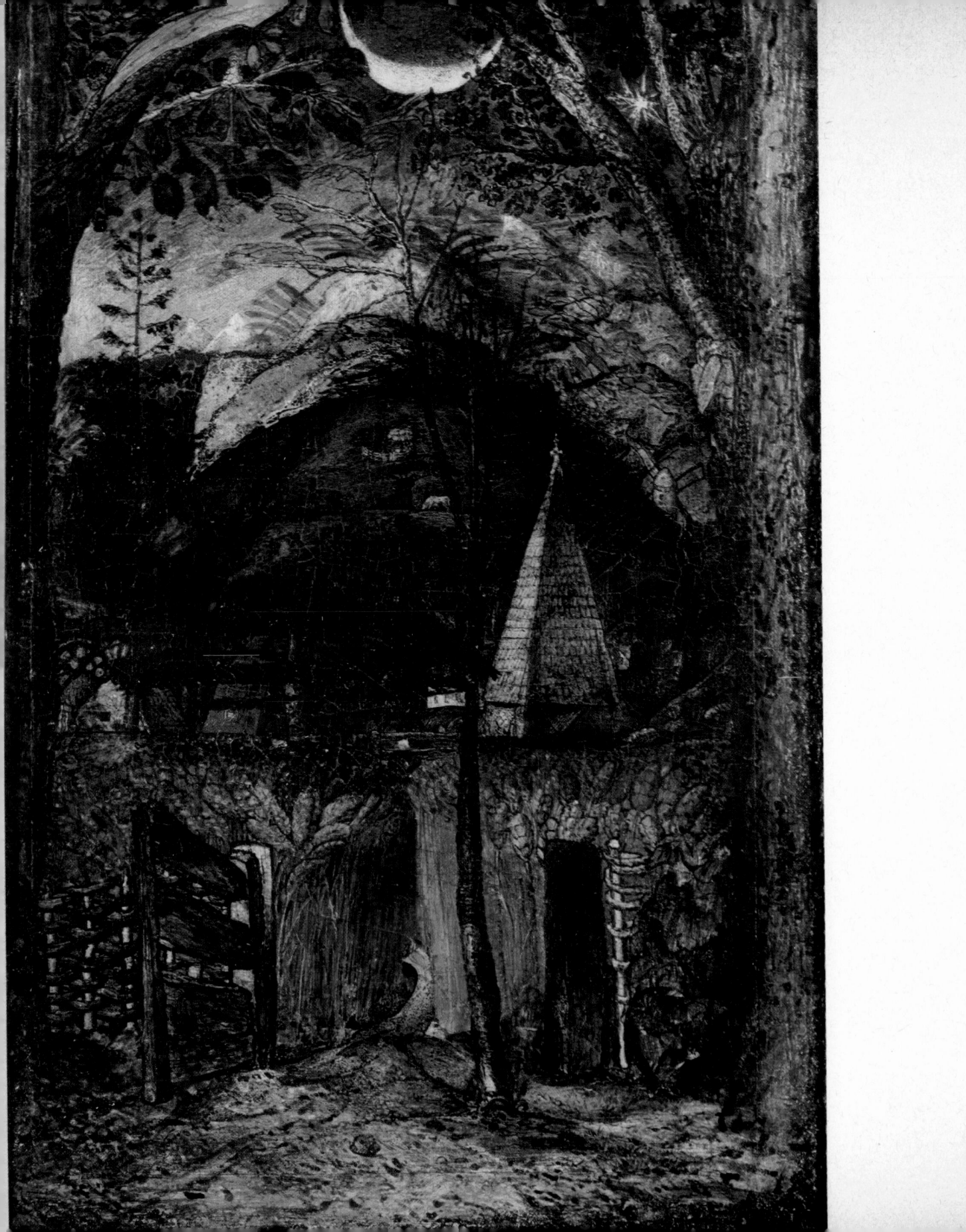

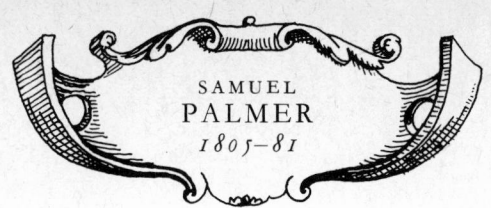

SON OF A LONDON BOOKSELLER; in childhood he lived on the southern fringe of London, facing the now built over hills of Dulwich. For a while he was a precocious imitator of the more free style of Turner; then coming to know John Linnell and William Blake he began to combine a close simplified objectivity of landscape forms with the consequences of a belief that the wonder of rich hilly scenery and the twilights of dawn and evening could only be explained as a 'proscenium of eternity': landscape was recording his mystical vision of the borders of Heaven as mirrored in his Surrey or Kentish hills. An inheritance enabled him to live for some years in the Kentish village of Shoreham, in a house on the edge of the Darenth, which draws light through willows and meadows under the swell of chalk hills. The Darenth valley, the North Downs, the Kentish hop gardens, the depth of dramatic fertility around Underriver, near Sevenoaks, became his special country; and the close neighbourhood of Shoreham village afforded him extra-

80. A HILLY SCENE, *c.*1826–8. *Tempera, watercolour, pen* $8\frac{1}{4} \times 5\frac{3}{8}$ *in. London, Tate Gallery.* Kentish forms, the chalkland hill, the chalk quarry, the windmill, thatched cottages, the spire roofed with shingles, combined in Palmer's highly personalized ideal of a landscape on the borders of Paradise. In this image of fruitfulness Palmer also had in mind two stanzas from Spenser (*Faerie Queene,* II.VI. 42–3):

> There is continuall spring, and haruest there
> > Continuall, both meeting at one time:
> > For both the boughes doe laughing blossomes beare,
> > And with fresh colours decke the wanton Prime,
> > And eke attonce the heauy trees they clime,
> > Which seeme to labour vnder their fruits lode:
> > The whiles the ioyous birdes make their pastime
> > Emongst the shadie leaues, their sweet abode,
> And their true loues without suspition tell abrode.
>
> Right in the middest of that Paradise,
> > There stood a stately Mount, on whose round top
> > A gloomy groue of mirtle trees did rise,
> > Whose shadie boughes sharpe steele did neuer lop,
> > But like a girlond compassed the hight,
> > And from their fruitfull sides sweet gum did drop,
> > That all the ground with precious deaw bedight,
> Threw forth most dainty odours, and most sweet delight.

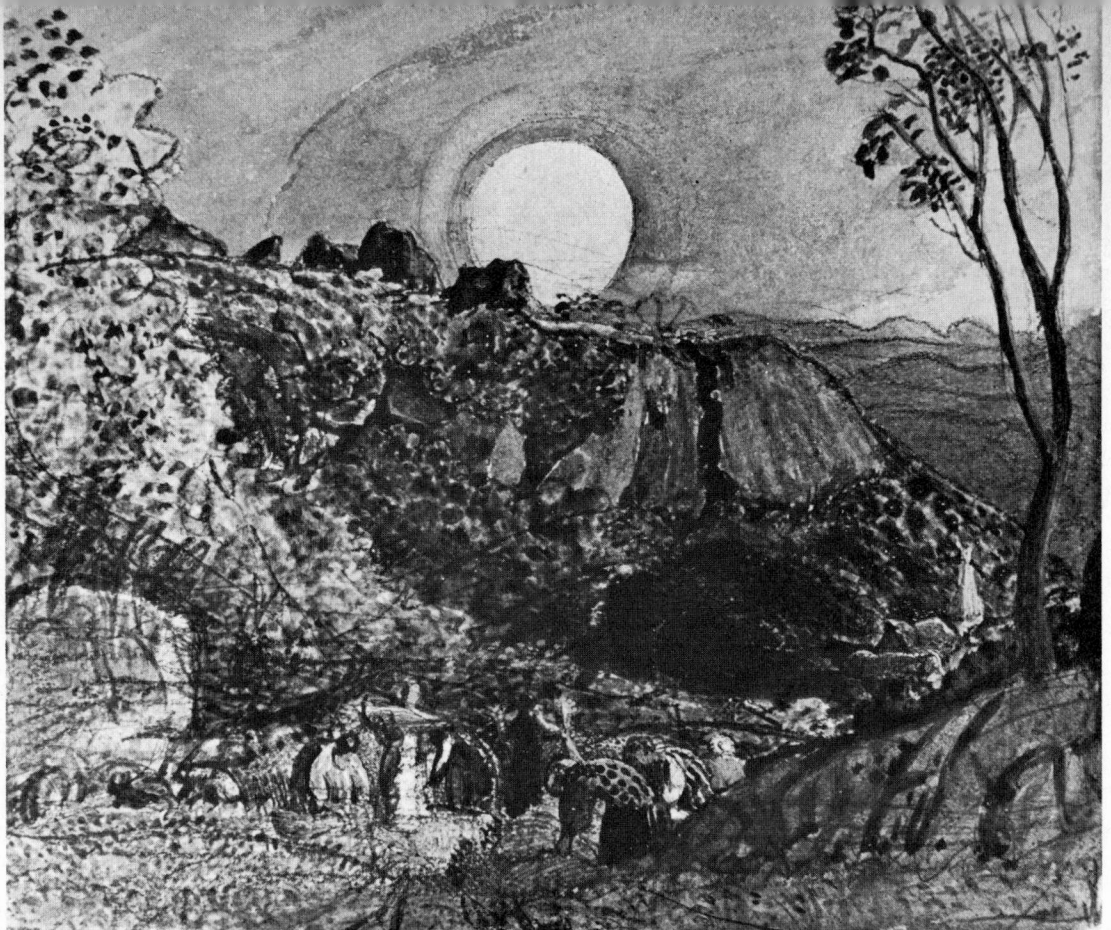

ordinary conditions of hallucinatory light revealing and enhancing rising and falling curves and rounded contours, out of which he invented the small sepia drawings and small paintings of his 'Shoreham period' (1825–35).

Palmer's art combined the multitudinous interests of the previous half century, medievalism, the inheritance of the Ideal in landscape derived from Claude, etcetera, a Christianized Neo-platonism, an emotional and mystical concern, a symbolical concern, for light and distance and colour and the fertility of nature, and a new objectivity, a new scrutiny of visual experience. The feeling of this artist's 'Shoreham period' makes him 'go out to draw some hops that their fruitful sentiment may be infused into my figures' or declare that 'By God's help I will not sell away his gift of art for money; no, not for fame neither, which is far better. Mr Linnell tells me that by making studies of the Shoreham scenery I could get a thousand a year directly. Tho' I am making studies for Mr Linnell, I will, God help me, never be a naturalist by profession' (1828).

Palmer's mystical enthusiasm could hardly survive in the sentimental materialism of the Victorian century, and he ceased to be a striking inventor of landscape arrangements. He found his later landscape ideal in Devonshire, North and South. 'Habitable latitudes' for him, 'began south of the railings of Hyde Park', and their 'kernel', he said, was Devonshire. He talked of the 'heaped up richness' of Devonshire, of himself as 'the utterly South-Devon-stricken one'. *Page* 193.

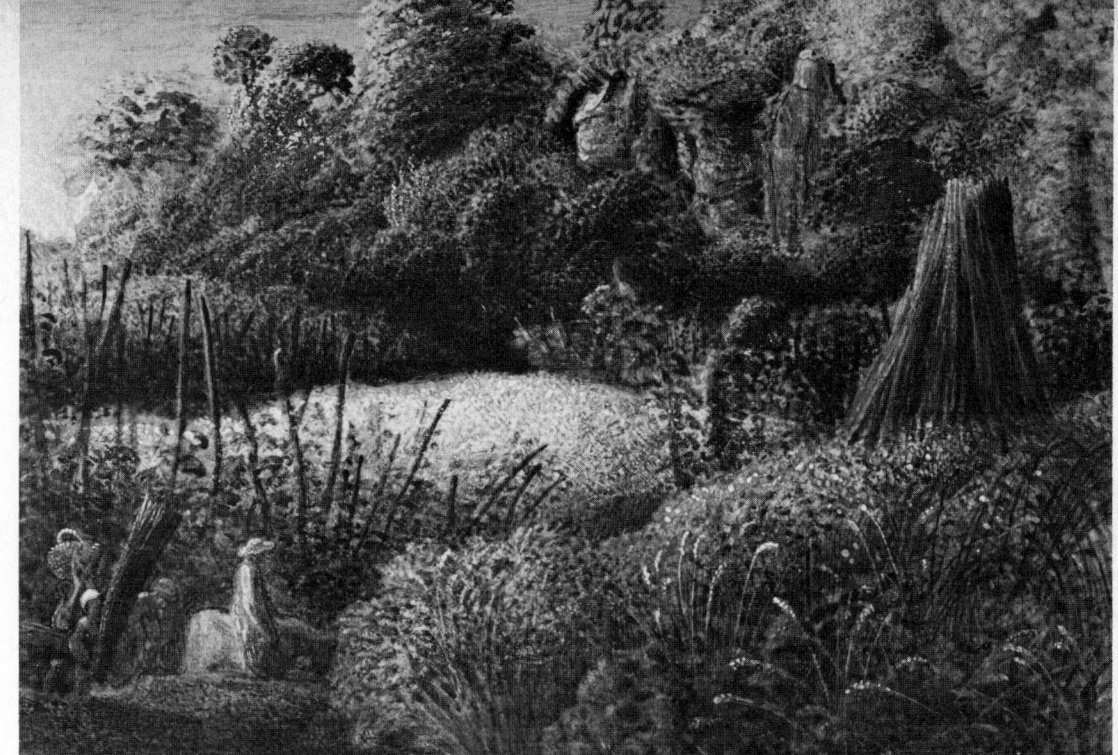

82. SCENE AT UNDERRIVER (THE HOP GARDEN), *c.* 1833–4. *Oil and tempera,*
7 × 10 *in. Private collection.*

Underriver in Kent lies under a wooded ridge just to the south-east of Knole
Park, near Sevenoaks. The neighbourhood is now rural-residential and has lost the
pastoral isolation which Palmer, and before him the poet Christopher Smart who
was born nearby at Shipbourne, so much enjoyed.

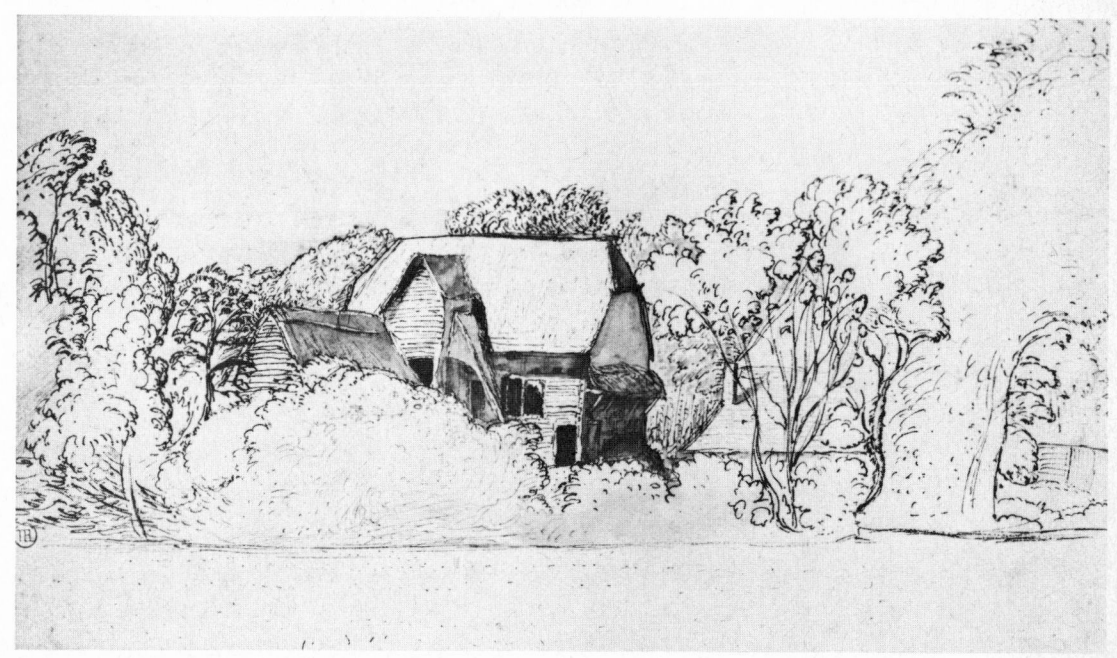

83. AN ANCIENT BARN, *c.* 1829. *Pen and wash,* 6 × 10¾ *in. Private collection.*

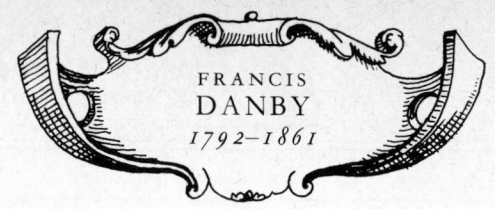

FRANCIS
DANBY
1792–1861

MANY OF THIS IRISH ARTIST'S LANDSCAPES have disappeared, and it seems, as we look at his surviving or recovered work, that he never managed to maintain his gifts in a developing freedom. He grew up in Dublin, and during his twenties, in Bristol, he was painting small, fresh, clear panels of landscape or landscape genre, before a period in which he attempted, with misguided encouragement from Sir Thomas Lawrence, the President of the Royal Academy, to rival John Martin in the hugely apocalyptic and sensational. Pursued by family difficulties and scandal, he lived abroad, in Paris and Geneva, returned to London, and finally settled at Exmouth. Pictures by him suggest repeated efforts to catch the market by the sentimental as well as the sensational; whereas his forte proved to be solemn landscape or seascape in which earth divides the colours of sky or sunset and their reflection on water; which explains his retirement at last to Exmouth and the wide sky-mirror of the Exe estuary. His skies were admired by Turner—whose follower he was in some degree—and many nineteenth-century artists were entranced by his landscapes and seascapes, especially his sunset picture *The*

84. CLIFTON ROCKS FROM ROWNHAM FIELDS, *c. 1822. Oil, 15¾ × 20 in. Bristol, City Art Gallery.*

A landscape of the tidal Avon at Bristol, downstream from the Suspension Bridge. Eric Adams, in his *Francis Danby: Varieties of Poetic Landscape* (1973), hazards that this, and other pictures by Danby of landscape genre with children, were Danby's response, in part, to poems by Clare and Blake about children at play—especially Blake's *The Echoing Green*:

> Old John with white hair
> Does laugh away care,
> Sitting under the oak,
> Among the old folk.
> They laugh at our play,
> And soon they all say,
> Such, such were the joys,
> When we all girls and boys,
> In our youth time were seen,
> On the Echoing Green.

There are reasons for supposing that Danby was acquainted with *The Village Minstrel* by Clare and with Blake's *Songs of Innocence*.

Evening Gun (known by a small replica), which moved French critics to high praise, among them Gautier: *Un chef d'œuvre, tout simplement . . . il y a dans cette toile une tranquillité, un silence, une solitude, qui impressionnent vivement l'âme. Jamais la grandeur de l'Océan n'a été mieux rendue. (Les Beaux-Arts en Europe, 1855).* Danby looked for his early landscapes especially in the Avon gorge at Bristol, finding subjects later on in North Wales, Cornwall, Lincolnshire and along the Thames, as well as around Exmouth, and in Norway, Switzerland and Brittany. *Page* 191.

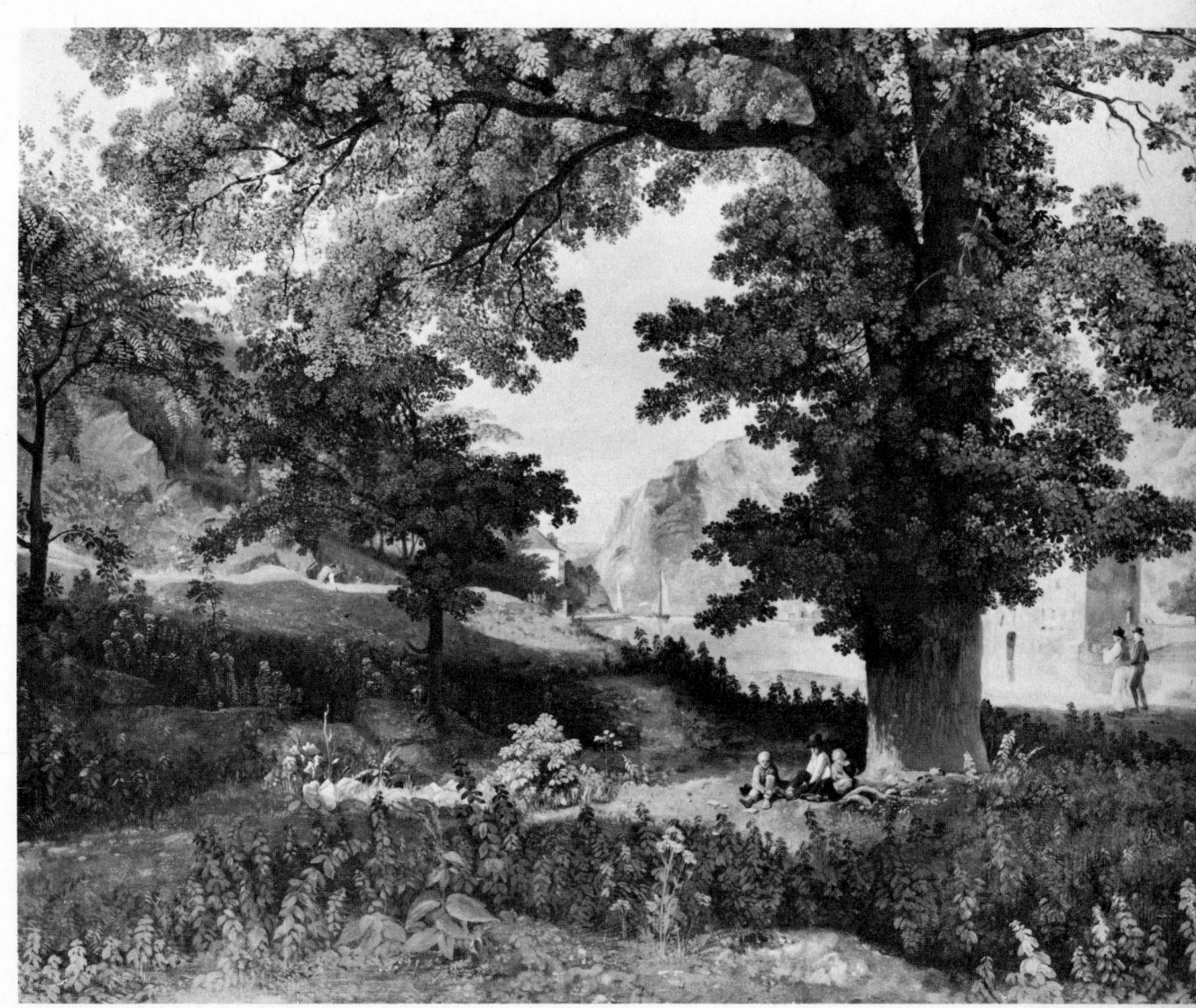

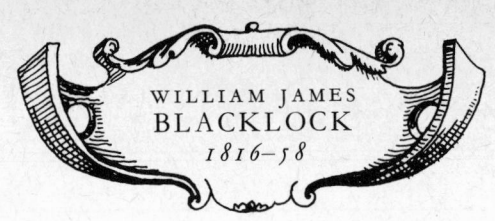

LANDSCAPE PAINTER of Courbet's generation and one of the few English artists who have made acceptable pictures out of the scenery of the Lake District. He was born in London, to a bookseller from Cumwhitton, near Carlisle, who took him back to Cumwhitton, when his health gave way, about 1820. Blacklock therefore grew up in fell and river country at no great distance from the Lakes. The distinctive tones and character of Lakeland rock, mountain and river scenery enter his pictures just as the tones and character of the Jura limestone enter Courbet's landscapes. He began to paint with some success in London, where Pre-Raphaelite influence helped to clarify his vision of Cumberland landscape, but never overpowered or destroyed the breadth and harmony of his later work. Like his father he became ill in London, and he went back to Cumberland in 1850, at a critical time in his career. He grew worse and just when his pictures were beginning to attract attention at the Academy he became nearly blind, and died at Dumfries in Scotland when he was only 42. His drawings have a remarkable purity and intensity, recalling the earlier naturalism of Samuel Palmer. But for his early death Blacklock might have matured into a landscape painter of great power.

85. THE ROOKERY, 1853–4. *Oil, 21½ × 39½ in. Carlisle, Art Gallery.*

The house is not certainly identified: it suggests both Haddon Hall in Derbyshire, and Naworth Castle in Cumberland, of which there is a painting by Blacklock, similar in manner but less successful, in the National Gallery, Dublin.

86. CATBELLS AND CAUSEY PIKE, 1853–4. *Oil, 12¾ × 21¾ in. Carlisle, Art Gallery.*

Cumberland. Catbells left, Causey Pike, right centre, bulking over Derwentwater, with the spire of Keswick Church to the right.

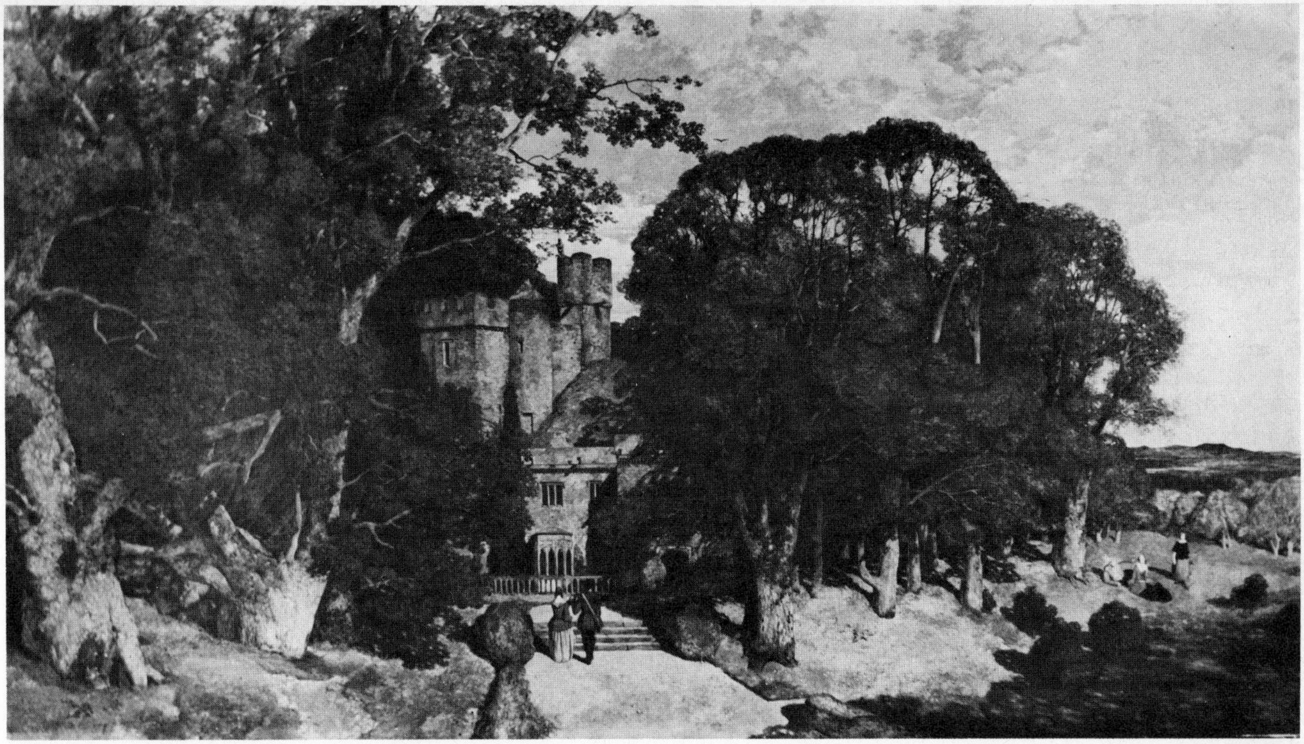

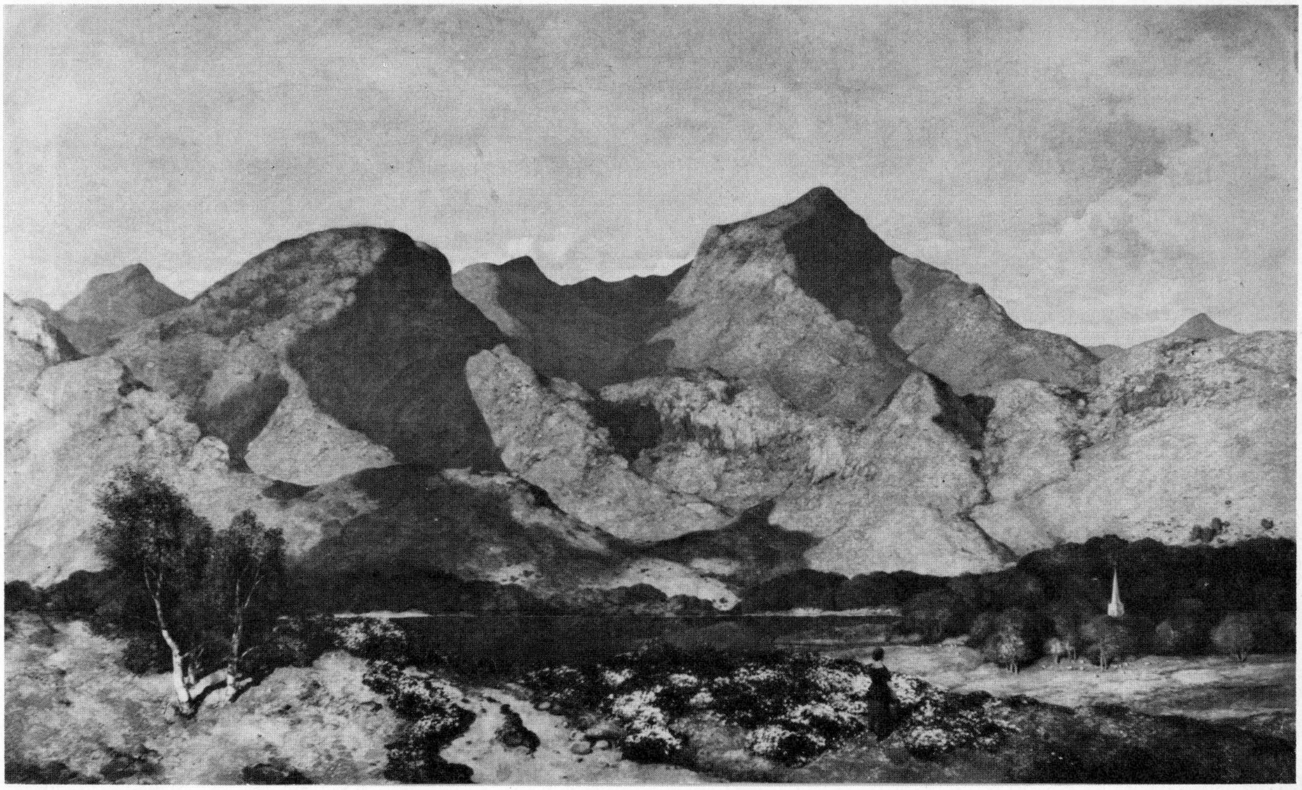

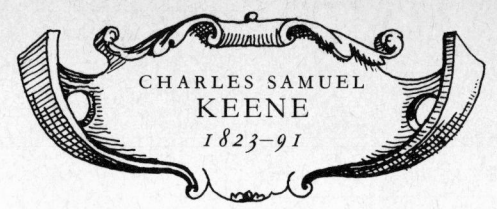

CHARLES SAMUEL
KEENE
1823–91

A DRAUGHTSMAN much admired by Pissarro and other Impressionists for the selective honesty of his depiction. Though born in Hornsey, the son of a solicitor, Charles Keene was one of the artists of East Anglia. He spent much of his childhood at Ipswich. Content and unambitious except for skill in drawing, he lived by illustrating for *Punch* every week a jest generally supplied to him by others. His friend Edward Fitzgerald wrote of him as 'a man who can reverence, though a droll in *Punch*'; and regarding his line one thinks of him as reverencing the visible facts of existence, and not faking or exaggerating its show. He effaced himself, in his London studio, in an era of art grandees, never pontificating or making more than the occasional remark about working from 'nature', which was a favourite word: 'I never could do any work without a foundation from nature', 'Draw a thing as you see it,' 'A man who can draw anything can draw everything.' Pissarro on Keene, to his son Lucien, June 13, 1883: 'England has Keene, he does not exhibit, he is not fashionable, and that is everything. England, like France, is rotten to the core, she knows only one art, the art of throwing sand in your eyes.' Keene drew landscape in his favourite Suffolk, on the coast around Dunwich and Southwold; around Witley, in Surrey, where he had a cottage; and also in South Devon. *Page* 196.

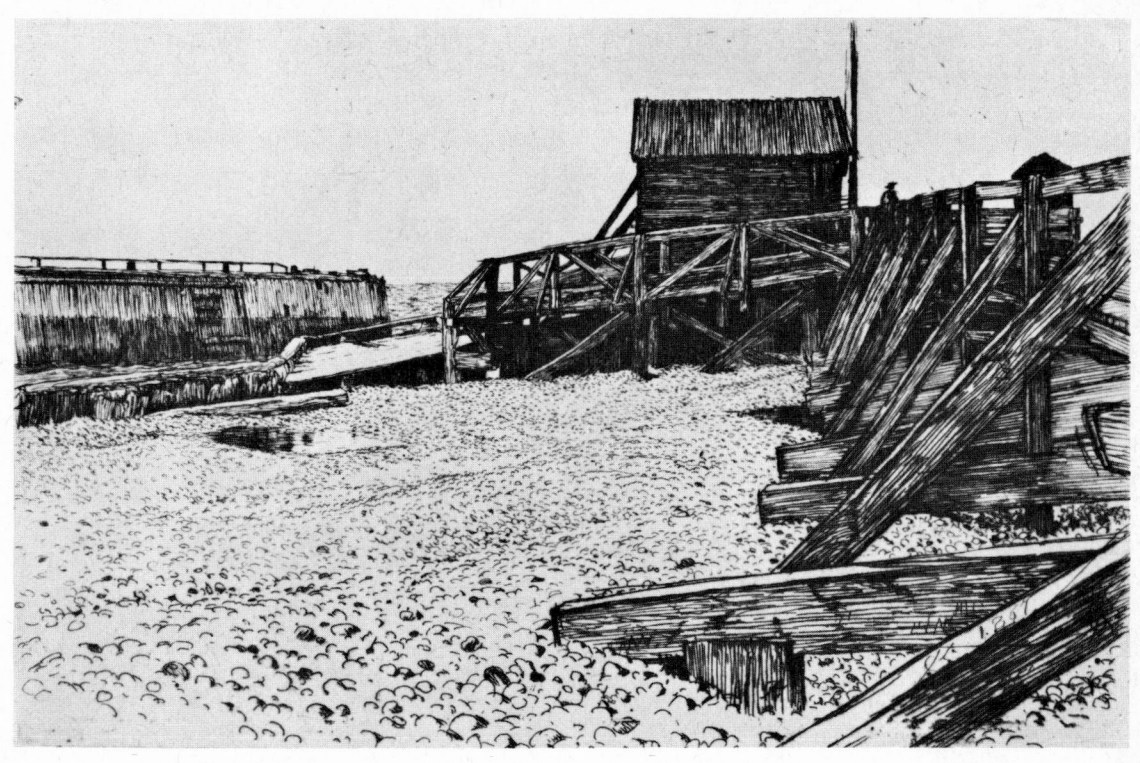

87. SOUTHWOLD HARBOUR, 1867. *Etching,* $3\frac{7}{8} \times 6$ *in. London, Victoria and Albert Museum.*
Southwold on the Suffolk coast, a little way north-east of Charles Keene's Dunwich.

88. LOCK ON A CANAL. *Etching, $3\frac{7}{8} \times 6$ in. London, Victoria and Albert Museum.*

A Hertfordshire scene, a lock on the old Grand Junction (now Grand Union) Canal, between Watford and King's Langley.

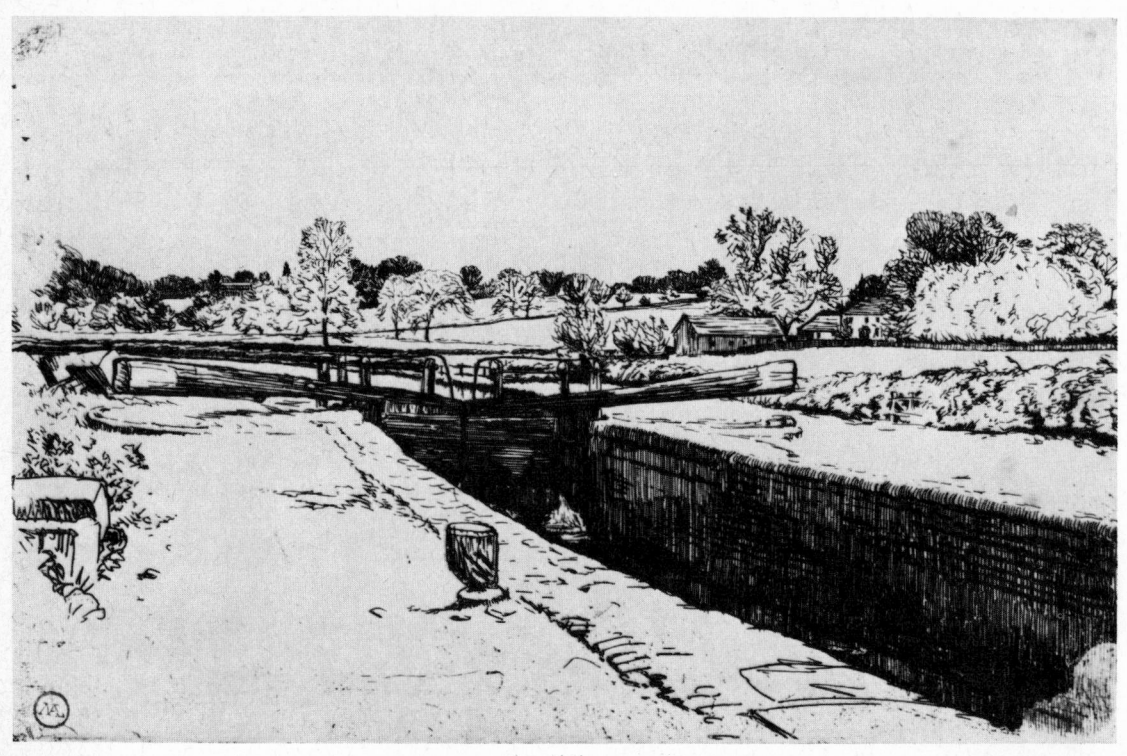

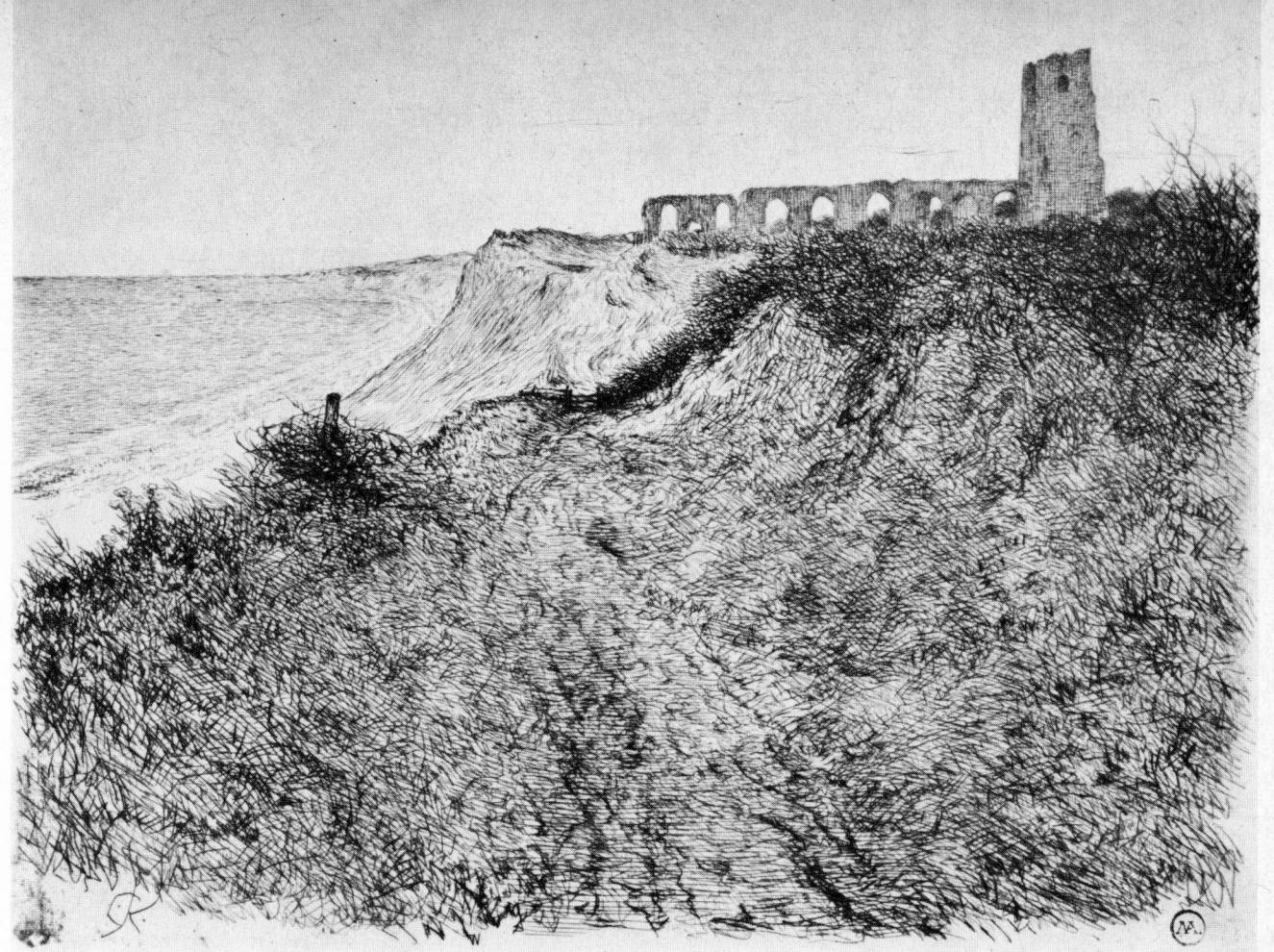

89. DUNWICH. *Etching, $5\frac{1}{2} \times 7$ in. London, Victoria and Albert Museum.*

'I defy any one, at desolate, exquisite Dunwich, to be disappointed in anything. The minor key is struck here with a felicity that leaves no sigh to be breathed, no loss to be suffered . . . Dunwich is not even the ghost of its dead self; almost all you can say of it is that it consists of the mere letters of its old name. The coast, up and down, for miles, has been, for more centuries than I presume to count, gnawed away by the sea. All the grossness of its positive life is now at the bottom of the German Ocean, which moves for ever, like a ruminating beast, an insatiable, indefatigable lip. . . . There is a presence in what is missing—there is history in there being so little. It is so little, today, that every item of the handful counts. The biggest items are of course the two ruins, the great church and its tall tower, now quite on the verge of the cliff, and the crumbled, ivied wall of the immense cincture of the Priory.'—Henry James, in 1897.

Dunwich was Charles Keene's favourite place on the coast of his native county of Suffolk; from the beach there he played the bagpipes to the North Sea (page 196). The cliff has long been eaten back to the west of the church, of which nothing is left.

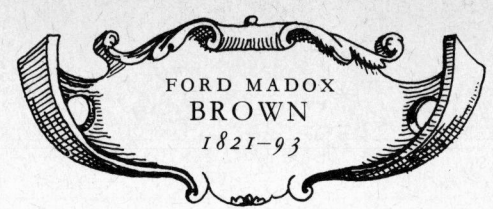

FORD MADOX
BROWN
1821–93

ONE OF THOSE VICTORIAN ARTISTS whose earnestness and application (and posthumous celebrity) outstripped rather modest talents, which they misapplied to concepts of uplift and didacticism. He was born at Calais, the son of a ship's purser, and had his training as an artist in Belgium and in Paris. England became his permanent home in 1846. He soon influenced the young Pre-Raphaelites and was influenced in turn by their version of the naturalism of the century, in what he called 'purity of natural colour' and 'simple imitation'. As an independent, he inclined a little more to landscape for its own sake, painting out of doors and adding local colour to local colour in shrill and brilliant addition sums. He made himself into a Londoner for the most part, finding his landscape motifs in the quiet surrounding country—the open country on the Kentish and Essex sides of the Thames Estuary, in Middlesex and in the artists' Hampstead. He painted in the Lakes in 1848, before his Pre-Raphaelite years, and was in the Isle of Wight in 1851 with Holman Hunt.
Page 195.

90. HEATH STREET, HAMPSTEAD. Detail from *Work*, 1852–62. *Oil, the whole picture,* 53 × 77 *in. Manchester, City Art Gallery.*

Brown painted the background of his picture out of doors in Hampstead in July and August. 'In July he had taken lodgings in Hampstead with the view of painting the background of *Work*. This he did, working assiduously in Heath Street, a proceeding which excited the admiration and astonishment of idle passers-by. The weather was by no means propitious, but on very rainy days he worked in an unhorsed four-wheeled cab.' *Ford Madox Brown,* by F. M. Hueffer, 1896.

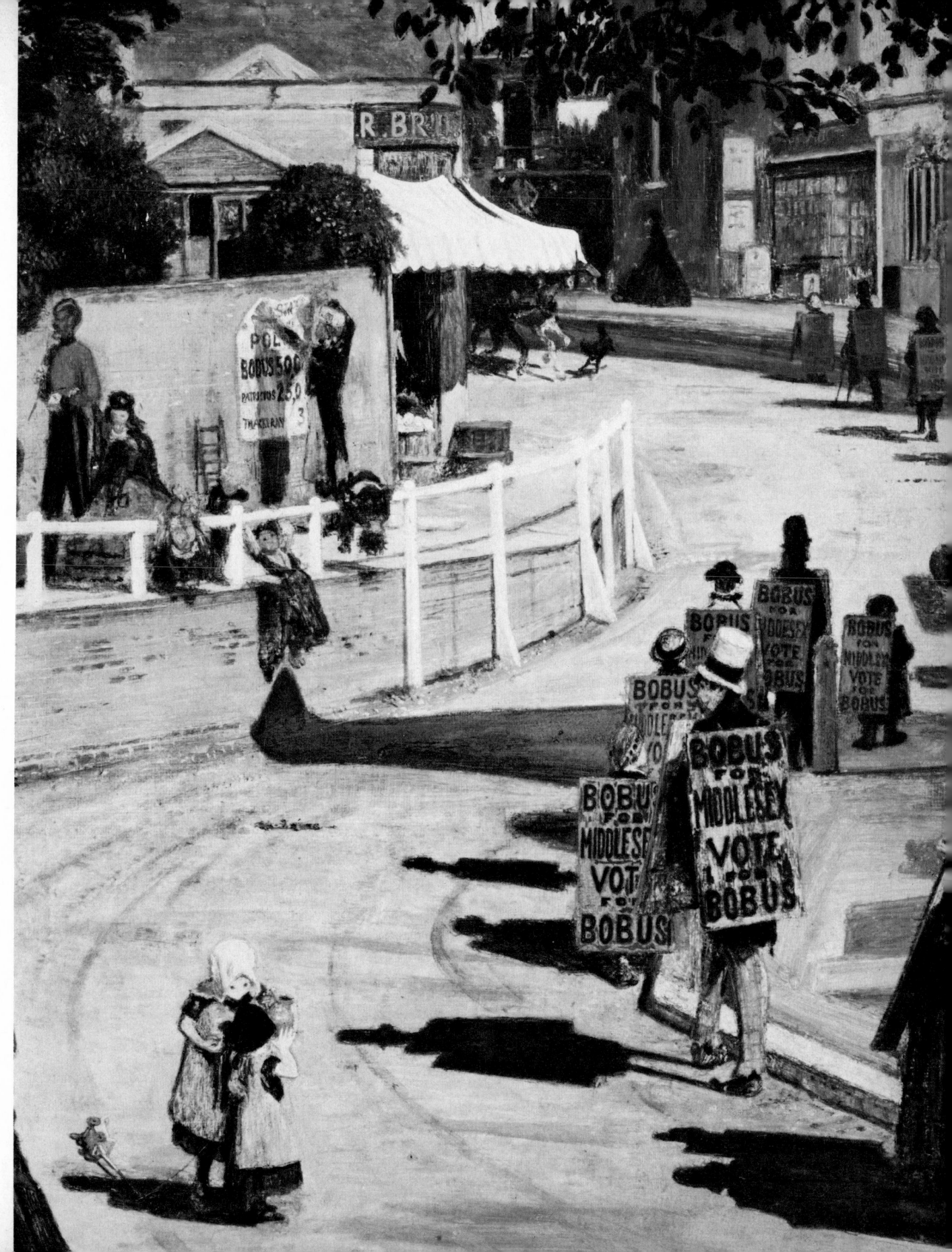

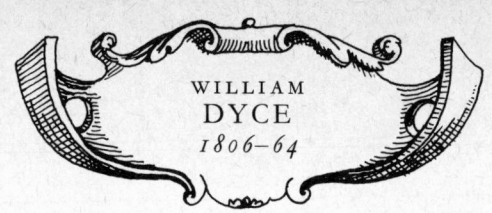
His *Pegwell Bay* seems to be the one landscape—indeed the one painting—of distinction by this learned Aberdeen Scot who was so able a busybody in the official art affairs of the mid-19th century, interested in art education, art history, aesthetics, fresco painting, church music and electro-magnetism. As an art student in Rome in the late 1820s he was in touch with the German Nazarene painters and so was the more inclined to paint devotional canvases which he then found unsaleable in Aberdeen or London. He took to portraits and subject pictures, and the provision of frescoes in the new House of Lords and elsewhere. Almost all his known painting is academic and worthless. Then in the 1850s he painted under the happily muted influence of Pre-Raphaelite naturalism, and produced his cool *Pegwell Bay*, in which the figures have a discreetly acceptable relationship with the scene from nature. It is the picture by which he escapes oblivion. In other Pre-Raphaelitish landscapes Dyce will insert, with a maximum of indiscretion and mawkish artificiality, a figure of Christ—so the landscape can be called *Gethsemane*; or a figure of George Herbert—so the landscape is Christianized by the double presence in it of the devotional poet and the dreaming spire of Salisbury Cathedral.

91. CULVER CLIFFS, ISLE OF WIGHT, *c.* 1855. *Watercolour,* $6\frac{1}{2} \times 10\frac{1}{4}$ *in. George Goyder collection.*

The view is of the Red Cliff and the Culver Cliff on the south coast of the Isle of Wight. See below, Plates 97 and 98.

92. PEGWELL BAY—A RECOLLECTION OF OCTOBER 5TH, 1858. 1859. *Oil, 25 × 35 in. London, Tate Gallery.*

The northern end of Pegwell Bay, in the Isle of Thanet in Kent. In the distance, left, the Norman tower of the grand church of Minster-in-Thanet. Careful inspection of the picture reveals Donati's Comet, which had appeared earlier in 1858. The foreground figures are one of Dyce's children, his wife (who is picking up cockles) and her two sisters.

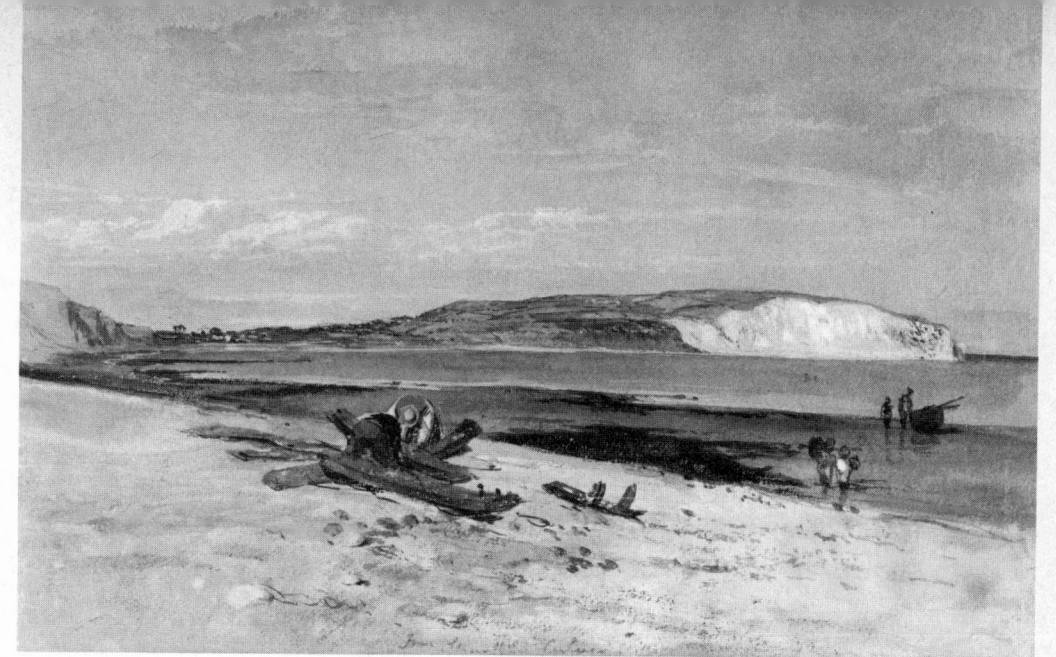

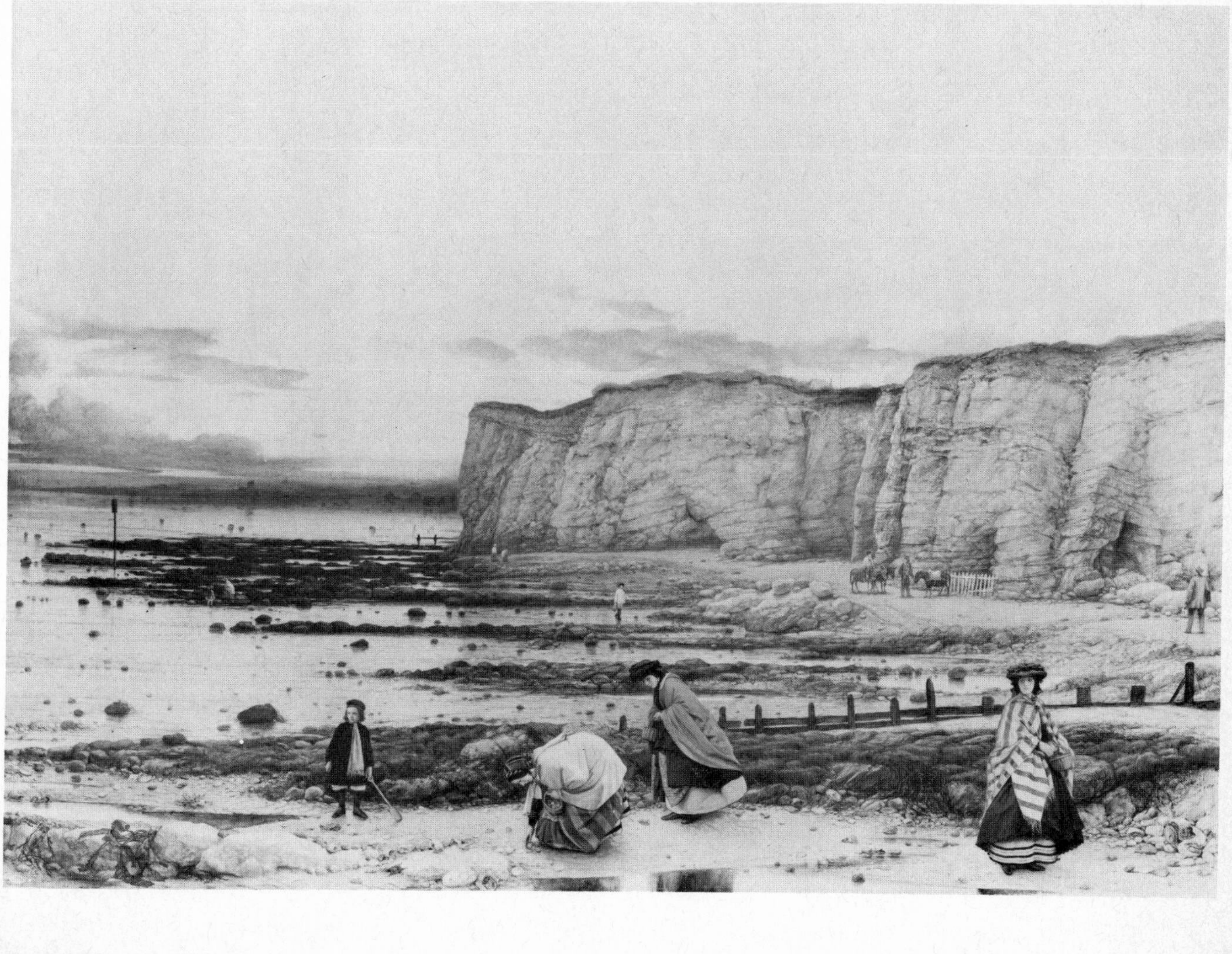

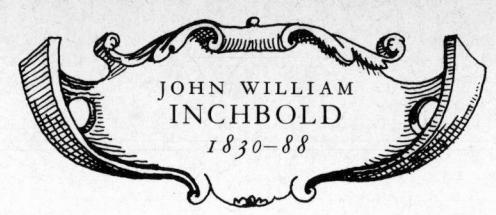

LANDSCAPE PAINTER, etcher and poet, on terms as a young man with Holman Hunt and the other Pre-Raphaelites, and a friend of Tennyson, Coventry Patmore and Swinburne. Ruskin encouraged him and hectored him on the need to paint from nature with detailed accuracy. As the son of a newspaper proprietor in Leeds, where he was born and where he died, he could afford the unpopularity of his work. He painted from the scenery of Cornwall, Devon, Yorkshire (Gordale Scar), Scotland; and then looked for many of his motifs abroad, in Switzerland, Italy, Spain, Algeria. Swinburne commemorated him in a long peom, recalling their early experiences of

> Tintagel, and the long Trebarwith sand,
> Lone Camelford, and Boscastle divine
> With dower of southern blossom, bright and bland
> Above the roar of granite-baffled brine

and speaking of him as a painter of light, which he was:

> To thee the sun spake, and the morning sang
> Notes deep and clear as life or heaven.

93. A STUDY IN MARCH, 1854–5. *Oil, 20 × 13¾ in. Oxford, Ashmolean Museum.*

When he exhibited this picture at the Royal Academy in 1855 Inchbold gave it a motto from *The Excursion* by Wordsworth, which he misquoted as if from memory: 'When the primrose flower peeped forth to give an earnest of the spring'. The full passage fits even better:

>   I returned,
> And took my rounds along this road again
> When on its sunny bank the primrose flower
> Peeped forth, to give an earnest of the Spring.
>   (*Book First*, 813–6)

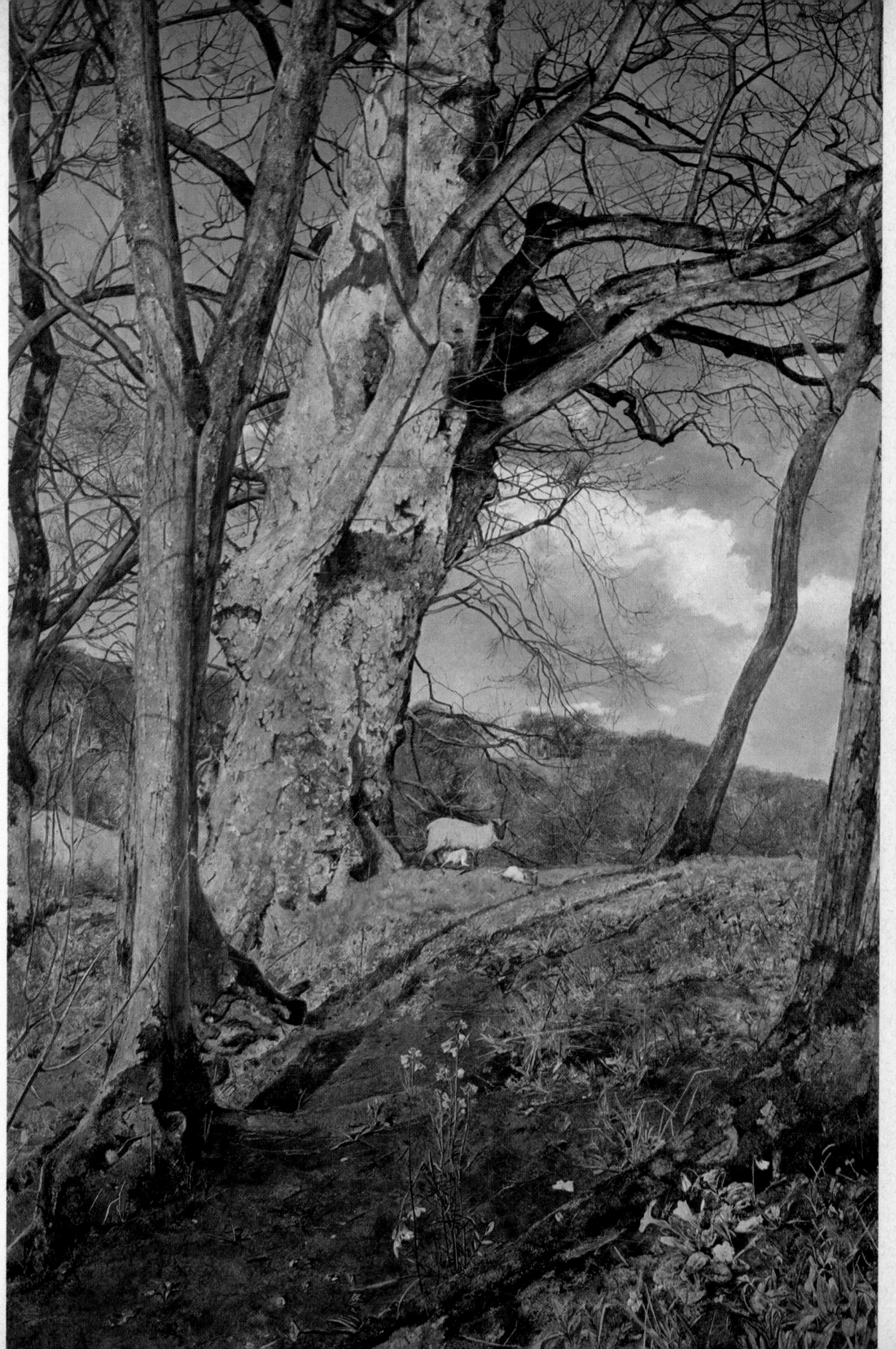

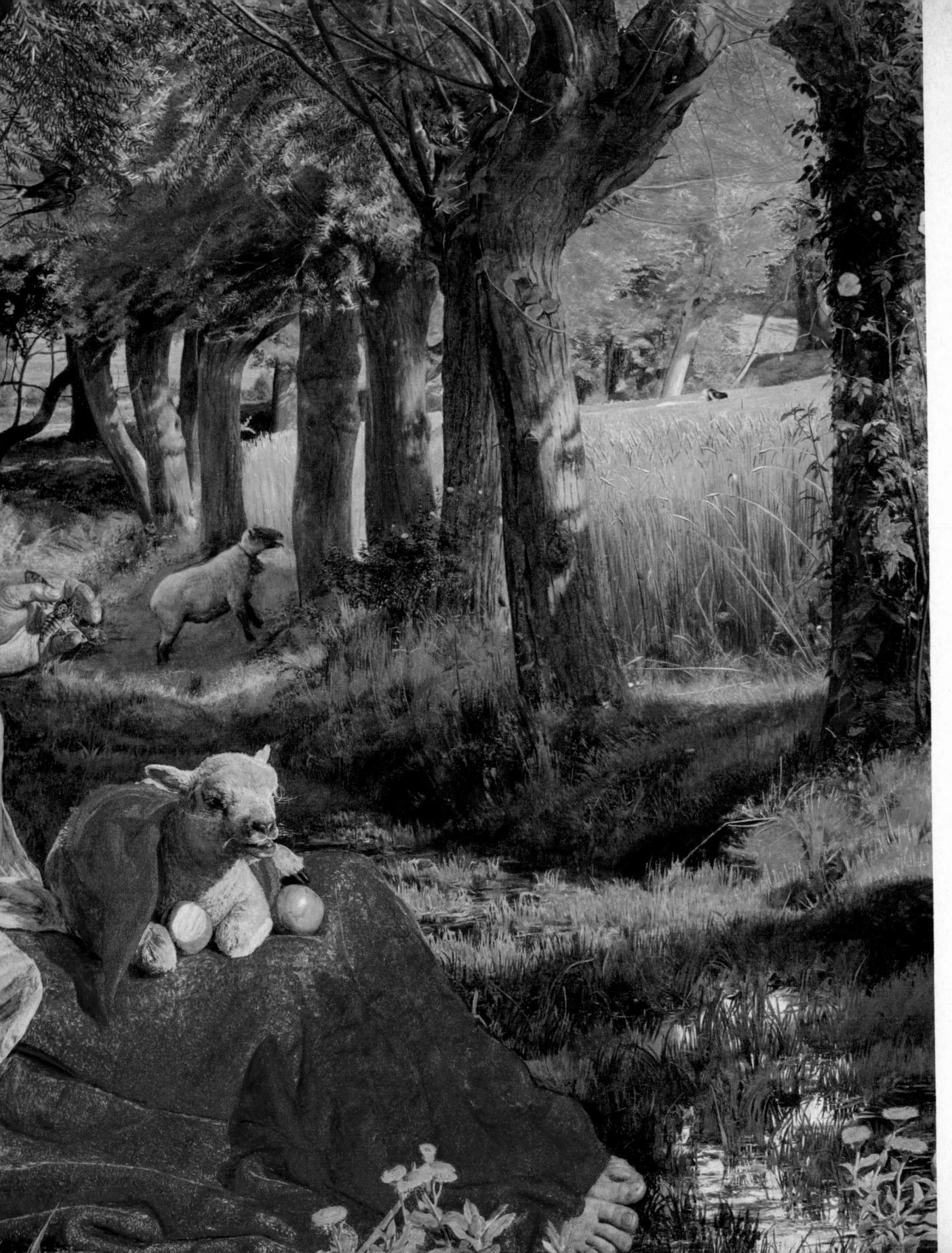

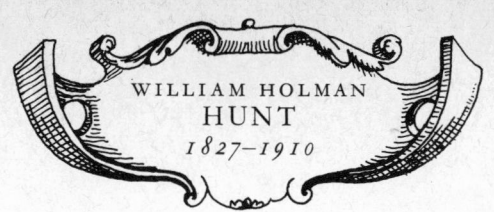

THOUGH he had some gift for landscape, Holman Hunt used it as an adjunct. Landscape gave him the mise-en-scène for his subject pictures of modern life or times past. In a neo-medieval way it filled the corners for him in such works of revolutionary but all the while extremely Victorian moralism and religiosity. As one of those who founded the Pre-Raphaelite Brotherhood in 1848, he stuck to the severest Pre-Raphaelite discipline. Like his figures, his landscape corners had to be 'real' or 'true', their colours glowing, or glaring, in full sunlight. For such use he made landscape studies on the Essex marshes; in Surrey; at Knole in Kent; along the Thames; around Rye and Winchelsea; in Devon and Cornwall, and elsewhere. Holman Hunt eked out his small talent with hard work and immeasurable self-esteem. For Impressionism (see page 197) as a betrayal of High Art and as another example of the well-known impudence of the French, he developed a sick hatred which no doubt helped to procure him his Order of Merit (1905), and his burial in St. Paul's, not far from the City warehouse which his father had managed. *Page* 196.

94. LANDSCAPE AT EWELL: landscape background from *The Hireling Shepherd,* 1851. *Oil, the whole picture,* 30 × 42½ *in. Manchester, City Art Gallery.*

For Holman Hunt on the painting of this landscape background at Ewell in Surrey, in company with Millais, who worked there on his *Ophelia,* see below, page 197.

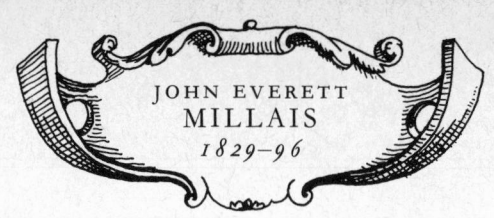

LIKE OTHER PRE-RAPHAELITES Millais (who founded the Pre-Raphaelite Brother-hood in 1848, with Rossetti and Holman Hunt) used landscape at first as an accompaniment to his story pictures. He had more interest in subject and portrait than in nature; and after his marriage to Ruskin's former wife in 1855, when he was 26, the stimulus of Pre-Raphaelite insistence on 'truth' and nature weakened in him, and the tension of his drawing and painting declined to a conventional expression of the shallowest feelings, which simply made use of landscape forms. The delightful landscape background of *The Blind Girl* was painted in 1854 when Millais was in the hyperaesthesia of his relationship with Effie Ruskin. The rest of the picture dates from 1856, the year in which it was exhibited. By then Millais was on the way to becoming the most celebrated and richest, and most vapid, of Victorian painters. Finally he became President of the Royal Academy, and like his friend Holman Hunt he was to be buried in St. Paul's. For Holman Hunt, Millais and nature, see page 197.

95. WINCHELSEA, SUSSEX, 1854. Background from *The Blind Girl*, 1856. *Oil, the whole picture,* 31¾ × 21 *in. Birmingham, Museum and Art Gallery.*

Painted from the meadows below Winchelsea, on the east, across the Royal Military Canal. Millais and his friend Thackeray were together at Winchelsea in 1854, Thackeray working on his unfinished novel *Denis Duval*, set in Winchelsea, while Millais did hard labour on his landscape background.

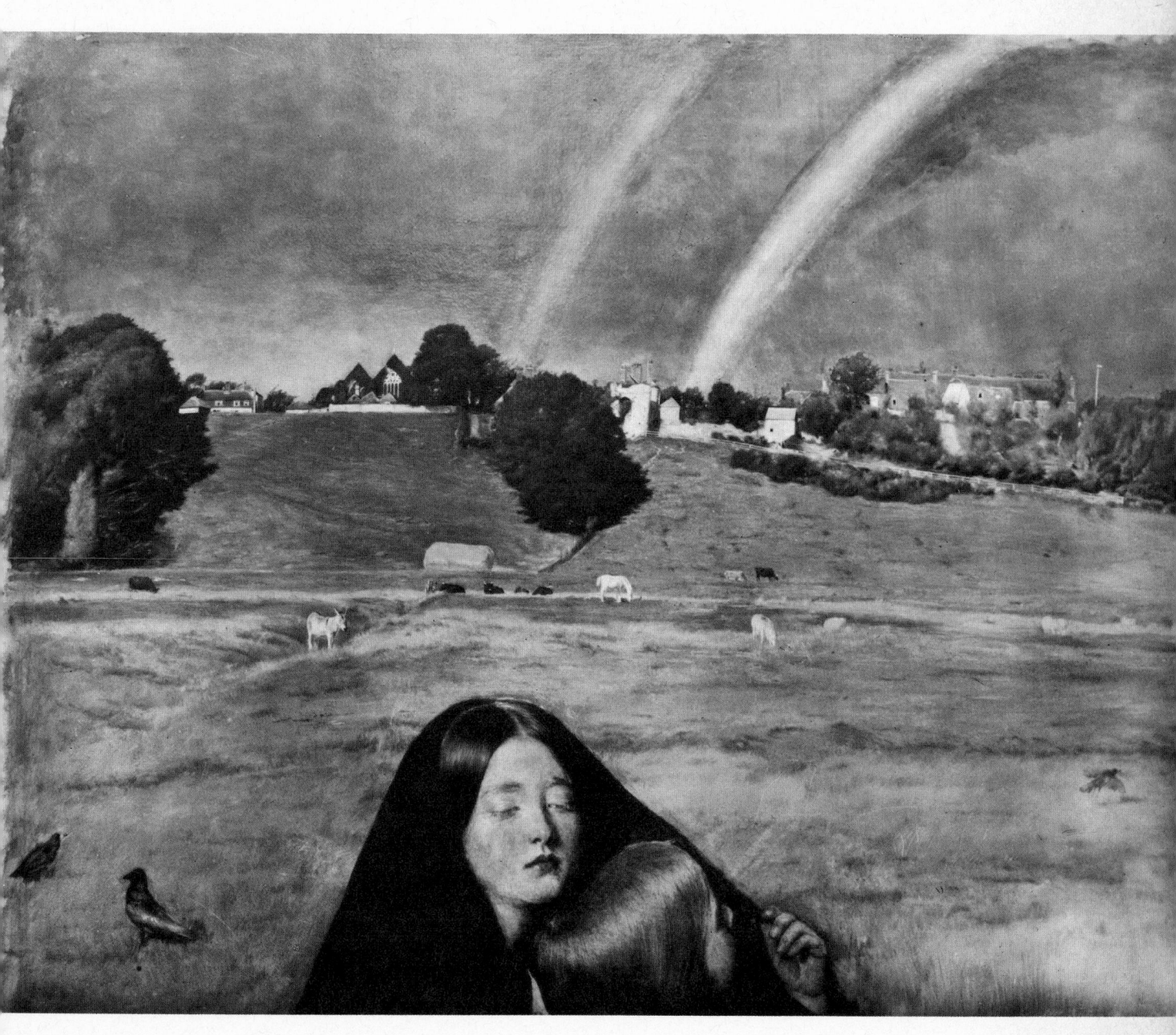

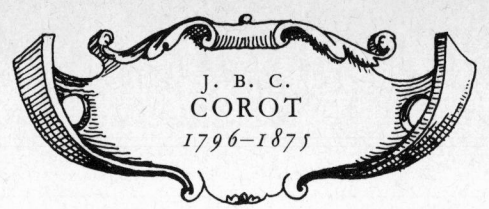

J. B. C.
COROT
1796–1875

'QUITE ALONE, I threw myself on nature, and here we are,' said Corot of himself as the young artist who had just finished a neo-classical training. Several English artists of Corot's generation, such as Linnell or Danby, began by throwing themselves on nature, and would have agreed with him that the artist should 'imitate' his scene conscientiously, while preserving at the same time and at all costs the first impression it had made on him: 'If we have been really touched, the sincerity of our emotion will transmit itself to others.' They were less strong, they were poor and they had to please, whereas Corot had money to support his independence of character. He could afford to say 'I paint a woman's breast exactly as I would paint an ordinary milk bottle', and he could afford to paint in his own way. Just as well, since he was getting old before he was accepted either in France or abroad. In his *Talks About Art* (1877) the American William Morris Hunt, who worked with Millet and the Barbizon painters, remarked 'Twenty years ago nobody in Europe would buy him. He was "so peculiar!" So was Christopher Columbus. The pioneer is always peculiar.' For Corot the light and forms of France and Italy were enough. He made no more than two late visits to England, first in 1851, then again in 1862, when he painted at least three pictures, one of the Thames at Richmond (Plate 96), one of the Serpentine, and one reckoned to be of the gardens around the Crystal Palace.

Page 191.

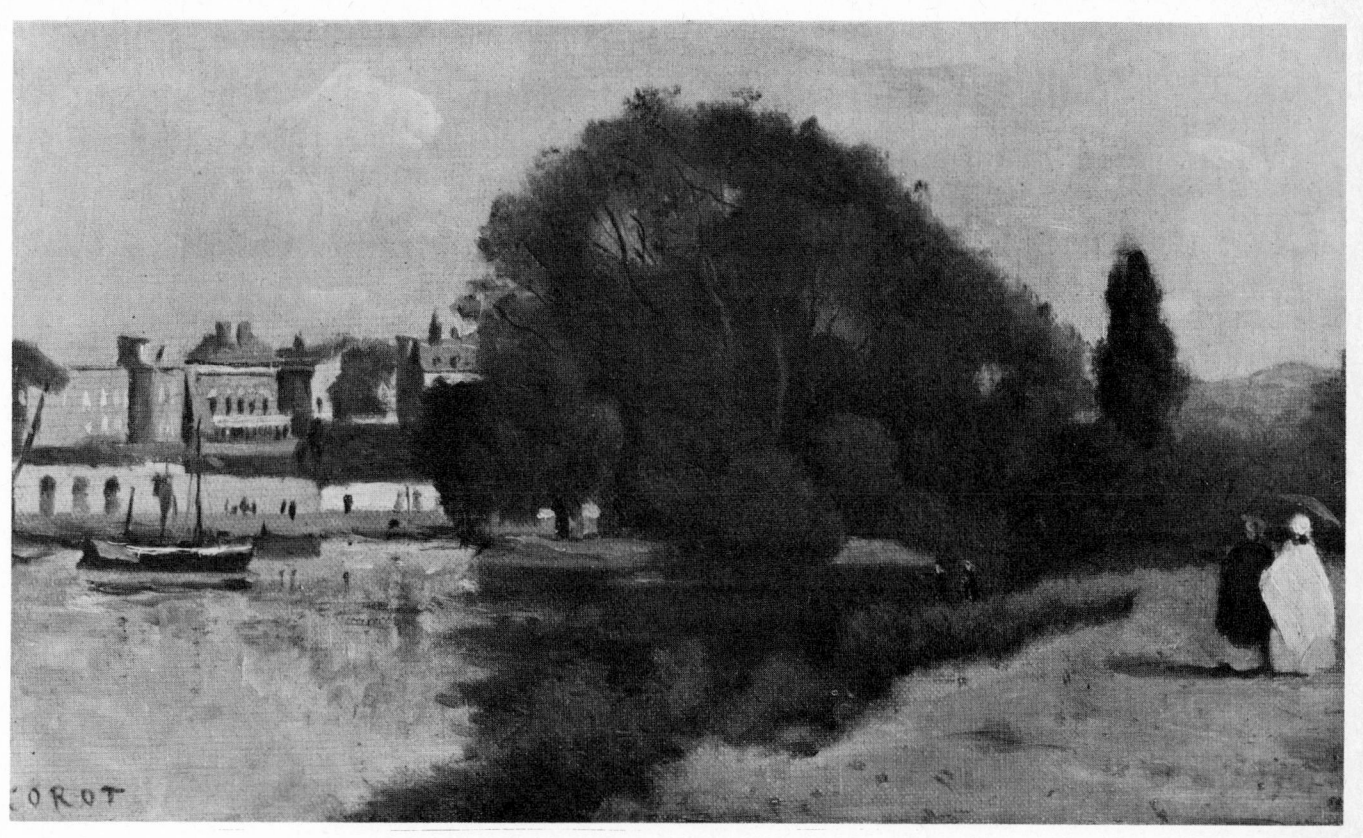

96. RICHMOND, SURREY, 1862–7. *Oil, 8½ × 14 in. Sir Anthony and Lady Hornby collection.*

The Thames at Richmond. Compare the mass of the willow trees with Corot's sentence in his account of the landscape painter's day (page 192): 'The small rounded willow trees seem to turn like wheels on the river-bank.'

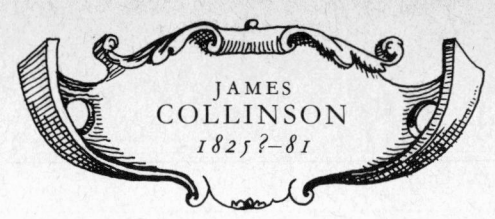

JAMES
COLLINSON
1825?–81

THE MOST REMARKABLE RESULTS of the life of this least successful of the Pre-Raphaelite Brotherhood were the poems in which the great Christina Rossetti wrote about her love for him. They were engaged, until Collinson reverted to Catholicism, left the Brotherhood for that reason, in 1850, and entered the novitiate of the Jesuits at Stonyhurst. The Jesuits found him wanting, and he took again to art and became a regular exhibitor of Victorian genre. Holman Hunt recalled him as amiable, painstaking and accurate in his drawing, 'but in his own person tame and sleepy, and so were all the figures he drew'. Perhaps that was too contemptuous. 'The Child Jesus', the long poem he contributed to *The Germ*, the little magazine of the P.R.B., has merit, and shows the Pre-Raphaelite eye for the details of landscape. He was the son of a bookseller at Mansfield.

97. MOTHER AND DAUGHTER, AND THE CULVER CLIFF, *c.* 1855. *Oil, 20¾ × 16⅝ in. Collection of Mr and Mrs Paul Mellon.*

A summer landscape, with figures, in the Isle of Wight, perhaps suggested to Collinson by Legh Richmond's Isle of Wight tales in his once famous and piously elevating *Annals of the Poor*. Collinson's picture, Burchett's *Isle of Wight* (Plate 98) and Dyce's watercolour (Plate 91) are no doubt connected and perhaps they result from a common trip to the island by all three artists. Collinson was living with Burchett in 1855 (both of them were Catholic converts), and Burchett had been a pupil under Dyce in the School of Design at South Kensington, and then one of his colleagues on the staff. For the view see note below on Burchett's painting.

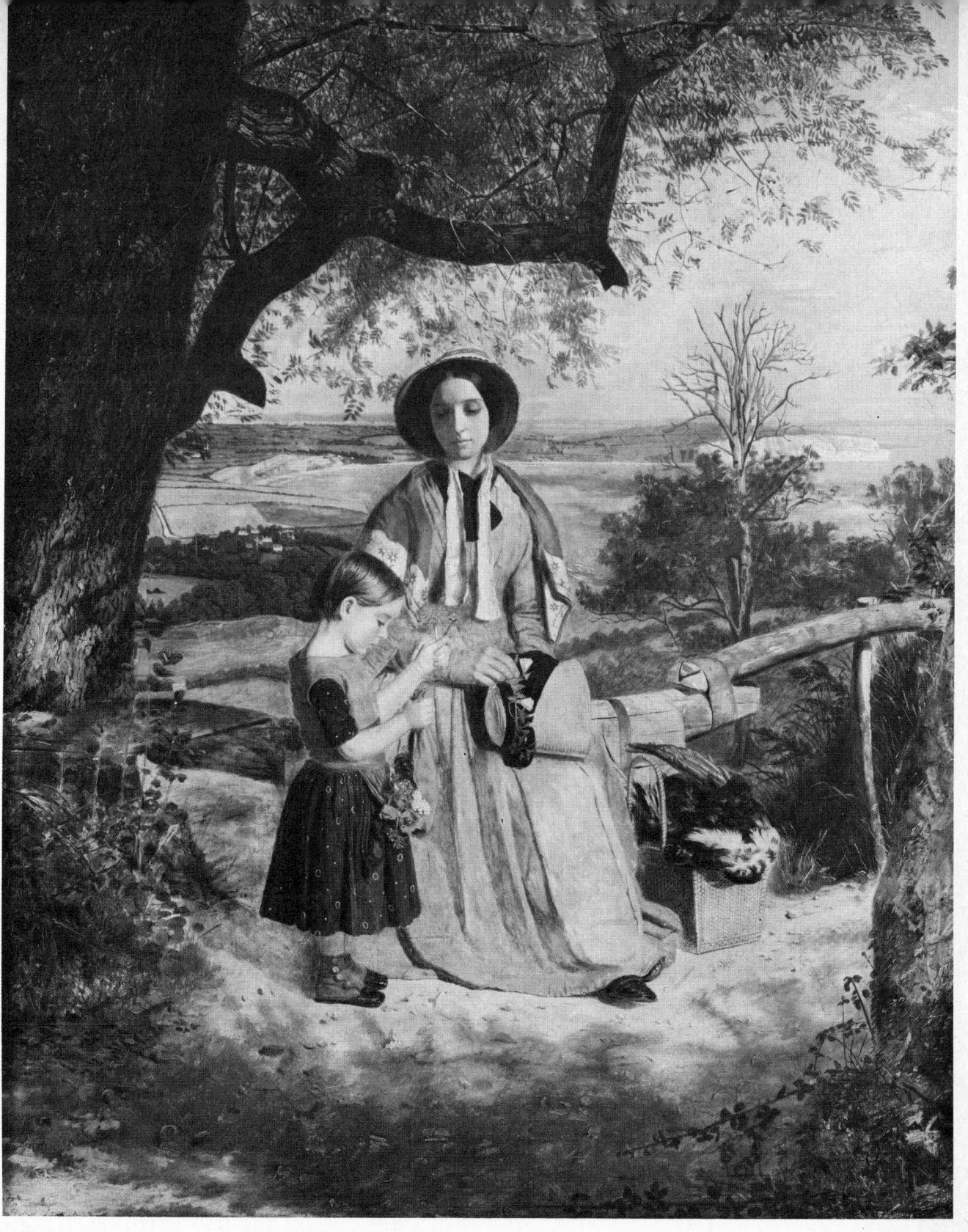

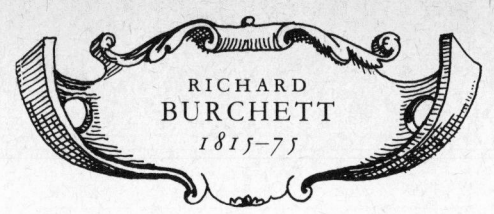

A PAINTER of landscape and history subjects who seldom exhibited and became wrapped in his career as an art teacher and a leading Victorian art official; in 1851 he became headmaster of the government's School of Design. Burchett had Pre-Raphaelite sympathies, and before the Pre-Raphaelite Brotherhood came into existence he had helped to found the Cyclographic Club, which circulated a portfolio of drawings and criticism. Members of the club included Millais, Holman Hunt, Arthur Hughes and Rossetti.

98. THE ISLE OF WIGHT, *c.* 1855. *Oil,* $13\frac{1}{2} \times 22\frac{1}{2}$ *in. London, Victoria and Albert Museum.*

See note above on Plate 97. Burchett and Collinson painted the Culver Cliff from more or less the same point, near Shanklin, which had not then developed into a maritime suburbia. From the footpath behind the old Shanklin church of St. Blasius (rebuilt in 1859), Burchett's view, like Collinson's is across Sandown Bay to Red Cliff and the striated chalk of Culver Cliff. On the down above he shows the Earl of Yarborough's memorial obelisk.

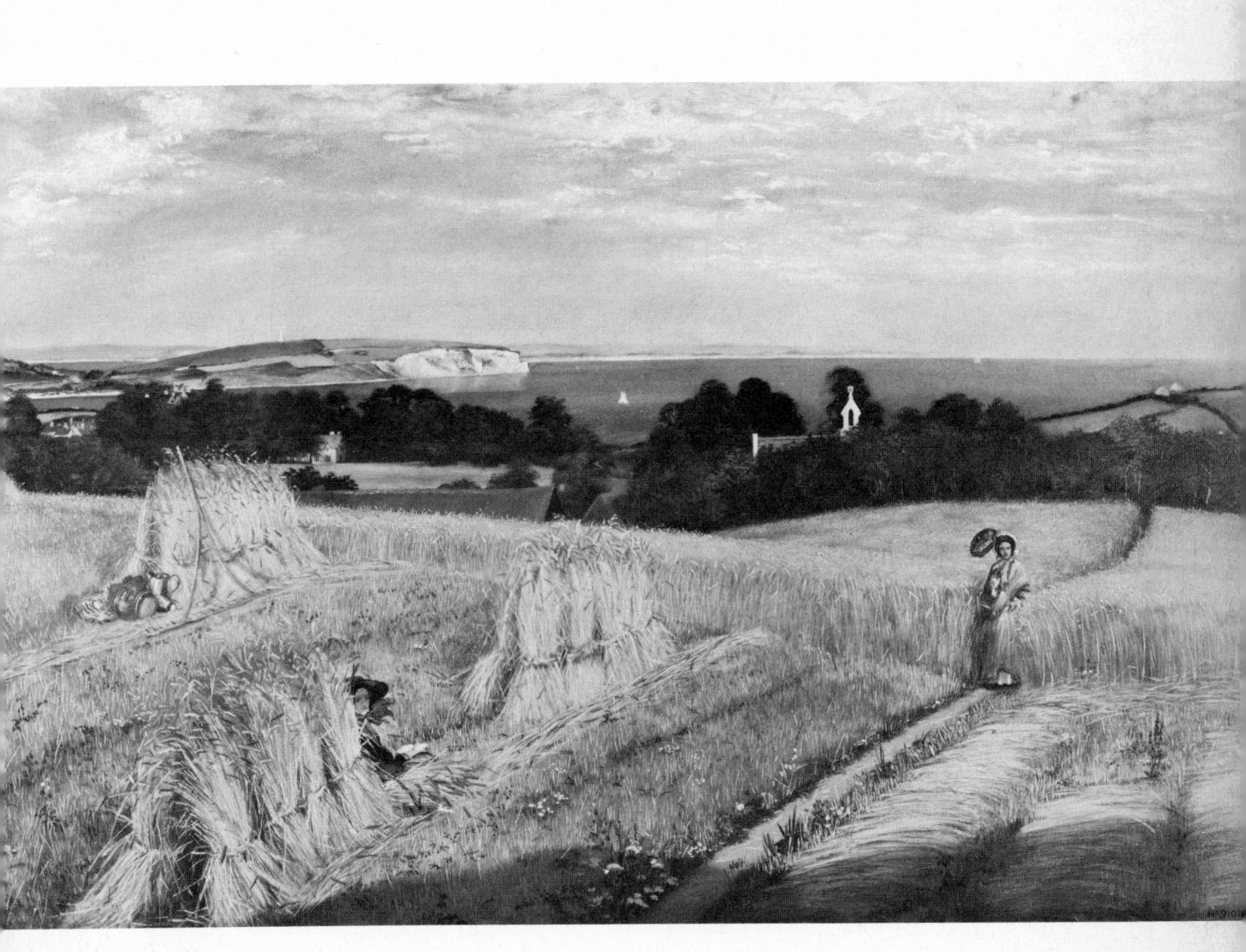

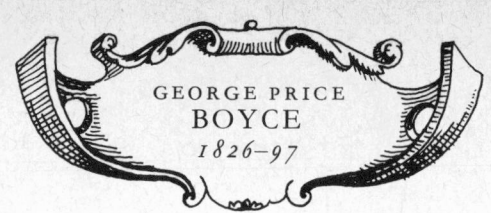

GEORGE BOYCE was a lifelong friend of Rossetti and other Pre-Raphaelites, and for some years his watercolour landscapes showed a shrillness of 'accurate' colour, and an extra attention to detail. But this Pre-Raphaelitism was absorbed in broader composition, and his landscapes became more tonal (and free of sentimental figures poised carefully in the foreground). They spoke for themselves in their construction of shape and colour. Boyce was less insular than many of his English contemporaries, and more independent. He added Charles Keene and the young Whistler to his friends, and in Paris he was on visiting terms with Corot, whose pictures he bought. The *peinture-verité* of the Barbizon landscapists evidently appealed to him, helping to modify and harmonize his effects. Allen Staley, who gives the best account of him, though he under-esteems his work, in his *Pre-Raphaelite Landscape* (1973), hazards that Boyce may have helped Whistler to the painting of his Thames nocturnes. He painted in Wales (David Cox was his first teacher), along the Thames below Oxford, in Devon, Surrey, Shropshire, Derbyshire, Co. Durham, Venice, Switzerland, Egypt, etc. One admirer of his work, not surprisingly, was the poet Gerard Manley Hopkins.

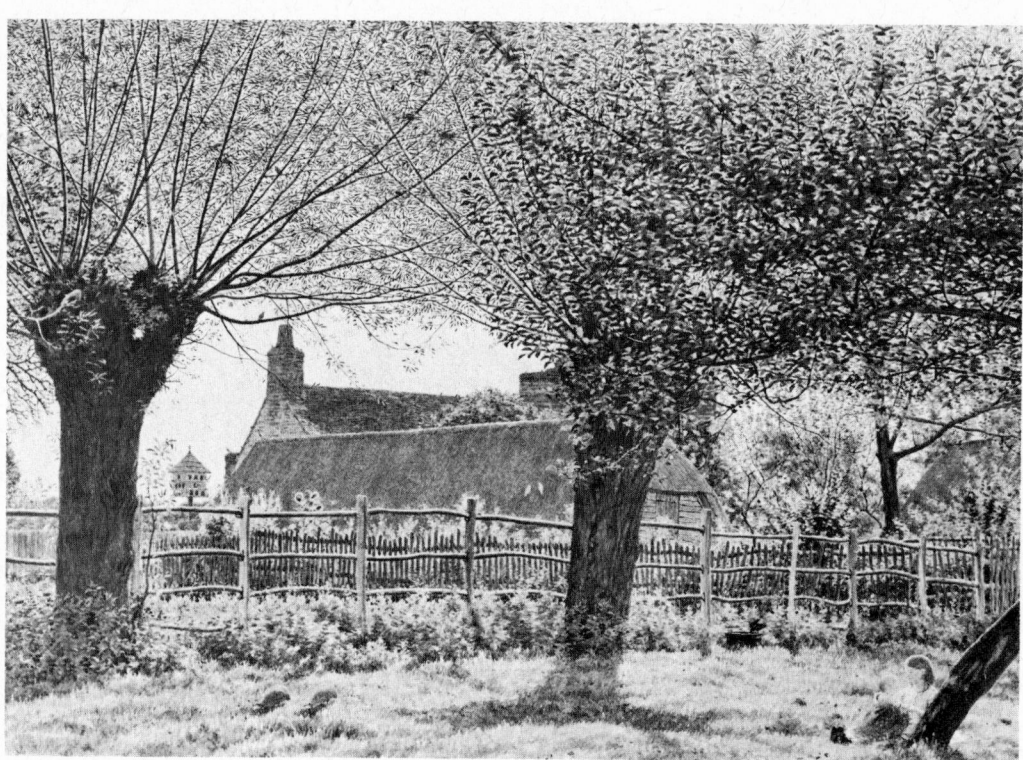

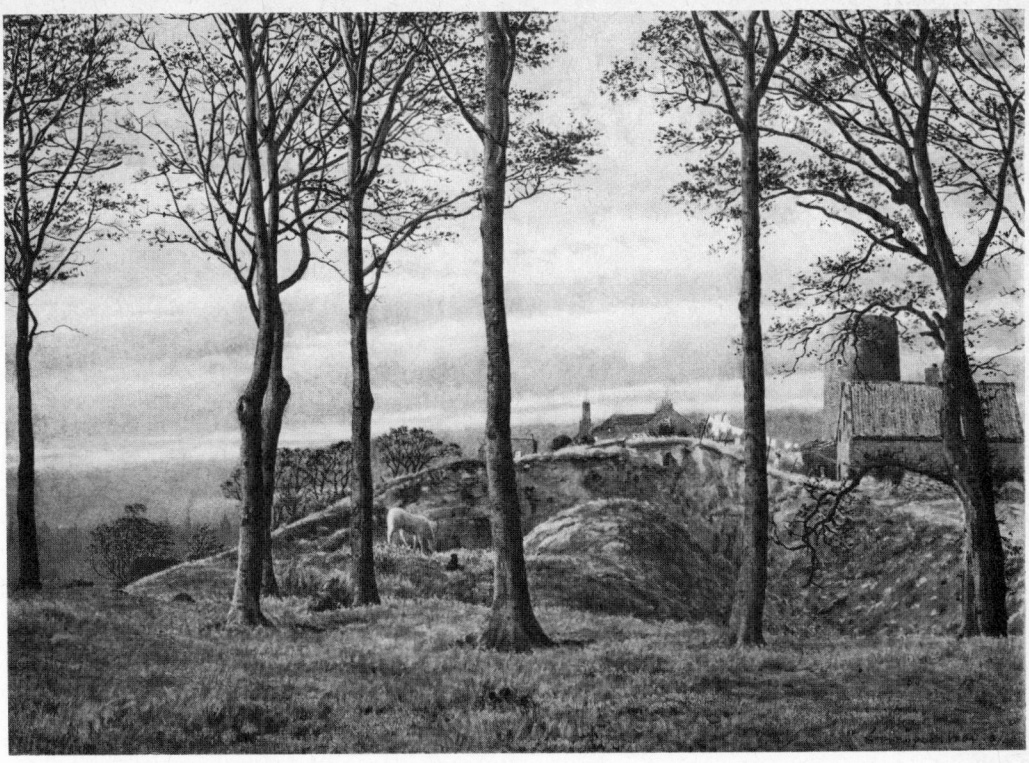

100. WINDMILL
HILLS, GATESHEAD-
ON-TYNE, 1864.
Watercolour,
11 × 15¾ in.
Newcastle upon Tyne,
Laing Art Gallery.
For the Tyne from
this point of view
which was once so
well known to
travellers and
landscape painters,
see Plate 67, Thomas
Miles Richardson's
*The Tyne from
Windmill Hills,
Gateshead.*

◁ 99. AT BINSEY,
NEAR OXFORD, 1862.
Watercolour,
12½ × 21⅛ in. Bedford,
*Cecil Higgins Art
Gallery.*

101. THE THAMES
BY NIGHT FROM THE
ADELPHI, 1855–6.
Watercolour, 8¾ × 13⅛
*in. London, Tate
Gallery.*
A watercolour at one
time in the collection
of the great William
Morris.

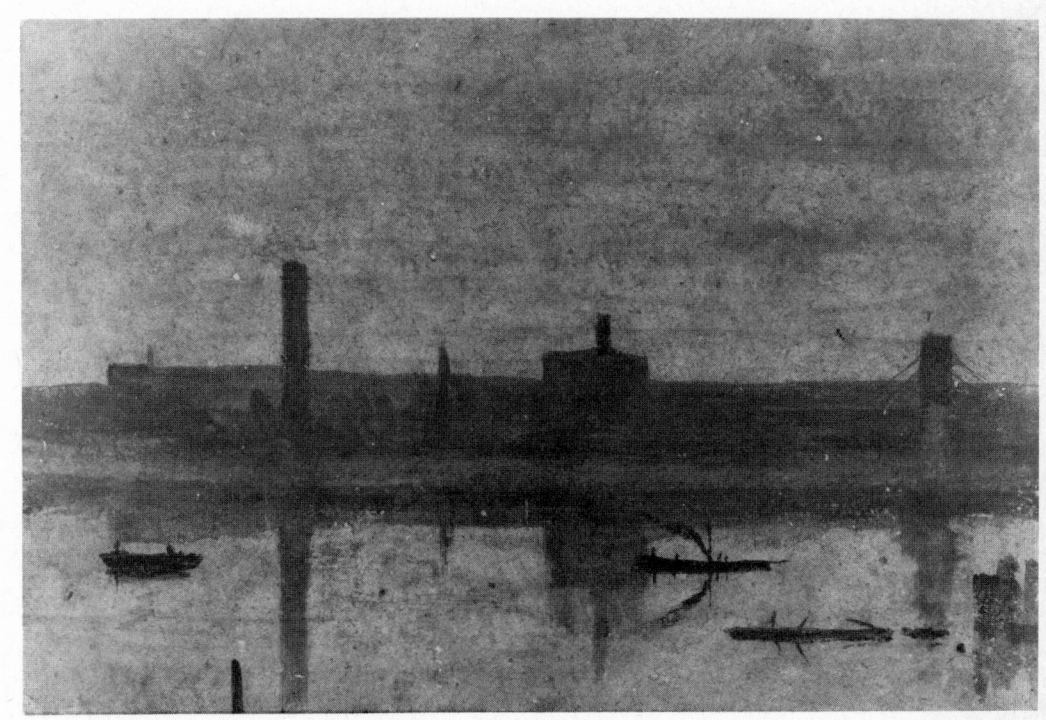

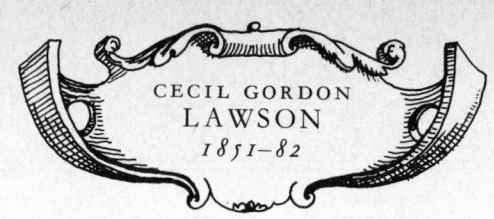

LANDSCAPE PAINTER, born at Wellington in Shropshire, son of a portrait painter from Scotland. With his family he later moved to Chelsea, to a house on Cheyne Walk, from which he painted *Cheyne Walk, Chelsea,* his first Royal Academy picture, exhibited in 1870 when he was only nineteen. In a short life he lived and worked at Wrotham in Kent, using a barn as a studio (1874) and at Haslemere in Surrey (1879); looking also for landscape subjects in North Wales, Wharfedale, Sussex and North Devon. Many of his landscapes are sentimentalized in one way or another, such as the introduction of women and children or of some literary reference. In his *Cheyne Walk* the figure on the left leaning on a stick is that of Carlyle.

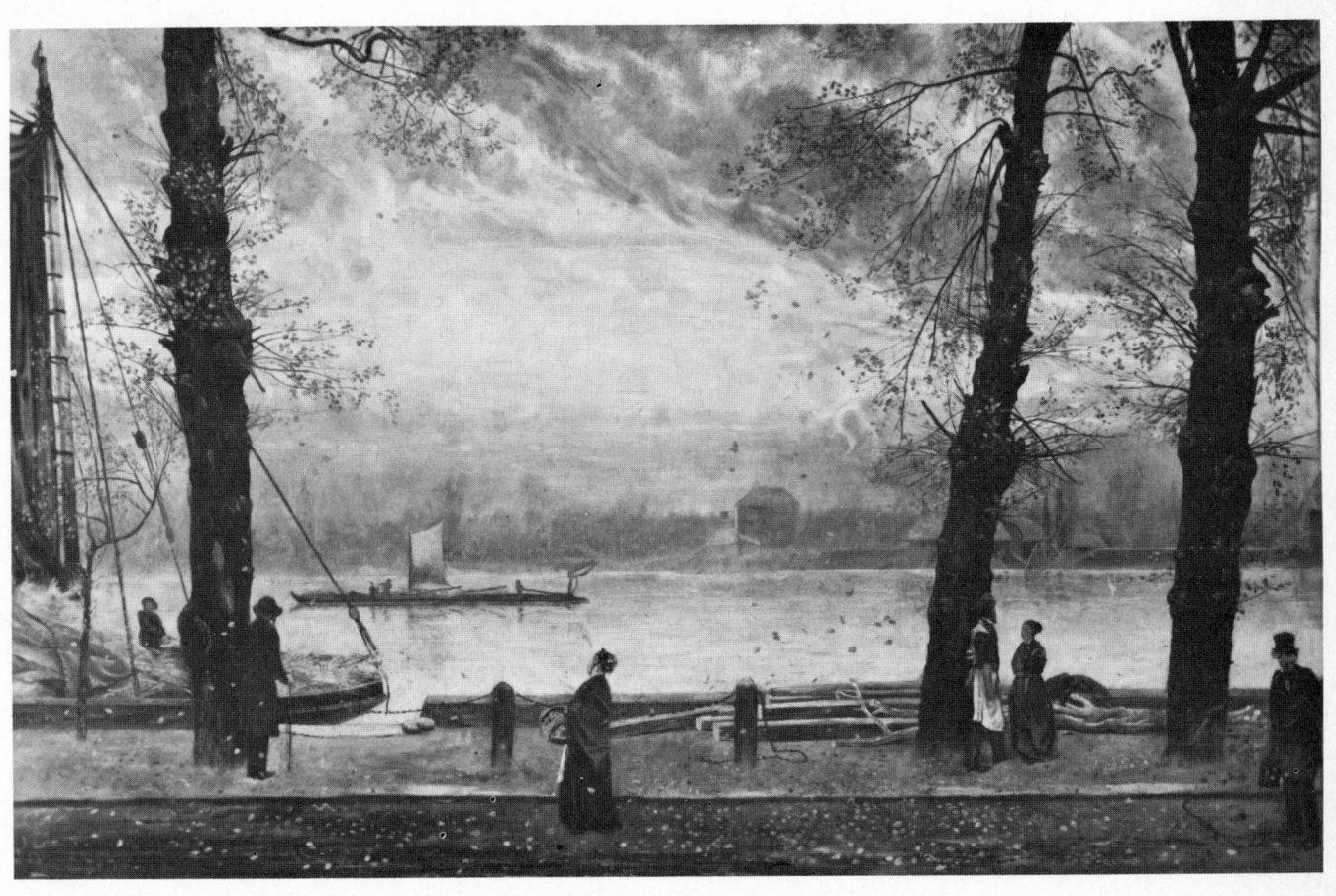

102. CHEYNE WALK, CHELSEA, 1869–70. *Oil,* $28\frac{3}{8} \times 38\frac{1}{4}$ *in. Private collection.*

Cheyne Walk, with barges moored alongside the road before the infinite attraction of the old Thames-side was damaged by the building of the Embankment in 1872.

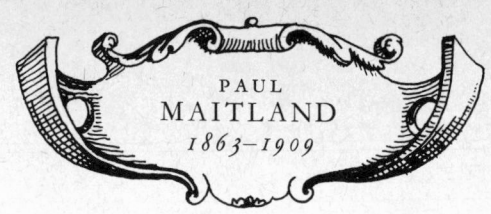

SICKERT has left descriptions of his friend Paul Maitland, Chelsea-born artist who painted Whistler's Chelsea in his own more realistic way. In 1889 Sickert brought together a group of young artists who exhibited as 'The London Impressionists'. Maitland was one of them. His teacher had been Whistler's close friend, the London Frenchman Théodore Roussel, colour-etcher and painter of *The Reading Girl,* in the Tate Gallery. He was a hunchback, small, strong, solitary, who was to be seen painting along the Chelsea Embankment or in Kensington Gardens. In argument about painting 'Maitland would agree, or else he would correct you with a tiny brief and grating *mot,* that was in its turn corrected by an affectionate upward gleam from his light eyes that was unforgettable. He had reason to be very sure of his own powers, and he treated *de pouvoir en pouvoir.*' Sickert writes of his last encounter with Maitland. He saw him from a bus in Kensington High Street 'walking home loaded with the apparatus of the painter from nature', he got off and caught him up, and Maitland took him back to his house in Wright's Lane, off the High Street, 'into a large studio that was piled like an arena from the tiny bit of clear floor in the centre to the ceiling, with his paintings, the whole work of his short life.' Maitland is one of those many painters pushed out of sight by the strident, neglected by art officials, and still waiting for adequate recognition.

103. BATTERSEA BRIDGE IN THE EIGHTIES. *Oil,* 10 × 12 *in. London, Private collection.*

104. CHEYNE WALK: THE CORNER OF BEAUFORT STREET. *Oil,* $8\frac{3}{4} \times 8\frac{1}{2}$ *in. London, Tate Gallery.*

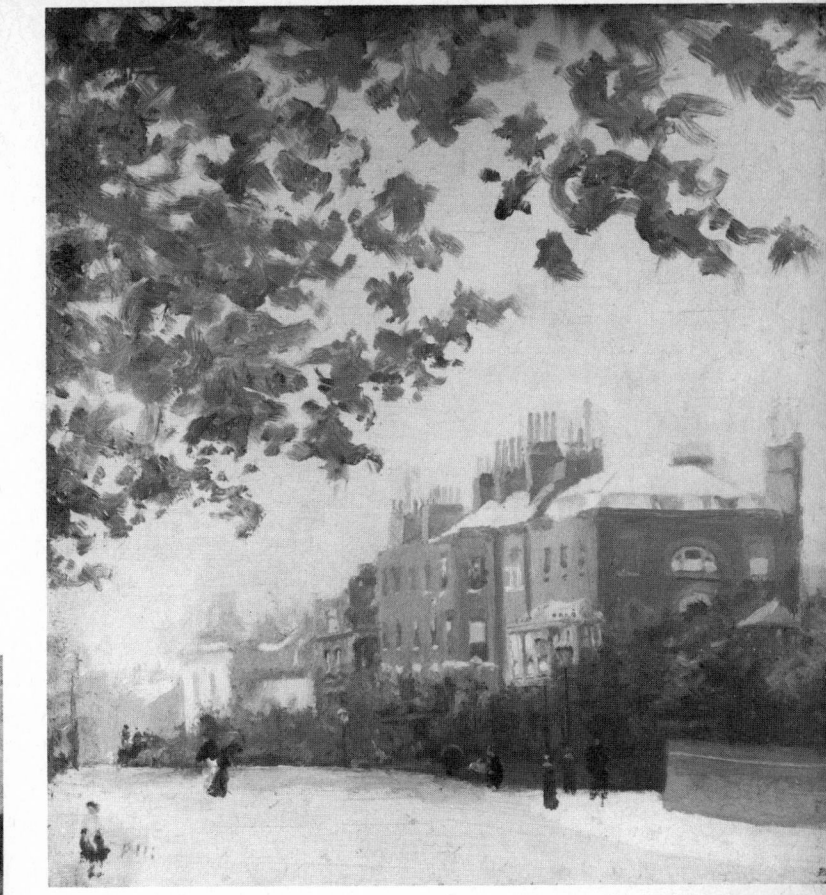

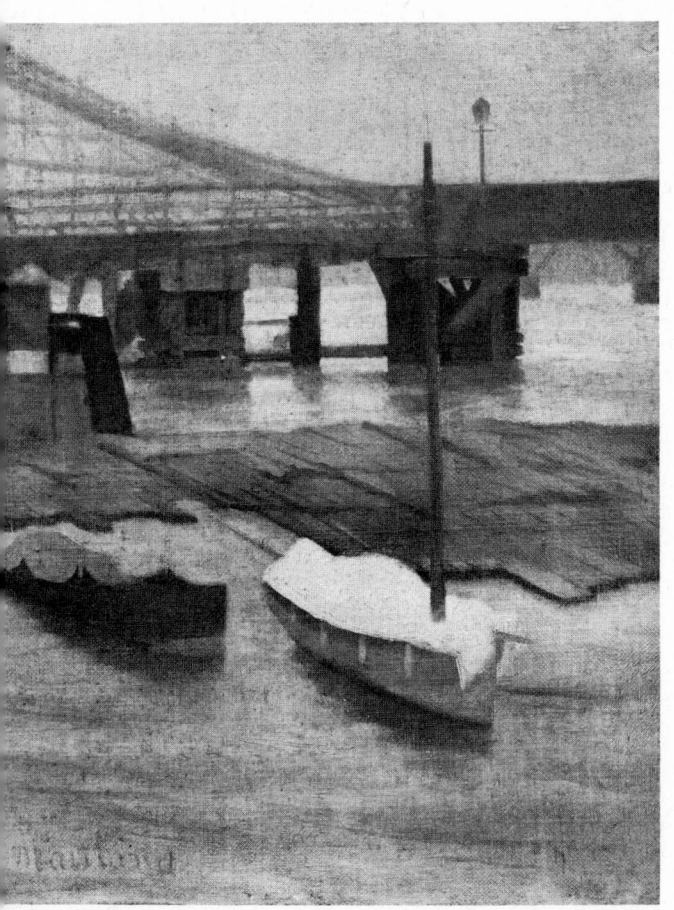

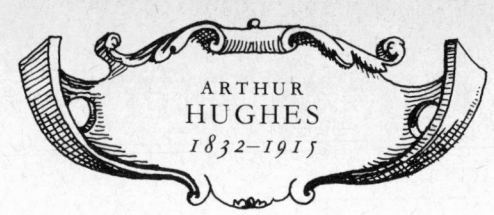

PAINTER AND ILLUSTRATOR, a Pre-Raphaelite friend and fellow-traveller, who sometimes enclosed his figures of genre or poetic narrative in fresh landscapes of acidly green spring or early summer. 'Young, handsome, silent' is how Ford Madox Brown described him in the company of other young artists. He lived modestly in a riverside house at Putney, later at Wallington, near Croydon, on the Wandle, later still at Kew Green, where he died; always about, always welcome, but unassertive and not greatly impressing himself on his friends. He enlisted among the 'Fine Art Workmen' of William Morris's famous firm of Morris, Marshall, Faulkner and Co., in 1861, withdrawing before the firm was registered, though he contributed one design for stained glass. Millais was his first inspiration (they met in 1852) and he looked up to him as to an archangel. Millais in turn looked down on him as to a mouse, in his *Proscribed Royalist*. Hughes was the model for the hunted man who peers out of the hollow tree in a mouselike attitude, true, no doubt, to life or character. After the 1860s his pleasantly sentimental art drifted into insipidity.

105. HOME FROM THE SEA, 1856–63. *Oil, 20 × 25¾ in. Oxford, Ashmolean Museum.*

The history of *Home from the Sea* (which Hughes also called *A Mother's Grave*) is given in Ironside and Gere, *Pre-Raphaelite Painters,* 1948. Hughes painted the background first of all, 'from nature during the summer of 1856, in the old churchyard at Chingford, Essex.' The small perpendicular church, with its brick porch of the sixteenth century, was then ruinated and grown over with ivy, as the picture shows. When Hughes painted Chingford churchyard and church they were not engulfed, as they are now, with housing. The view from this high situation westward across the River Lea was then rural, and open country stretched northward to Epping Forest.

In this landscape background Hughes set his favourite dog roses, a symbol for him of spring or May time, and evanescence. About their presence in the picture which became *The Long Engagement* he wrote to the poet William Allingham that painting them in had 'been a kind of match against time with me, they passing away so soon, like all lovely things *under* the sun (eh?) and as sensitive as beautiful. The least hint of rain, just a dark cloud passing over, closes them up for the rest of the day perhaps.' (*Letters to William Allingham*, ed. H. Allingham and E. B. Williams, 1911.)

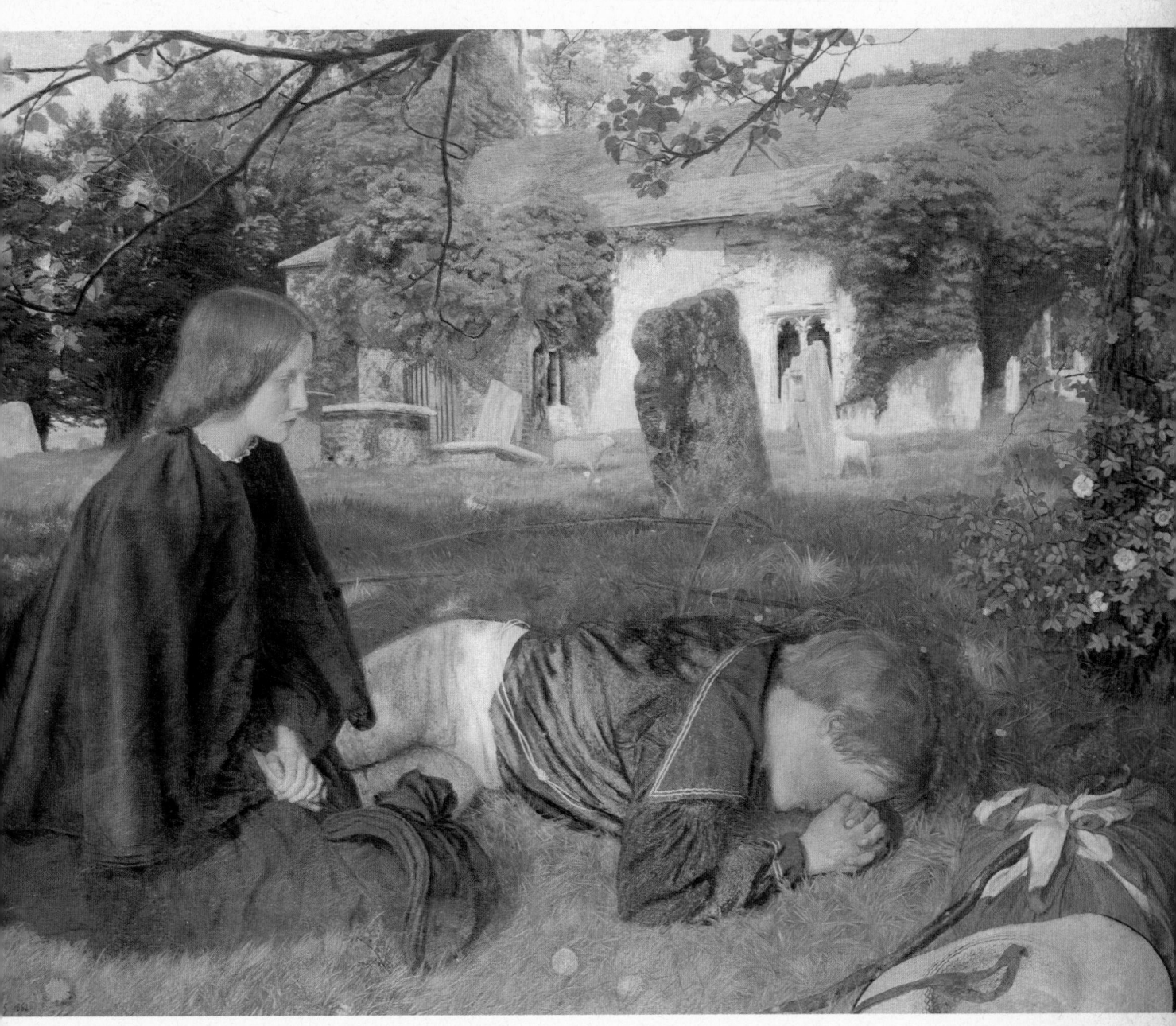

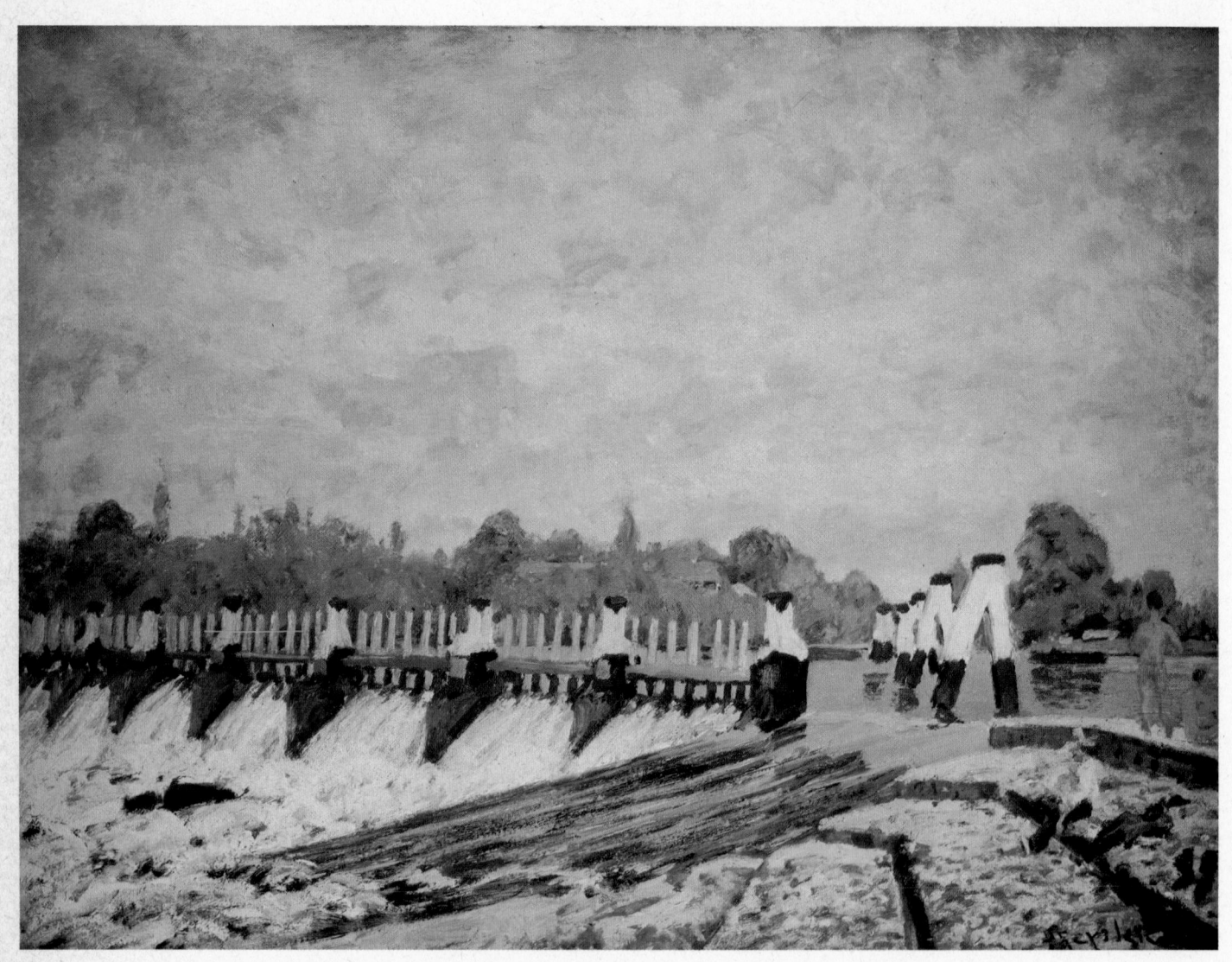

106. THE WEIR AT MOLESEY NEAR HAMPTON COURT, MORNING EFFECT, 1874.
  Oil, 19½ × 29⅜ in. Edinburgh, National Gallery of Scotland.

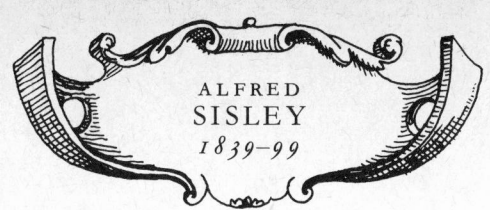

ALFRED
SISLEY
1839–99

THE SISLEY FAMILY were part English, part French. Alfred Sisley's grandmother was a Frenchwoman, his father and mother were English residents in Paris, where Alfred Sisley was born and where his father worked in the silk trade, which he had pursued earlier in London. The painter always kept his English nationality, and presumably he had no lack of English acquaintances when he was invited to London in 1874 by the art collector and opera star Jean-Baptiste Faure. For most of his four months, from summer till early autumn, he worked along the river around Hampton Court and Molesey, at home enough to settle to a known total of fifteen landscapes. Also he painted one landscape of the metropolitan Thames. This great Impressionist painter of the realization of pleasure and love through landscape, or through nature, who said that every picture shows a place the artist has fallen in love with, came back to England again in 1881, and explored the Isle of Wight. Nothing survives from that visit. He was back once more in 1897. This time he travelled down to Cornwall, stayed three days at Falmouth, and then went on to Penarth, on the coast outside Cardiff, moving on to Langland Bay on the Gower peninsula. He liked the scenery round Penarth, and the approaches to Cardiff, with great ships moving in and out. But his Welsh pictures have rather weak or pallid qualities, as if his power was diminishing, whether or no he fell in love with his view points. *Page* 199.

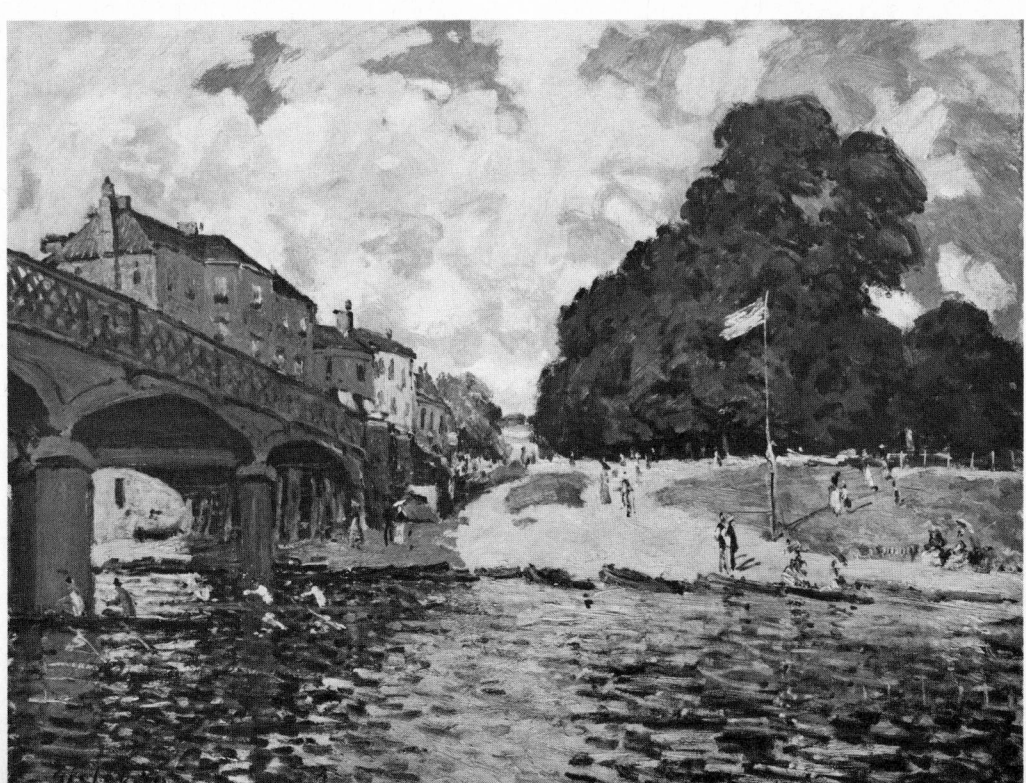

107. BRIDGE AT HAMPTON COURT, 1874. *Oil*, 18⅛ × 24 *in. Cologne, Wallraf-Richartz Museum.*

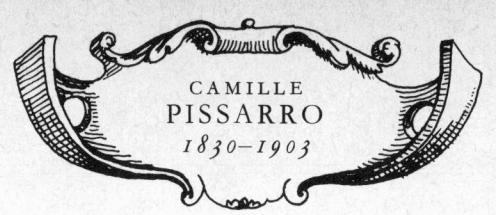

LUCKILY FOR US this grandest and humblest of landscape painters, who thought it might be a good idea to burn museums and prevent art deriving from art, came several times to England. In 1870, in face of the Prussian invasion of France, Pissarro abandoned his house at Louveciennes, just north of Versailles, first for Mayenne, then for London, where his married half-sister was living in the still countrified suburb of Norwood. So we have (or for the most part American collectors have) his Norwood paintings of 1870 and 1871, his *Dulwich College* and his *Crystal Palace*. Pissarro recalled that he and Monet, who was in London also taking refuge from the war, both submitted pictures to the Royal Academy. 'Naturally we were rejected.' He found subjects enough to paint, but wrote of encountering contempt, indifference and rudeness, more sense of commerce than art, and 'egotistical jealousy and resentment' among colleagues, meaning presumably such English artists as he met, himself a mature painter in his forties. His son Lucien transferred himself to London in 1883, a presence which brought Pissarro back in 1890, 1892, and 1897. Each stay resulted in landscapes: from 1890, pictures of Kensington Gardens, Hampton Court, the Thames at Charing Cross Bridge, and Hyde Park; from 1892, brilliantly coloured landscapes of Kew Gardens, and Kew, and a fine *Primrose Hill*; from 1897, pictures painted in Bedford Park, the first of the planned garden suburbs, which, with its carefully kept trees and its 'boiled lobster' houses by Norman Shaw, was still the home 'of the elect in the art world', where the Yeats family lived, and where Lucien Pissarro had just taken a house, in Bath Road (No. 62). Among the Bedford Park landscapes are two elmy, summery ones of cricket matches in progress.
Page 197.

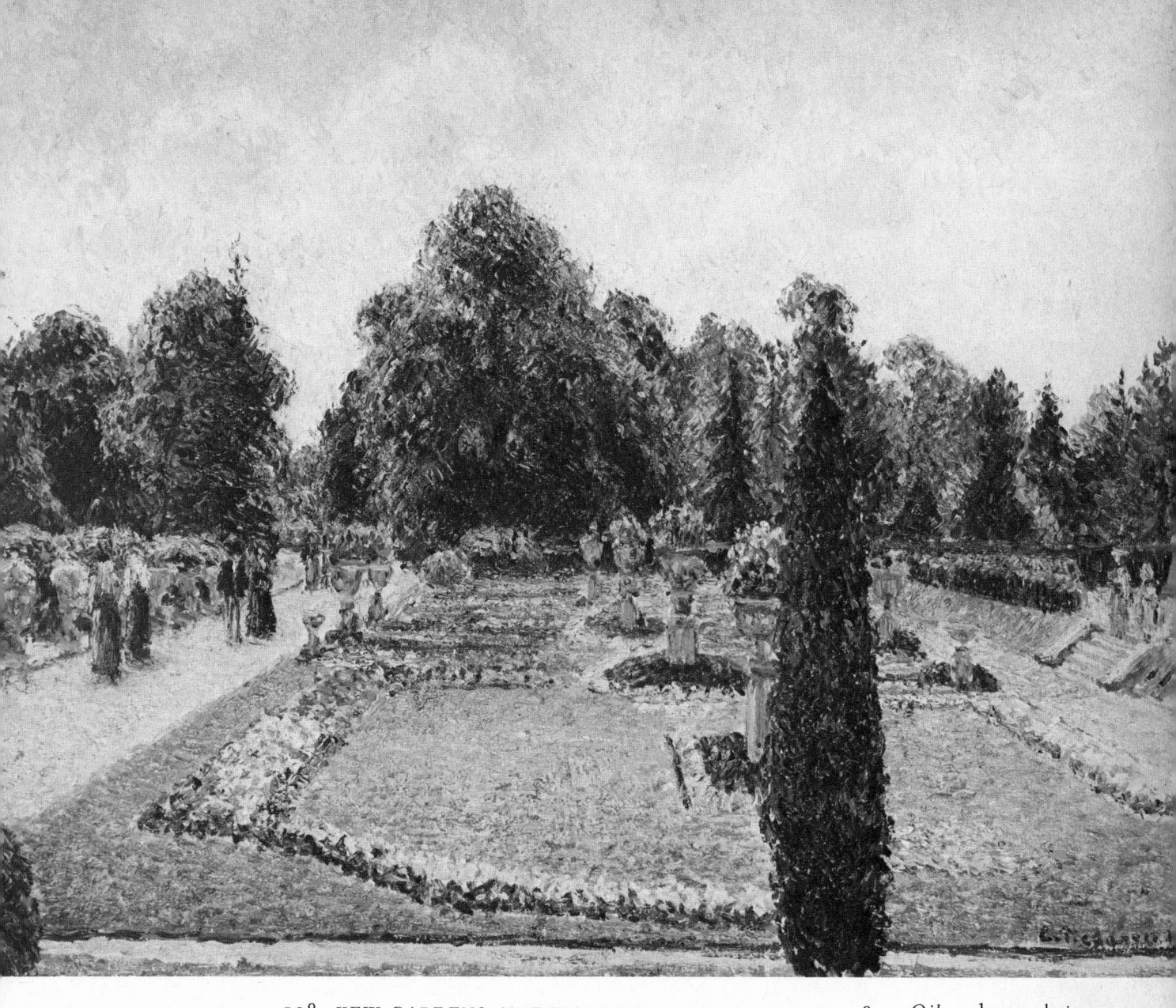

108. KEW GARDENS, THE WALK TO THE PALM HOUSE, 1892. *Oil, 21¼ × 25½ in. Private collection.*

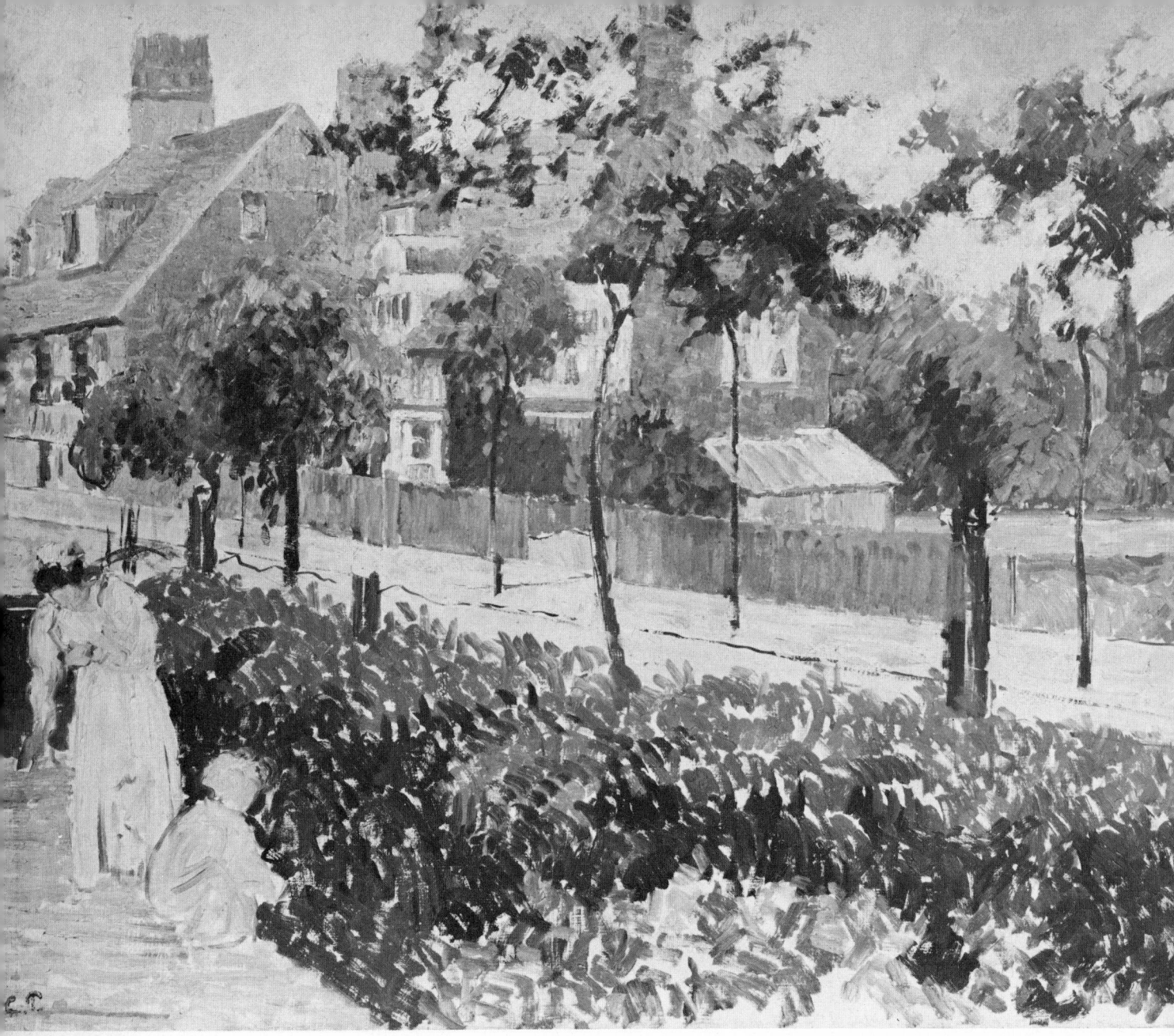

109. BEDFORD PARK, BATH ROAD, LONDON, 1897. *Oil, 21¼ × 25½ in. Oxford, Ashmolean Museum.*

110. DULWICH COLLEGE, 1871. *Oil, 19¾ × 25 in. Toronto, Collection Mrs Maurice*
     B. Taylor.
When Pissarro was living at Upper Norwood in 1870–1 the Dulwich College
buildings were new. They were opened in fact in 1870.

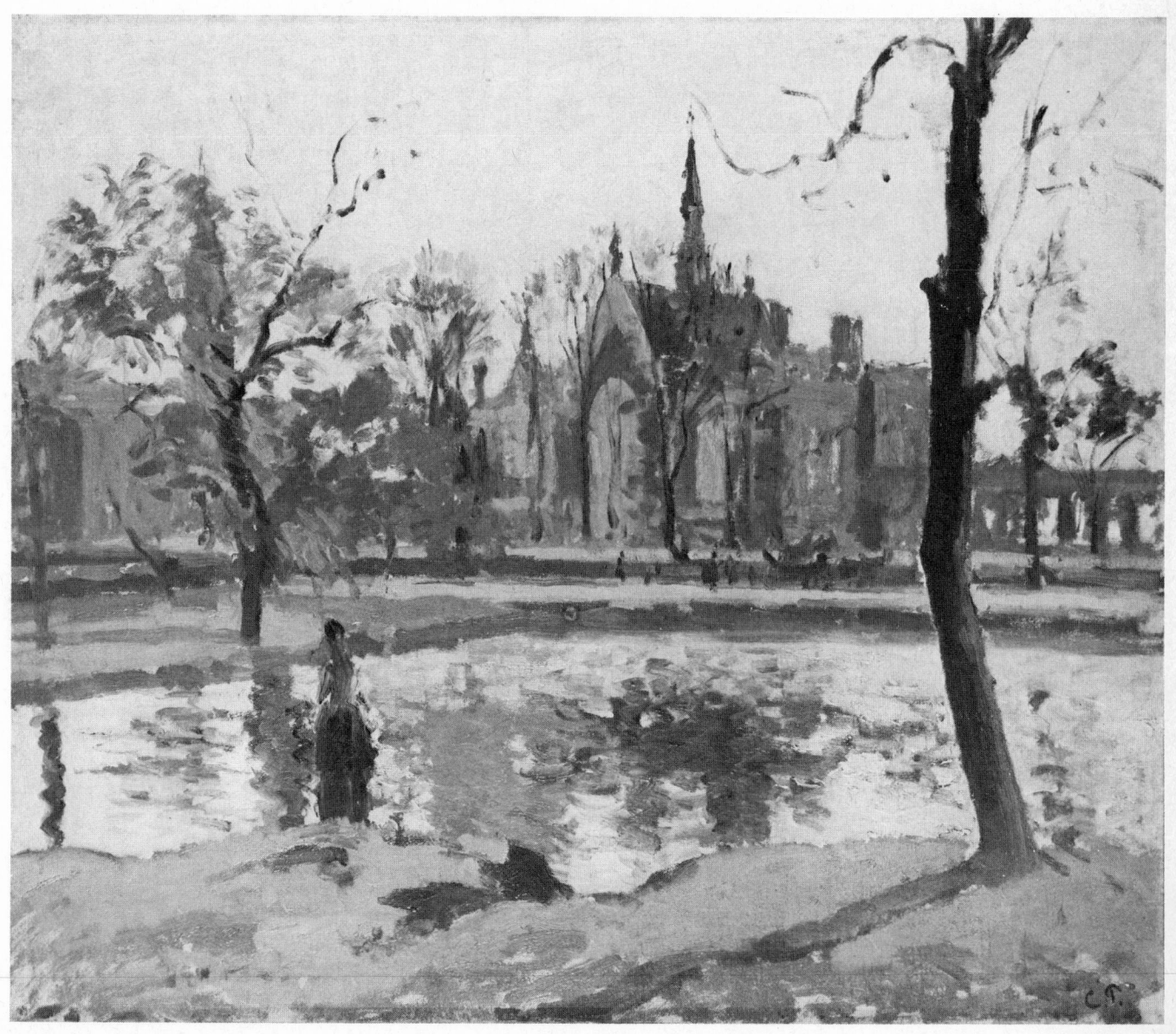

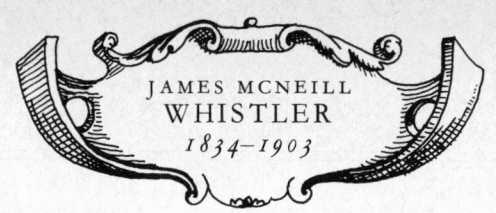

WE KNOW WHISTLER BEST for his colour symphonies, harmonies and nocturnes of the crepuscular or the foggy Thames, with the triangular sails of the old Thames barges. America of the mid century was no place for him as an artist, and he first turned his eye on the Thames in 1859, the year in which he chose London rather than Paris for his arena. Chelsea, at one address and another, became his customary home from 1862 until his death 41 years later. Everything he needed, first for his etchings, then for his colour arrangements and for his lithographs, was at hand within walking or rowing distance—downstream, the Pool and Wapping (there were also watercolours to be derived from the Thames at Erith and from the estuary at Southend); upstream, the bridges, the Battersea and Chelsea reaches; round about, the streets under snow and by lamplight.

Broadly he required extent—of sky, sand, foreshore, water, colour. Extent was everywhere along the river, and occasionally he would find it in other places where land and water bordered each other, at Sandwich in Kent, along the Sussex coast at Selsey Bill, on visits to Speke Hall near Liverpool from 1873, at St. Ives in the winter of 1883–4, and then at Lyme Regis in Dorset in 1895. Wortley in the West Riding, and Chester, visited in 1900, also figure in his work. But in essence this great American made himself into the Londoner whose funeral service in the end was at Chelsea Old Church and whose grave is at Chiswick. The sad thing is that English galleries have so few of his pictures—the Tate along his river should have a room of them—to which they were nearly as indifferent as they were to the London paintings of Monet, Pissarro and Sisley. George Moore wrote of Whistler's witty and provocative art polemics that 'Mr. Whistler is only serious in his art—a grave fault according to academicians, who are serious in everything except their "art".'

Page 198.

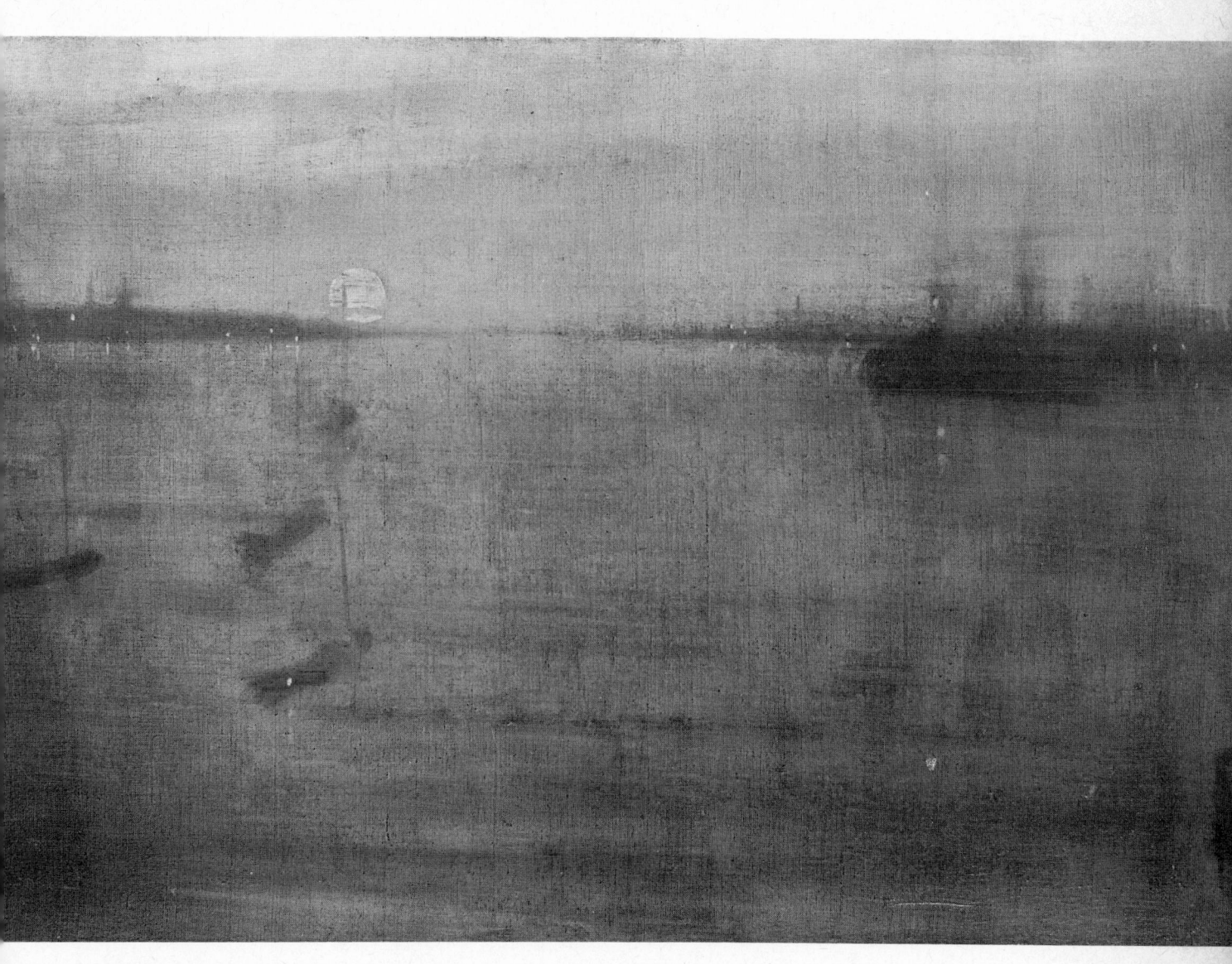

III. NOCTURNE IN BLACK AND GOLD: ENTRANCE TO SOUTHAMPTON WATER,
c. 1875–82. *Oil,* 20 × 30 *in. Chicago, The Art Institute.*

113. THE BEACH AT SELSEY BILL, *c.* 1865. *Oil,* 24 × 18¾ *in. New Britain, Connecticut, New Britain Museum of American Art.*

The wide, blunt, sandy headland in Sussex, now given over to beach huts and caravans. Whistler stayed at Selsey with Charles Augustus Howell, the witty, not at all scrupulous, on and off friend of Rossetti, Burne-Jones and many artists of the time.

112. DORSETSHIRE LANDSCAPE, 1895. *Oil,* 12⅝ × 24¾ *in. Washington D.C., Smithsonian Institution, Freer Gallery of Art.*

Painted from a subject near Lyme Regis.

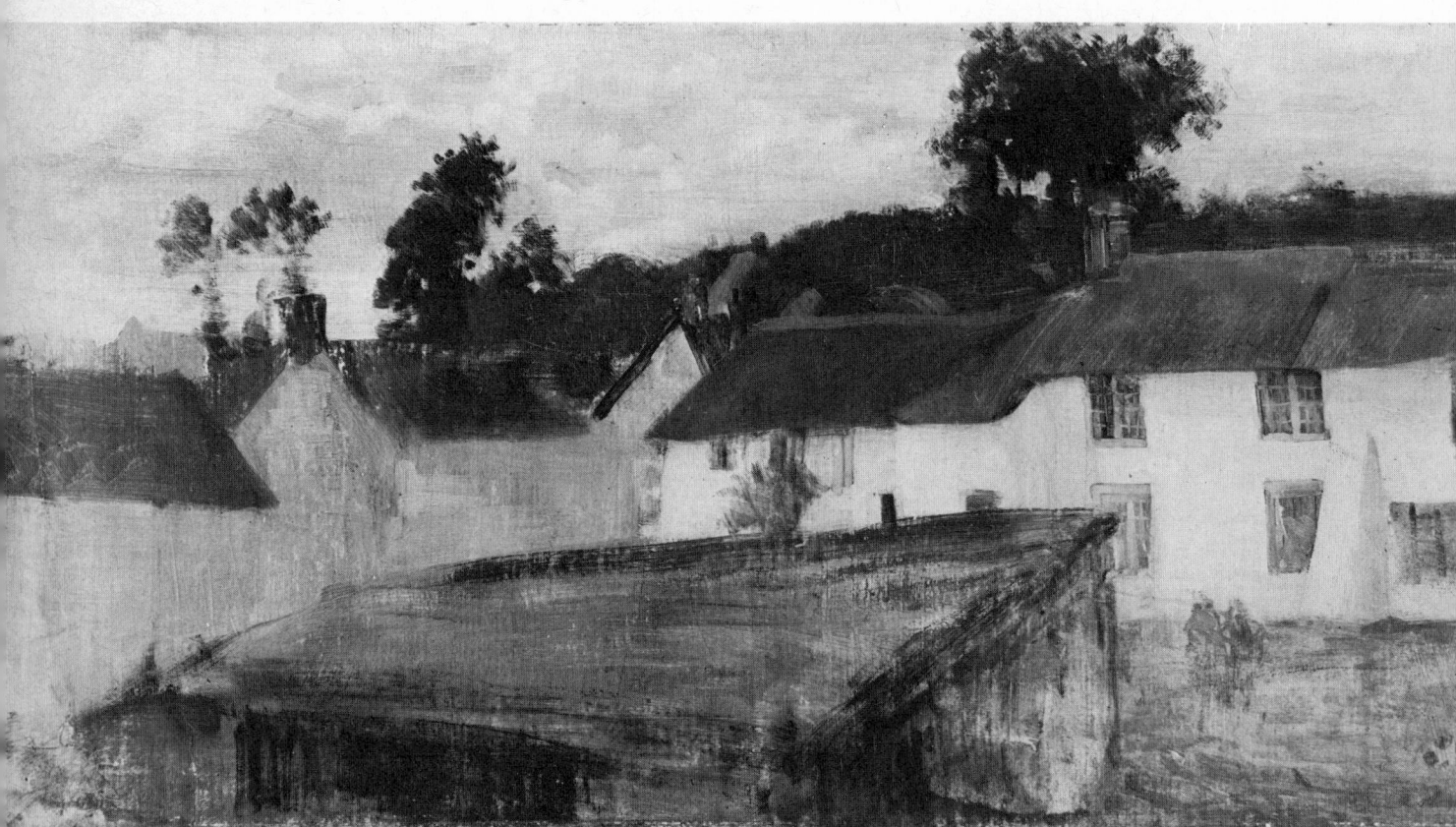

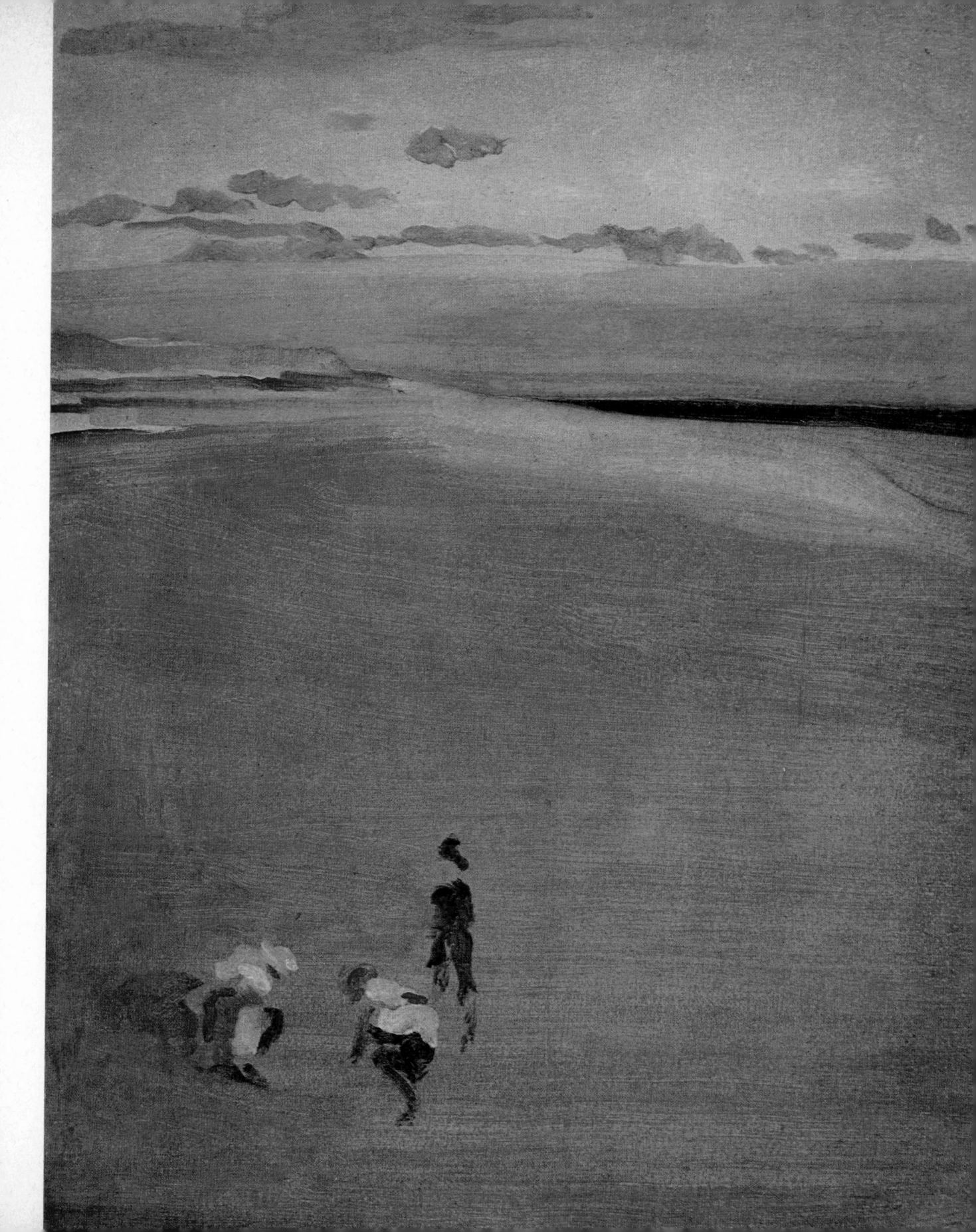

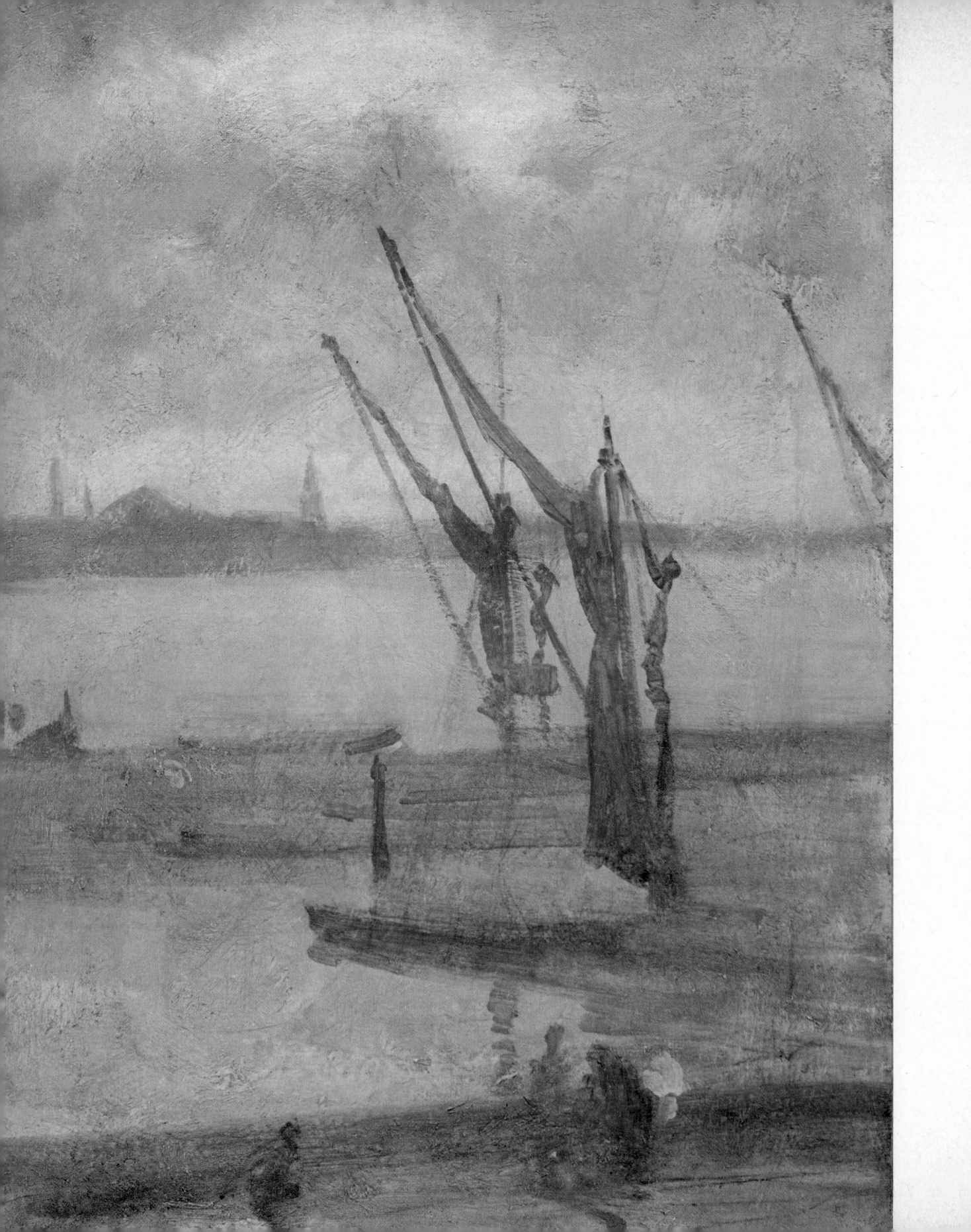

114. CHELSEA WHARF: GREY AND SILVER, *c.* 1875. *Oil,* $24\frac{1}{4} \times 18\frac{1}{8}$ *in. Washington D.C., National Gallery of Art.*

115. THE CRYSTAL PALACE, LONDON, 1871. *Oil,* $18\frac{7}{8} \times 28\frac{3}{4}$ *in. Chicago Art Institute.*

The Crystal Palace, the wonder of the Great Exhibition in 1851, was rebuilt in 1854 at Upper Norwood (and then burnt down in 1936).

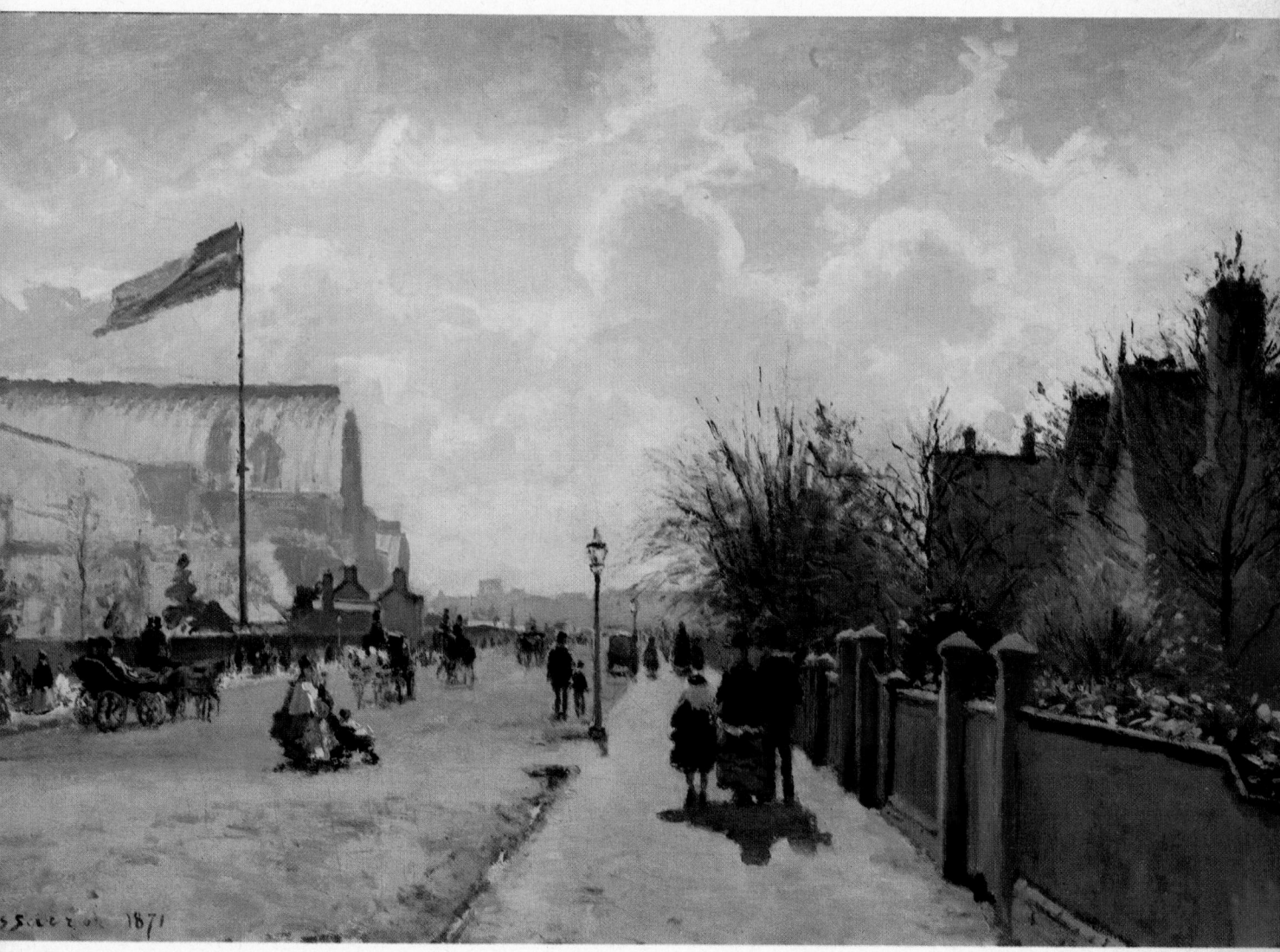

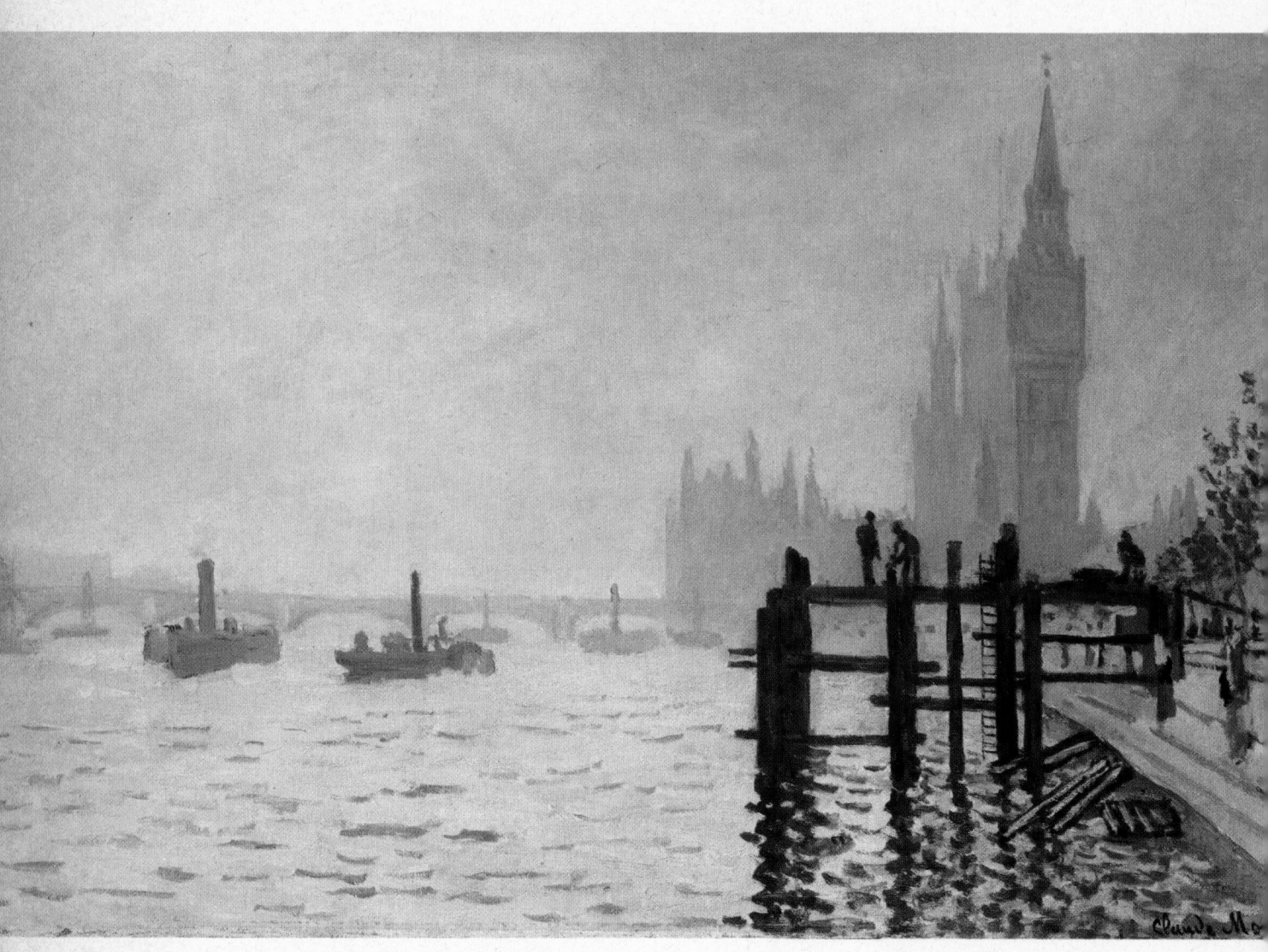

116. THE THAMES AND THE HOUSES OF PARLIAMENT, 1871. *Oil*, 18½ × 28½ *in.*
London, National Gallery.

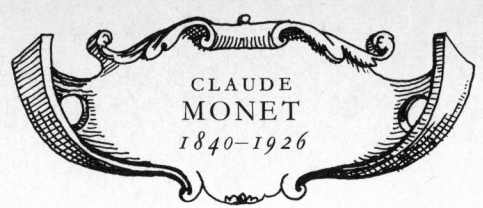

MONET, 29 years old, came to London in the autumn of 1870, sheltering from the Prussian invasion of France and the siege of Paris. He painted his first London pictures in 1871. If they are not among his greatest things, a look, for instance, at the *Green Park* or *The Thames and the Houses of Parliament* reveals imaginative existence in tones slightly melancholy, yet true at once to London and to the tenderness of his own perception. On this first visit the young Monet also painted the Pool of London. By December 1871 he was back in France.

London impressed him, but on the whole, in his long painting life Monet preferred the manifestation of light and colour out of cities, in a nature less cumbered. He came back to London several times, but not to paint until 1899, when he was nearly sixty. By then Monet was the grand master for whom the incised forms of nature were dissolving in radiance, the master of the series of the Haystacks and Rouen Cathedral. Staying at the Savoy Hotel (he could well afford it by this time, after his years of poverty) he began his Bridges, from a balcony room which overlooked the river, Charing Cross Bridge to the right and Waterloo Bridge to the left. In that era of fog and smoke the open river in front of him was a laboratory of coloured atmosphere. Study by study according to weather and times of day, he started on Charing Cross Bridge; to which the heavy Waterloo Bridge was a contrast of megalopolitan strength, sometimes intimidating, captured and beautified by colour. He was back again in the Savoy in February 1900; and in this stay (which lasted till April) he began the Houses of Parliament series, painting in a room immediately across the river in St. Thomas's Hospital. In the winter and spring of 1901 he was once more busy in London on what he called '*mes Londres*', which still required his attentions at home in France in 1902, 1903 and 1904. In all he painted ninety or a hundred of these miracles-in-sequence, of blue and purple with passages of vermilion and madder and emerald green and cadmium yellow. The largest number of them ever to have been exhibited together was 37, in Paris in 1904. Then 26 of them were exhibited together in 1973, in a London which had shown them small regard. Monet produced as well some late colour medleys suggested by Leicester Square.   *Page* 200.

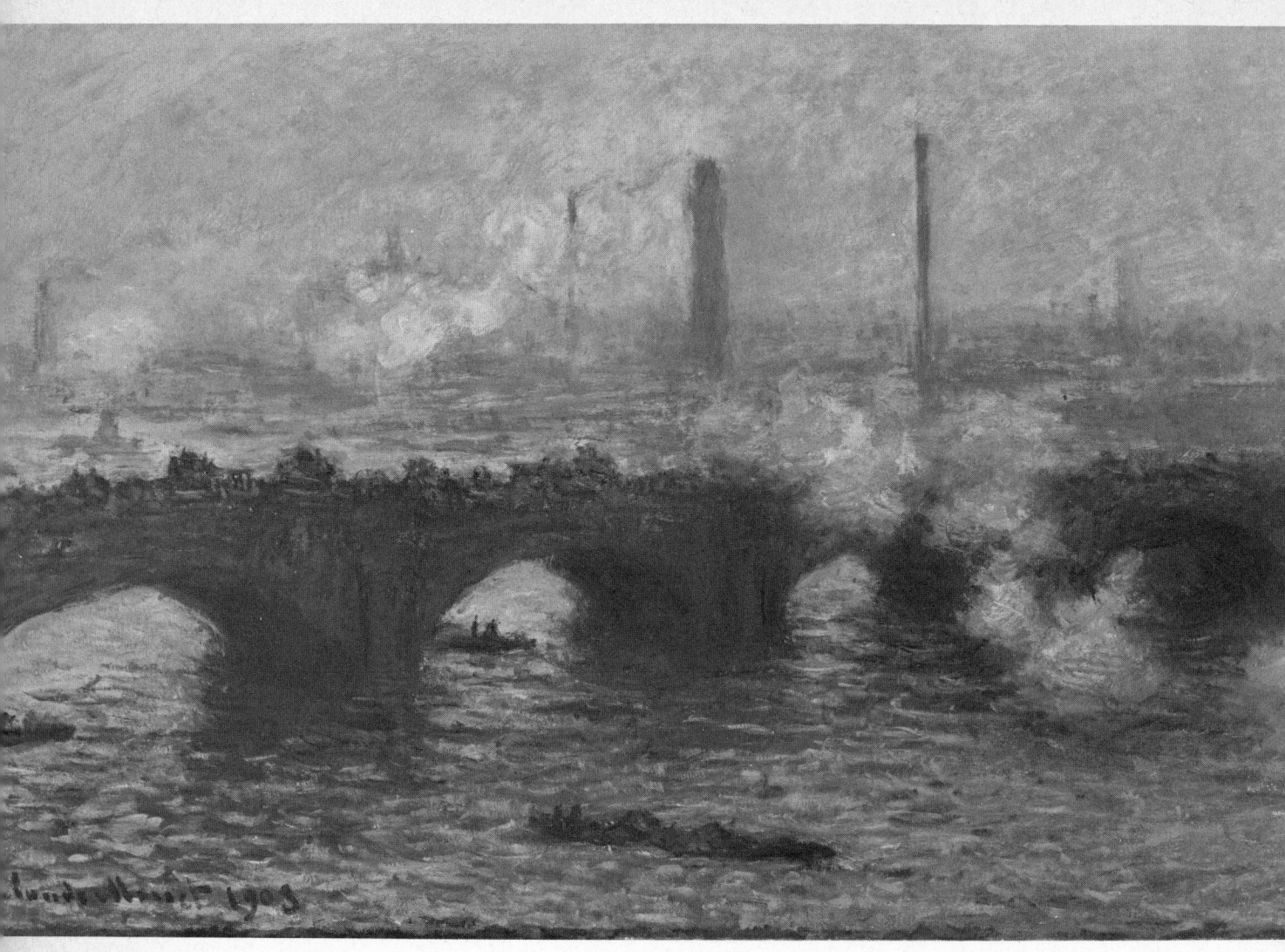

117. WATERLOO BRIDGE, GRAY DAY, 1903. *Oil, 25⅜ × 39⅜ in. Washington D.C., National Gallery of Art.*

118. GREEN PARK, LONDON, 1870–1. *Oil, 13½ × 28½ in. Philadelphia, Museum of Art,*
The W. P. Wilstach collection.

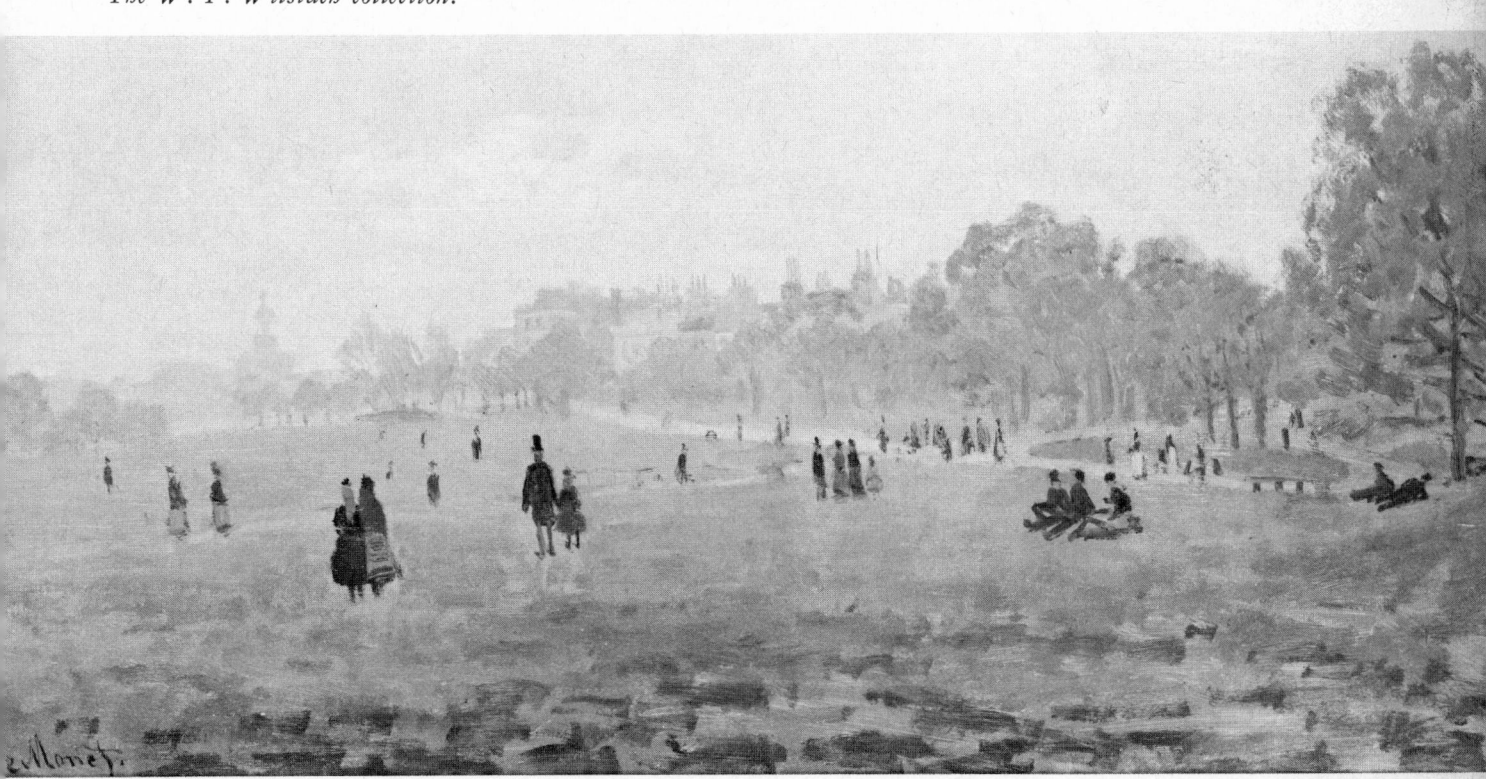

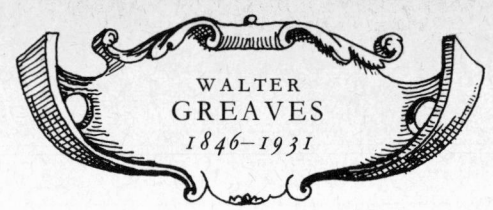
WALTER GREAVES BEGAN by painting crests and coats of arms on boats built by his father, who like himself was a Chelsea waterman. Then he took to painting pictures of the Chelsea shore, and he was working on a picture one day, near Cheyne Walk, when Whistler ran into him and was intrigued enough to invite him round to his studio. If that wasn't the beginning of Greaves as an artist, it was the beginning of a peculiar relationship by which Greaves was both captured and liberated.

When Greaves was an old pensioner in the Charterhouse, John Rothenstein asked him how early he had started to paint. His reply was 'I never *could* help it, Chelsea was so beautiful you couldn't but paint.' He also told Rothenstein that he lost his head over Whistler when he first met him and saw his painting. 'Before that my brother and I had painted grey, and filled our pictures with numerous details. But Whistler taught us the use of blue and made us leave out detail. At first I could only try to copy him, but later I felt a longing for my own style, and something more my own did come back.' Sickert, converted by the Greaves exhibition of 1911, called him 'a little master of the first rank' and rightly intimated that the professionalism of Whistler and the excitement of knowing him and his work stripped away uncertainty in Greaves and sharpened his vision of the river scenery. He declared that a Whistlerian nocturne by Greaves is a very different thing from a Whistlerian nocturne by Whistler. 'If in *Old Battersea Bridge*'—that rather poor picture by Greaves in the Tate Gallery—'Greaves caught badly the slippery strip touch which was Whistler's worst fault, in *The Balcony* we have an august Nocturne with a quality of intricate and monumental design that Whistler never reached.'
Page 200.

119. THE BALCONY. *Oil,* 30 × 24 *in. Private collection.*
Painted from Whistler's window in Lindsey Row, Chelsea.

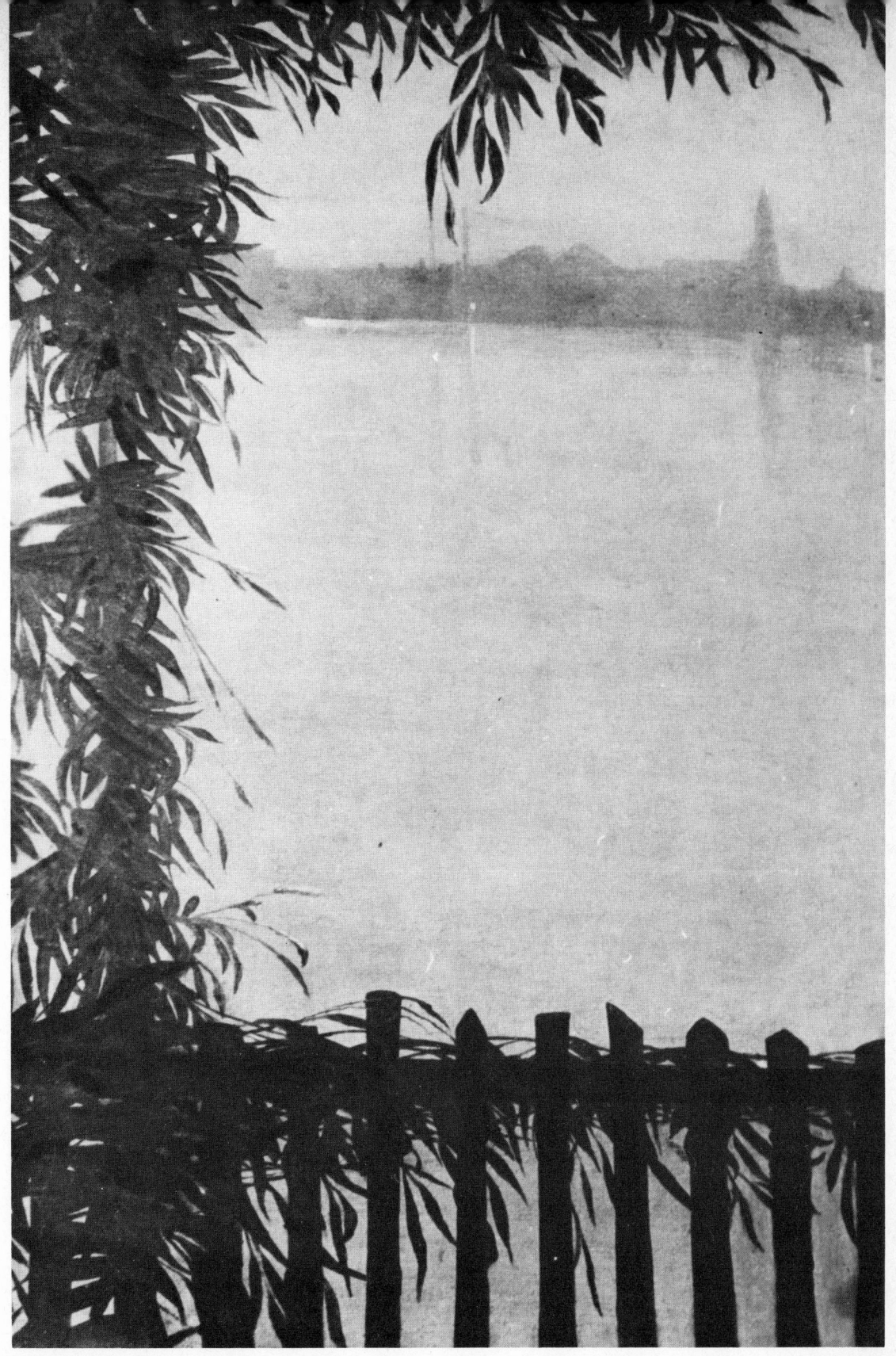

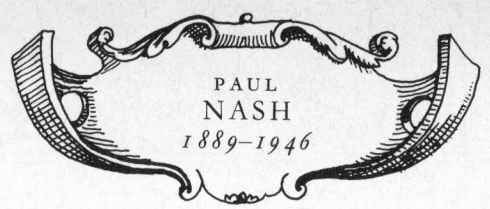

PAUL NASH was born in London, a barrister's son, and grew up in the semi-suburbanism of Iver Heath in Buckinghamshire. At various times he painted landscape at Dymchurch in Kent ('wastes of sand and shingle and the long dykes traversing the Romney Marsh'); at Iden and Rye; in Wiltshire, where he was moved by the avenues in Savernake Forest, the Marlborough downland and its copses, and the standing stones of Avebury; and at Swanage in Dorset. He lived

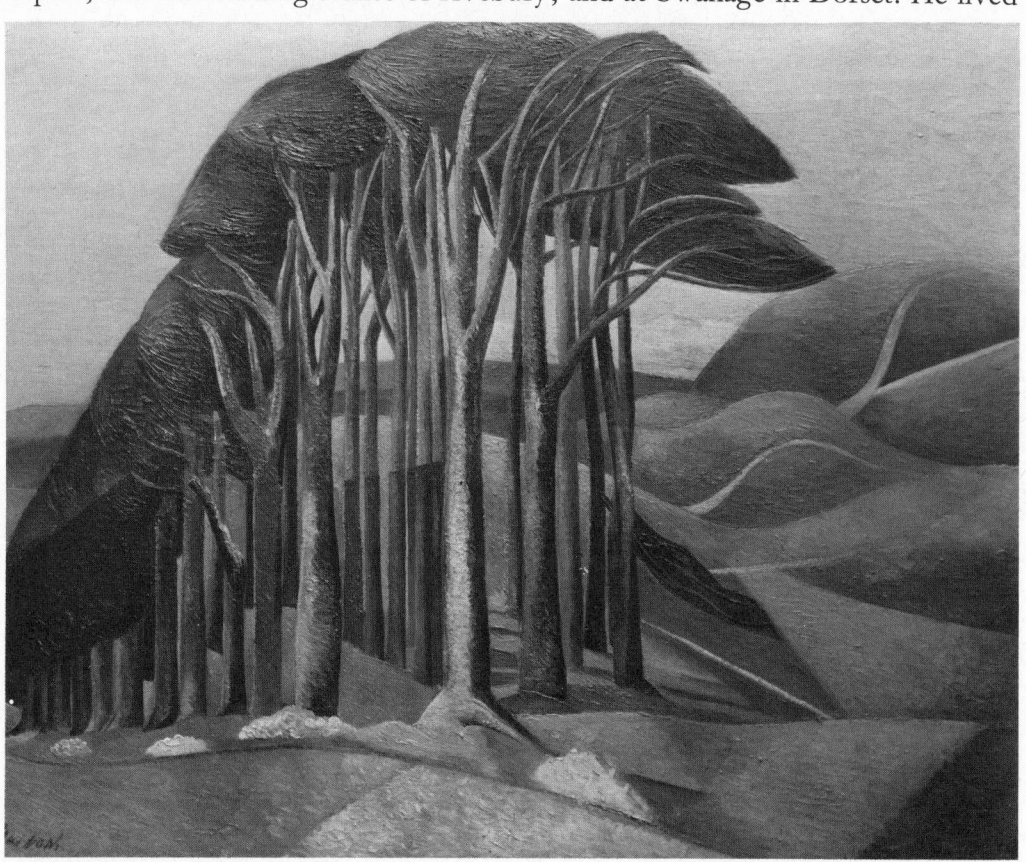

120. WOOD ON THE DOWNS, 1929. *Oil, 28 × 36 in. Aberdeen, Art Gallery.*

Nash made a drawing of beech trees near Ivinghoe Beacon, in Buckinghamshire, on which the trees in this famous picture are based. Otherwise the scene was probably suggested to him by the ridge road across the Marlborough Downs between Marlborough and Hackpen, in Wiltshire—a rolling road accompanied by windbreaks and clumps of beech trees.

uneasily between the old and the new in twentieth-century art, and the visible scene became for him less a self-interpretative reality than a peep-show of symbols of not easily definable mystery. In his writings he will talk about 'that terrifying element, water' or that 'love of the monstrous and the magical' which led him, from his early years, 'beyond the confines of natural appearances into unreal worlds or states of the known world that were then unknown.' Even his famous picture *We are Making a New World* (1918) is more a malign symbol of a No Man's Land than an image of what lay in *his* sight between the trenches. Form in his pictures gradually becomes little more than an approximation good enough for the symbolic; and in his weak later work (as in the parallel writing) there is more and more of the *voulu*.

Page 202.

121. THE SHORE, 1923. *Oil, 24 × 35 in. Leeds, City Art Galleries.*

Groins, sand and sea along the shore of Romney Marsh, at Dymchurch in Kent.

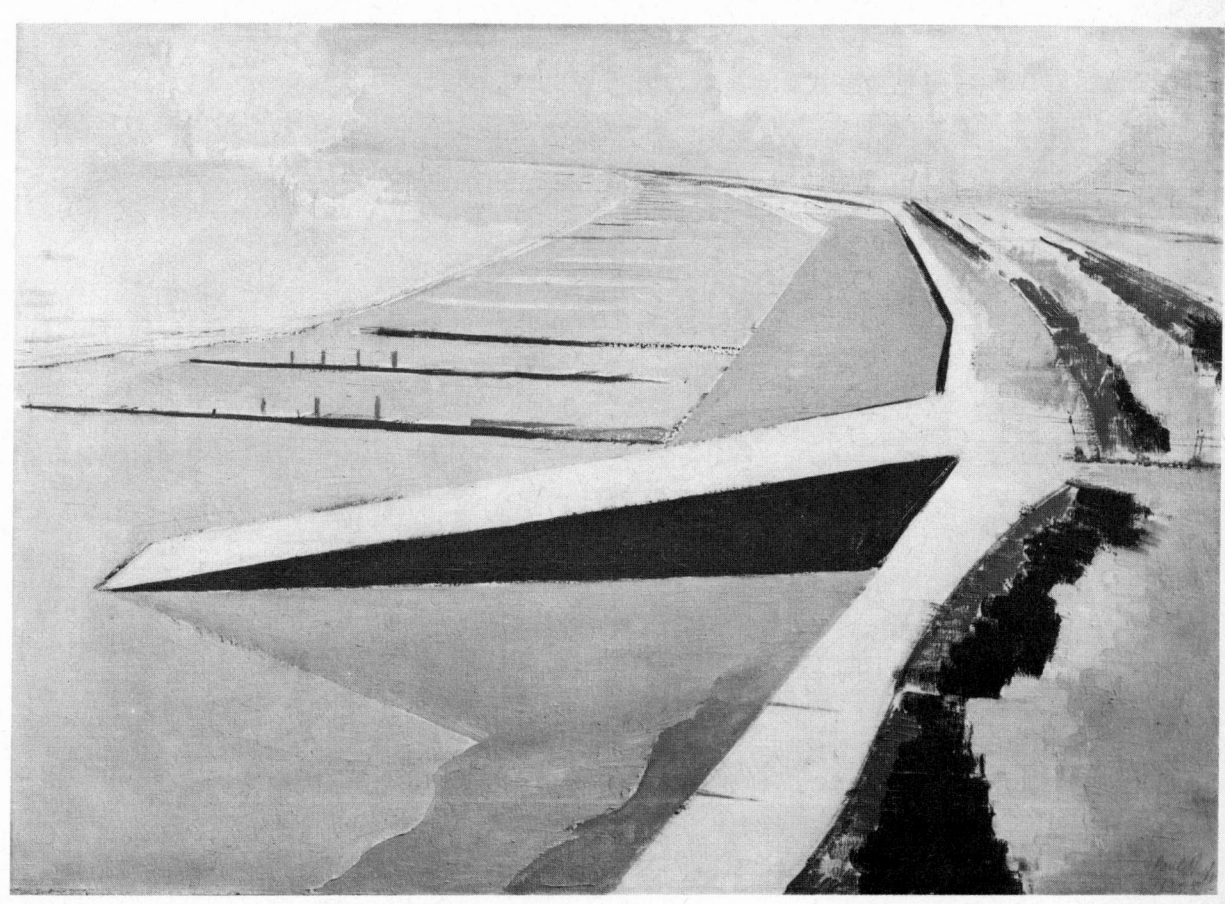

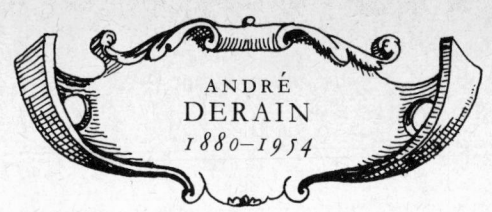

THE YOUNG DERAIN began his painting with extraordinary brilliance and gaiety. Working with Matisse at Collioure in the Mediterranean sun he had divined that shadow amounted to a world of clarity and luminosity contrasting with the direct light of the sun. He set himself against the division of tones and he was beginning to move towards these new principles when his dealer Ambrose Vollard suggested that he should paint a series of London canvases. He came over from Paris to London in 1905, in the late summer or autumn, and again in April 1906. He followed the tradition of Whistler, and Whistler's friend Monet, at any rate in one thing, in finding his subjects, or most of them, along the Thames, with its bridges and its great sailing barges. Otherwise his London pictures, built up with areas of unbroken colour, helped to initiate the basic revolution in twentieth-century art, the ultimate rejection of landscape and all other kinds of naturalism or realism. They were happy pictures, from a happy time in Derain's life; and if the Pool of London wasn't Collioure, he was delighted with the abundance of local colour which he found everywhere in London, along the river and in the parks. *Page* 201.

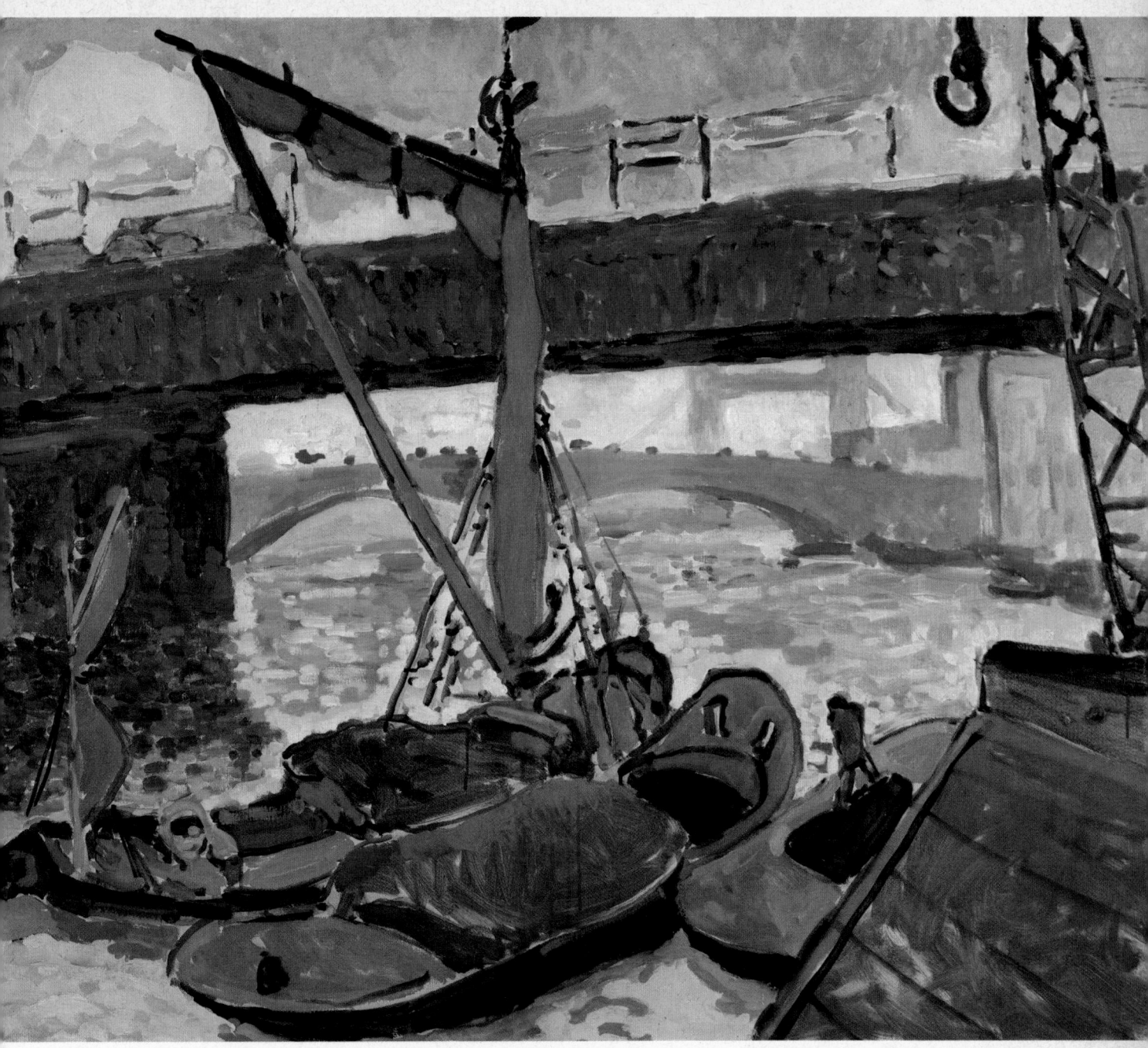

122. BARGES ON THE THAMES, 1905–6. *Oil, 32 × 39 in. Leeds, City Art Galleries.*

Looking down river from the Southwark shore, under Alexandra Bridge to London Bridge and Tower Bridge.

123. THE HILL ABOVE HARLECH, *c.* 1917. *Oil,* 21⅛ × 23⅜ *in. London, Tate Gallery.*

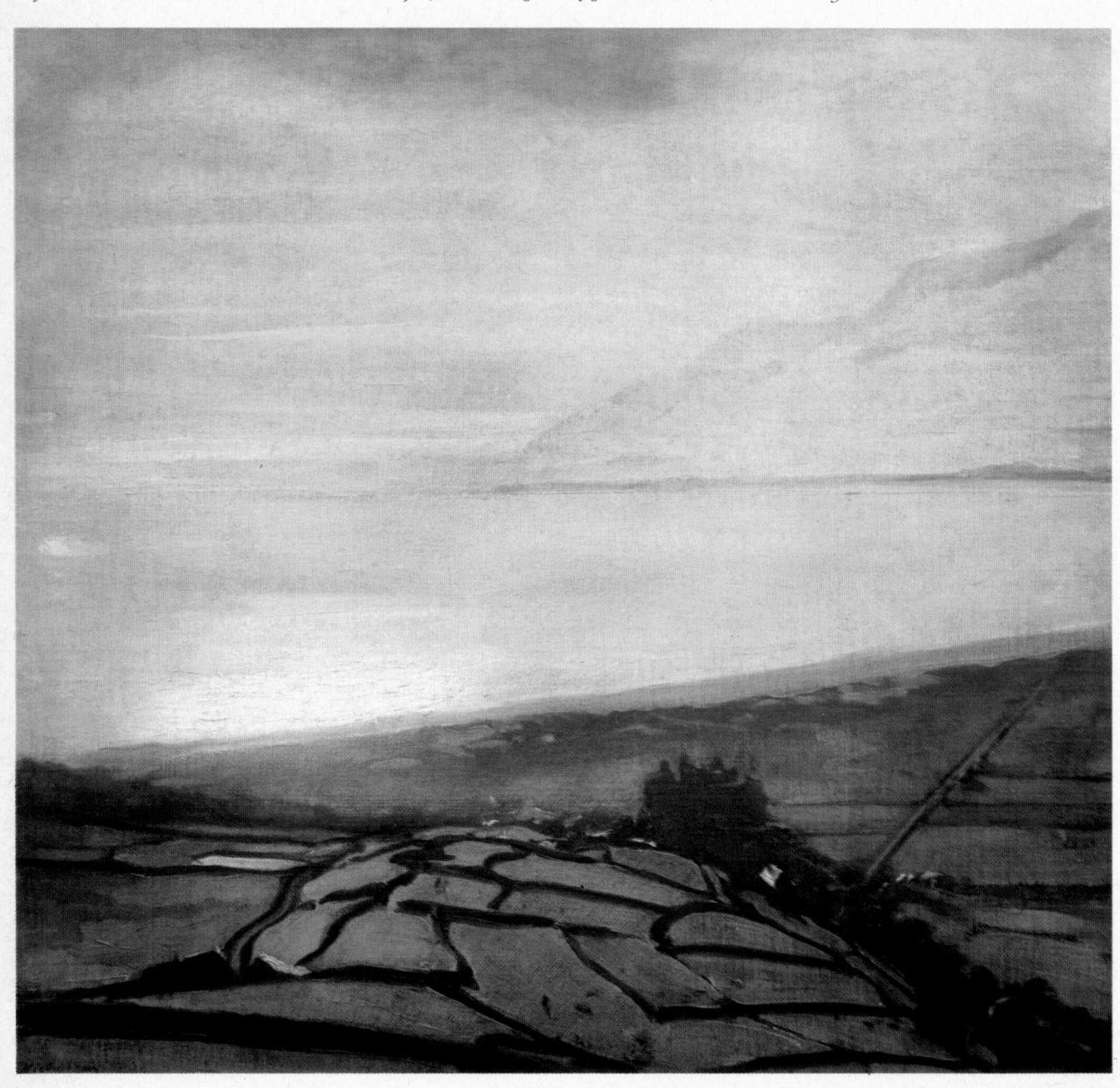

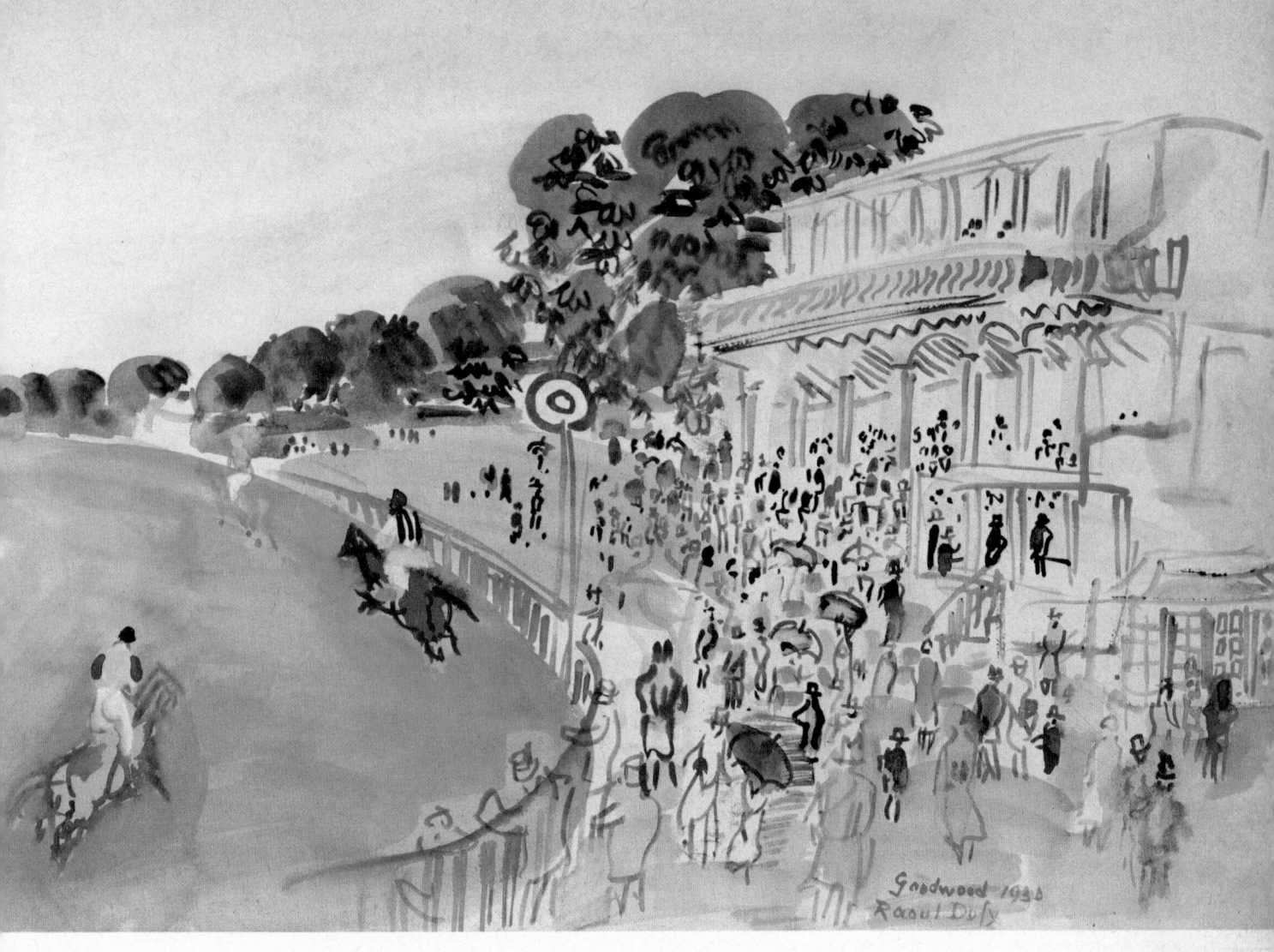

124. RACES AT GOODWOOD, 1930. *Watercolour*, 19½ × 26 *in. New York, Collection Mr and Mrs Abraham L. Bienstock.*

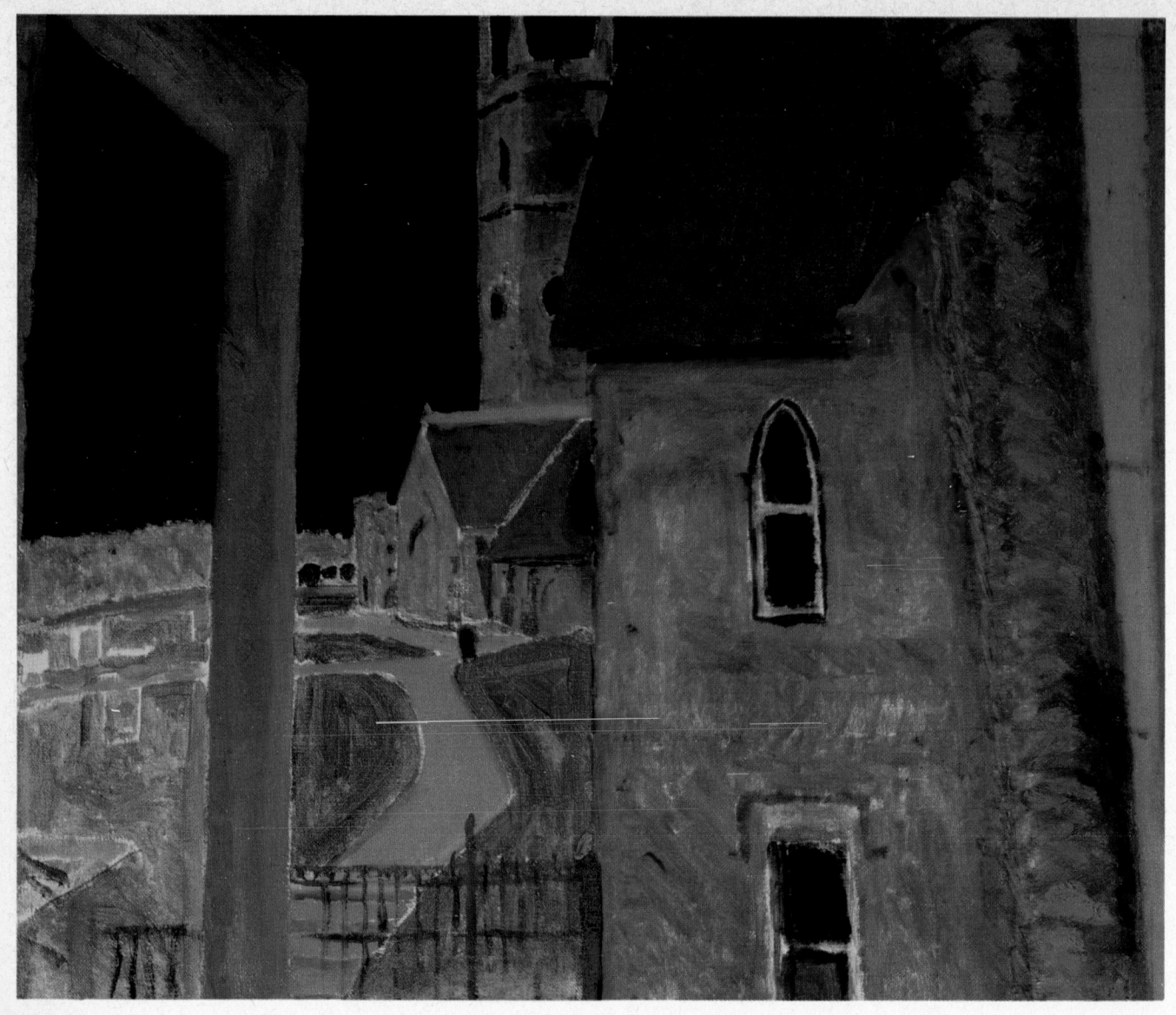

125. CORNISH CHURCH, 1920. *Oil, 21 × 25½ in. London, Tate Gallery.*

The church of St. Columb Major, between Newquay and Bodmin in North Cornwall.

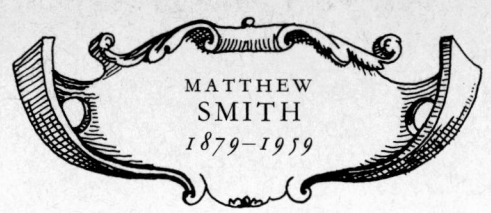

THE SPREADING DAHLIAS and flowing nudes of Matthew Smith were the colour excesses of a slight, shy, almost grey man who entered and left the room like an after-thought. In the phrase used for Turner when he was young, his art developed into pushing the colours around—in his case pushing the heavy pigments around—until his picture idea was complete. But there was a time until the 1920s when Matthew Smith still reacted to the colour architecture of Derain and other Fauve painters and built with colours, above all in the landscapes he painted at St. Columb Major in East Cornwall between the summer and autumn of 1920. These are surprising and satisfying, the work of an artist who then as always could afford to be an independent. He was a Yorkshireman, the son of a well-to-do wire manufacturer at Halifax. Most of his landscapes were painted in the south of France, around Cagnes and Aix-en-Provence.

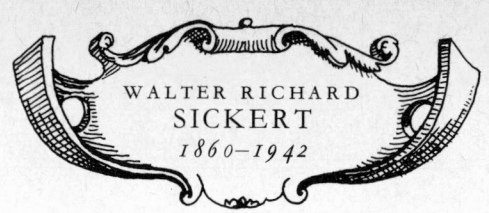

WALTER RICHARD SICKERT
1860–1942

A WALK AROUND even the modern Camden Town, or any other shabby Victorian or Edwardian suburb of London, gives some of the base of Walter Sickert—of more in him than his sombre, well shaped urban landscape. If Camden Town would need supplementing with the black grandeurs of a peeling Bath, as it used to be, London remains his city. He was city born, in Munich, and city reared in London, where his German father, a comic draughtsman, settled in 1868. For a time he worked in Paris. He had been a pupil of Whistler's, then in Paris he attached himself to Degas. Thereafter one associates him variously with Dieppe, Venice, Brighton, Broadstairs, Hove, Bath—and London. Ordinarily squalid people had to be about, in their ordinarily squalid streets, bedrooms, theatres; the urban mess of insides and outsides, the lineaments of which Sickert tried to possess. This painter, who wrote so wittily and with every degree of insight and personal bias and exaggeration about other artists, left himself alone, remarking on one occasion 'It is safer, ruthlessly to brush aside all statements of a painter's claim made by himself. *A painter must be judged by his canvases and not by his patter.*' He liked a remark by Millet, which is a test for landscape, and applies to the varieties of his own work, '*La nature ne pose pas.*'

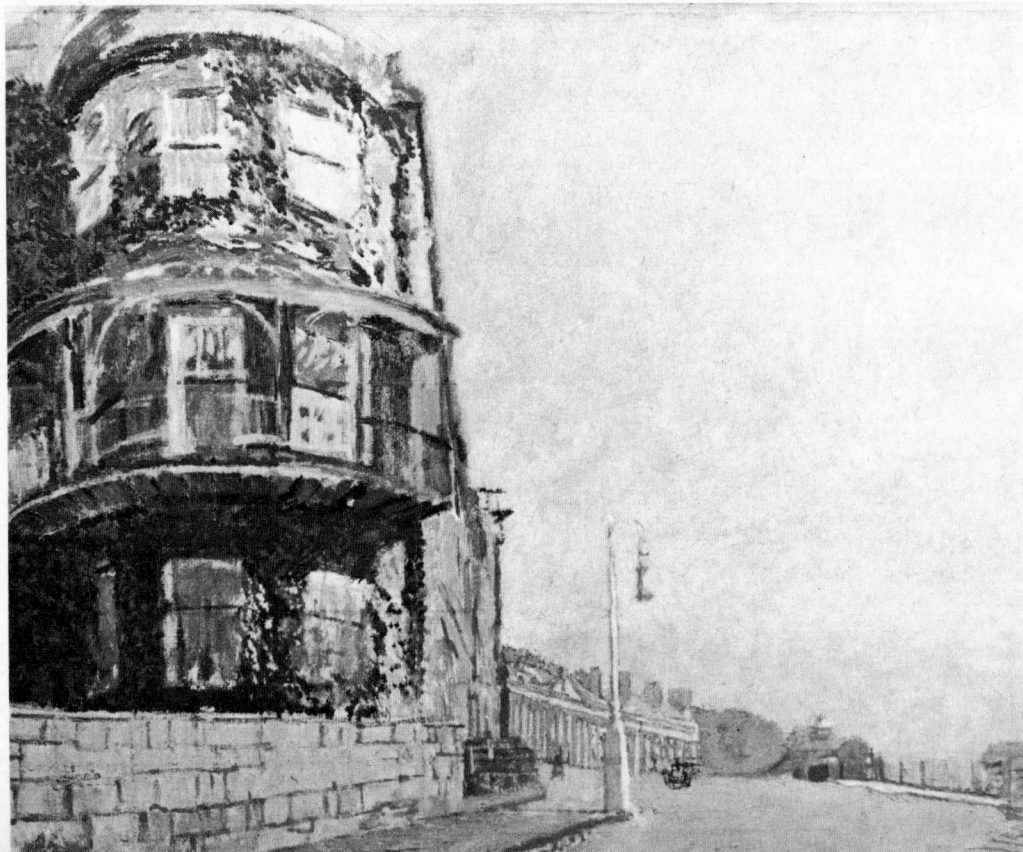

126. MR. SHEEPSHANK'S HOUSE, BATH, *c.* 1917–18. *Oil,* 24½ × 30¼ *in. Durban Museum and Art Gallery, Natal.*

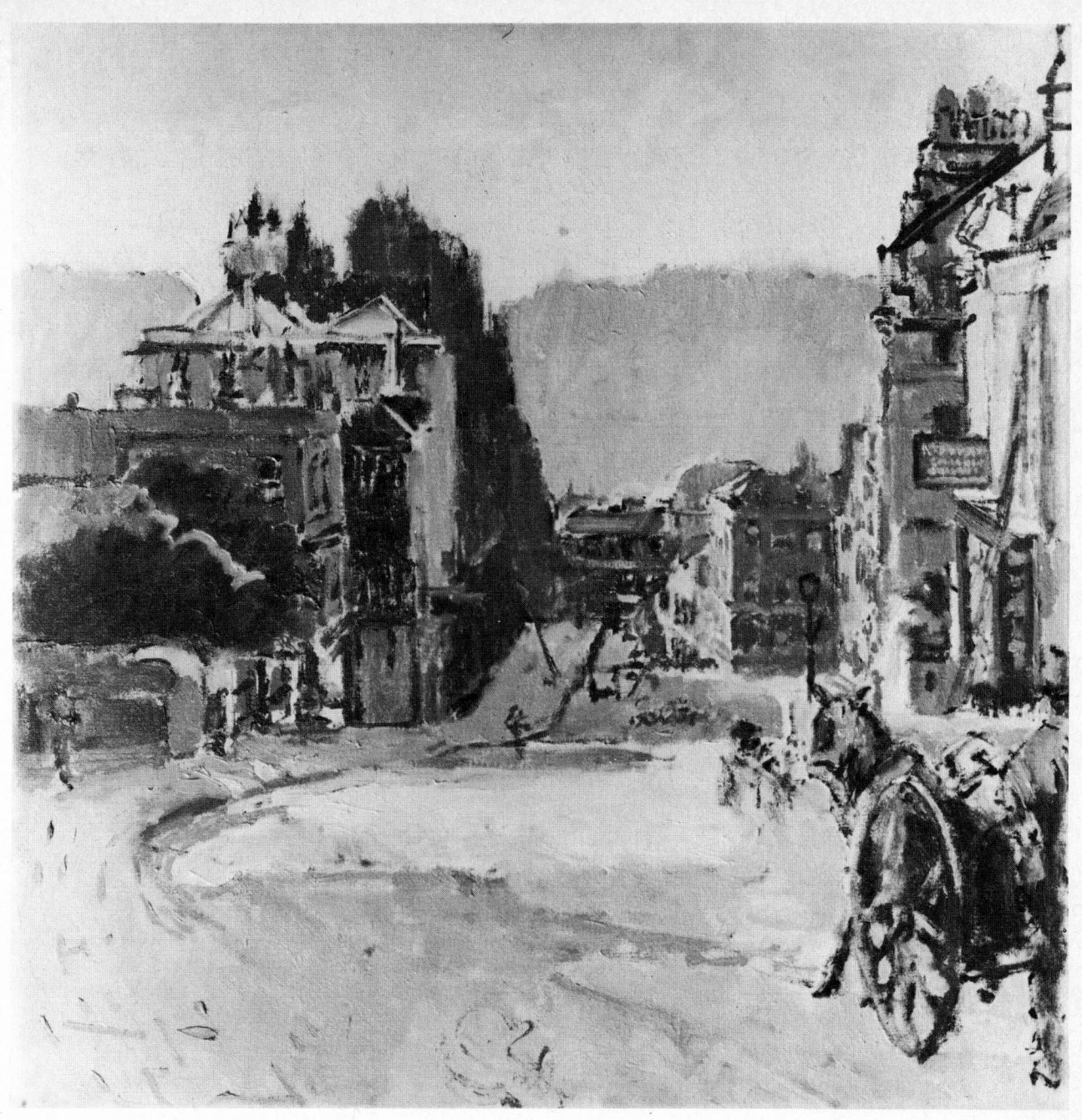

127. THE BELVEDERE, BATH, *c. 1917. Oil, 28 × 28 in. London, Tate Gallery.*

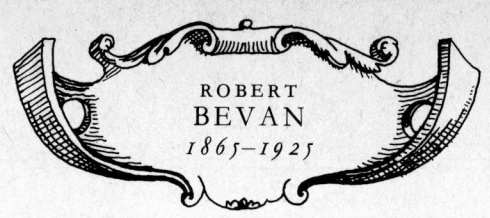

ROBERT
BEVAN
1865-1925

PAINTER AND LITHOGRAPHER, a banker's son, born in London, and brought up
at Cuckfield in Sussex, where he painted some of his landscapes, and where he is
buried. For a time he was a student in Paris. In 1890 he took to Brittany, and there,
at Pont Aven, he came to know Gaugin in 1894. At this time, in his late twenties,
he was also friendly with Renoir, who encouraged him in his painting of horses,
and he was familiar with Cézanne's landscapes. He worked in Somerset, in the
hilly country of the Blackdowns, at Clayhidon and along the valleys of the Culme
and its tributary the Bolham; further south at Luppitt in Devonshire; in Poland
(he had married a Polish art student); and in London (pictures of cabs and horses
and horse sales), changing from an individual impressionism to an individual
Fauve style, evidently well aware of the early work of Matisse and Derain. Like
the Fauve painters, he inclined to use colour undivided, building landscapes from
unbroken shapes of colour (hitting incidentally on those combinations of green
and mauve so observable in English spring scenery, near and far). He felt himself
linked especially to the big heaped up hills of the Honiton region in Devon,
already divided into a medley of small fields, each one of them a hedge-defined
facet. He was an unassertive, uncommunicative man, given to painting in solitude
in bare cottages.

Page 201.

128. HAZE OVER THE VALLEY, *c.* 1913. *Oil,* 17 × 21 *in. London, Tate Gallery.*

One of the deep Somerset valleys under the Blackdown Hills, painted when Bevan
was at Clayhidon, south of Wellington. The view is probably from the slopes of
Clayhidon Hill.

129. THE SMITHY, LUPPITT, 1920. *Lithograph,* $9\frac{1}{4}$ × $12\frac{1}{4}$ *in.*

Luppitt, where Bevan painted in the summer of 1920, is a few miles north of
Honiton in Devonshire. The view (in reverse from a painting) is from the hillside
below Luppitt church across the valley to Hartridge Hill.

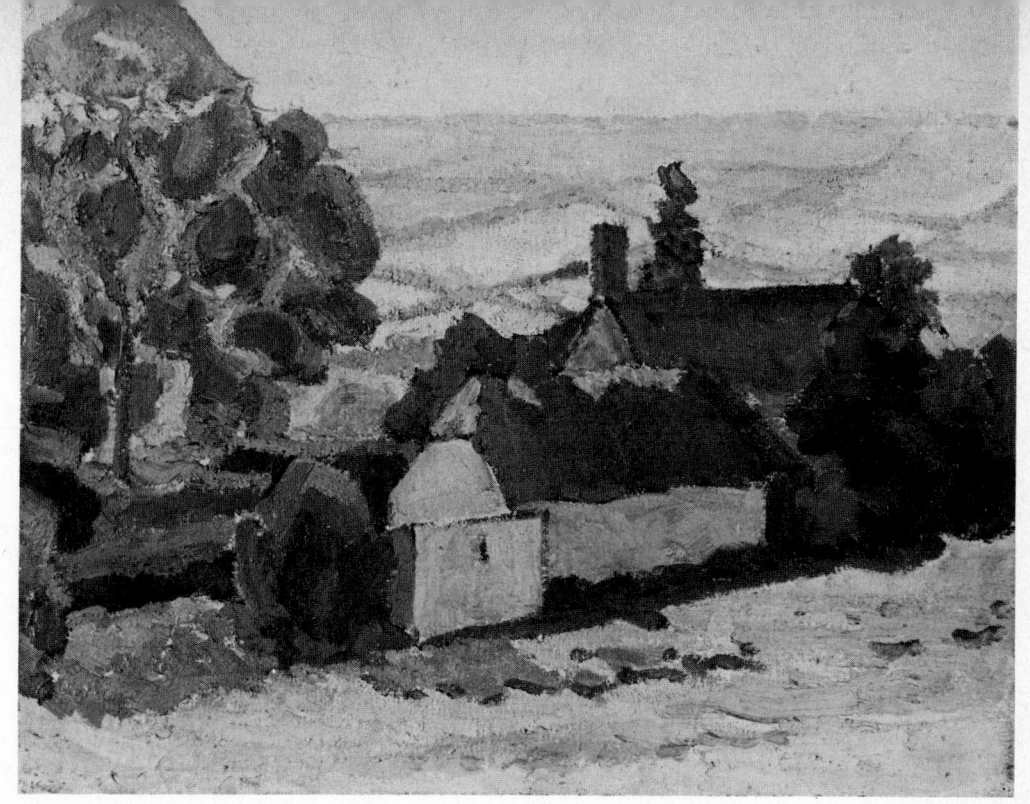

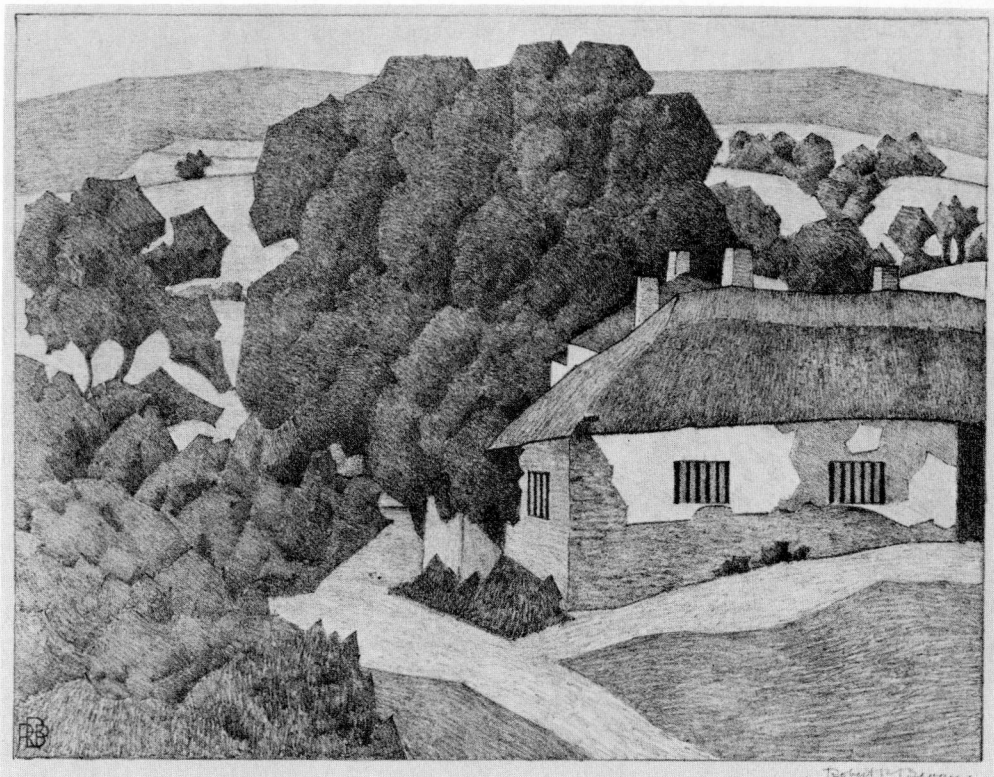

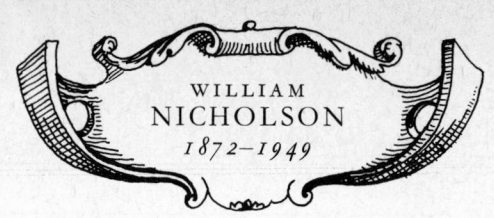

LANDSCAPE was important in the versatility of William Nicholson. He and his brother-in-law James Pryde designed posters, as the Beggarstaff Brothers; he made colour woodcuts, and cartoons for stained glass; he designed for the theatre; he painted still life, and, for bread and butter, the portraits which no doubt led to the knighthood he received in 1936. But it was his landscapes, happy and serene, which were 'the true barometer of Nicholson's state of mind.' Nicholson came from Newark-on-Trent, the son of a Midland industrialist and Conservative politician, who could afford his passage through the schools of art. Painters who affected him were Velasquez, Manet, and Whistler, whom he knew and who approved of his early work. He married young, and the family moved from house to house, Nicholson happiest below open rolling country which gave him sweeps of sunlight and of earthly and atmospheric colour. He called himself 'the painter of the Downs'—the South Downs, near Rottingdean, where he took a house in 1909, the Wiltshire downland, near Sutton Veny, his home from 1923 to 1933; and he died under the Berkshire Downs at Blewbury. His landscapes were not limited to such country. Paris, London, Dieppe, La Rochelle, Avignon, Brittany, Spain, the Venetian Lido, Cumberland, Cornwall, Wales around Harlech, Oxford and Oxfordshire (around Woodstock), Yorkshire, the Sussex coast and Brighton, as well as the Sussex Downs—he found his pictures everywhere, strengthening their direct innocence and simplification more and more with a basis of structural subtlety. Another of his works of art was to be the father of Ben Nicholson.

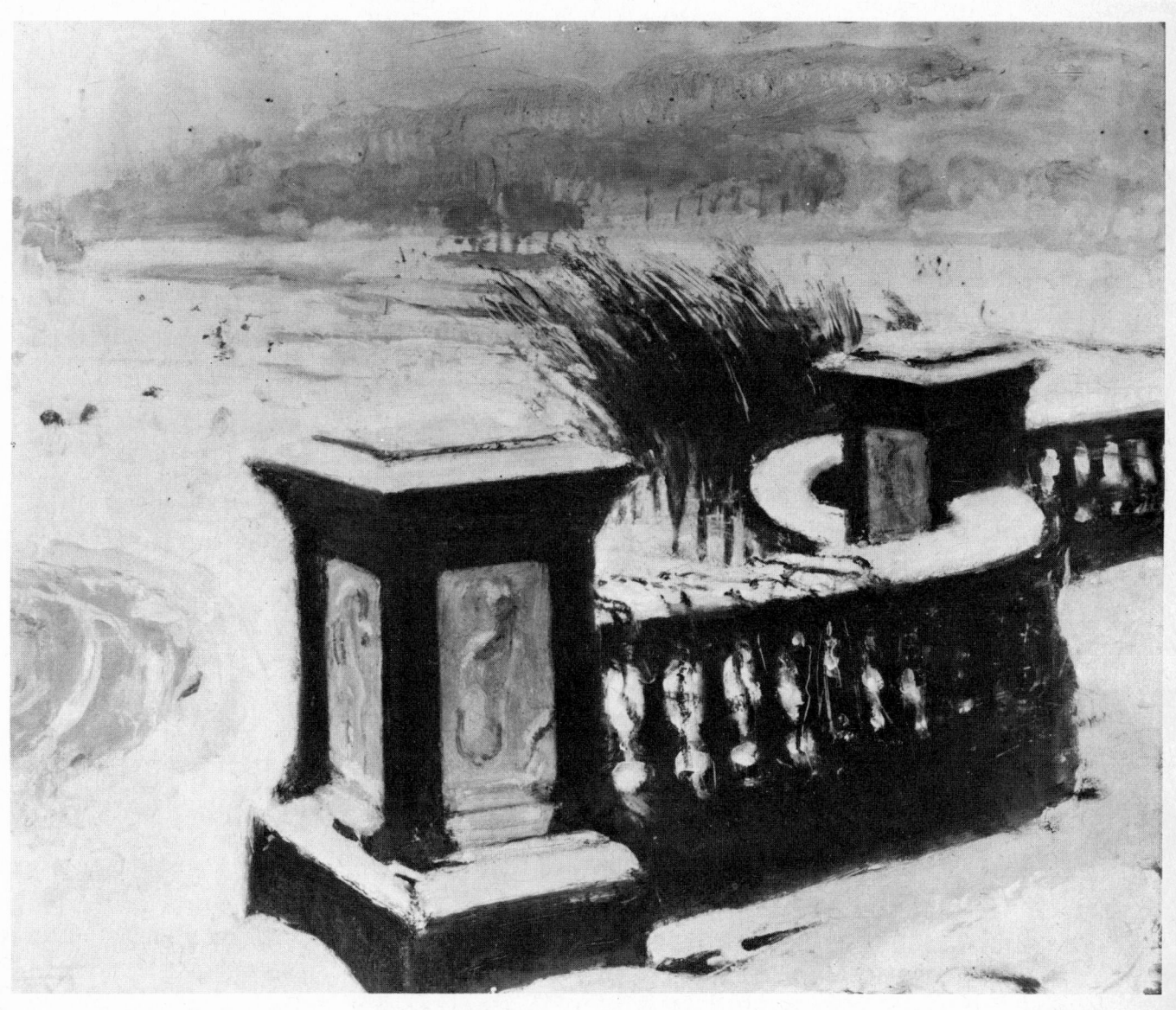

130. SNOW AT BRETTON PARK, 1939. *Oil, 18 × 15 in. Collection Mrs Hanbury-Kelk.*
Bretton Park surrounds the mansion of Bretton Hall (partly by the architect Sir
Jeffry Wyatville), near Wakefield in the West Riding. The Hall is now a training
college.

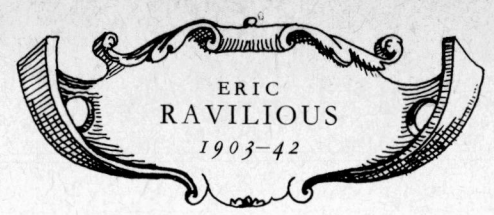

THE LATE TWENTIES and the thirties were a period of hesitation for many young English painters, in a limbo between English landscape traditions and the modernism of the School of Paris. Ravilious was one of them, a pupil of Paul Nash, who became a designer of formal asceticism, at once attracted by non-figurative art and hesitant to abandon English landscape; of which he made a semi-abstract restatement, finding subjects in the smooth planes of south country chalk hills and scarps, Sussex, Wiltshire, Dorset, etc. The Second World War postponed his resolution of the problem. And then he died on service as an official war artist.

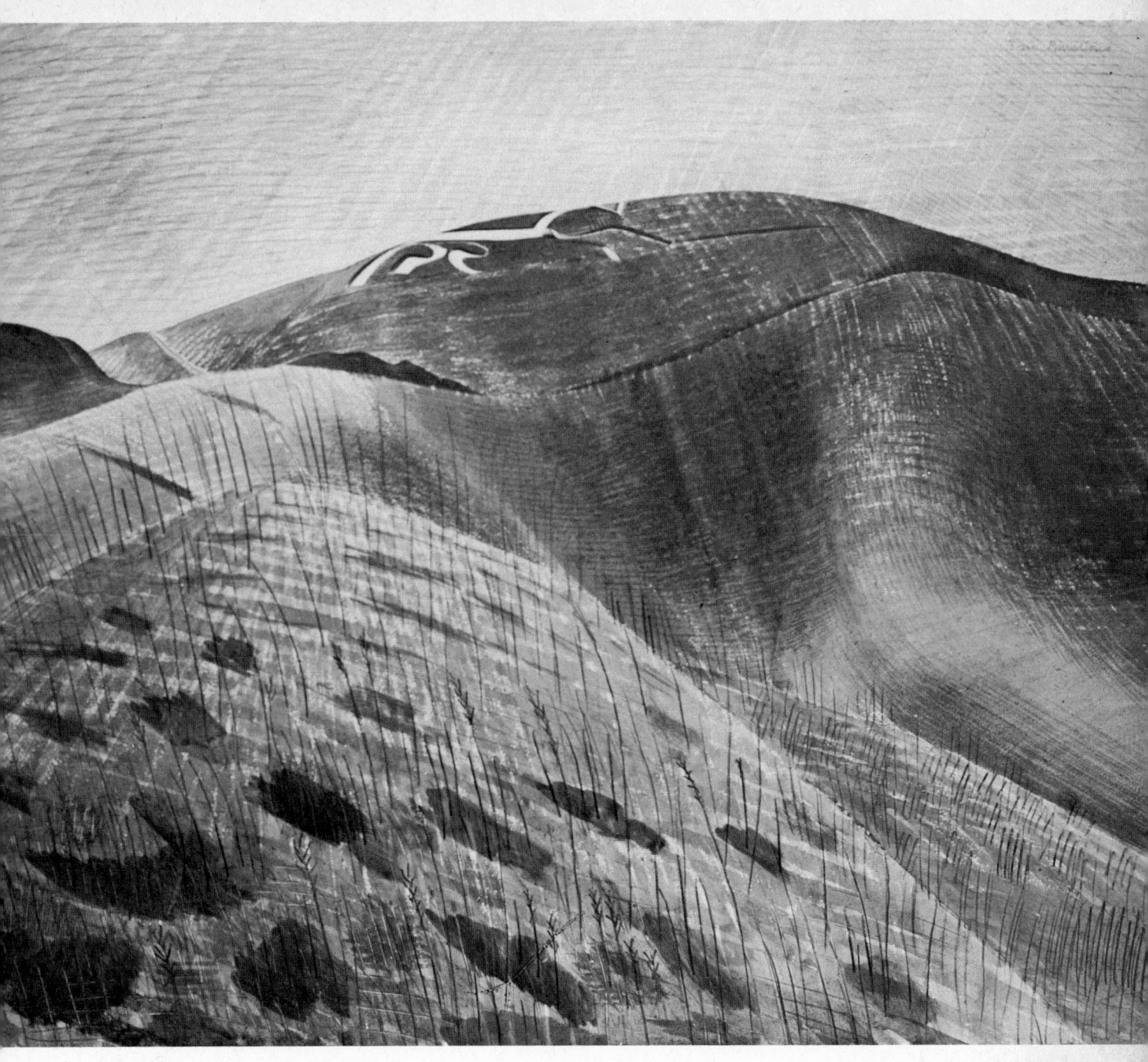

131. THE VALE OF THE WHITE HORSE, *c.* 1939. *Watercolour,* $17\frac{3}{4} \times 21\frac{3}{4}$ *in. London, Tate Gallery.*

The oldest of the White Horses of the chalkland scarps, on the edge of the Berkshire downs above Uffington.

'MENACING', it is frequently said of Edward Burra's clear, bright coloured, unshadowed statements of extraordinary facts, his patterned night life of flash pimps and bulging women, his dance of death, and his human or sub-human events on the edges of the mind. A landscape of menace, neither praised nor condemned, has also grown on Edward Burra. In his sixties he has painted huge watercolour landscapes of fells, moors, and valleys in Yorkshire, in the bleakness of the North Riding near Whitby, in the West Riding—Wharfedale, Penyghent, Kilnsey Crag, etc., broad and terse watercolours of reds, browns, greys, yellows, blacks, and startling greens. The beautiful indifference of these landscape images is at once bullying and fascinating. Burra has painted sardonic landscape, or sardonic environment of life, the hard shell not protecting the soft meat, in the neighbourhood of Rye, where he has always lived, in East Anglia, South Wales, Cornwall (china clay workings near St. Austell), and in the Irish Gaeltacht.

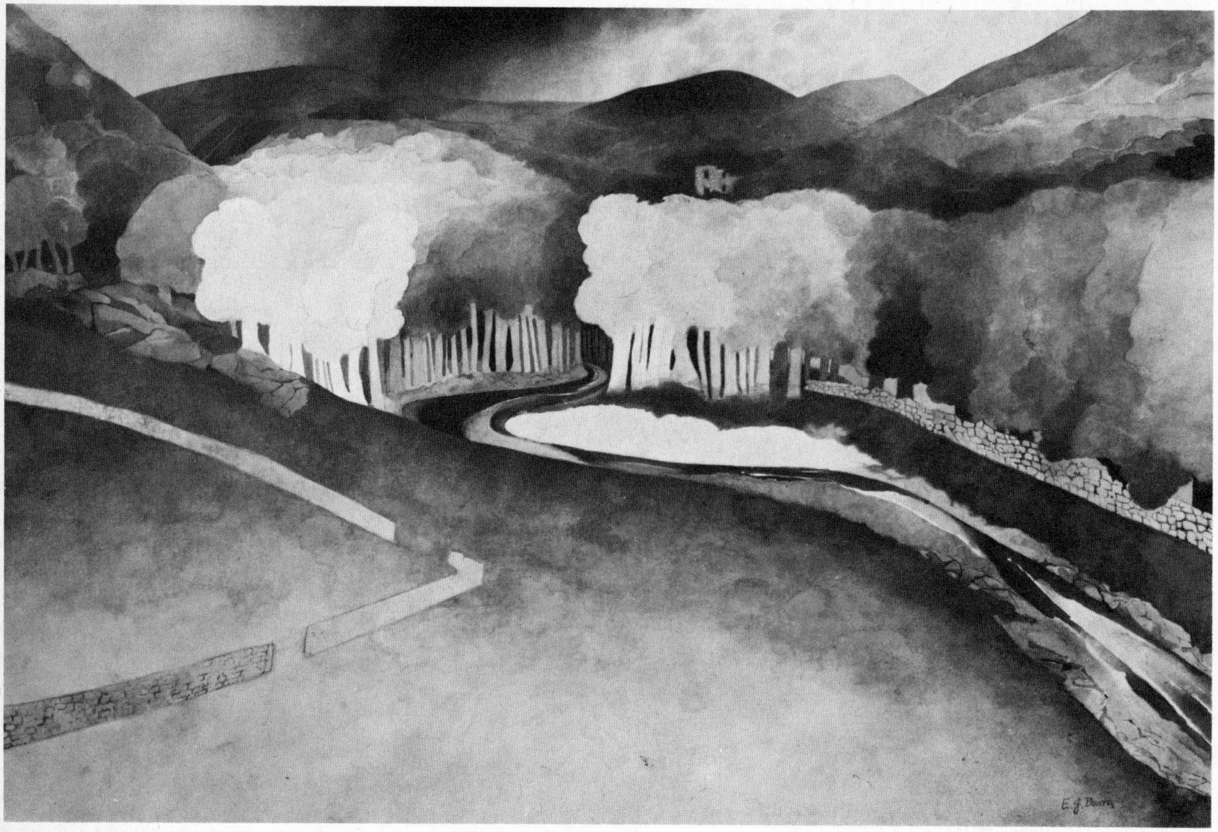

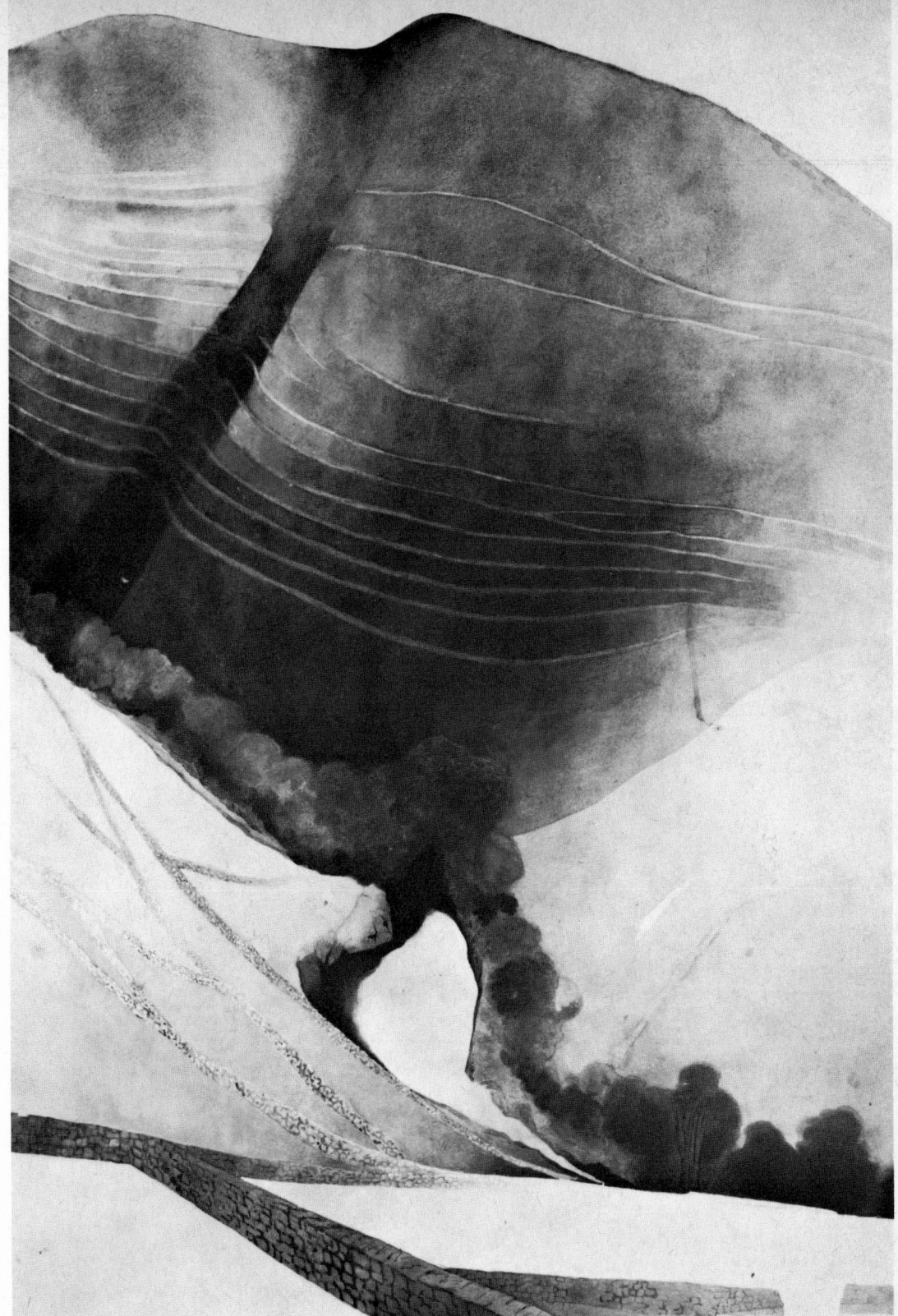

132.
WHARFEDALE,
YORKSHIRE,
1972. *Watercolour,*
$26\frac{1}{2} \times 40$ *in.*
Lefevre Gallery.

133. VALLEY
AND RIVER,
YORKSHIRE,
1972. *Watercolour,*
$39\frac{1}{2} \times 26\frac{3}{4}$ *in.*
Lefevre Gallery.

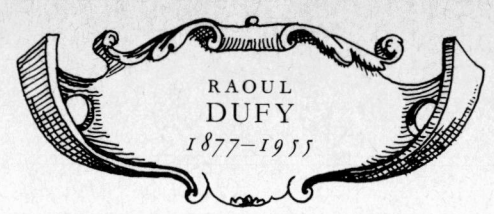

MATISSE exhibited his picnic landscape of *Luxe, calme et volupté* in 1905, the year of Derain's first paintings of London. Dufy saw it and years later he recalled its effect on himself: it was a 'miracle of the imagination expressed in colour and drawing', it showed him the new reasons for painting precisely as the Impressionists had *not* painted. Add another of his remarks, that 'What matters isn't the subject, but the way the subject is presented', and a third remark, that in his painting he wanted to exhibit the way he saw things 'with my eyes and in my heart', and you have Dufy's achievement. He had to be free to imagine, in colour and in drawing, yet he still presented a subject in every painting; and we accept Dufy's imagining, and his presentation, all the more because his subjects of coloured action of every complex and pleasurable kind are equally familiar to us all. He paints the *bonheur de vivre*, and why shouldn't a violin by Dufy be red, bright red, if the 'real' violin and the real 'red' combine as Dufy's reality? It was in the thirties that this witty painter from Le Havre, this rococo semi-realist, took English subjects into the play of his colour and drawing—the activity of the Thames from Tower Bridge to Westminster, the changing of the guard, regattas at Cowes and Henley, racing at Ascot and Epsom and Goodwood, the cavalcade of George VI's coronation. Also Dufy travelled in 1930 and 1932 to paint the Kessler family (84 inches by 108) in a Norfolk landscape.

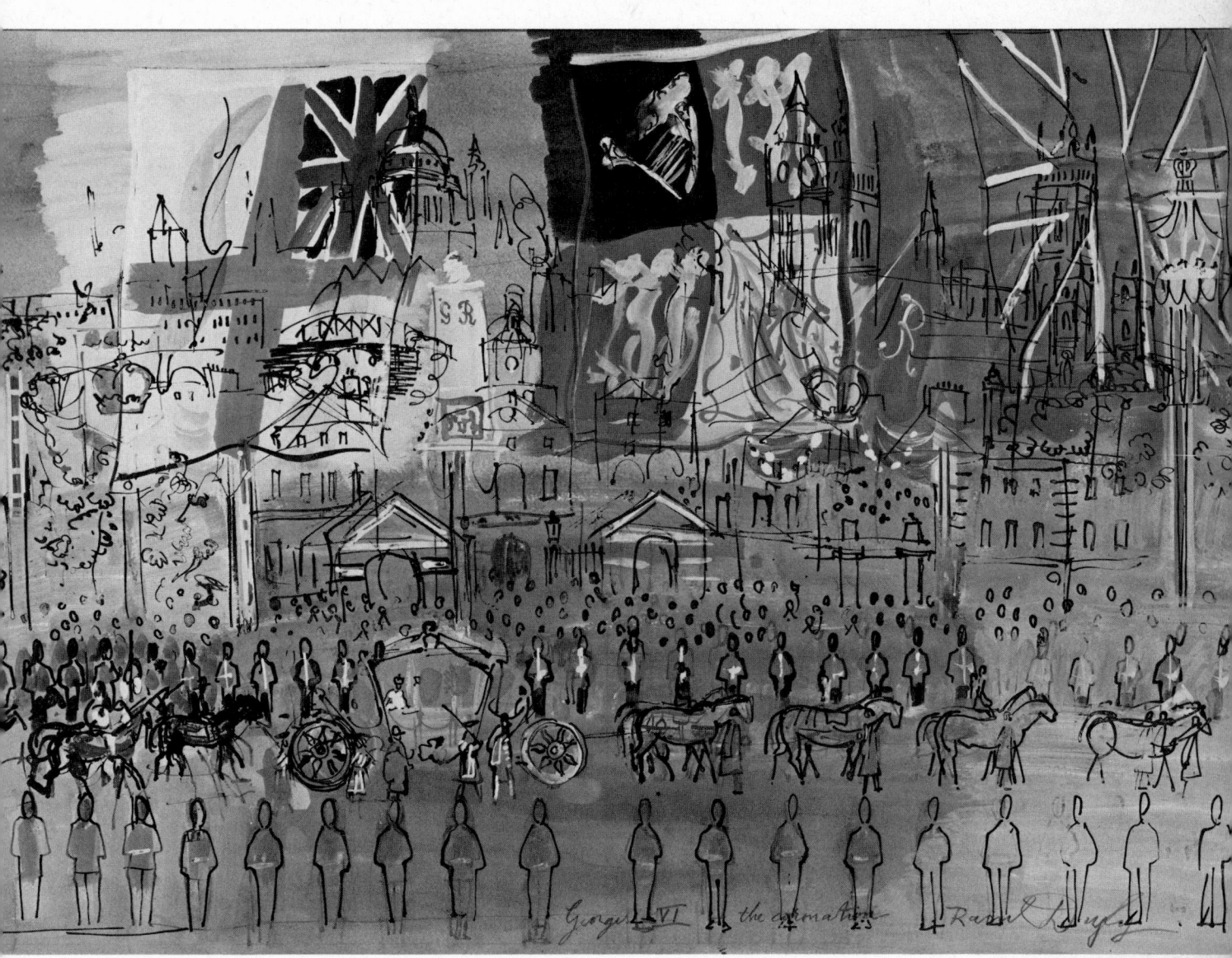

134. CORONATION OF GEORGE VI, 1937. *Watercolour, 16 × 26 in. Créteil, Collection
M. Boulard.*

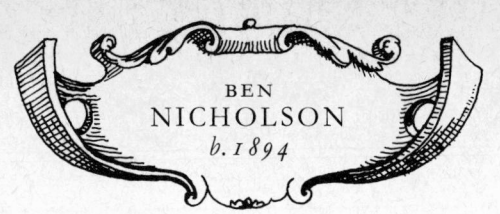

BEN
NICHOLSON
b. 1894

IT IS NATURAL and necessary that an abstract painter should be in continual rapport with landscape, since we inescapably live among its constituents of light, colour, tones, lines, surface, relief. Ben Nicholson, son of the now much under-esteemed painter William Nicholson, made his first English landscapes from the scenery of Cumberland and Cornwall (1927–30), having tasted before that of the light of Touraine, the Ticino and the coast of Spain. A modern journey up the motorway towards Carlisle may suggest something definitive of this painter's work. Followed, edged, endlessly preceded by traffic, the driver as he goes north from Birmingham to Lancashire is harassed by the need to attend and yet is forced to realize how land left and right is fouled disgustingly by the scramble for markets. Then coming out of Lancashire and into Cumberland, and on to the fells, at last the driver can afford to see more of his transient surroundings, taking note of the colour and the light across hills on which field walls and only scattered farmhouses restore an equilibrium between man and landscape, under liquidly clear skies empty of industrial smoke: through the sense of vision he enters an outward and inward happiness, if he can respond to it.

The preferred country of Nicholson's English landscape has been the Land's End or Penwith district of Cornish moorland, cliff, harbour and sea (through the 1940s), and intermittently from 1955 the scenery of the Yorkshire Dales, especially Wharfedale. He likes scenery which is bare, allowing a universality of light, like an uneven canvas or panel. Across this the cleanest lines—of hills, roads, walls—can be traced in movement, tension, and stillness; scenery in which horizontals are in a never vicious relation with the verticality of branching trees, buildings, chimneys, roof tops, telegraph poles. The interaction between fact and invention is so vital that an abstract relief can be called 'English Landscape' or 'Holkham Sands' (both works of 1969), though there is no question of an abstract being other than abstract or a landscape other than landscape, however much the scene is induced to reveal its composed and tense relationship of stillness and motion, and shape and line.

Nicholson's landscapes are not allowed to be vehicles of selfconsciousness or attitudinizing: they are discoveries of what an admired scene contains and offers in itself, through this painter; they afford, like the rest of his work, Delacroix's desired 'spectacle of eternal youth' (see page 19—Delacroix on English artists). *Page* 202.

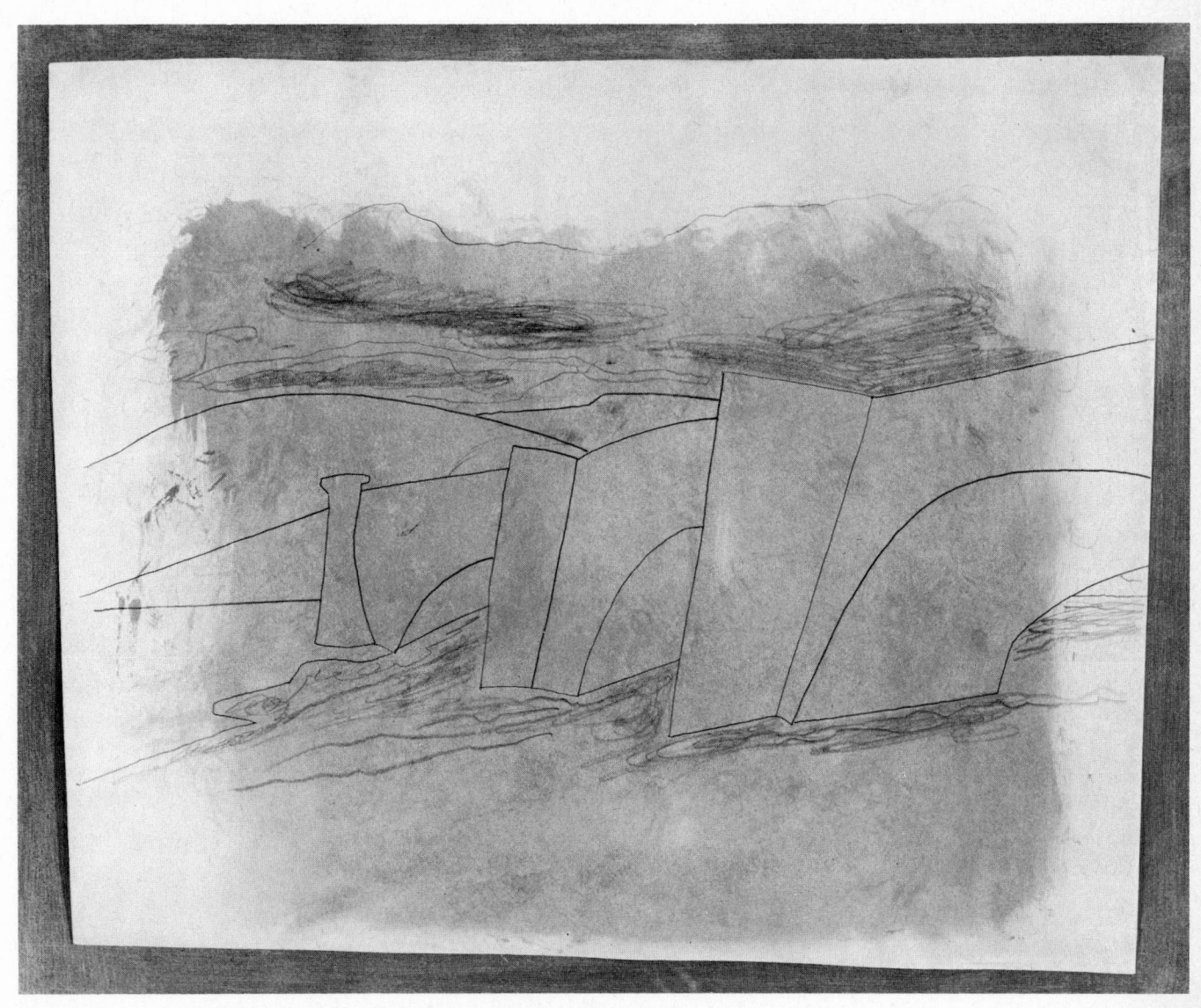

135. BURNSALL, BRIDGE, 1972. *Pen, pencil and wash. Collection the artist.*

Bridge over the Wharfe at Burnsall, north of Skipton, Yorkshire. For Nicholson on Wharfedale, see page 203.

136. ST. IVES, 1940. *Oil, $12\frac{3}{4} \times 15\frac{3}{8}$ in. Reddihough collection.*

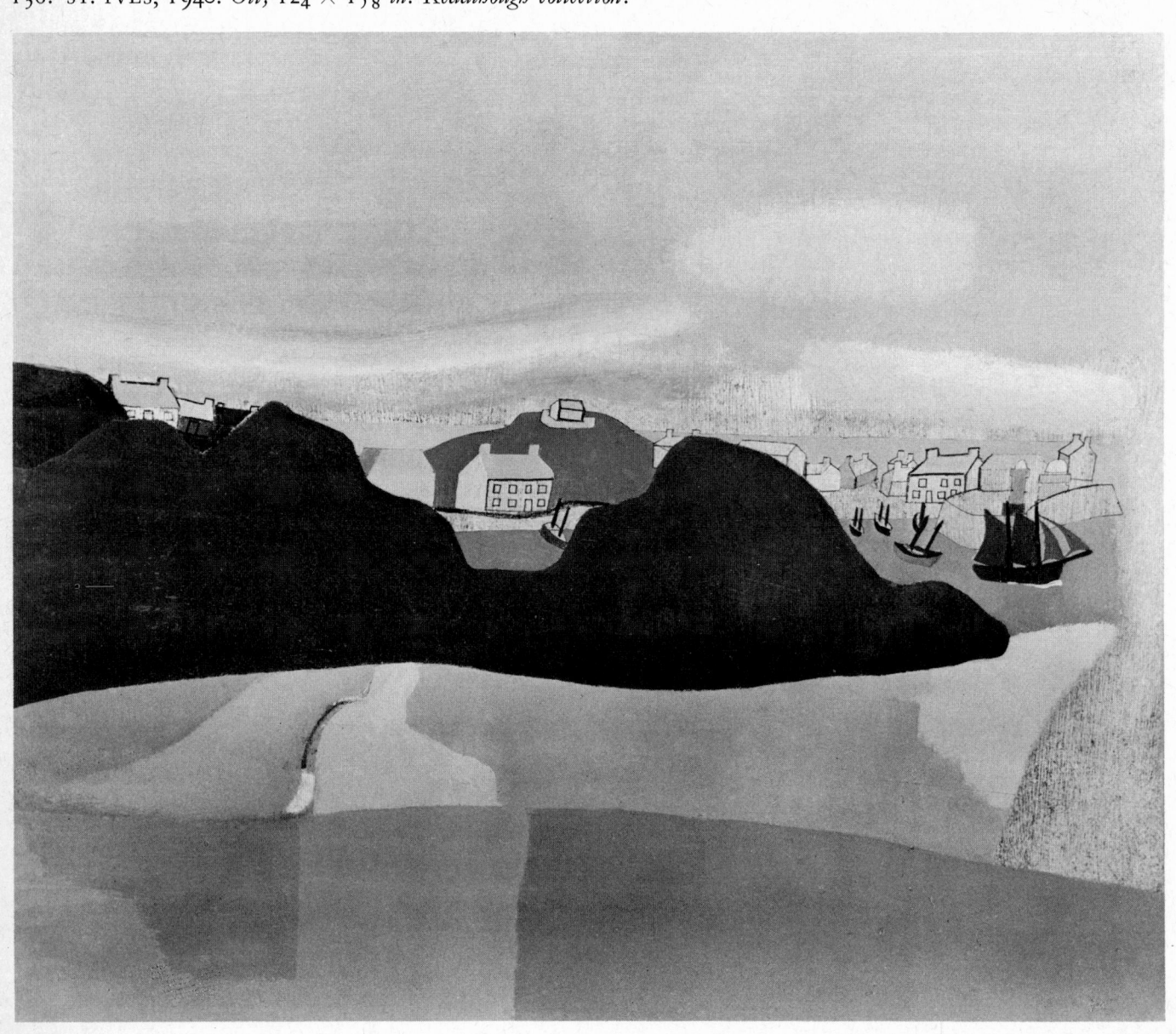

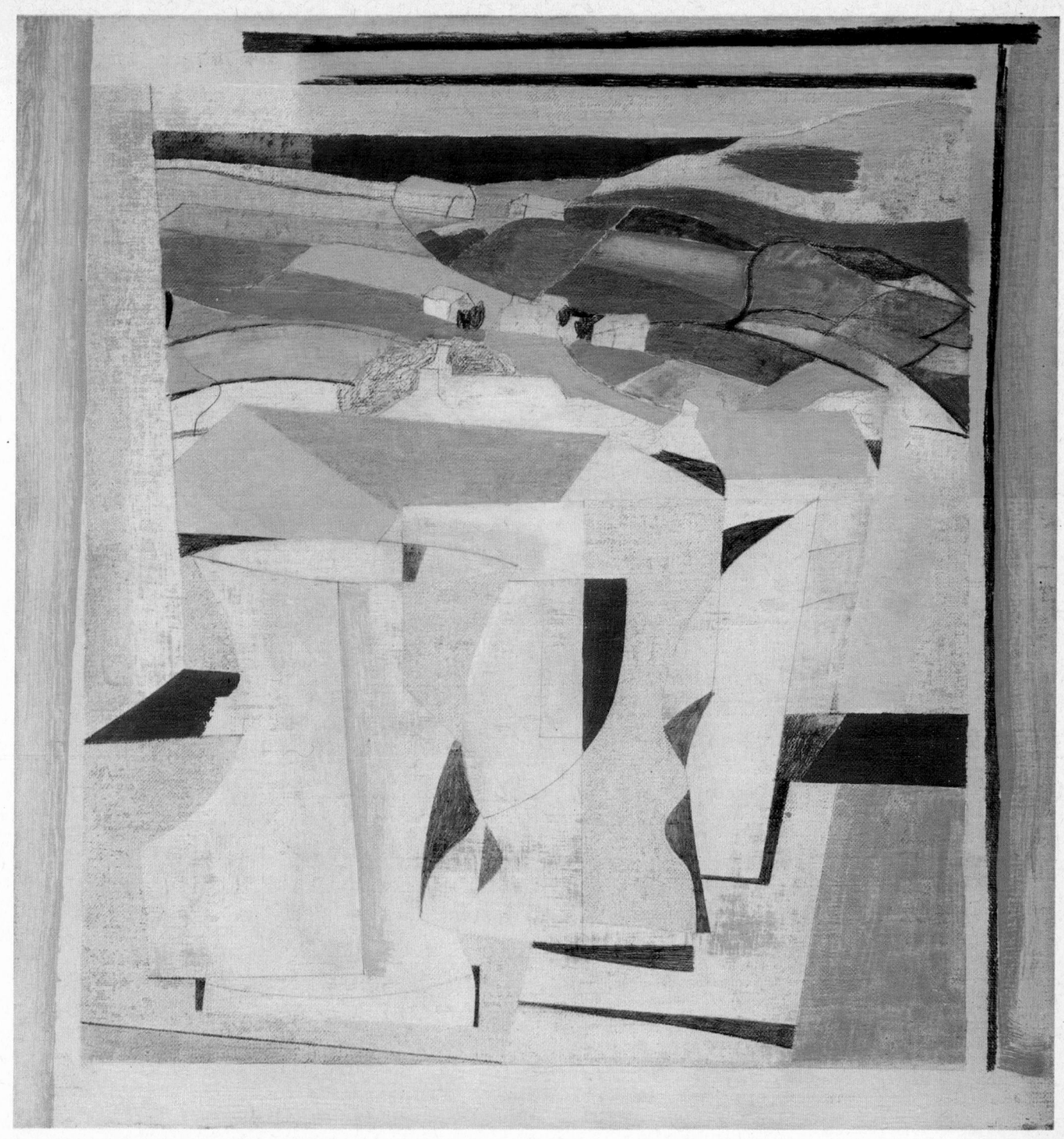

137. DECEMBER 1947 (TRENDRINE, CORNWALL), 1947. *Oil, 15 × 14½ in. Washington, Phillips Collection.*

A landscape from the hamlet of Trendrine, on the road from St. Ives to Zennor, looking towards the Atlantic.

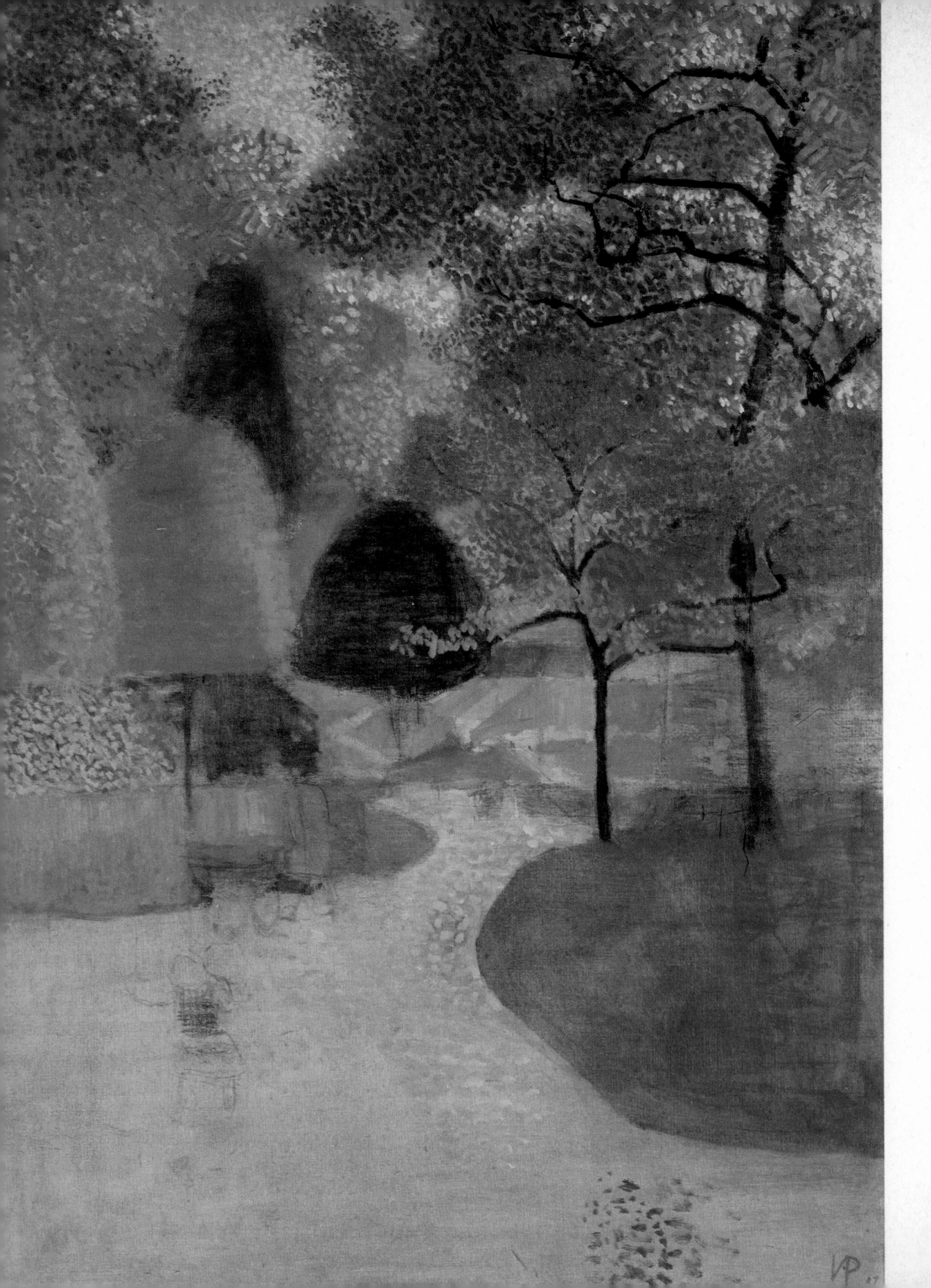

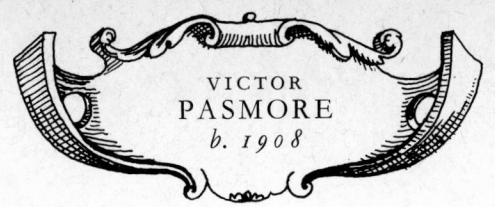

THERE WAS A TIME—he was in his twenties—when this painter could stand in the Louvre in front of a Courbet landscape and slap his thigh with a huge gesture and exclamation of delight that made the attendants, and everyone else, look round. In the thirties and into the forties he was a latter day Impressionist or Post-Impressionist associated with the reactionary (and rather defiant) Euston Road School. He painted naturalistic landscapes which seemed to start decades late with Whistler among the coloured hazes of the Thames—though higher upstream, at Hammersmith and Chiswick where something remained of the old amalgamation of light and shore and water which Whistler had known before the lower Thames was embanked. Then as if believing in an evolution of sensibility he worked through the precepts and the example of Whistler, Cézanne, Van Gogh, Seurat and Gaugin, concluding that they had looked and worked towards a colour art akin to music. At the end of the forties and in the fifties he was convinced and converted by this strange recapitulation in himself and began to combine shapes unrelated to nature, in tension or balance, often in a sonorous and thrilling inter-action of colours. Before this crystallization the best landscapes of this consider-able artist derived from Chiswick and Hammersmith and then from the Porthmeor Beach at St. Ives in Cornwall, where he passed the summer of 1950 in sympathetic contact with Ben Nicholson.

Page 203.

138. THE PARK, 1947. *Oil, 43 × 31 in. London, Collection Adrian Heath.*

Based on drawings made in Chiswick Park in London.

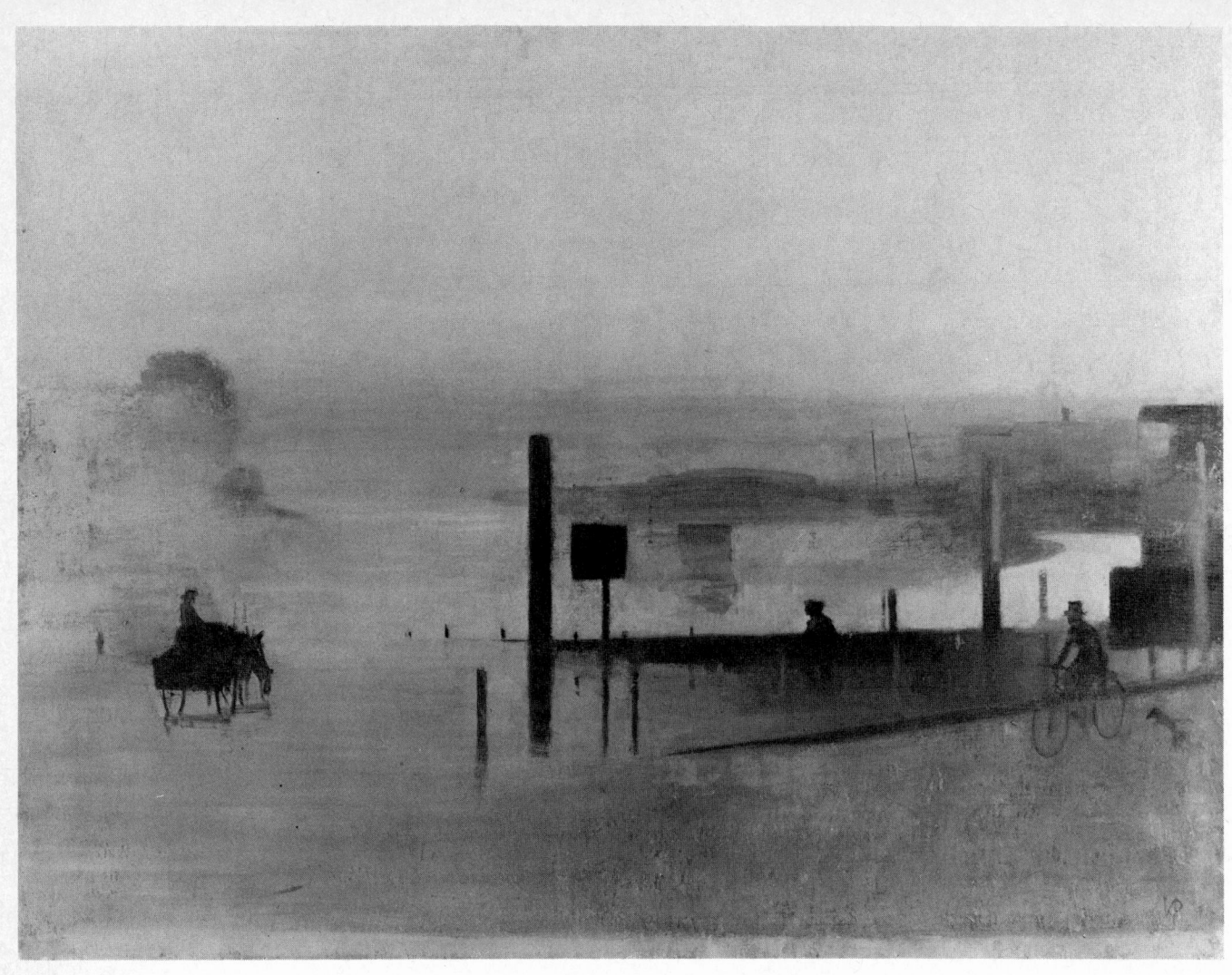

139. THE QUIET RIVER: THE THAMES AT CHISWICK, 1943–4. *Oil, 30×40 in.*
London, Tate Gallery.

140. EVENING, HAMMERSMITH, *c.* 1945. *Oil,* $34\frac{1}{4} \times 47\frac{1}{4}$ *in. Ottawa, National Gallery of Canada.*

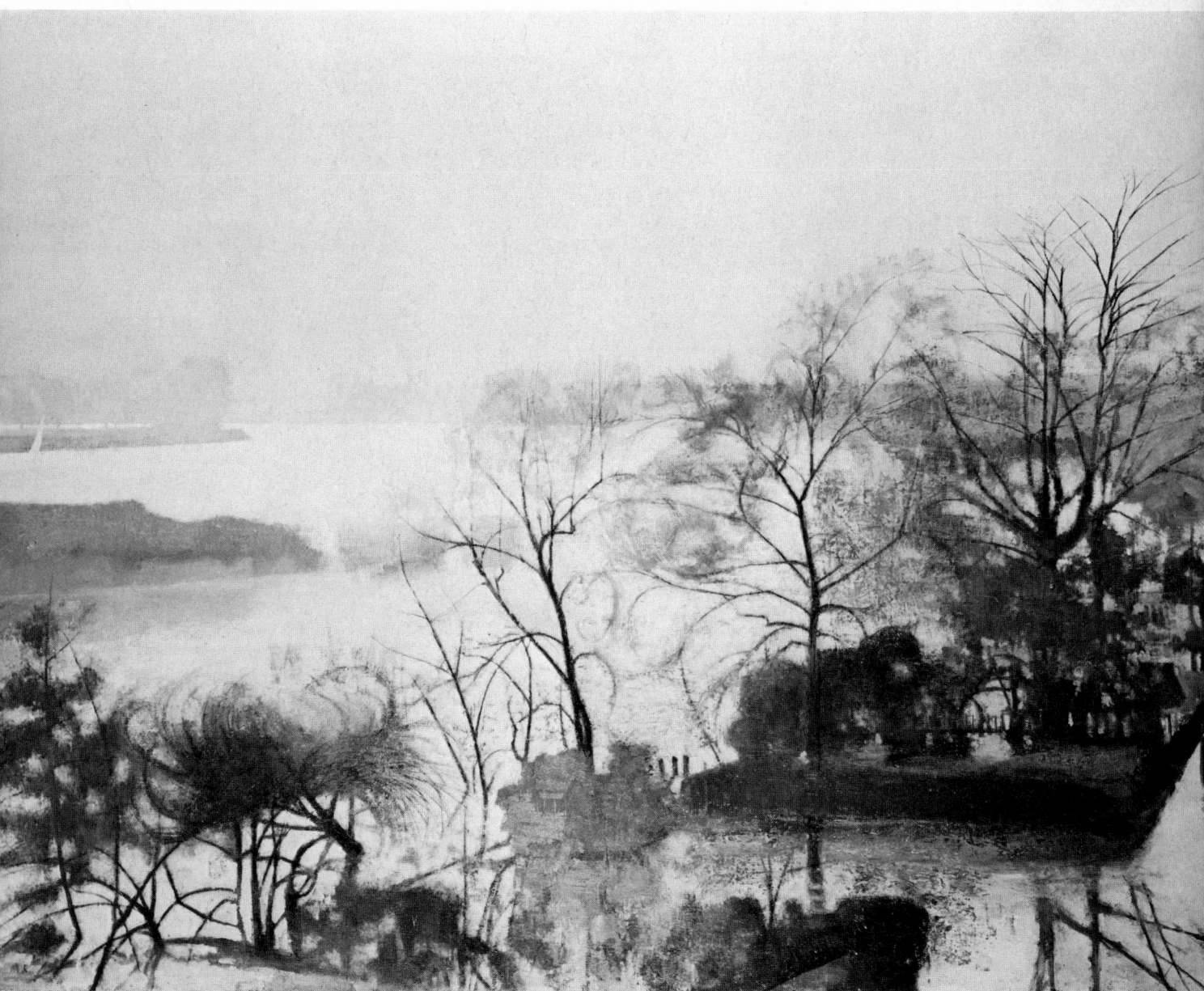

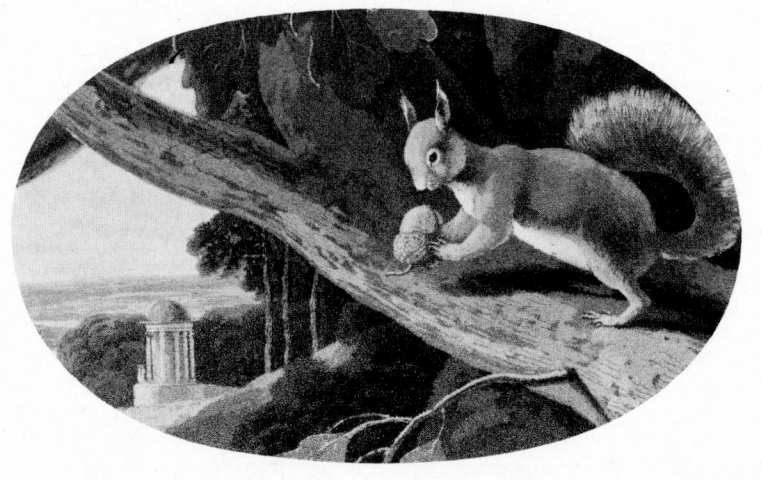

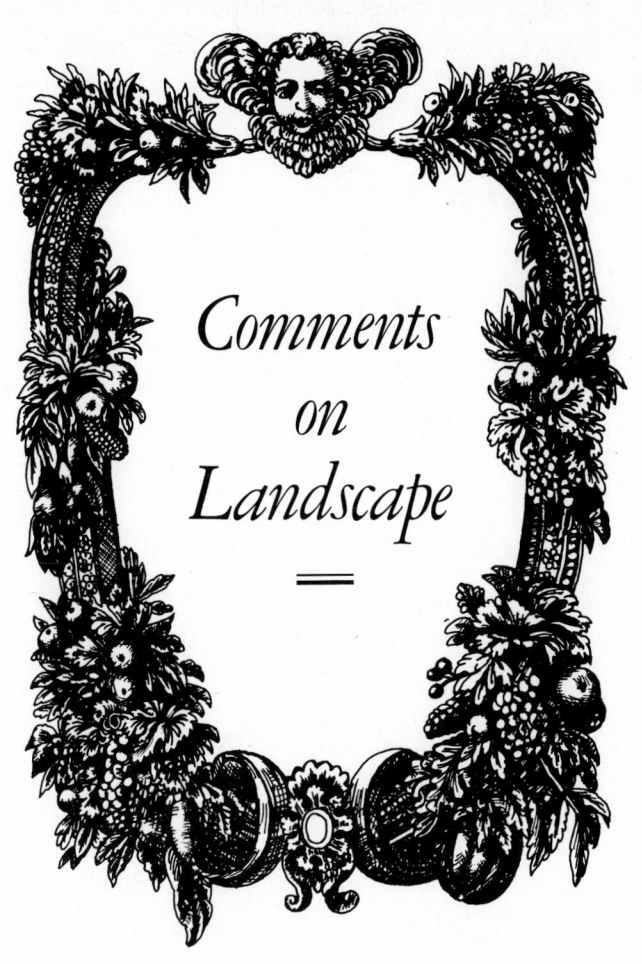

Comments
on
Landscape
=

WHEN ARTISTS speak formally about their art—or about art in general—they are often stilted or unconvincing; they manage to hide themselves in words they seldom use as well as they use paint. Most of these comments on landscape are different. All of them are by artists whose work is reproduced in this book, and they are generally in the nature of asides and exclamations, revealing—though the two cannot be separated—something of the kind of man, in each case, as well as the kind of artist.

To begin with I had intended to collect statements only about the places in Great Britain which the artists had visited and painted—about the land they transformed into landscape. But statements of that kind are mostly made in paint. Verbal ones are infrequent. So I added remarks on painted landscape, from Wilson calling Gainsborough's trees 'fried parsley' to Victor Pasmore signing off from landscape and assuring himself that an earlier generation of great landscapists believed that they were the primitives of a new non-figurative art, akin to music.

In my note on Sickert (page 162) I quoted Sickert's remark that 'a painter must be judged by his canvases and not by his patter.' To which one replies 'Of course'—and to which one may add that good artists are not always so silent as we suppose. Against, for example, Turner who had difficulty with words and next to no coherent speech except line, form and colour, we have to set Constable, Delacroix, Palmer, Corot, Whistler, Van Gogh, etcetera, and in our day Ben Nicholson, whose letters should become one of the artists' classics of the future. It is the mandarins of the studio, the highly successful, loudly puffed Followers, who have nothing to say, because they have invented nothing, and often they have been wise enough not to turn their nothing into words. The more the artist's true vitality, the more it is likely to break into exclamation. When we face their pictures, or other men's pictures, we are not the worse off for remembering Constable on his bloom and freshness, or Corot talking of nature as a guest in his studio or of

the vulgarity and pretentiousness of over-explosive sunsets; or Whistler on what nature does pull off now and again, or tongue-tied Sisley managing to enunciate that 'every picture exhibits a place the artist has fallen in love with'.

Richard Wilson 1713 or 1714–82

(His reply to the question who were the best painters of landscape). Why, sir, Claude for air and Gaspar for composition and sentiment; you may walk in Claude's pictures and count the miles. But there are two painters whose merit the world does not yet know, who will not fail hereafter to be highly valued, Cuyp and Mompers.

He used to call Barret's pictures *Spinach and Eggs* and Gainsborough's *Fried Parsley*. (Recorded by Sir (William Beechey.)

(His exclamation at the sight of the waterfall at Terni.) Well done, water, by God! 1751.

Wilson used to say, that 'everything the landscape painter could want, was to be found in North Wales.' (Recorded by Edward Dayes.)

Alexander Cozens c. 1717–86

THE INVENTION OF LANDSCAPE
The powers of art and invention, impart picturesque beauty, and strength of character to the works of an artist in landscape painting; as a noble and graceful deportment confers a winning aspect on the human frame. Composing landscapes by invention, is not the art of imitating individual nature; it is more; it is forming artificial representations of landscape on the general principles of nature, founded in unity of character, which is true simplicity; concentring in each individual composition the beauties, which judicious imitation would select from those which are dispersed in nature ... How far the incapacity of combining our ideas with readiness and propriety in the works of art, may arise from neglecting to exercise

the invention, or from not duely cultivating the taste and judgment, cannot perhaps be easily determined: but it cannot be doubted, that too much time is spent in copying the works of others, which tends to weaken the powers of invention; and I scruple not to affirm, that too much time may be employed in copying the landscapes of nature herself.   *1784.*

ART AND NATURE

(Quotations from Shakespeare and Pope used by Cozens to explain his views on landscape.)

This is an Art
Which does mend Nature, change it rather; but
The Art itself is Nature.

Those Rules which are discover'd, not devis'd
Are Nature still, but Nature methodiz'd:
Nature, like Monarchy, is but restrain'd
By the same Laws which first herself ordain'd.

Thomas Gainsborough 1727–88

REAL VIEWS FROM NATURE

Mr. Gainsborough presents his Humble respects to Lord Hardwicke; and shall always think it an honor to be employ'd in anything for his Lordship; but with respect to *real Views* from Nature in this Country he has never seen any Place that affords a Subject equal to the poorest imitations of Gaspar or Claude. Paul Sanby is the only Man of Genius, he believes, who has employ'd his Pencil that way—Mr. G. hopes Lord Hardwicke will not mistake his meaning, but if his Lordship wishes to have anything tolerable of the name of G, the subject altogether, as well as figures etc. must be of his own Brain; otherwise Lord Hardwicke will only pay for Encouraging a Man out of his way and had much better buy a picture of some of the good Old Masters. (Letter to Lord Hardwicke.)
About 1764.

FACES AND LANDSCAPES

I'm sick of Portraits and wish very much to take my Viol da Gamba and walk off to some sweet Village where I can paint Landskips and enjoy the fag End of Life in quietness and ease. But these fine Ladies and their Tea drinkings, Dancings, *Husband huntings* and such will fob me out of the last ten years, & I fear miss getting Husbands too—But we can say nothing to these things you know Jackson, we must jogg on

and be content with the jingling of the Bells, only damn it I hate a dust, the Kicking up of a dust, and being confined *in Harness* to follow the track, whilst others ride in the waggon, under cover, stretching their Legs in the Straw at Ease, and gazing at Green Trees & Blue skies without half my *Taste*, that's damn'd hard. (Letter to William Jackson.)

HAVE YOU ROCKS AND WATERFALLS?

If the People with their damn'd Faces could but let me alone a little I believe I should soon appear in a more tolerable light but I have been plagued very much. Thank God I shall now shut myself up for the summer and not appear til September comes in . . . The weather Sir, is *settled* in very fine in these Parts but rather too warm for Riding in the middle of the day especially upon Lansdown where there is no shade.

I suppose your Country is very woody—pray have you Rocks and Waterfalls! for I am as fond of Landskip as ever. (Letter from Gainsborough in Bath to James Unwin in Derbyshire.)   *1768.*

FIGURES IN LANDSCAPE

Do you really think that a regular Composition in the Landskip way should ever be fill'd with History, or any figures but such as fill a place (I won't say stop a Gap) or to create a little business for the Eye to be drawn from the Trees in order to return to them with more glee. (Letter to William Jackson.)

LITTLE DUTCH LANDSKIPS

How happy should I be to set out for Yarmouth and after recruiting my poor Crazy Frame, enjoy the coasting along til I reach'd Norwich and give you a call—God only knows what is for me, but hope is the Pallat Colors we all paint with in sickness—'tis odd how all the Childish passions hang about me in sickness, I feel such a fondness for my first imitations of little Dutch Landskips that I can't keep from working an hour or two of a Day, though with a great mixture of bodily Pain—I am so childish that I could make a Kite, catch Gold Finches, or built little Ships. (Letter to Thomas Harvey.)   *1788.*

HIS 'CORNARD WOOD'

Mr. Boydell bought the large landscape* you speak of for seventy-five guineas last week at Greenwood's. It is in some respects a little in the *schoolboy style*—but I

* Plates 28, 29.

do not reflect on this without a secret gratification; for as an early instance how strong my inclination stood for Landskip, this picture was actually painted at Sudbury in the year 1748; it was begun *before I left school*;—and was the means of my Father's sending me to London.

It may be worth remark that though there is very little idea of composition in the picture, the touch and closeness to nature in the study of the parts and *minutiae* are equal to any of my later productions. In this explanation I do not wish to seem vain or ridiculous, but do not look on the Landskip as one of my riper performances.

It is full forty years since it was first delivered by me to go in search of those who had *taste* to admire it! Within that time it has been in the hands of twenty picture dealers, and I once bought it myself during that interval for *Nineteen Guineas.* Is not that curious? (Letter to Henry Bate, later Sir Henry Bate Dudley.) *1788.*

Joseph Wright of Derby 1734–97

STEALING OFF TO LANDSCAPES

I have just prepared a canvas the size of Tate's 'Moonlight', for an evening effect on another view on the River Tay at Dunkeld, which, if care and study will accomplish it, I intend it to be the best picture I ever painted. I know not how it is, tho' I am engaged in portraits and made a complete dead colour of a half length yesterday, I find myself continually stealing off and getting to Landscapes. (Letter to John Leigh Philips.) *1792.*

WATER, REFLECTION, AIR AND DEPTH

Mr. Wm. Hardman called last night. I showed him the pictures by candle-light, but I don't think he could see them well. They did not seem to reach his feelings, except a small one of an effect of fire, seen through a dark group of trees, with a large piece of water reflecting the objects about it . . . 'Tis a new subject, and rather a favourite with me. If there should be an exhibition this year, independent of the Royal Academy, I perhaps may show it to the public, as also the companion to the 'Moonlight', in my friend Tate's hands, which, now being near finished, and if I flatter not myself, will be a tolerable picture. 'Tis full of air, and has depth, two necessary requisites for a Landscape. (Letter to John Leigh Philips.) *1793.*

NATURE OBSERVED

The picture of the little elegant bit of scenery at Rydall,* which my friend Holland mentioned to you, is not near being finished. The water indeed is further advanced than the rest of the picture, for I was keen to produce an effect I had never seen in painting of shewing the pebbles at the bottom of the water with the broken reflections on its surface. But I have not succeeded to my wish, & Holland who sees all my works thro' the most partial medium, has colored his description too highly. So highly finished is that little bit of nature that to do it justice it should be painted upon the spot.

Your account of the Isle of Man makes me wish to see it. We [more] often see fine shaped rocks than fine coloured ones; the patches of different colours are not large and distinct enough to have effect at a distance. The different hues are produced by small mosses rather than by original colours in the stones. (Letter to John Leigh Philips.) *1795.*

Edward Dayes 1763–1804

ON GOING TO ITALY

The vast importation of fine pictures has, in a great degree, removed the necessity of the young artist going to Italy . . . Almost all our landscape painters bring away as much prejudice as spoils them through life; for it is by no means uncommon to see the air of that climate brought into all their English scenes; a thing just as absurd as Dutch figures in an Italian view; or, as once occurred in a picture of the Apostles awakening Christ in the Storm, where the figures were Dutch, with a Dutch boat, and even Dutch colors . . . Countries, as well as men, have their peculiar character, and should, no doubt, be equally attended to. The beautiful silvery tone of distance that attends some of our tolerably clear days, is highly fascinating, and must interest every one but the coxcomb, who can talk of nothing but the serenity of an Italian atmosphere. Some men have carried the infatuation so far, as to suppose that a man cannot become an artist of any celebrity, who has not inhaled the air of Italy; as if the atmosphere had a divine virtue, and could make painters. *c. 1798.*

* *Rydal Waterfall,* 1795. Derby Museum and Art Gallery.

SOME LOCAL SPOT

When an artist gives a representation of some local spot, we feel obliged by his extending our topographical knowledge; but if, in his fancy pictures, we are ever presented with common-place stuff, such as might ouze out of any futile pate, we feel disgusted, and turn away dissatisfied, and uninformed. What makes the little rural representations of the Dutch school delight, is, in a great measure, their locality, and the idea of the primitive simplicity and happiness we connect thereto. Farington made a long stay at the Lakes of Cumberland; but the grandeur of those scenes does not appear to have infused any of their dignity into his imagination. (From a note on Joseph Farington.)   *c. 1804.*

John Crome 1768–1821

INAPPROPRIATE FIGURES

The man who would place an animal where the animal would not place itself, would do the same with a tree, a bank, a human figure—with any object, in fact, that might occur in Nature, and therefore such a man may be a great colourist, or a good draughtsman but he is no artist. (Compare Gainsborough, page 184 and Constable, page 189.)

BREADTH, DIGNITY AND CLOUDS

In your letter you wish me to give you my opinion of your picture, I should have liked it better if you had made it more of a whole, that is the trees stronger, the sky running from them in shadow up to the opposite corner; that might have produced what I think it wanted, and have made it a much less too-picture effect . . . I cannot let your sky go off without some observation. I think the character of your clouds too affected, that is, too much of some of our modern painters, who mistake some of our great masters because they sometimes put in some of those round characters of clouds, they must do the same; but if you look at any of their skies, they either assist in the composition or make some figure in the picture, nay, sometimes play the first fiddle. I have seen this in Wouerman's and many others I could mention.

Brea[d]th must be attended to, if you paint but a muscle give it brea[d]th. Your doing the same by the sky, making parts broad and of a good shape, that they may come in with your composition, forming one grand plan of light and shade, this must always please

a good eye and keep the attention of the spectator and give delight to every one. Trifles in Nature must be overlooked that we may have our feelings raised by seeing the whole picture at a glance, not knowing how or why we are so charmed. I fear I have written a long rigmarole story about giving dignity to whatever you paint. (Letter to James Stark.)   *1816.*

J. M. W. Turner 1775–1851

LIGHT AND SHADE AND ENGLISH LANDSCAPE

Among the mutable and infinite contrasts of light and shade, none is so difficult either to define or [to make] deductable to common vision as reflexes.* They enter into every effect in nature, oppose even themselves in theory, and evade every attempt to reduce them to anything like rule or practicality. What seems one day to be equally governed by one cause is destroyed the next by a different atmosphere in our variable climate, where [all] the seasons are recognizable in one day, where all the vapoury turbulance involves the face of things, where nature seems to sport in all her dignity in dispensing incidents for the artist's study . . . how happily is the landscape painter situated, how roused by every change of nature in every moment, that allows no langour even in her effects which she places before him, and demands most peremptorily every moment his admiration and investigation, to store his mind with every change of time and place . . .

As it is my pride that these should be English lectures, it is natural that they should speak of English effects; and if the Italian masters are but slightly recalled [?] of, it is not to follow they are to be lightly thought of in our pursuits. On the contrary, what they have done are to be duly weighed in our estimation, as far as contrast to ours . . . They have provided what they saw to be practicable in their atmosphere, and we should prove what is so in ours. An endless variety is on our side and opens a new field of novelty . . . The soil is British and so should be the harvest. (Lecture fragment.)   *c. 1810.*

A STORM AT FARNLEY HALL, ABOVE THE WHARFE

One stormy day at Farnley Turner called out to me loudly from the doorway, 'Hawkey! Hawkey! Come here! Come here! Look at this thunder-storm. Isn't it grand?—isn't it wonderful?—isn't it sublime?' All this time he was making notes of its form and colour on

* i.e. lights reflected from a lighted surface to a shaded surface.

the back of a letter. I proposed some better drawing-block, but he said it did very well. He was absorbed—he was entranced. There was the storm rolling and sweeping and shafting out its lightning over the Yorkshire hills. Presently the storm passed, and he finished.

'There! Hawkey,' said he. 'In two years you will see this again, and call it *Hannibal Crossing the Alps.*' (Hawkesworth Fawkes's account of an incident in 1810.)

THE ARTIST'S IMAGINATION

If theory dared to stipulate for aerial hues, peculiar colors or tones of color, she would here step to self-destruction . . . [The] imagination of the artist dwells *enthroned* in his own recess [and] must be incomprehensible as from darkness; and even words fall short of illustration, or become illusory of pictorial appreciations. (Turner's fifth Royal Academy lecture.) *1818.*

RECOLLECTIONS OF WALES

Now for Aberiswith—I think you have well chosen—it is well sheltered, from the East—the Town close to the sea, no doubt must be much improved, in regard to comfort and good quartering since my seeing it, and the scenery of natural valley, the Estwith, the Ridol and the Devil's Bridge are beautiful and Grand features. The view from the Inn near the Devil's Bridge commands the falls of the Ridol—the Devil's Bridge torrent rushes down a deep chasam, under two Bridges one over the other—viz the new one built upon the old one—You are in the neighbourhood of Havord or Hawvaford, know[n] I dare say yet known by being the Seat of Esquire Johns a fine place well wooded and he employ'd Stothard to paint the same so think you will find some Pictures by him there. I do not think [?] you [could] have hit upon a more desirable spot for your pencil and hope you may feel—just what I felt in the days of my youth when I was in search of Richard Wilson's birthplace. (Letter to Hawksworth Fawkes.) *1847.*

May. Blossoms. Apple, Cherry, Lilac.
Small white flowers in the Hedges
in Clusters, D. Blue Bells,
Buttercups and daisies in the fields
Oak, Warm, Elm G. [i.e. Grey] Ash, Yellow, &c.

May 30. Margate, a small opening along the horizon marked the approach of the sun by its getting yellow. (From Turner's last surviving sketchbook, when he was 70 or 71.) *1845–6.*

John Constable 1776–1837

NATURE AT EAST BERGHOLT

I shall shortly return to East Bergholt where I shall make some laborious studies from nature—and I shall endeavour to get a pure and unaffected representation of the scenes that may employ me with respect to colour particularly and anything else—drawing I am pretty well master of.

There is little or nothing in the exhibition worth looking up to—there is room enough for a natural painture. The great vice of the present day is *bravura,* an attempt at something beyond the truth. (Letter to John Dunthorne.) *1802.*

BANKS OF THE STOUR

How much I can Imagine myself with you on your fishing excursion in the new forest, what River can it be. But the sound of water escaping from Mill dams [? 'delights me' omitted], so do Willows, Old rotten Banks, slimy posts, & brickwork. I love such things . . . As long as I do paint I shall never cease to paint such Places. They have always been my delight—& I should indeed have delighted in seeing what you described in your company . . .

But I should paint my own places best—Painting is but another word for feeling. I associate my 'careless boyhood' to all that lies on the banks of the *Stour.* They made me a painter (& I am grateful) that is I had often thought of pictures of them before I had ever touched a pencil. (Letter to John Fisher.) *1824.*

SKIES IN THE LANDSCAPE

I have often been advised to consider my *Sky*—as a '*White Sheet drawn behind the Objects*'. Certainly if the Sky is *obtrusive*—(as mine are) it is bad, but if they are evaded (as mine are not) it is worse, they must and always shall with me make an effectual part of the composition. It will be difficult to name a class of Landscape, in which the sky is not the '*key note*', the '*standard of Scale*', and the chief '*Organ of sentiment*'. You may conceive then what a '*white sheet*' would do for me, impressed as I am with these notions, and they cannot be Erroneous. The sky is the '*source of light*' in nature—and governs every thing. (The same letter to John Fisher.) *1824.*

LIGHTNESS AND BRIGHTNESS

My picture is liked at the Academy. Indeed it forms a decided feature and its light cannot be put out, because it is the light of nature . . . My execution annoys most of them and all the scholastic ones—perhaps the sacrifices I make for *lightness* and *brightness* is too much, but these things are the essence of landscape. (Letter to John Fisher.) *1824.*

MY LIMITED ART

My limited and abstracted art is to be found under every hedge and in every lane, and therefore nobody thinks it worth picking up; but I have my admirers, each of whom I consider an host. (Letter to C. R. Leslie.) *1832.*

FRSESHNESS OF SPRING

I never did admire the autumnal tints in nature, so little of a painter am I in the eye of commonplace connoisseurship—I love the exhilarating freshness of spring. (Letter to C. R. Leslie.) *1833.*

THE DEWY FRESHNESS

Calling upon Constable, one day, I found him with a palette-knife, on which was some white, mixed with a viscous vehicle, and with which he touched the surface of a beautiful picture he was painting. Upon expressing my surprise, he said 'Oh! My dear Hart, I'm giving my picture the dewy freshness.' He maintained that the process imparted the dewy freshness of nature, and he contended that the apparent crudeness would readily subside, and that the chemical change which would ensue in a short time, would assume the truthful aspect of nature.' (Recorded by Solomon Hart.)

Your regard for me has at least awakened me to believe in the possibility that I may yet make some impression with my 'light'—my 'dews'—my 'breezes' —my *bloom* and my *freshness*—no one of which qualities has yet been perfected on the canvas of any painter in this world. (Letter to C. R. Leslie.) *1833.*

A PICTURE OF THE MORNING

The 'Morning Post' speaks beautifully of my 'House'.* S[hee] told me that it was 'only a picture of a house', and ought to have been put into the Architectural Room. I told him it was a 'picture of a summer morning, including a house.' (Letter to Samuel Lane.) *1833.*

* *Englefield House, Berkshire—Morning.*

ON THE MEZZOTINTS IN HIS 'ENGLISH LANDSCAPE'

The most of these subjects, chiefly consisting of home scenery, are from Pictures exhibited by the Author at the Royal Academy during the past few years; they are taken from real places, and are meant particularly to characterize the scenery of England; the effects of light and shadow being transcripts only of such as occurred at the time of being taken. (From the *Introduction*.) *1833.*

ENGLAND'S 'ENDLESS VARIETIES OF EFFECT'

[Constable's 'List of the Engravings' in his *English Landscape*.]

Frontispiece, Paternal House and Grounds of the Artist. Evening.

Spring. East Bergholt Common, Hail Squalls. Noon.

Sunset. Peasants returning homewards.

Noon. The West and Fields, Hampstead.

Yarmouth Pier, Norfolk. Morning Breeze.

Summer Morning. The Vale of Dedham.

Summer Evening. A Homestead, Cattle reposing.

Dell in the Woods of Helmingham Park. Autumn.

Hampstead Heath, Stormy Noon. Sand Diggers.

A Sea Beach, Brighton, Heavy Surf. Windy Noon.

Stoke Church, by Neyland, Suffolk. Rainbow at Noon.

River Stour, Suffolk, near Flatford Mill. An Avenue.

Head of a Lock on the Stour. Rolling Clouds.

Mound of the City of Old Sarum. Thunder Clouds.

A Summerland, Rainy Day; Ploughmen. Noon.

Barges on the Stour: Gleams of Light on the Meadows.

A Water Mill, Dedham. Burst of Light at Noon.

Weymouth Bay, Dorset. Tempestuous Evening.

Summer Afternoon, Sunshine after a Shower.

The Glebe Farm, Green Lane; Girl at a Spring.

The Nore, Hadleigh Castle. Morning, after a Stormy Night.

Vignette, Hampstead Heath. Labourer returning. *1833.*

EAST BERGHOLT AND THE VALE OF DEDHAM

The beauty of the surrounding scenery, the gentle declivities, the luxurious meadow flats sprinkled with flocks and herds, and well cultivated uplands, the woods and rivers, with farms and picturesque cottages, all impart to this particular spot an amenity and elegance hardly anywhere else to be found; and which has always caused it to be admired by all persons of taste, who have been lovers of Painting, and who can feel a pleasure in its pursuit when united with the contemplation of Nature.

Perhaps the Author in his over-weaning affection for these scenes may estimate them too highly, and may have dwelt too exclusively upon them; but interwoven as they are with his thoughts, it would have been difficult to have avoided doing so; besides, every recollection associated with the Vale of Dedham must always be dear to him, and he delights to retrace those scenes, 'where once his careless childhood strayed', among which the happy years of the morning of his life were passed, and where by a fortunate chance of events he early met those, by whose valuable and encouraging friendship he was invited to pursue his first youthful wish, and to realize his cherished hopes, and that ultimately led to fix him in that pursuit to which he felt his mind directed. (Letterpress for the mezzotint of *East Bergholt, Suffolk*.)   *1835.*

ARUNDEL, SUSSEX
The Castle is the cheif ornament of this place—but all here sinks to insignificance in comparison with the woods, and hills. The woods hang from excessive steeps, and precipices, and the trees are beyond everything beautifull: I never saw such beauty in *natural landscape* before. I wish it may influence what I may do in future, for I have too much preferred the picturesque to the beautifull—which will I hope account for the *broken ruggedness of my style* . . . The meadows are lovely, so is the delightfull river, and the old houses are rich beyond all things of the sort—but the trees above all, but anything is beautifull. (Letter to C. R. Leslie.)   *1833.*

SKETCHING FROM NATURE
When I sit down to make a sketch from nature, the first thing I try to do is, *to forget that I have ever seen a picture.*

A FREEHOLD
Whatever may be thought of my art, it is my own; and I would rather possess a freehold, though but a cottage, than live in a palace belonging to another.

THE APPROPRIATENESS OF NATURE
[On a painting by him with a bird in it.]

Yes, I saw it. I had sat a long time without a living thing making its appearance. I always sit still until I see some living thing; because if any such appears, it is sure to be appropriate to the place. If no living thing shews itself, I put none in my picture. (Reported by W. P. Frith.)

SEEING NATURE
The art of seeing nature is a thing almost as much to be acquired as the art of reading the Egyptian hiero-glyphics. (Lecture given at Hampstead.)   *1836.*

Cornelius Varley *1781–1873*

CADER IDRIS, 1803
When I ascended from Dolgelly to Cader Idris with Cristal, Havel and several others, as evening approached all the party except Cristal and I were cautious to descend while day light remained, but the increasing grandure & brilliancy of the scene above detained us against all risks to behold the splendour. We were much higher than the nabouring hills which were all covered by an enormous sheet of clouds causing early dark nights below—where cottage lights were seen febly glimmering while all above was glorious sunshine mid an upper stratum of bright clouds and the luminous surface of the lower ocean of clouds—Soon after golden vapour began to play upon our mountain. [he describes how Cristall and himself then saw the phenomenon of the Glory or Spectre of the Brocken] As the sun went down this bright vision faded leaving us in grey twilight and whilst noticing our freedom from clouds we were suddenly covered & they became so dense that at arms length our finger ends touching we could not see each other when we hastned lower to get below them & to find the horse track, but we could not, so we returned & hastned down the natural slope of many falln stones sometimes sliding with a number & having to jump aside to avoid those that rolled after. Having stiff boots I was in advance of Cristal & had to avoid the stones which he loosned, several splashing on the Pool below the light from which was our chief guide. (See Plate 68.)

CLOUDS OVER SNOWDON *
In 1805 I travelled in North Wales quite alone, for the whole season was so rainy that in most places I was the only traveller. This apparent solitude mid clouds & mountains left me more at large 'To hold converse with Natures charms & view her stores untold.'

* Varley's watercolour *Snowdon from Llanllyfni* (Birmingham Museum and Art Gallery) pictures the process he describes.

Having been familiar with the known Electrical experiments I was better prepared & more at liberty to observe and understand what I saw . . . In 1805 while seated on the North bank of the Vale of Llanllyfni . . . Snowdon to the East. The whole sky was clear except a line of a few small separate clouds floating over the southern range. These were moving eastwards and following each other correctly over the same summits, & the foremost led the way & passed direct over the Peak of Snowdon & then it assumed a pecululiar definite and stratified form, showing some decided action between the two, though they did not touch. The second and third followed exactly the same path and paid the same peculular respect as they passed Snowdon Peak. Some whilst passing over a vale left an end as lingering towards a hinder peak & sent out one towards a lateral peak whilst a foremost portion stretched out faster towards Snowdon. These hinder parts were gathered in when fairly over Snowdon, but when clearly past Snowdon they resumed their shapless form, but while intending to watch the last over Snowdon I found there were quite as many others following, their number still increasing, & they were larger. I watched the hindermost one, it had little ragged portions of no account following, but they were swelling into clouds & passed on, & their minute rags were swelling after them at a greater rate toward the west than the wind could carry them east. They now obscured the outline of the southern range. Then rain began at the east and very slowly extended westward till the whole range was under rain. By this time the line of clouds had grown some miles over the sea, thus meeting the wind that fed them, the distant horizon being still visible under them, but the rain extended gradually to the sea and verry progressively obscured the distant horizon.

I had yet fine weather over head, but the clouds kept increasing in size till the whole sky was overcast & a cheerless rainy afternoon ensued—Here I believe I saw and understood the gradual progress from a cloudless morning to universal rain, here was a silent invisable flow of electricity to the mountains.

John Sell Cotman 1782–1842

CROYLAND ABBEY, PETERBOROUGH CATHEDRAL AND ELY CATHEDRAL

Croyland is most delicious. You know how I esteemed my Howden. This, oh! is far, far superior. Castle Acre to it is as nothing. I am sorry I am obliged to paint this in so brilliant a manner as it precludes all hope of my ever seeing it now with you. Yet I feel my pen incapable of describing it—'tis so magnificent. The old part full of Sketches, the Door, the Window—in short the whole, wonderful.

I passed through Thorney and sketched the Abbey, but it is nothing worth. Peterborough is too perfect for my pencil. Every architect can make a better drawing from that than I can. Therefore to them I will yield up my claims. . . . I visited Ely from Cambridge. The day was bad, but the Minster is superb, very superior to Peterborough in my opinion, as to grotesque beauty. I saw it during my getting completely wet, though to great advantage—lighted up by the last rays of the sun and a violent storm passing over. The lightning seemed to dart immediately upon the roof. (Letter to Dawson Turner.)   *1804.*

NORFOLK AND MOUSEHOLD HEATH

I galloped over Mousehold Heath on that day, for my time was short, through a heavy hail-storm, to dine with my Father—but was obliged to stop and sketch a magnificent scene on the top of the hill leading down to Col. Harvey's house, of trees and gravel pit. But Norfolk is full of such scenes. Oh! rare and beautiful Norfolk. (Letter to Dawson Turner.)   *1841.*

David Cox 1783–1859

GENERAL OBSERVATIONS ON LANDSCAPE PAINTING

The principal art of Landscape Painting consists in conveying to the mind the most forcible effect which can be produced from the various classes of scenery; which possesses the power of exciting an interest superior to that resulting from any other effect; and which can only be obtained by a most judicious selection of particular tints, and a skilful arrangement and application of them to differences in time, seasons, and situation. This is the grand principle on which pictorial excellence hinges; as many pleasing objects, the combination of which renders a piece perfect, are frequently passed over by an observer, because the whole of the composition is not under the influence of a suitable effect. Thus, a Cottage or a Village scene requires a soft and simple admixture of tones, calculated to produce pleasure without astonishment; awakening all the delightful sensations of the bosom, without trenching on the nobler provinces of feeling.

On the contrary, the structures of greatness and antiquity should be marked by a character of awful sublimity, suited to the dignity of the subject; indenting on the mind a reverential and permanent impression, and giving, at once, a corresponding and unequivocal grandeur to the picture. In the language of the pencil, as well as of the pen, sublime ideas are expressed by lofty and obscure images; such as in pictures, objects of fine majestic forms, lofty towers, mountains, lakes margined with stately trees, rugged rocks, and clouds rolling their shadowy forms in broad masses over the scene . . . the Student should ever keep in view the principle object which induced him to make the sketch: whether it be mountains, castles, groups of trees, corn-field, river scene, or any other object, the prominence of this leading feature should be duly supported throughout; the character of the piece should be derived from it; every other subject introduced should be subservient to it; and the attraction of the one, should be the attraction of the whole. *1813.*

Francis Danby 1792–1861

SIMPLICITY, TRUTH, EXAGGERATION

Ruisdael never attempted anything extraordinary, but from his simplicity and truth he impresses the mind with a feeling of grandeur if not poetry. Indeed, poetry beside it (unless it be truly sublime) looks tricky and artificial. But his storm [*Storm off the Dykes of Holland*, in the Louvre] at first does not strike, as it is not exaggerated in any way and is quite grey in colour. (Letter to his patron John Gibbons.) *1837.*

LIKE A BIRD IN THE FIELDS OR ON THE SANDS

The days at present are woefully dark. In approaching the winter I find I calculate on so many months, but it would be better to count on the probable number of hours, of *good clear daylight*. In the latter I am often sadly out in my reckoning. When taken by the month I do not regret having lived like a bird in the fields or on the sands all the summer, for this pleasure is what I most care for in life, and I am contented to fag hard all the winter for its repetition if but *once* more, and so on as long as it may please God. (Letter written in November to his patron John Gibbons.) *1848.*

PAINTING THE SUN

I consider I have been very unfortunate this last month from illness and the great difficulty I have had in bringing the 'Home, Home' to a conclusion. The effect is the most difficult I have ever attempted, being an attempt to represent the sun in full golden richness unobstructed by clouds, just before setting, which is really too much for anyone, if I had been fully aware of the difficulty. I am lost in the endless work of balancing tones. I hope Mr. Pryor will not find this out; I would rather he supposed that I painted it off-hand than know I had painted and repainted 100 times, leaving off at last full of imperfections. The fact is, one might as well paint the picture and write the word 'Sun' where I mean it to be. (Letter to John Gibbons.)

THE ELIXIR

Let us exult in the confidence that we belong to that class of our fellow-men, who by the elixir you describe, 'the true enjoyment of nature', retain the heart of youth, though the eye grow dim, the hand tremble, and the head fade grey. (Letter to Sir George Petrie.)

Jean-Baptiste-Camile Corot 1796–1875

THE FIRST IMPRESSION

Only be guided by what you feel. As ordinary human beings we are subject to error, so listen to what people say, but do not go along with more of it than you can understand or than blends with your feelings. Firmness; submissiveness.—Follow your convictions. Better be nothing than an echo of other painters. As the wise man said, when you follow someone, you are always behind. Beauty in art is truth steeped in the impression we have received from nature. I am struck by the look of a particular place. I try for a conscientious imitation of it, but never for a moment do I forget the emotion it stirred in me. Reality is a portion of art; which is completed by feeling. In nature look first of all for the form; then for values or tone relationships, and colour, and execution; and submit to the feelings you have experienced. What we experience is definitely real. We are moved by the elegance and grace of some locality, some object. We must stick to it and as we strive for truth and accuracy we must always give it the appearance we were so much taken by. Whatever the locality, whatever the object; we must submit to our first impression. If we have been really touched, we shall transmit the sincerity of our emotion to others. (Note on the cover of a sketchbook.)

NATURE IN THE STUDIO

After my expeditions, I invite Nature to come and spend a few days with me; that's when my madness begins. Brush in hand I go nutting in the woods of my studio, where I hear the birds singing, and the trees shivering in the wind and where I see the streams and rivers flowing along with a thousand reflections of earth and sky; the sun goes down and gets up as my guest.

A LANDSCAPE PAINTER'S DAY

[There have been doubts about the authenticity of this next piece, which was first published in 1863. Was it fathered on Corot, did he write it or not? Corot was asked and wouldn't say. According to Pierre Courthion's *Corot raconté par lui-même*, Corot in fact roughed out *La Journée d'un Paysagiste* one day when he was staying with his friend Daniel Bovy at the Château de Gruyères in Switzerland. Someone else touched it up afterwards, and punctuated it. In spite of its whimsicalities about sylphs and nymphs and flowers which are patient and utter thank you's to God, this piece does say much about landscape painting as an act of love and identification with the theatre of existence—as one would like it to be the whole time.]

Yes, it's delightful, the landscape painter's day. He gets up early, at three in the morning, before sunrise, he goes and sits under a tree; and watches, and waits. He cannot see much to begin with. Nature is like a whitish veil, on which some of the masses are barely sketched in outline; everything is misty, everything shivers in the cool breath of dawn. *Bing!* The sky has grown lighter—the sun has still to tear the gauze which is hiding the meadows and the valley and the hills along the horizon—The vapours of the night still trail round like silvery tufts of wool over grass of a cold green. *Bing!—Bing!*—a first ray from the sun—the small flowers seem to be waking up happily—there isn't one of them without its trembling drop of dew—the leaves feel the chill and they are stirring in the morning air . . . Birds are singing under the foliage and you can't see them and you might think it was the flowers saying their prayers—Butterflies in love flutter across the meadow and set the tall grasses rippling—Everything is there—everything is invisible—The whole landscape lies on the far side of that gauze of transparent mist which is rising—rising—rising, drawn upwards by the sun—and as it lifts it reveals the silvery twinkling of the river, the meadows, the trees, the small houses, the distant recession. At last you can distinguish what you could only guess at before.

Bam! the sun is up—*Bam!* there's the peasant at the bottom of the field with a couple of oxen yoked to his cart—*Ding! ding!* that's the bellweather leading the sheep—*Bam!* everything flashes and glitters—it's broad daylight—light which is still golden and caressing. The pure outline and harmony of tones in the background are swallowed up by an infinity of sky, in the misty blue air—Flowers lift their heads up—birds are fluttering round—A countryman riding a white horse disappears down the hollow lane—The small rounded willow trees seem to turn like wheels on the river-bank.

Adorable!—and the artist paints! and paints!—Oh! that beautiful brown heifer up to her flank in the wet grass—I will paint her in—*Crac!* there! Splendid! splendid! Dear me, that's it, exactly! There is a peasant watching and afraid to come nearer—let's see what he makes of it. 'Hi, Simon!' Simon comes up and has a look. 'What do you think of it, Simon?' 'Oh! Well! m'sieur—it's pretty, all right!' 'You see what I've painted there?' 'I think I do—I think tes a big yellow rock you've put there!'

Boum! boum! midday! The sun is a-blaze, the ground burns—*Boum!* Everything has become dull and heavy—The flowers hang their heads—The birds have stopped singing, noises are coming up from the village. That's heavy work—that's the blacksmith, that's his hammer ringing on the anvil—*Boum!* let's go home! You can see everything and nothing. We'll go and eat at the farm—A good slice of home-made bread, with some freshly churned butter—eggs—cream—ham! *Boum!*—Work away, friends, I am going to take a rest—it's time for my siesta—and I dream a landscape of the morning—I dream my picture—Afterwards I shall paint my dream.

Bam! bam! The sun drops to the horizon—Time to get back to work—*Bam!* the sun is having a go at the big drum—*Bam!* it is setting in an explosion of yellow, and orange, and red fire, and cerise, and purple—How pretentious and vulgar! I don't care for it—Wait—let's sit down under that poplar—by that smooth looking-glass of a pool—Nature looks tired—But the flowers are picking up—Poor things—They are not like us men, they don't complain about everything. The sun's to their left—they are patient—'Good', they say, 'it will soon be on our right—' They are thirsty—they wait! They know the sylphs of the evening will come and wet them with vapour from their invisible watering-cans—they are patient and they say thank you to God.

But the sun drops lower and lower behind the horizon—*Bam!* it shoots out a last ray, a flare of gold and purple, fringing that cloud which passes by—Good! everything has vanished—Good! Twilight is beginning—Dear me, how delightful! The sun has gone. There is nothing left in this toned down sky but a vaporous tint of pale citron, which melts away into the blue of night via greenish tones of a sick turquoise, quite extraordinarily fine, of a fluid, elusive delicacy—The colour is going, all round—the trees have become nothing but masses of grey or brown—the dark water is reflecting the soft tones of the sky—You cannot see anything any more, you can only feel it is there—Everything is vague, confused—Nature drops off to sleep—while the cool evening air sighs in the leaves—dew impearls the velvet of the turf—Nymphs run off—and hide—and hope to be seen—*Bing!* down comes a star from the sky and dives into the pool—What a charming star, the pool trembles, and it sparkles all the more, and looks at me—It smiles at me, and winks—*Bing!* there is star No. 2 in the water, a second eye opens there. How welcome they are, these fresh smiling stars—*Bing! bing! bing!* three stars, six stars, twenty stars—Every star in the sky has fixed up a rendez-vous in this happy pool—Everything has gone to sleep once more—Only the pool is twinkling—It's swarming with stars—It's all illusion—The sun has gone down, and the sun we have inside our souls gets up, the sun of art—Good, there's a picture finished!

Samuel Palmer 1805–81

HILLS AND VALLEYS OF VISION
Note that when you go up to Dulwich it is not enough on coming home to make recollections in which shall be united the scattered parts about those sweet fields into a sentimental and Dulwich looking whole. No. But considering Dulwich as the gate into the world of vision one must try behind the hills to bring up a mystic glimmer like that which lights our dreams. And those same hills (hard task) should give

us promise that the country beyond them is Paradise—for to the wise and prudent of this world what are Raffaelle's backgrounds but visionary nonsense, what the background of the Last Supper but empty wind—and its figures but a party of old Guys at supper?

1824.

VERY LATE TWILIGHT
Remember the Dulwich sentiment at very late twilight time with the rising dews (perhaps the top of the hills quite clear) like a delicious dream. *1824.*

SHOREHAM
And now the trembling light
Glimmers behind the little hills, and corn,
Lingring as loth to part: yet part thou must
And though than open day far pleasing more
(Ere yet the fields and pearled cups of flowers
    Twinkle in the parting light;)
Thee night shall hide, sweet visionary gleam
That softly lookest through the rising dew:
    Till all like silver bright
    The faithful Witness, pure, and white,

Shall look o'er yonder grassy hill,
At this village, safe, and still.
All is safe, and all is still,
Save what noise the watch-dog makes
Or the shrill cock the silence breaks
    —Now and then.—
      And now and then—
      Hark!—once again,
      The wether's bell
      To us doth tell
Some little stirring in the fold.

  Methinks the ling'ring, dying ray
    Of twilight time, doth seem more fair,
And lights the soul up more than day,
    When widespread, sultry sunshines are.
Yet all is right, and all most fair,
    For Thou, dear God, hast formed all;
    Thou deckest ev'ry little flower,
    Thou girdest ev'ry planet ball—
      And mark'st when sparrows fall.
    Thou pourest out the golden day
      On corn-fields rip'ning in the sun
    Up the side of some great hill
      Ere the sickle has begun. . . .

1824 or 25.

AERIAL PERSPECTIVE

Often, and I think generally, at Dulwich, the distant hills seem the most powerful objects in colour, and clear force of line: we are not troubled with aerial perspective in the valley of vision.   *1825.*

SHOREHAM

I have begun to take off a pretty view of part of the village, [Shoreham, Kent] and have no doubt but the drawing of choice portions and aspects of external objects is one of the varieties of study requisite to build up an artist, who should be a magnet to all kinds of knowledge; though, at the same time, I can't help seeing that the general characteristics of Nature's beauty not only differ from, but are, in some respects, opposed to those of Imaginative Art; and *that,* even in those scenes and appearances where she is loveliest, and most universally pleasing. . . . However, creation sometimes pours into the spiritual eye the radiance of Heaven: the green mountains that glimmer in a summer gloaming from the dusky yet bloomy east; the moon opening her golden eye, or walking in brightness among the innumerable islands of light, not only thrill the optic nerve, but shed a mild, a grateful, an unearthly lustre into the inmost spirits, and seem the interchanging twilight of that peaceful country, where there is no sorrow and no night.

After all, I doubt not but there must be the study of this creation, as well as art and vision; tho' I cannot think it other than the veil of Heaven, through which her divine features are dimly smiling; the setting of the table before the feast; the symphony before the tune; the prologue of the drama; a dream, and ante-past, and proscenium of eternity. (Letter to John Linnell.)   *1828.*

WALES AND TINTERN ABBEY

Our Ossian Sublimites are ended—and with a little more of McPherson's mist & vapour we should have had much more successful sketching—but unfortunately when we were near Snowdon we had white light days on which we could count the stubbs & stones some miles off—we had just a glimpse or two one day through the chasms of stormy cloud which was sublime—however we have this evening got into a nook for which I would give all the Welch mountains grand as they are & if you & Mrs. Richmond could but spare a *week* you might see Tintern & be back again. . . . I think of the Abbey—& such an Abbey! the lightest Gothic—trellised with ivy & rising from a wilderness of orchards—& set like a gem amongst the folding of woody hills. (Letter to the artist George Richmond.)   *1835.*

CLOVELLY

I have several times been going to write to you—thinking you would so much like the sentiment of some park outskirts which run along by the cliff edge here. . . . You should come by *express* train to Exeter & will then find the Bideford coach waiting to start directly. Then you will see again the beautiful Torridge. Just beyond Torrington if you ride outside, notice Wear Gifford—such a bit of English sentiment—would I could get a sketch of it! You will if not upset into the river arrive at Bideford at 7 p.m.—thence there are eleven miles to Clovelly. (Letter to the artist George Richmond.)   *1849.*

NORTH DEVON

I coasted round as far as Ilfracombe—waterfall into the sea—then back, and landed at Combe Martin, walking home to Berryarbor. We must take the trouble to map out and paint with the different local colours arable land and garden, which come in every variety of rows and patterns. Also woods and woody hills must be juicy and rich; real TREE COLOUR, not anything picture colour. Detached elegant trees sometimes stand out into the glade; and above the woody or arable hill-tops, a bit of much higher hill is sometimes visible, all heaving and gently lifting themselves, as it were, towards the heavens and the sun. It is of no use to try woody hills without a wonderful variety of texture based on the modelling.

In the solemn moor-tops, the furze &c. is the dark, and the barer ground a graduating half-tint—but all dark and solemn. WHAT CAN BE THE REASON that they delight so much?

NEVER FORGET THE CHARM of running water. In Berryarbor valleys it gushes everywhere. O! the playful heave and tumble of lines in the hills here. (Letter to a pupil.)   *c. 1850.*

Ford Madox Brown 1821–93

TIMETABLE OF A LANDSCAPE

25th September [1848]—Began painting a view of Windermere*: worked six days at about four hours a day, last day in rain under an umbrella.

2nd October—started on foot for Patterdale; then over the mountains past the Greenside lead-mine to Keswick.

3rd—Through the Borrowdale pass to Wast-water.

4th—Rain all day; stopped there.

5th—Started in the rain over the mountains by Easkdale to Windermere . . .

6th—By rain to Liverpool . . .

31st March [1849]—Painted at the view of Windermere . . .

5th April—Painted at *Windermere*, cows and foreground (five hours).

6th—Painted at idem, horses, etc. (five hours) . . .

10th—Painted in the day-time, and in the evening from nine till eleven: finished it, and carried it to the Royal Academy (seven hours work.)   *1848, 1849.*

SUNLIGHT AND LAMBS

The *Baa Lamb** picture was painted almost entirely in sunlight, which twice gave me a fever while painting. . . The lambs and sheep used to be brought every morning from Clapham Common in a truck: one of them ate up all the flowers one morning in the garden, where they used to behave very ill. The background was painted on the Common.   *1852.*

THE PROGRESS OF 'CARRYING CORN'*

1st September—Out by quarter to eight to examine the river Brent at Hendon; a mere brooklet, running in most dainty sinuosity under overshadowing oaks and all manner of leafiness. Many beauties, and hard to choose amongst, for I had determined to make a little picture of it. However, Nature, that at first sight appears so lovely, is on consideration almost always incomplete; moreover there is no painting intertangled foliage without losing half its beauties. If imitated exactly, it can only be done as seen from one eye and quite flat and confused therefore . . .

Monday—Up late, shower-bath—to work at Brent by ten till half-past one—dinner and sleepy. About three out to a field, to begin the outline of a small landscape. Found it of surpassing loveliness. Corn-shocks in long perspective form, hayricks, and steeple seen between them—foreground of turnips—blue sky and afternoon sun. By the time I had drawn-in the outline they had carted half my wheat: by to-day all I had drawn in was gone . . .

12th September—yesterday . . . To work at the Brent by 11 a.m. Emma and the child brought me my dinner there at two, in a little basket.

20th . . . Got to the Brent late, at eleven; worked till one, when it was raining pretty freely. I endeavoured to work through it; but, the big drops piercing the foliage overhead, I had to give over; spent twenty minutes under a thicket of leafage. Tried to begin again when the rain was a little cleared, but found the weight of water quite displaced the different branches from their normal position, making confusion; so came home to dinner. . . .

21st—To the Brent by half-past nine: worked well till half-past one. Begins to look bravely, and beautiful colour; but still requires all my energy and attention to master the difficulties attending a style of work I have not been bred to . . . After dinner to the corn-field for about three hours; interrupted by a shower, and somehow did very little. Altogether these little landscapes take up too much time to be profitable . . .

26th . . . To the Brent by ten, worked till one—finished the landscape part as much as I can do to it from nature . . . Home to lunch, after a splendid walk in the broiling sun. Afternoon, to the corn-field . . .

30th . . . Lunch, and to the field from three to half-past five . . .

3rd October—To work at the cornfield from quarter past three till quarter to six: did next to nothing. It would seem that very small trees in the distance are very difficult objects to paint, or else I am not suited to this sort of work; for I can make nothing of this small screen of trees, though I have pottered over them sufficient time to have painted a large landscape, the men of English schools would say . . .

6th . . . Off to the field; rain; worked about one hour and a half under an umbrella, at the swedes. Rain drove me off . . .

11th—The field again—Sunshine when I did not want it, cold and wind when it went. Worked at the trees and improved them—found the turnips too

---

* *Windermere*, 1848–55, Port Sunlight, Lady Lever Art Gallery.
* *The Pretty Baa Lambs (Summer Heat)*, 1851–9, in the Birmingham Art Gallery.
* Plate 79.

difficult to do anything with of a serious kind. I don't know if it would be possible to paint them well; they change from day to day. An unpleasant and profitless day (eight hours).

12th—Up latish—bath. Saw my turnips were all false in colour: ruminated over this disgrace, and tried to retrieve it. Put it in some shape, ready to take out in the afternoon. Set to work at the coat from lay-figure in back yard—very cold—worked till four at it. Then to the swedes. Found the gate nailed up and brambled; had to go round by a *détour*, but in and set to work; but not much good. Tried to get the main tree more in harmony; a little to the swedes—men in the field pulling them . . .

13th . . . Exquisite day: hedges all gold, rubies, and emeralds, defying all 'white grounds' to yield the like . . . Afterwards to the field—for last time, thank Heaven. I am sick of it; I have now only to work at home at it to put in a little harmony. *1854.*

THE DREAM OF POSSESSION

21st August—Looked out for landscapes this evening; but, although all around one is lovely, how little of it will work up into a picture! that is without great additions and alterations, which is a work of too much time to suit my purpose just now. I want little subjects that will paint off at once. How despairing it is to view the loveliest of nature towards sunset, and know the impossibility of imitating it!—at least in a satisfactory manner, as one could do, would it only remain so long enough. Then one feels the want of a life's study, such as Turner devoted to landscape; and even then what a botch is any attempt to render it! What wonderful effects I have seen this evening in the hayfields! the warmth of the uncut grass, the greeny greyness of the unmade hay in furrows or tufts with lovely violet shadows, and long shades of the trees thrown athwart all, and melting away one tint into another imperceptibly; and one moment more a cloud passes and all the magic is gone. Begin to-morrow morning, all is changed; the hay and the reapers are gone most likely, the sun too, or if it is not it is in quite the opposite quarter, and all that *was* loveliest is all that is tamest now, alas! It is better to be a poet; still better a mere lover of Nature, one who never dreams of possession. *1855.*

Charles Keene *1823–91*

THE DUNWICH LANDSCAPE

This Dunwich is a curious little place, but interesting. All along at the base of the sandy cliff (striped with layers of rolled pebbles) you come upon human bones that have dropped from the shallow alluvial soil at the top. The land is sinking all along this coast, and a great city that flourished in Saxon times and was decaying at the Norman Conquest lies miles under the sea. There is one ruined church left just at the edge of the cliff. I believe 'the oldest inhabitant' can just remember when it was used for service, but its only congregation now is the owls and bats! Some of the cliff has fallen away lately and disclosed the shaft of a well. The bricks look to me Roman, but nothing has been found. There is a good lot of it, and it looks likely to fall, so one gives it a wide berth. The green marches at the back of the place are dotted with the fine cows and sorrel horses that this county is famous for. 'Cows and churches' is the motto at the head of 'Suffolk' in old Fuller's 'Worthies.' My big pipes are 'going' well just now from the practice I've had in my holiday, and so secluded is this place that at any time two or three hundred yards down the beach I can strut on the hard sand and skirl away at 'Fingal's Lament' or 'The Massacre of Glencoe' (my favourite pibroch) out of earshot of a soul. (Letter to the artist Joseph Crawhall.) *1877.*

WORKING FROM NATURE

What do you mean, that you have been working, but without success? Do you mean that you cannot get the price you ask? then sell it for less, till, by practice, you shall improve, and command a better price. Or do you only mean that you are not satisfied with your work? nobody ever was that I know, except J— W—,* Peg away! While you're at work you must be improving . . . Do something from Nature indoors when you cannot get out, to keep your hand and eye in practice. Don't get into the way of working too much at your drawings away from Nature. (Letter to the artist J. M. Stewart.)

William Holman Hunt *1827–1910*

PAINTING A LANDSCAPE BACKGROUND

I went off to the Lea marshes for a month; the river and the meadows were pure and beautiful at that date [1849], the lucid streams were stocked with innumer-

* Whistler.

able roach and dace and other silvery fish, and the gorgeously panoplied dragonflies, preying upon the careless butterfly, darted with lightning speed over the water. The region was well appreciated by anglers, but appeared to be out of the route of the landscape painter. All, all, alas! have now disappeared; the actors have gone, and the stage itself has sadly changed, but then it was not difficult to find a rich landscape for my 'Christian and Druid' picture. I painted the hut and its appendages from a shed near to my lodgings there.

Millais agreed with me that for the subject of 'Ophelia in the Stream' which he had settled upon, and made a hasty sketch for, and for mine of 'The Hireling Shepherd', there was good probability of finding backgrounds along the banks of the little stream taking its rise and giving its name to our favourite haunt, Ewell; accordingly we gave a day to the exploration. Descending the stream for a mile from its source, I soon found all the material I wanted for my landscape composition, but we looked in vain during a long tracing of the changing water, walking along beaten lanes, and jumping over ditches and ruts in turn, without lighting upon a point that would suit my companion. Many fresh hopes were shattered, until he well-nigh felt despair, but round a turn in the meadows at Cuddington, we pursued the crystal driven weeds with reawakening faith, when suddenly 'Millais' luck' presented him with the exact composition of arboreal and floral richness he had dreamed of.

ALL THE COLOUR OF LUSCIOUS SUMMER
Shakespeare's song [Edgar's song, in *King Lear* III 6, Holman Hunt's text for 'The Hireling Shepherd'] represents a shepherd who is neglecting his real duty of guarding the sheep . . . He was the type of muddle-headed pastors, who, instead of performing their services to the flock—which is in constant peril—discuss vain questions of no value to any human soul. My fool has found a Death's Head Moth, and this fills his little mind with forebodings of evil, and he takes it to an equally sage counsellor for her opinion. She scorns his anxiety from ignorance rather than profundity, but only the more distracts his faithfulness. While she feeds her lamb with sour apples, his sheep have burst bounds and got into the corn. I did not wish to force the moral, and I never explained it till now. For this meaning was only in reserve for those who might be led to work it out. My first object as an artist was to paint, not Dresden china *bergers*, but a real shepherd, and a real shepherdess, and a landscape in full sunlight, with all the colour of luscious summer, without the faintest fear of the precedents of any landscape painters who had rendered Nature before. (From a letter.)   *1897*.

IMPRESSIONISM
I must, in taking leave of the subject, insist that as a rule the greater part of the work figuring under the name of 'Impressionism' is childishly drawn and modelled, ignorantly coloured and handled, materialistic and soulless. Let it be clearly realised that it is so, in being destitute of that spirit of vitality and poetry which every true master, ancient or modern, painter, sculptor, or architect, has given to his simplest work, this supermundane spirit coming instinctively from his responsible soul, whether he intended or not to teach any lesson.   *1905*.

Camille Pissarro 1830–1903
IMPRESSIONISTS IN LONDON
In 1870 I found myself in London with Monet, and we met Daubigny and Bonvin. Monet and I were very enthusiastic over the London landscapes. Monet worked in the parks, whilst I, living at Lower Norwood, at that time a charming suburb, studied the effects of fog, snow, and springtime: We worked from Nature, and later on Monet painted in London some superb studies of mist. We also visited the museums. The water-colours and paintings of Turner and of Constable, the canvases of Old Crome, have certainly had influence upon us. We admired Gainsborough, Lawrence, Reynolds, etc., but we were struck chiefly by the landscape painters, who shared more in our aim with regard to *plein air*, light, and fugitive effects. Watts, Rossetti, strongly interested us amongst the modern men. About this time we had the idea of sending our studies to the exhibitions of the Royal Academy. Naturally we were rejected. (Letter to Wynford Dewhurst.)

PAINTING AT KEW
I am now very busy at Kew Gardens where I have found a series of splendid motifs which I am trying to render as well as I can. The weather helps—it's quite exceptional, it seems. But the difficulty! More than ever I feel how weak I am when faced with such a hard job. (Letter to Durand-Ruel.)   *June, 1892*.

I try to do the best I can here despite the continual change of weather. Kew Gardens are marvellous and the surroundings are superb. But time is so short and the work takes so long that I'm driven to despair at last! (Letter to Durand-Ruel.)   *July, 1892.*

BEAUTY IN MODEST CORNERS
Georges says Epping is not very beautiful. But then beautiful things can be made with so little and motifs which have too much beauty can look theatrical—look at Switzerland. Didn't old Corot make beautiful little pictures in Gisors out of a couple of willow trees, and a tiny stream, and a bridge, like that picture of his at the Exposition Universelle? What a masterpiece that was! Happy the people who can see beauty in a modest corner where others can't see a thing.* Everything is beautiful, the secret is putting it across. And from the way you describe it, Epping must be very interesting at least. (Letter to Lucien Pissarro.)   *1895.*

SEEING AND FEELING NATURE
Tell your wife of course I shall come to Epping, but that I shall have to work the whole while, I haven't many years to live and as long as I can see clearly and feel nature with intensity I cannot waste my time— Not if I am to bring my life to a fitting end. (Letter to Lucien Pissarro.)   *1894.*

James Abbott McNeill Whistler 1834–1903
WHISTLER, THE JUDGE, AND BATTERSEA BRIDGE
[From the report of the libel action, Whistler *v.* Ruskin.] The picture called the nocturne in blue and silver* was now produced in Court.

'That is Mr. Grahame's picture. It represents Battersea Bridge by moonlight.'

BARON HUDDLESTON: Which part of the picture is the bridge? (*Laughter.*)

His Lordship earnestly rebuked those who laughed. And witness [i.e. Whistler] explained to his Lordship the composition of the picture.

'Do you say that this is a correct representation of Battersea Bridge?'

'I did not intend it to be a "correct" portrait of the bridge. It is only a moonlight scene, and the pier in the centre of the picture may not be like the piers of Battersea Bridge as you know them in broad daylight.

* Compare Constable, page 188.

* Now in the Tate Gallery, London, renamed by Whistler *Nocturne in Blue and Gold: Battersea Bridge.*

As to what the picture represents, that depends upon who looks at it. To some persons it may represent all that is intended; to others it may represent nothing.'

'The prevailing colour is blue?'

'Perhaps.'

'Are those figures on the top of the bridge intended for people?'

'They are just what you like.'

'Is that a barge beneath?'

'Yes. I am very much encouraged at your perceiving that.* My whole scheme was only to bring about a certain harmony of colour.'

'What is that gold-coloured mark on the right of the picture like a cascade?'

'The "cascade of gold" is a firework.'

A second nocturne in blue and silver was then produced.

WITNESS: That represents another moonlight scene on the Thames looking up Battersea Reach.   *1878.*

NOCTURNES AND HARMONIES
Why should not I call my works 'symphonies,' 'arrangements', 'harmonies', and 'nocturnes'? I know that many good people think my nomenclature funny and myself 'eccentric'. Yes, 'eccentric' is the adjective they find for me.

The vast majority of English folk cannot and will not consider a picture as a picture, apart from any story which it may be supposed to tell.

My picture of a 'Harmony in Grey and Gold' is an illustration of my meaning—a snow scene with a single black figure and a lighted tavern. I care nothing for the past, present, or future of the black figure, placed there because the black was wanted at that spot. All that I know is that my combination of grey and gold is the basis of the picture. Now this is precisely what my friends cannot grasp.

They say, 'Why not call it "Trotty Veck", and sell it for a round harmony of golden guineas?'—naively acknowledging that, without baptism, there is no . . . market!

But even commercially this stocking of your shop with the goods of another would be indecent—custom alone has made it dignified. Not even the popularity of Dickens should be invoked to lend an adventitious aid to art of another kind from his. I should hold it a vulgar and meretricious trick to excite people about

* Compare Corot, the Peasant and the Cow, page 192.

Trotty Veck when, if they really could care for pictorial art at all, they would know that the picture should have its own merit, and not depend upon dramatic, or legendary, or local interest.

As music is the poetry of sound, so is painting the poetry of sight, and the subject-matter has nothing to do with harmony of sound or of colour.

The great musicians knew this. Beethoven and the rest wrote music—simply music; symphony in this key, concerto or sonata in that.

On F or G they constructed celestial harmonies—as harmonies—as combinations, evolved from the chords of F or G and their minor correlatives.

This is pure music as distinguished from airs—commonplace and vulgar in themselves, but interesting from their associations, as, for instance, 'Yankee Doodle', or 'Partant pour la Syrie'.

Art should be independent of all clap-trap—should stand alone, and appeal to the artistic sense of eye or ear, without confounding this with emotions entirely foreign to it, as devotion, pity, love, patriotism, and the like. All these have no kind of concern with it, and that is why I insist on calling my works 'arrangements' and 'harmonies'. (From 'The Red Rag'.)   *1878.*

POETRY OF THE THAMES

Nature contains the elements, in colour and form, of all pictures, as the keyboard contains the notes of all music.

But the artist is born to pick, and choose, and group with science, these elements, that the result may be beautiful—as the musician gathers his notes, and forms his chords, until he bring forth from chaos glorious harmony.

To say to the painter, that Nature is to be taken as she is, is to say to the player, that he may sit on the piano.

That Nature is always right, is an assertion, artistically, as untrue, as it is one whose truth is universally taken for granted. Nature is very rarely right, to such an extent even, that it might almost be said that Nature is usually wrong: that is to say, the condition of things that shall bring about the perfection of harmony worthy a picture is rare, and not common at all.

This would seem, to even the most intelligent, a doctrine almost blasphemous. So incorporated with our education has the supposed aphorism become, that its belief is held to be part of our moral being, and the words themselves have, in our ear, the ring of religion. Still, seldom does Nature succeed in producing a picture.

The sun blares, the wind blows from the east, the sky is bereft of cloud, and without, all is of iron. The windows of the Crystal Palace are seen from all points of London. The holiday-maker rejoices in the glorious day, and the painter turns aside to shut his eyes.

How little this is understood, and how dutifully the casual in Nature is accepted as sublime, may be gathered from the unlimited admiration daily produced by a very foolish sunset.

The dignity of the snow-capped mountain is lost in distinctness, but the joy of the tourist is to recognise the traveller on the top. The desire to see, for the sake of seeing it, is, with the mass, alone the one to be gratified, hence the delight in detail.

And when the evening mist clothes the riverside with poetry, as with a veil, and the poor buildings lose themselves in the dim sky, and the tall chimneys become campanili, and the warehouses are palaces in the night, and the whole city hangs in the heavens, and fairy-land is before us—then the wayfarer hastens home; the working man and the cultured one, the wise man and the one of pleasure, cease to understand, as they have ceased to see, and Nature, who, for once, has sung in tune, sings her exquisite song to the artist alone, her son and her master—her son in that he loves her, her master in that he knows her.

To him her secrets are unfolded, to him her lessons have become gradually clear. He looks at her flower, not with the enlarging lens, that he may gather facts for the botanist, but with the light of the one who sees in her choice selection of brilliant tones and delicate tints, suggestions of future harmonies. (From 'The Ten O'Clock Lecture'.)   *1885.*

Alfred Sisley 1839–99

SKIES IN LANDSCAPE

Every picture exhibits a place the artist has fallen in love with. That is one of the things which make up the superlative charm of Corot and Jongkind. One of the really difficult problems is to make the canvas alive. It is an essential task for the true artist, this animating of his picture. Form, colour, surface, everything must serve that end. What imparts the liveliness is the impression made on the artist, which is the one cause of the impression made on the spectator . . . Objects require to be shown in their proper context, bathed in light as they are in nature. That is the line of future progress. Everything depends on the sky. It mustn't be a mere background. On the contrary the sky not only helps to give depth to the picture by its planes (the sky has planes no less than the earth), it gives it movement as well by its form, by the way it is arranged in harmony with the effect or composition of the picture.

There can't be anything more splendid, more thrilling, than the kind of sky we get so often in summer, blue sky with beautiful wandering white clouds. What motion, and style! It's like a wave when we are on the sea. We are lifted up by it, and swept along. Then later, in the evening, there is another sky: the clouds lengthen, they're like the wake behind a ship, they're eddies which seem immobilized in mid-air. Little by little they dissipate, absorbed by the sun as it goes down. That is a more tender sky, more melancholy, it has the charm of the evanescent, and I'm particularly fond of it. I emphasize this part of a landscape to make you realize how important it is to me. An indication of this is that I begin every one of my pictures with the sky. Artists I like? Thinking of contemporaries, Delacroix, Corot, Millet, Rousseau, Courbet, are masters. In fact I like all artists who have loved nature and shown a deep feeling for it. (Letter to Adolphe Tavernier.) *1893.*

Claude Monet 1840–1926

NATURE INSTEAD OF PARIS

Fécamp . . . I am surrounded here by everything I love. I spend my time out of doors on the shingle, when it's rough or when the fishing-boats are going out. Or I go into the country, which is so beautiful here that I find it more agreeable winter than summer; and naturally I am working all the time, and I believe this year I shall do some serious things. Then in the evening, my dear friend, I find a nice fire in my little house and a nice little family . . . Thanks to that gentleman from Le Havre, who came to my help, I am enjoying the most perfect tranquility. I wouldn't mind staying the whole time in a corner of nature as peaceful as this. Your being in Paris doesn't make me in the least envious. To tell the truth I don't believe we can do a thing in surroundings like that. Wouldn't you agree that we do our best work where there is nothing but nature around? In Paris we are too preoccupied with things to see and listen to, however strong-minded we are, and what I do here will at least have the merit of not resembling anyone else, it will simply be the impression of my own feelings. (Letter to the painter Bazille.) *1868.* (Soon after Monet was turned out of the house, and tried to drown himself.)

PAINTING THE THAMES

Savoy Hotel . . . I am hard at it as you may suppose, I am full of enthusiasm, but it's so difficult, above all everything changes so that it's the devil to get at what I want, all the same I am full of enthusiasm and I hope to get some pictures more or less as I want them. (Letter to Durand-Ruel, his dealer.) *1901.*

When I began, I was like everyone else, I thought two canvases were enough, one for dull weather, one for sun. Then I painted some hayricks which struck me and which made a splendid group, a little way from here; one day I saw my light had changed and I asked my daughter-in-law if she would mind going back to the house and bringing me another canvas. She brought me one, but it wasn't long before the light had changed again. Another canvas, and another! And I worked on each till I had my effect—and that was that. Not very difficult to understand.

Where the process became really awful was on the Thames. Appearance changed all the time. At the Savoy Hotel or at St. Thomas's Hospital, where I had my viewpoints, I kept almost a hundred canvases on the go—for one subject. I would search feverishly through my sketches till I found one not too different from what I could see. Then in spite of everything I would change it entirely. When I finished work, I would move the canvases and see that I had overlooked just the one which would have served—there it was in my hand. That wasn't very bright! (From an interview.) *1927.*

Walter Greaves 1846–1931

GREAVES AND WHISTLER ON THE RIVER

One day we [i.e. Graves and his brother] were painting on the river bank near our place, when Whistler, whom we knew by sight as a neighbour in Lindsey Houses, came up to us and watched us at work. He said suddenly, 'Come over to my place,' and we went there and he showed us his work and his Japanese things. I lost my head over Whistler when I first met him and saw his painting. But Whistler taught us the use of blue and made us leave out detail. At first I could only try to copy him, but later I felt a longing for my own style, and something more my own did come back.

We often used to stay up all night on the river with him, rowing him about. When he came to a view which interested him he would suddenly stop talking and sketch it with white chalk on brown paper, just showing the position of the lights and the river banks and bridges. Just as suddenly he would start laughing and talking again. The next day I'd go round to his studio and he'd have it all on the canvas. He got me into the way of working like that. (Greaves to John Rothenstein.)

WATCHING THE RED-SAILED BARGES

I still draw. In fact, I couldn't pass the time without it. I think I could draw all old Chelsea by heart. I don't suppose I'd get it extraordinarily exact, but I can *see* the place all right as I do it.

I never seemed to have any ideas about painting—the river just *made* me do it. You see, you have to have them if you paint in a studio; but if you are outside all day, as I was, by the river, all you've got to do is to watch the red-sailed barges passing. And then there was the bridge—I suppose Battersea Bridge got a bit on the brain of all of us. (Greaves to John Rothenstein.)

Robert Bevan 1865–1925

THE ANATOMY OF TREES

A painter of landscape has to know the anatomy of trees much more than in botany: Shape, colour and movement, that's what you want to know to distinguish trees and give character to landscape.

PATTERNS OF LANDSCAPE

So much of the landscape painted since the eighteenth century has been man made. The patterns of hedgerows and copses, of orchards and parks are all man made.

ROADS

He once asked me [his son R. A. Bevan] what I thought was the greatest change in English landscape since he started painting it. I hazarded 'telegraph poles and wires' but his answer was 'the change in the roads from light macadam to black tarmac.'

THE ESSENCE OF HILLS

My father and I [R. A. Bevan] were once on the Aylesbury line. It was a fine clear day. He looked out of the train window and said 'I see the Chilterns quite differently since John Nash started painting them. And that doesn't happen with many landscape painters. Courbet I think almost certainly got the essence of those odd heavy hills though I hardly know the Jura country. I've tried to do it myself in the Blackdown Hills ever since I started painting at Applehayes ten years ago. And I hope I've succeeded.'

André Derain 1880–1954

LANDSCAPE

There is only one kind of painting: landscape. It's the most difficult of all. Also there is composition, but that isn't half so difficult, in my view. Because no one can stop us imagining the world in the way that suits us best. (Letter to Vlaminck.)   ?1906.

NATURE AND THE ARTIST

Delacroix's saying is true: 'Nature is a dictionary; we draw our words out of it.' But on top of the dictionary there is our will to write, there is the unity of our particular thought; all we do is to translate into space our virility, our timidity, our sensibility, our intelligence. All these things together constitute that personality which realizes itself in a plastic way. (Letter to Vlaminck.)   1909.

IN LONDON

'I always associate with London much of my early happiness and the fun that I got out of life before the First World War.' He told us that he had spent many delightful hours wandering about London, popping into pubs and frequenting the music halls, which had evidently made a great impression on him. He had also discovered Wapping; there it didn't matter in the least if you were a foreigner, you always found sympathy and amusement. In the Pool of London, too, he had come across those gaily coloured steamers that appear in several of his Fauve paintings. He reminisced gently about meals at the Cheshire Cheese and related how on one occasion he had made Picasso eat so much steak and oyster pudding and toasted cheese that the latter fell ill and jokingly accused Derain of trying to poison him.

London had not only stimulated his imagination with its gusto and local colour; it was clear that the museums had meant much to him. He told us that in 1905 he had studied primitive art in the British Museum and began to be interested in negro sculpture; and this, he added, before any of the others. He still kept many examples of negro sculpture in his collection (and very fine ones they were, especially the Benin heads), but he was no longer interested in them now that they had ceased to stir by their emotional impact alone and had become a subject for classification. Yes, he continued, London presented a dazzling spectacle to the painter, and who could forget Hyde Park with its horsemen and nursemaids? (From conversation with Denys Sutton.)

Paul Nash 1889–1946

LANDSCAPE SYMBOLS

Blake's life was spent in seeking to discover symbols for what his 'inward' eye perceived, but which alas, his hand could seldom express. Turner, again, sought to break through the deceptive mirage which he could depict with such ease, to a reality more real, in his imagination. In the same way, we, today, must find new symbols to express our reaction to environment. In some cases this will take the form of an abstract art, in others we may look for some different nature of imaginative research. But in whatever form, it will be a subjective art.

For myself, my sympathies are too clearly exposed by this essay to need further explanation. Last summer, I walked in a field near Avebury where two rough monoliths stand up, sixteen feet high, miraculously patterned with black and orange lichen, remnants of the avenue of stones which led to the Great Circle. A mile away, a green pyramid casts a gigantic shadow. In the hedge, at hand, the white trumpet of a convolvulus turns from its spiral stem, following the sun. In my art I would solve such an equation.   *1934.*

Ben Nicholson born 1894

VIEWPOINTS

When people living in a past world state that all modern painting is distorted or out of drawing, they are, according to their own standards, perfectly correct. But what standards are those? They believe, for instance, to take one limitation, in a fixed point of view in perspective, and the only support for retaining this point of view is their knowledge that certain painters and carvers have restricted themselves to a

stationary viewpoint . . . There is no reason why we should be limited to a fixed viewpoint once we have discovered that in life itself there are an unlimited number of points of view.   *1932.*

MUSIC AND ARCHITECTURE OF PAINTING

The kind of painting which I find exciting is not necessarily representational or non-representational, but it is both musical and architectural, where the architectural construction is used to express a 'musical' relationship between form, tone and colour and whether this visual, 'musical', relationship is slightly more or slightly less abstract is for me beside the point.   *1941–8.*

COLOUR IN ITS OWN RIGHT

Blue exists in a painting in its own right—no sea, no sky, no 'key' is required to experience this blueness.

In a painting it should be as impossible to separate form from colour or colour from form as it is to separate wood from wood-colour or stone-colour from stone. Colour exists not as applied paint but as the inner core of an idea and this idea cannot be touched physically any more than one can touch the blue of a summer sky.   *1955.*

THE VISUAL POETRY OF LANDSCAPE

St. Ives and its surrounding sea and landscape did indeed, I hope, have an effect on my work. Living here in Switzerland also is most stimulating to my work, but by the way this is not Switzerland as most British people think of it, but the Ticino, which is Italian Switzerland a mile or two from the Italian border and with Italian as its native language. The landscape is superb, especially in winter and when seen from the changing levels of the mountain side— the persistent sunlight, the bare trees seen against a translucent lake, the hard, rounded forms of the snow-topped mountains, and perhaps with a late evening moon rising beyond in a pale, cerulean sky—is entirely magical and with a kind of visual poetry which I would like to find in my painting.   *1959.*

THE STONES OF CORNWALL AND BRITTANY

I feel very much at home with the huge standing stones at Carnac in Brittany and the quoits of West Penwith in Cornwall in which the sea also plays a big part. There is perhaps an especial feeling of life because these are not considered 'works of art.'   *1968.*

WHARFEDALE

I am just back from Wharfedale where my special friend and I went—a terrific event and I have never drawn under such fiendish and delightful conditions—cold winter winds and incessant rain but what a landscape—I think one of the most beautiful in England—that and W. Penwith. We did get some work done however mostly from inside a small sports Cortina . . . I did make 2 rather spiffing drawings of Burnsall bridge—and of a small squat church with the sky going by at a tremendous pace—and also one of the whole landscape going by ditto . . . Do you know Holkham Sands? More or less miraculous—I think it's in Norfolk. *1972.*

Victor Pasmore born 1908

PICTORIAL FORMS

By imitating the objects and effects of nature, the painter is able to acquire endless pictorial forms and combinations of forms with which to express himself... The abstract painter must have similar material at his disposal without which he cannot construct the picture. Indeed he must find fresh pictorial forms sufficiently potent to strike the imagination. The use of geometric forms which are universally recognized both for their beauty and their implication, together with other forms of a symbolic nature can serve his needs in this respect. *1948.*

SPACES, TONES AND COLOURS

As the rhythmic divisions of time and sound in music find an echo in the deepest recesses of the mind, so do the spaces, the tones and the colours of painting. *1949.*

AFTER IMPRESSIONISM

After centuries of dependence upon its power of natural representation, painting at last emerges on its own and has developed along lines analogous to the symphony and the sonata in music. This does not mean that descriptive painting is invalidated, only that a new form of pictorial expression has been added . . . What I have done . . . is not the result of a process of abstraction in front of nature, but a method of construction emanating from within. I have tried to compose as music is composed, with formal elements which, in themselves, have no descriptive qualities at all . . . The writings of Cézanne, Van Gogh, Seurat, Gaugin and Whistler reveal quite clearly that these masters regarded Impressionism not as an end, but as a beginning and, further, that they considered themselves as the primitives of a new art, 'an art of the future, closer to music, where colour would reign supreme', as Van Gogh put it . . . Like nature a painting is solid and made up of parts; the same eye that looks at it, looks at nature: the same mental and emotional machinery which reacts to its appearance, reacts to the natural scene. There cannot be one law for nature and another for art. In reality a painting is like a bunch of flowers; it shines upon the spectator like a sun and warms his heart by the power of its own form. *1951.*

I found that all attempts to extend the boundaries of Impressionism along cubist or fauvist lines led to a breakdown in rational technique and rational interpretation. The only field which appeared open to rational development was in terms of purely abstract forms. *1960.*

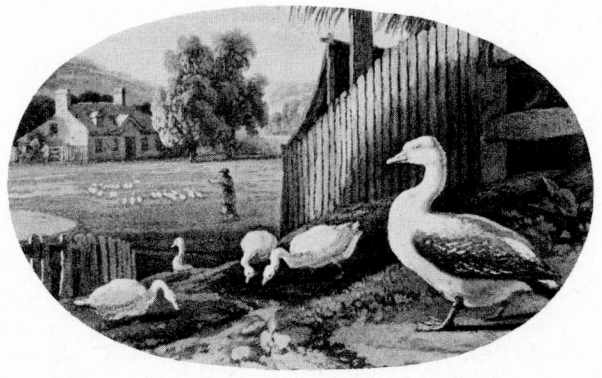

Richard Wilson: 1, 2, Whitley. *Artists and their Friends in England 1700–1799*, 1928. 3, Matthew, *Diary of an Invalid*, 1820. 4, Edward Dayes, *Works*, 1805.

Alexander Cozens: Cozens, *New Method of Assisting the Invention in Drawing Original Compositions of Landscape*, 1784.

Gainsborough: all from *Letters of Thomas Gainsborough*, ed. Mary Woodall, 1963.

Wright of Derby: all from Bemrose, *Life and Letters of Joseph Wright A.R.A.*, 1885.

Edward Dayes: *Works*, 1805.

Crome: Wodderspoon, *John Crome and his Works*, 1876.

Turner: 1, John Gage, *Colour in Turner*, 1969. 2, Thornbury, *Life of Turner*, 1862. 3, Gage, op. cit. 4, Finberg, *Life of J. M. W. Turner*, 1961. 5, 6, Finberg, *Inventory of the Drawings of the Turner Bequest*, 1909.

Constable: 1–6, 8, 9, 13, *John Constable's Correspondence*, ed. R. B. Beckett, 1962–8. 7, Solomon Hart, *Reminiscences*, 1882. 10–12, 16, *John Constable's Discourses*, ed. R. B. Beckett, 1970. 14, 15, Leslie, *Memoirs of the Life of John Constable*, 1843. 16, W. P. Frith, *Further Reminiscences*, 1888.

Cornelius Varley: *Cornelius Varley's Narrative Written by Himself*, Catalogue of the Varley exhibition, Colnaghi's, London, 1973.

Cotman: S. D. Kitson, *Life of John Sell Cotman*, 1937.

Cox: David Cox, *Treatise on Landscape Painting and Effect*, 1813.

Danby: 1–3, Eric Adams, *Francis Danby*, 1973. 4, William Stokes, *Life of George Petrie*, 1868.

Corot: 1, Théophile Silvestre, *Histoire des Artistes vivants*, 1856. 2, Pierre Courthion, *Corot raconté par lui-même*, 1946.

Palmer: 1–3, *Samuel Palmer's Sketchbook*, intro. by M. Butlin, 1962. 4–6, 8, A. H. Palmer, *Life and Letters of Samuel Palmer*, 1892. 7, Richmond MSS.

Ford Madox Brown: all from *Praeraphaelite Diaries and Letters*, ed. W. M. Rossetti, 1900.

Charles Keene: Layard, *Life and Letters of Charles Keene*, 1892.

Holman Hunt: 1, 2, 4, Holman Hunt, *Pre-Raphaelitism and the Pre-Raphaelite Brotherhood*, 1905. 3, *The Art of William Holman Hunt*, in the Catalogue of the Walker Art Gallery, Liverpool, 1907.

Pissarro: 1, Wynford Dewhurst, *Impressionist Painting*, 1904. 2, 3, Venturi, *Les Archives de l'Impressionisme*, 1939. 4, 5, *Camille Pissarro: Letters to his son Lucien*, tr. John Rewald, 1943.

Whistler: all from Whistler, *The Gentle Art of Making Enemies*, 1890.

Monet: 1, G. Poulain, *Bazille et ses amis*, 1932. 2, Venturi, *Les Archives de l'Impressionisme*, 1939. 3, *La Revue de l'Art ancien et moderne*, Feb. 1927.

Greaves: Sir John Rothenstein, *The Artists of the 1890s*, 1928.

Bevan, communicated by R. A. Bevan, Esq.

Derain: 1, 2, Derain, *Lettres à Vlaminck*, 1955. 3, Denys Sutton, 'André Derain: Art as Fate', *Encounter*, Oct. 1955.

Paul Nash: *Unit 1*, ed. Herbert Read, 1934.

Ben Nicholson: 1–4, Ben Nicholson, *A Studio International Special*, ed. M. de Sausmarez, 1969. 5, Nicholson exhibition catalogue, Galerie Bayeler, Basel, 1968. 6, Personal communication.

Pasmore: 1, Pasmore exhibition catalogue, Redfern Gallery, London, Dec. 1948. 2, Pasmore exhibition catalogue, Redfern Gallery, London, Nov. 1949. 3, *Art News and Review*, Feb. 24, 1951. 4, Reply to a questionnaire by Leif Sjoberg, King's College, University of Durham, 1960 (see Alan Bowness, in *Burlington Magazine*, CII, 1960).

Index

Page numbers in italic refer to illustrations; ff after a page number refers to unpaged colour plates following.